WADE HAMPTON III

WADE HAMPTON III

Robert K. Ackerman

THE UNIVERSITY OF SOUTH CAROLINA PRESS

© 2007 University of South Carolina

Published by the University of South Carolina Press
Columbia, South Carolina 29208

www.sc.edu/uscpress

Manufactured in the United States of America

16 15 14 13 12 11 10 09 08 07   10 9 8 7 6 5 4 3 2 1

Library of Congress Cataloging-in-Publication Data

Ackerman, Robert Kilgo, 1933–
  Wade Hampton III / Robert K. Ackerman.
    p. cm.
  Includes bibliographical references and index.
  ISBN-13: 978-1-57003-667-5 (cloth : alk. paper)
  ISBN-10: 1-57003-667-5 (cloth : alk. paper)
    1. Hampton, Wade, 1818–1902. 2. Generals—Confederate States of America—
Biography. 3. Confederate States of America. Army—Biography. 4. Governors—
South Carolina—Biography. 5. Legislators—United States—Biography. 6. United
States. Congress. Senate—Biography. 7. South Carolina—Politics and govern-
ment—1865–1950. 8. South Carolina—History—Civil War, 1861–1865. 9. Recon-
struction (U.S. history, 1865–1877)—South Carolina. I. Title.
  E467.1.H19A28 2007
  973.8092—dc22
  [B]
                                        2006037507

This book was printed on Glatfelter Natures, a recycled paper with 50 percent post
consumer waste content.

To my wife, May, and to our children and their families, whose support has been inestimable: Mark and Mandy Ackerman; Roxanne and Eddie Spencer and Robert, Andrew, and Rachel Spencer; and Bettye Ackerman and Michael Garvin and Cassidy Ackerman-Garvin

CONTENTS

ILLUSTRATIONS

South Carolina is represented in the Statuary Hall of the U.S. Capitol by statues of two of the most famous of its statesmen: John C. Calhoun and Wade Hampton III. Both have been virtually idolized by South Carolinians; both live in the mythology of this state. Calhoun has attracted the attention of an impressive number of scholars, resulting in a lengthy list of books, including multiple volumes of Calhoun papers. In sharp contrast more than fifty years elapsed between one biography of Hampton in 1949 and three in the first years of this century. There have also been a limited number of studies of Hampton's role in the Confederate military and in Reconstruction. There are two obvious reasons for this contrast: Hampton lost three of his homes to fires that consumed the bulk of his papers, and, unlike Calhoun, Hampton was not an intellectual who wrote treatises and whose ideas were widely quoted.

Those limitations notwithstanding, a biography of Hampton is a worthy project, largely because a study of his life is helpful in understanding a crucial period in American history, especially that of South Carolina. He was representative of the ante bellum planter class, a significant military leader in the Confederate army, and he played a key role in the Reconstruction and post-Reconstruction eras. Hampton's life is one of tragedy and repeated failures. His disappointed intentions were in essence failures for South Carolina, which influenced the state for generations.

This remarkable man represents much that was the most interesting of nineteenth-century South Carolina. He was a wealthy planter, an owner of hundreds of slaves, and a moderate political leader who opposed secession but loyally supported his state once the fateful decision was made. He was an astoundingly successful military leader who lacked the advantages of a West Point education. In defeat he flirted with the possibilities of desperate guerrilla warfare or immigrating to Brazil but then made the right and courageous decision to stay in his state. In the era of radical Reconstruction, he went from bitter denunciation of the black troops in occupation duty to appealing to the freed black population to join with whites in overthrowing the radicals and returning the state to the control of native whites with limited black participation. His election as governor in 1876 ended the radical period. In power he made reasonable efforts to fulfill his promises of equal treatment of both races, but it was a losing battle in the face of acrid bitterness and increasing resentment from nonaristocratic South Carolinians, who with some justice became disillusioned with the leadership of conservative aristocrats who proved to be ineffective in improving the lot of the mudsill classes. The commoners could no longer be lulled into complaisance by tales of the state's aristocratic past. After two rather uneventful terms in the U.S. Senate, forces that shaped South Carolina for the next two generations defeated him.

To understand Wade Hampton III it is necessary to know something of his roots, especially the two earlier Wade Hamptons. The late J. H. Easterby wrote that "the first Wade represented the rising tide, the second the flood tide, the third the turning tide, and the ebb of an epoch that is gone. . . . In the sum total of their lives they epitomize the old South—its time of spacious empire building; a genteel civilization in full flower; a heroic struggle for preservation and the deep tragedy of defeat."[1]

Most students of this state and of the South would agree that the antebellum South was a Greek tragedy, and the fatal flaw was slavery. The three Wade Hamptons were indeed a part of the slave-holding South. One of the significant features of this story is that the scion of one of the South's greatest slave-holding families played a leading, albeit ineffective, role in the first attempt at bringing the two races together in some kind of realistic cooperation with at least a measure of justice. Wade Hampton had as good a claim to aristocracy as America affords: he was of the third generation of landed wealth, he was classically educated, and he embodied a sense of noblesse oblige responsibility to his society.

This author is immodest enough to believe that an understanding of Hampton's career will assist moderns in understanding present conditions. I subscribe to the creed of the nineteenth-century historian Friedrich Karl von Savigny: "History is the only true way to attain a knowledge of our own condition." Writing history is always a matter of selectivity, choosing what to treat and what not to treat. The presence and absence of papers in part determined this study. In addition to South Carolina, Hampton also lived in Mississippi, Virginia, and Maryland. I chose to concentrate on those parts of his life that had the most influence on South Carolina. Obviously, his military career affected South Carolina and the entire South. While the Mississippi plantations figured importantly in Hampton's life, the records pertaining to those efforts are sparse and scattered, forcing the researcher to speculative conclusions, fraught with possible errors. The precise details of the Mississippi plantations are not, however, vital to his influence on South Carolina. The same can be said about his experience as commissioner of Pacific Railroads.

Readers should understand that the paucity of personal papers meant that we often do not know what Hampton thought on some issues; we have to settle with what he said and did. All too often we have to depend on newspapers, which thankfully gave Hampton generous coverage. I tried for balance by considering newspapers of contrasting attitudes. It would have been better if there had been letters to his wife, revealing his innermost thoughts. Alas there are few of these.

ACKNOWLEDGMENTS

My sincere thanks to my wife, May, for her assistance and patience with what seemed an interminable project. I am grateful to the able staff of the South Caroliniana Library, especially Allen Stokes and Robin Copp. The staff of the South Carolina Department of Archives and History, especially Robert Mackintosh, was of great help. My thanks also go to the staffs of Perkins Library, Duke University, and the Southern Historical Collection, University of North Carolina. Thanks especially are owed to Paul Hardin, the former chancellor of the University of North Carolina, Chapel Hill, who made the arrangements for my access to the Duke and UNC collections. I also received invaluable assistance from the staffs of the Library of Congress; the Center for American History, University of Texas; the Mississippi Department of Archives and History, especially Clinton Bagley; and the courthouses of Washington and Issaquena counties of Mississippi, especially Erline D. Fortner of the Issaquena County Courthouse and Nellie Taylor of the Washington County Courthouse. Special thanks go to son Mark and his colleague Carey Blizzard, daughter Bettye, and son-in-law Michael Garvin for assistance with the mysteries of the computer. Ann Fripp Hampton, whose publication of the letters of Sally Baxter Hampton was valuable, was helpful and encouraging. I am of course grateful to my acquisitions editor, Alexander Moore of the University of South Carolina Press, for his assistance and patience.

WADE HAMPTON III

~◊ONE◊~

From Frontiersmen to Aristocracy

The South Carolina saga of the Hampton family begins with Wade Hampton I, who came to this colony as a frontiersman, fought as a leader in the American Revolution, acquired great quantities of land and slaves, exercised entrepreneurial skills in building a fortune, served as a leader in South Carolina, and when he died in 1835 was believed to be the wealthiest planter in the United States.[1] The progenitors of Wade Hampton I first settled in Virginia. William Hampton came from England in 1620 in the *Bono Nova* to settle in the vicinity of Elizabeth City, where the family established a plantation known as Hamfield. The son of William and Abigail, Thomas, became an Anglican priest, cementing the family relationship with the Anglican and Episcopal churches. The Hamfield plantation passed to John Hampton, Jr., son of the priest, Thomas. John Hampton II in 1712 married Margaret Wade, introducing to the family a name that will be "given" for generations. Anthony Hampton, the second son of John and Margaret, married Elizabeth Preston, thereby establishing an enduring tie between the Hampton and Preston families of Virginia and South Carolina.

Around the middle of the eighteenth century Anthony and his brother James and their families moved to the North Carolina frontier, in what was then Rowan County.[2] The first Wade Hampton was born in 1751 in either Virginia or North Carolina. Wade I was the third child of Anthony and Elizabeth (Preston) Hampton.[3] Anthony quickly emerged as a leader in North Carolina. He served as a captain in a militia company during the North Carolina Regulator movement in the 1770s, and he served in the North Carolina colonial assembly, representing the newly created Surrey County, beginning the family tradition of military and political leadership. Four of the sons of Anthony Hampton who survived the American Revolution served in the South Carolina Assembly. They also served in the revolutionary forces, but the real leadership roles went to Wade Hampton I.

In 1774 three of the sons moved to the South Carolina frontier, followed by Anthony and the rest of the family. The Hampton family settled in the valley of the Middle Tyger River, bordering on the Cherokee nation. They engaged in farming and trade with the Indians.[4] Disputes about broken treaty promises and the influence of the French in the French and Indian War (1756–1763) led to the Cherokee War, which ravaged the South Carolina frontier for several years beginning in 1760.[5] Treaty negotiations obtained temporary peace, but there were periodic outbursts of violence for years to come. In the summer of 1776 a Cherokee raiding party attacked the Hampton homestead and massacred Anthony Hampton, his wife, their son Preston, and an unnamed grandson. The surviving sons, John, Richard, Edward, Henry, and Wade, all participated in retaliatory raids against the Cherokee Indians. The Treaty of DeWitt's Corner (present-day Due West) in 1777 finally and formally concluded this war. The Cherokees ceded the four northwestern counties in South Carolina.[6]

The Hamptons were both farmers (not yet planters) and merchants. Preston Hampton had been a trader with the Cherokees. By 1778 the Hamptons had a flourishing mercantile business with locations in Charles Town and the Congarees (near the soon-to-be-established Columbia). In 1779 Wade and Richard Hampton purchased land at Granby (east of present-day Cayce), where they established their largest operation; Wade also won election to the state House of Representatives that year.[7] During the war the Hamptons were major suppliers for the revolutionary troops. When the state settled unpaid accounts after the war, the Hampton brothers received 4,946 pounds in compensation.[8]

During the Revolution Wade Hampton catapulted himself into the state's leadership. He made a fortune by combining his mercantile business with military service. He served as paymaster for Thomas Sumter's Sixth Rifle Regiment. In 1780 Wade joined the prestigious South Carolina Society, and thenceforth, the Hamptons were part of South Carolina aristocracy.[9] From entering the colony as a frontiersman in 1774 to membership in the state's elite in 1780 was heady progress, even in a frontier society.

Circumstances of the war forced Wade to compromise. He was not in Charleston when Gen. Benjamin Lincoln surrendered that city in May 1780, but the Hampton brothers were presently accosted by the British near Winnsboro and relieved of about thirty slaves.[10] Faced with the threat from British commander Sir Henry Clinton that rebels would have their estates seized, Wade Hampton, in September 1780, took the oath of allegiance to the crown. In doing this he was in the good company of such leaders as Rawlins Lowndes, Henry Middleton, and Daniel Huger. Signing the oath of allegiance was an act of expediency for this new member of the landed aristocracy.[11]

Wade soon found reason to repudiate his oath of allegiance, as did many other South Carolinians. One result of the British conquests was their establishing a fort at Granby, which actually included the Hampton house.[12] Wade left his property in the hands of the British and joined the state militia commanded by Thomas Sumter. Hampton played an important role in seizing

Friday's Ferry, close by Fort Granby. Then on May 16, 1781, Col. Henry "Light Horse Harry" Lee took the fort at Granby. Hampton himself was at that time engaged in operations near Charleston. Establishing another important family tradition, Hampton became Sumter's cavalry commander. He figured importantly in the Battle of Eutaw Springs, which, although not a rebel victory, contributed to the depletion of the British forces.[13]

Wade Hampton I managed to combine military and political leadership. He represented Saxe Gotha in that remarkable state assembly that met as a capital-in-exile in Jacksonborough in 1782. Francis Marion and Thomas Sumter were also members. After the Jacksonborough assembly Hampton continued his military career as the commander of a regiment of state cavalry. He emerged from the war with an excellent military reputation and with wealth, obtained from his mercantile business.[14]

Wade set about building his fortune and family. After the fighting ceased he married Martha Epps Goodwyn Howell, owner of Greenfield Plantation in Richland District. In 1790 he built a new home, which he named Woodlands—that name also applied to his other Richland holdings. Hampton was the first in Richland District to plant short-staple cotton. Using the newly invented cotton gin, he was one of the early up-country cotton aristocrats. His first wife died in 1784, and in 1786 he married Harriet Flud, daughter of a prominent Santee planter.[15] Harriet gave birth to two sons: Wade II in 1791 and Frank in 1793.[16]

True to family tradition, the first Wade Hampton was a superb horseman. He began trading and training horses before the Revolution. At various times he was a member of the Statesburgh Jockey Club, the St. George Jockey Club, and the South Carolina Jockey Club. Hampton, Charles Cotesworth Pinckney, Gabriel Manigault, William Moultrie, and others owned the Washington Race Course in Charleston, Hampton being the largest shareholder.[17]

Hampton's wealth and power grew geometrically. By 1799 he was producing six hundred bales of cotton worth ninety thousand dollars, a staggering sum for the time. He was the first in the region to own a gin, and he was the first in the state to use waterpower to operate a gin.[18] His political life developed with his success as a man of business. He was elected to the state assembly in 1779. In 1783 he resigned that office to become the ordinary for the Camden District. He again entered the state assembly in 1791. In that same year he became the sheriff of Camden District. In 1788 he was a member of the convention to decide whether South Carolina should ratify the new United States constitution; he opposed ratification.[19] In the new nation he served as a Republican member of Congress from 1795 to 1797 and from 1803 to 1805. In 1800 he was an elector for President Thomas Jefferson and Vice President Aaron Burr. President Jefferson offered Hampton the office of postmaster general, which he declined. Wade Hampton I was one of the founding trustees of South Carolina College, chartered in 1801. Other trustees were Gov. John Drayton, Henry W. DeSaussure, C. C. Pinckney, Judge Hugh Rutledge, John F. Grimké, and Thomas Taylor. Hampton was present at the first meeting of the trustees of South Carolina College.[20] Taylor and Hampton were on the committee to arrange for a proper site for the college.[21] This established a long and meaningful relationship between the Hampton family, South Carolina College, and its successors. In 1794 Harriet Flud Hampton died, and in 1800 Hampton married his third wife, Mary Cantey.[22]

Typical of this generation, Wade Hampton I sired a large family. Of the two sons born to Harriet Flud Hampton, Wade II was the most promising. Frank proved to be something of a black sheep. While serving in the War of 1812 Frank was court-martialed at least once, and he killed one man in a duel. He died in Charleston in 1816 after a youth of dissipation. Hampton's third wife, Mary Cantey, produced five daughters and one son. Harriet, born in 1803, died unmarried in 1826. Louisa Wade, born in 1805, died unmarried in 1827. Caroline Martha, born in 1807, married John S. Preston of the distinguished Virginia family; they lived for some years at Houmas (a sugar plantation developed by Wade Hampton I) and then became residents of what became known as the Hampton-Preston Mansion in Columbia; Caroline died in 1883. Mary Sumter, born in 1810, married Thomson T. Player of Nashville, Tennessee. She died in childbirth at age twenty-one. The infant did not survive. Thomson Player later married the stepdaughter of John Bell, the distinguished Whig leader and one-time candidate for the presidency. Alfred, born in 1815, died at age ten. He was the first member of the family to be buried in the Trinity graveyard. Susan Frances, born in 1816, married John L. Manning. They built the mansion Milford near Pinewood, South Carolina. Manning served as governor of the state from 1852 to 1854. Susan died in 1845.[23]

Like many of the more enterprising of American entrepreneurs of the time, Hampton engaged in speculation with land on the frontier. He was especially shrewd in purchasing lands and then selling them in a timely fashion. He bought shares in a number of land companies, including the Virginia Yazoo Co., the Upper Mississippi Co., and the Georgia Mississippi Co. The Yazoo grants became embroiled in a deep and infamous scandal, but Hampton again emerged wealthier, even receiving compensation from Congress for some grants that had been canceled by the Georgia legislature.[24] In 1811 he purchased sugar plantations in Louisiana. After several additions, he owned as much as 148,000 acres along the Mississippi in a plantation known as Houmas, a tract the origins of which went back to Spanish grants. He also purchased cotton lands in Mississippi, but the greatest wealth came from the sugar cane of Houmas.[25] His principal residence was Woodlands, near Columbia, South Carolina. Woodlands was worth $128,039.52 at the time of the death of Wade Hampton I. In 1823 the *Niles Weekly Register* indicated that Wade Hampton was "probably the richest planter in the South." That estimate was doubtlessly based largely on his holdings on the Mississippi. In 1829 the *Niles Register* named Hampton as the leading producer of sugar and molasses in Louisiana.[26] The Louisiana lands brought his heirs $1.5 million in 1852.[27] Hampton I disposed of the Mississippi lands, but he kept and enhanced the Louisiana lands known as Houmas.[28]

An important reason for the Hampton fortune was the ownership of land in both the old South and also the newly developing Southwest—that is, Alabama, Louisiana, and Mississippi. In 1807 the South Carolina plantation was producing 1,500 bales of top quality cotton, most of which was shipped to Charleston on two riverboats owned by Hampton himself, by the Santee Canal. Because of soil erosion, depletion of land by the failure to rotate crops, and competition from more fertile lands, the center of financial growth was shifting southwestward.[29] A visitor to Columbia in 1846 wrote of the holdings of Wade Hampton II, "the Louisiana estate is said to be eminently valuable while the Carolina plantation has greatly declined in value."[30] The holdings in the new Southwest enabled the Hamptons to do far better than their South Carolina neighbors.

Wade Hampton described himself as a loose Christian. He acquired some of his wealth by somewhat questionable means; still, he was a philanthropist. The Trinity Cathedral in Columbia dates from 1812 with the building of the first church at the present site near the capitol. Wade Hampton I was one of its most generous benefactors.[31]

He was officially a Republican, but he was often sympathetic to policies that were Federalist and later Whig.[32] Those Whig leanings will be an important influence on Wade Hampton III at a time when many of the Whig policies were being carried forth by the Republican Party.

In 1807, when the British attacked the USS *Chesapeake*, there was a large public outcry, in the midst of which Hampton offered his services to the military. He was commissioned as a brigadier general, replacing Gen. James Wilkinson in command of the army on the Mississippi, when that notorious general was ordered to Washington for an investigation of charges that he had been involved in the Aaron Burr schemes.[33]

These were the years when the two sons born of Harriet Flud Hampton were reaching maturity. Both Wade II and Frank attended preparatory schools in Connecticut and then enrolled in South Carolina College. Neither son graduated from college.[34]

During the War of 1812 Wade Hampton I became a major general, and both sons served as commissioned officers. Wade Hampton II served as a lieutenant in the Light Dragoons.[35] In 1813 Hampton I was involved in the abortive Canadian campaign. Friction between Hampton and Gen. James Wilkinson was just one of the problems in that failed effort.[36]

Wade Hampton II gained military fame after resigning his commission in May or June of 1814. He then went to his father's estates on the Mississippi. He was present on business in New Orleans in 1815 at the time of Gen. Andrew Jackson's defense of that city. Wade II rejoined the military to play an important role in the Battle of New Orleans. Jackson selected Lieutenant Hampton to be his Pheidippides, that is, to carry the important news of the greatest American victory in the War of 1812 to Washington, where officials awaited news of peace negotiations in Europe. Fortunately, Hampton survived his journey better than Pheidippides did after that first Battle of Marathon. Wade II rode one horse from New Orleans to Columbia and then went on to Washington by boat. The great victory at New Orleans actually came after the peace treaty had been signed. Jackson gave the young Hampton special praise in his general orders of January 21, 1816. The young Hampton again resigned from the army as a lieutenant. He became known in South Carolina as Colonel Hampton, but that title was based on Gov. David R. Williams's appointing him deputy inspector general of the state troops in 1816 with the rank of lieutenant colonel.[37]

In 1817 Wade Hampton II married Ann Fitzsimons, daughter of an influential Charleston family. Ann's sister Catherine married James H. Hammond, soon-to-be prominent in South Carolina politics.[38] The maturing of the second Wade Hampton represented a significant step in the development of the Hamptons as members of Southern aristocracy. The historian J. H. Easterby described Wade Hampton I as a frontiersman who "made it" in a short span of time, a man characterized by "boldness and originality" with "an almost pagan lust for life,"[39] an apt description of the enterprising frontiersman. Easterby described the second Wade Hampton, certainly no frontiersman, as a man of gentility. He grew up with the wealth of a successful plantation family. Although he did not graduate from South Carolina College, he became a man of culture and influence.[40]

In 1823 Wade Hampton I purchased from Ainsley Hall the house later known as the Hampton-Preston Mansion. This became the home of choice for Mary Cantey Hampton, whereas the general preferred Woodlands.[41] In 1830 General Hampton transferred to his son part of the Houmas plantation on the Mississippi, passing the mantle to the next generation. Another indication of the transition was that Wade Hampton II became a trustee of South Carolina College in 1826, a position he held until his death in 1858.[42] Wade Hampton III also served in this capacity.

Wade Hampton I died at age eighty-one in 1835, leaving a thriving plantation business, a tradition of public service, and a reputation for leadership in the affairs of South Carolina. According to tradition, Wade Hampton II destroyed his father's will, because that document left the bulk of the estate to him. Without the will, the younger Hampton received letters of administration and proceeded to divide the estate into equal shares for the four heirs. Each share of the estate was worth $410,266.14. The Hampton-Preston Mansion in Columbia was excluded from the division and went to Hampton's widow, Mary Cantey Hampton. Wade II had already received control of Woodlands, which included 2,054 acres of swampland and 4,230 acres of highland appraised at $128,039.52. Hampton II ceded the Louisiana plantations to Mrs. Wade Hampton I, Caroline Preston, and to Susan F. Hampton Manning.[43] He retained ownership of the Mississippi cotton plantation Walnut Ridge. In 1827 the *Niles Register* had estimated that Wade Hampton I had an annual income of $100,000 from the Louisiana plantations alone.[44] That journal estimated that Hampton in 1826 owned 2,001 slaves on all of his lands. The Louisiana lands were the most profitable. In 1834 an overseer named Strong reported to Hampton I that the Houmas plantation had produced in that year a total of 1,700 hogsheads of molasses, greater by 300 than any previous year.[45] Contrary to the age-old wish that great estates be kept intact, the heirs divided the wealth of Wade Hampton I into four parts. Within a generation much of this wealth was gone. Debts incurred in the 1850s and the devastation of the Civil War left only the Prestons with any degree of wealth, and even that did not last. Ironically, the Prestons sold the Hampton-Preston Mansion to the wife of the radical governor Franklin Moses, Jr. With the deaths of Susan Hampton Manning in 1845, of Wade Hampton II in 1858, and of Mary Cantey Hampton in 1863; the War; and crushing debts; the lands were either sold or lost until little remained of the first Wade Hampton's princely domain.[46]

Another indication of the maturing of the Hamptons from Southern frontiersmen into plantation aristocrats is their changing attitude toward slavery. There is some indication that Wade Hampton I was capable of cruelty to slaves,[47] a trait not uncommon among those on the Southern frontier. More typical of the planter-aristocrat, Wade Hampton II had a reputation of kindness to his slaves. In 1850 this Hampton wrote with obvious pleasure of his distributing Christmas gifts to his slaves at Walnut Ridge on the Mississippi. Each received a blanket, a pair of stockings, a handkerchief, a calico dress and checked apron (to each woman), and a fine bleached shirt and fancy pants (to each man).[48] William Kauffman Scarborough concluded in his study of the great slave owners, *Masters of the Big House, Elite Slaveholders of the Mid–Nineteenth-Century South*, that Hampton II was exceedingly indulgent with his slaves. Dr. Robert W. Gibbes, who treated the Hampton slaves, stated his belief that this master was indeed kind to his human property.[49] A perusal of the Slave Schedule of the Census of 1850 found an impressive number of very old slaves in the possession of Wade Hampton II, a number aged one hundred and over, surely an indication of less-than-severe treatment.[50]

Wade Hampton II carried on the family tradition of fondness for horses and outdoors sports. He established a summer retreat at Cashiers Valley,

North Carolina, known to the family as "the valley." This became a family site for hunting, fishing, and general relaxation.[51] The present-day resort High Hampton is the descendant estate of the Hampton family's mountain retreat.

This wealthy aristocrat became deeply involved in the political and financial matters of the state. He served in the state senate from 1826 until 1830. He was a director of the Bank of South Carolina. Hampton, Franklin Elmore, and Pierce Butler invested in the Nesbitt Manufacturing Co., an iron company chartered in 1835. A Swedish company bought them out in 1850.[52] In 1836 the stock for the Louisville, Cincinnati, and Charleston Railroad was offered to the public. The idea of a transmontane railroad from Charleston to Cincinnati was a visionary scheme, which gained much attention and some investments from South Carolinians anxious to draw at least some of the trade from the Midwest to Charleston. These investors hoped to stave off or reverse the economic decline of South Carolina relative to the new states of the Southwest. The charter would be valid only if there were a public sale of a minimum of $4 million. That minimum was obtained only through the substantial personal purchases of Wade Hampton II.[53] He invested $209,050 in order to bring the total to the level required by the charter.[54]

Wade Hampton II, like his father, had inclinations toward the policies of the Whigs, inasmuch as they carried on the policies of federalism. Notably, Hampton II avoided much of the hysteria of nullification. He doubtlessly thought that nullification was a constitutional remedy of the state's woes, but he opposed disunion. Hampton, John Springs, W. C. Preston, and other wealthy South Carolinians not of the coastal region had a wide range of entrepreneurial interests in banks, railroads, manufacturing, and in lands in the Southwest. This group generally supported the Whig programs for economic development. Those planters devoted more exclusively to planting, yeoman farmers and subsistence farmers, tended to be Democrats. In 1840 the Whig-leaning group, including Hampton, supported William Henry Harrison for president, thus opposing John C. Calhoun, who backed Martin Van Buren. Largely because of the power of Calhoun, the Whigs lost in South Carolina in 1840 and won only one seat in Congress (William Butler of Greenville).[55] Hampton II admired the leading Whig Henry Clay, entertaining the Kentucky statesman at Millwood, Hampton's palatial home.[56] In 1847 another great Whig, Daniel Webster, visited Millwood. That eminent New England Whig found the Hampton's "establishment very handsome, and his family very well educated and agreeable."[57]

With all of the prosperity and influence of this grand aristocrat, there was genuine sadness. Ann Fitzsimons Hampton died in 1833 soon after the birth of Mary Fisher, their eighth child. Wade III was born in 1818; Christopher, born in 1821, died in 1886; Harriet Flud, born in 1823, died unmarried in 1848; Catherine, born in 1824, died unmarried in 1916; Ann, born in 1826, died unmarried in 1914; Caroline, born in 1828, died unmarried in 1902; Frank, born in 1829, married the very interesting Sally Baxter of New York and died in combat in 1863; and Mary Fisher, born in 1833, died unmarried in 1866.[58]

While this Hampton took some interest in political affairs, he was essentially a planter, businessman, and leader in South Carolina society. He used the most modern methods of planting, and he took considerable interest in acquiring and developing the best breeds of stock: cattle, sheep, swine, and especially horses. He even bought horses from the stables of King William IV, the most famous purchase being Monarch. Hampton's horses were frequent winners at South Carolina racing events.[59] Frank Forrester dedicated his book *Field Sports of the United States and British Provinces of North America* to Wade Hampton II, as "the First Sportsman of the land."[60] Millwood was the social center of South Carolina. In the late 1830s Hampton renovated Millwood to make it one of South Carolina's great mansions. Important, influential people, as well as the young friends of Hampton's children, enjoyed the hospitality of Millwood. The Hampton mansion became famous for its sumptuous entertainment. Hampton was influential in the election of Gov. William Aiken (1844–1846), and he staged a great celebration after the election. Benjamin F. Perry attended that party:

> When we reached the avenue leading from the public road to the house, we saw on both sides of it huge lighted torches of pine. Making the road as bright as if it were day. The supper was most luxurious and very handsomely decorated. . . . I never saw it surpassed in Washington, New York, or Boston. It was a very large assembly of ladies and gentlemen. But Colonel Hampton was distinguished for his frequent and magnificent entertainment and especially during the sittings of the legislature. . . . He possessed a princely fortune, and he spent his income with the munificence and liberality of a prince.[61]

Another indication of the sophisticated nature of Hampton was the fact that he was a patron of the arts. James DeVeaux was a well-known artist of this time. After studying in Philadelphia, DeVeaux painted portraits of such notables as George McDuffie, Thomas Cooper, and John L. Manning. Hampton helped finance DeVeaux's trip to Europe, where the artist was to copy some of the works of the masters for various South Carolina homes.[62]

Although Hampton II was never himself a political leader, he exercised significant influence, becoming known as the South Carolina Warwick. Benjamin F. Perry, who obviously knew Hampton well, wrote that many urged Hampton to offer himself for the office of governor, but "he preferred making governors to being one himself. For more than twenty years he was the great Warwick of South Carolina and took an active part in the gubernatorial elections. Seldom did anyone succeed to the chief magistracy of the state without his support."[63] The best-known example of Hampton as Warwick pertained to James H. Hammond, who was married to Catherine Fitzsimons, one of the sisters of Mrs. Wade Hampton II. Hammond became involved in an indiscretion with the daughters of Hampton, an indiscretion that Hammond did not deny. In 1846 Hammond, having served as governor in 1842–1844, decided to offer himself for election to the U.S. Senate, to replace George McDuffie. Hampton used his influence to stop the support for Hammond. The legislature instead chose F. H. Elmore. Hammond went into voluntary exile to his plantation, thinking he could never again be elected. When Calhoun died in 1850, the legislature considered Hammond but chose instead Robert Barnwell Rhett.[64] Hammond did not return to Columbia until 1857, when he won election to the U.S. Senate. Obviously time had worked its cures.[65]

Not one of the Hampton daughters ever married. Hampton III always felt responsible for his unmarried sisters, and they assisted in raising their brother's children. The relationship between the third Wade and his uncle-by-marriage Hammond was distant.

The second Hampton was an important influence in the events of the mid-century. In 1850 John C. Calhoun died while negotiations were underway that led to the package of legislation known collectively as the Compromise of 1850. Calhoun had opposed this move as failing to secure the guarantees he thought necessary for the security of his beloved South. The radicals in the state legislature succeeded in getting passed a call for an election of a convention, ostensibly to consider secession. In this entire furor Wade Hampton II was a moderate, quite in keeping with his Whig leanings. Southern Whigs persisted in seeing more value in the national government than their Democratic neighbors. The Whiggism of Hampton II was likely strengthened by his holdings along the Mississippi, where the major landholders saw a threat to their well-being from any division of sovereignty governing the Mississippi River, which stretched through the heart of the United States. He was a member of the group known as cooperationists—those who opposed South Carolina's seceding without the support of other Southern states. Hampton's associates in this position were Robert Woodward Barnwell, Andrew Pickens Butler, Langdon Cheves, Christopher Memminger, James L. Orr, and Benjamin F. Perry. Perry observed that those pushing for immediate and singular secession were not in general the large slaveholders; they were instead young, glory-seeking hotheads.[66] Those younger radicals became known as the fire-eaters. The fire-eaters did not have their way in the ensuing convention; the cooperationists prevailed.

The opposition of Wade Hampton II to the fire-eaters should not be misunderstood. He was a Southern moderate, willing to defend slavery, but with

reasonable caution. In 1849 Hampton had represented his district in a convention called to consider the growing threat to slavery coming from the North.
That convention resolved its willingness to take "firm, united and concerted
action" with other Southern states.[67] The wording of this is important. The
more radical group was willing, even anxious, to take the state out of the Union
alone. This convention selected a standing committee of five to carry on correspondence with other states. Hampton was a member of that committee. In
1852 Wade Hampton II and James Chesnut were considering the wisdom of
underwriting a newspaper in Columbia to present the case of the moderates.[68]

In 1858 the second Wade Hampton was going west to check on his plantations when he became ill on a Mississippi steamboat. He was put ashore at
Natchez, where he died. Hampton's son Christopher brought the remains
back to Columbia, where they were interred in the cemetery of Trinity Episcopal Church, the present-day Trinity Cathedral. The eulogies were significant in their praise.

One newspaper described Hampton as "a gentleman and citizen of untir-
ing public spirit, gallant demeanor, and high toned courtesy and hospitality—
in all parts a noble representative of the best old school and class of Carolina
planters . . . of the purest integrity and Roman firmness . . . , the first gentleman of his state in whatever was graceful and attractive . . . , beau ideal of a
Southern country gentleman."[69] The death of the second Wade Hampton
was a severe blow to the family. His surviving children were Wade III, Christopher (called Kit), Kate, Ann, Caroline, Frank, and Mary Fisher. Wade III
wrote from the plantation Wild Woods in Mississippi to his sister Mary
Fisher, "I want to do all in my power to replace him who has gone, to show
my love and reverence for him by my devotion to those dear daughters who
made his happiness on earth."[70]

In August 1855 Wade Hampton II had conveyed to his sons Wade III
and Christopher the plantation in Issaquena County, Mississippi, known as
Walnut Ridge, totaling 2,529 acres. This carried with it the obligation to pay
off mortgages of approximately $400,000, to be paid in installments to the
Bank of Louisiana in New Orleans. In July 1858 Christopher conveyed Walnut Ridge to his brother Wade III, with the indebtedness and 250 slaves.
Wade III assumed ownership of Walnut Ridge and signed notes promising
to make annual payments, typically $10,000, by January 1 of each year, with
several payments as high as $27,000. The first obligated payment was for
January 1, 1856. Hampton made the appropriate payments until the Civil
War began. There were no payment in 1862 or thereafter. Wade III had
earlier acquired the plantations Wild Woods and Bayou Place (or Richlands)
in Washington County, Mississippi. The production of cotton was
profitable enough in the 1850s for the owners to assume that the payments
could be made without difficulty. The coming of the war was the problem

that led to bankruptcy in 1868.[71] Christopher assumed ownership of the plantation Linden, adjacent to Wild Woods on Lake Washington. Frank inherited Woodlands and the Machines near Columbia. The four daughters received the Millwood mansion and 1,079 acres near Columbia, South Carolina.[72]

TWO

The Mantle Passes to the
Third Wade Hampton

Wade Hampton III was forty years old when his father died. He had had a long and meaningful apprenticeship before assuming the role as the senior Hampton, the wealthy owner of extensive plantations in South Carolina and on the Mississippi, as true an aristocrat as this country could produce, a Carolinian imbued with a sense of noblesse oblige. While he had grown up much under the influence of his grandfather and his father, men with distinguished and proud military records, his own education was classical, not military. This is of special interest because Hampton would become a very successful military leader, one of only three lieutenant generals in the Confederate army who had not been trained at the U.S. Military Academy. He followed the pattern of his father and grandfather in being a great outdoorsman, an almost fabled sportsman. That trait and the influence of the military achievements of his forebears likely gave him the best preparation for his military service. This can scarcely be overstated, because he reached the pinnacle of his effectiveness as a military leader. He did not achieve political distinction before the war, and, while he played an extremely important role in South Carolina politics after the war, he was not brilliantly successful. He was in fact a brilliant cavalry leader, who seemed to have had an instinctive understanding of terrain and tactics. Still, his education was classical and his speeches were laced with classical allusions. One can almost picture Hampton riding into battle citing *dulce et decorum est pro patria mori*.[1]

The third Wade Hampton was born in Charleston on March 28, 1818. He was born in the home of his mother's (Ann Fitzsimons) family. The young Hampton's formative years were spent at Millwood, his father's estate near Columbia. This impressive house was the center of much of the social life of Columbia and South Carolina. His father often entertained governors and presidents of South Carolina College. A correspondent from the *New York Herald* described Millwood as being built like an English manor house and located on a hill with a fine view of Columbia. The plantation had a frontage of about two miles on the Congaree River.[2] He undoubtedly learned the skills of hunting and fishing from his father and grandfather. The youngest Wade Hampton spent many formative hours at Woodlands, his grandfather's home. His mother died in 1833 when Wade was fifteen. Wade Hampton I, a towering figure in the young Hampton's life, died in 1835. Wade III inherited the sword that his grandfather had used in the Revolution. He practiced the skills of outdoor sportsmanship at the summer retreat in Cashiers Valley, North Carolina. He, of course, learned much about the management of the extensive Hampton plantations in South Carolina and on the Mississippi. He attended Rice Creek Academy, operated by Jimmy Daniels, and he entered South Carolina College at age fourteen.

Hampton and his fellow students received a classical education from the state's institution of higher education. The college expected its entering freshmen to have an accurate knowledge of Greek and Latin grammar, to have read the whole of Virgil, Cicero's orations, Xenophanes' Cyropedia, one book of Homer, and more,[3] and Hampton's orations often reflected his classical education. While not much is known about his experiences as a college student, it is known that he was a student of one of the great intellectuals of the age, Francis Lieber, whose liberal philosophy was much out of sympathy with the prevailing thought in South Carolina.[4] Lieber influenced Hampton's thinking about the possibility of reopening the slave trade in the 1850s[5] and might have influenced his treatment of freedmen after the war. Lieber took the side of the Union in the Civil War and became an advisor to President Lincoln, but his son Oscar joined the Hampton Legion and died of wounds in the Peninsula campaign.[6] In 1836 Hampton graduated from college.[7] He studied law, but apparently never had interest in practicing.

At age twenty he married Margaret Preston, the daughter of the late Gen. Francis Smith Preston of Virginia and the sister of John Smith Preston, who was married to Wade III's aunt Caroline. Margaret's father had served in both the Virginia House of Delegates and in the U.S. Congress, and he served as a colonel in the War of 1812 and later as a general in the Virginia militia. Caroline's husband, John Smith Preston, was educated at Hampden-Sydney College, University of Virginia, and Harvard. John's older brother William Campbell Preston had graduated from South Carolina College. Afterward William read law and began a practice in Columbia. In 1836 he became a U.S. senator from South Carolina, and he became president of South Carolina College in 1845. Obviously, Wade Hampton's marriage was advantageous.[8]

Wade Hampton II's expansive and expensive lifestyle left a joint heritage of a sense of aristocratic noblesse oblige and a large indebtedness. As stated above, Wade Hampton III assumed from his deceased father responsibility for a large indebtedness on the Mississippi estate Walnut Ridge, and Wade and his brother Kit assumed responsibility for a number of notes totaling about another eighty-two thousand dollars. This debt was indeed a princely sum for the mid–nineteenth century.[9] While most of these estates were operating quite profitably, the problem was in the timing of these debts. Within a few years the South plunged into a destructive war, and early in that war invaders took the lands along the Mississippi. Hampton lost his entire crop in 1861. After the war he faced the huge debt acquired in the late 1850s, and the repayment of those sums in an infinitely harder time was virtually impossible. In 1868 Hampton declared bankruptcy. Yet, he redeemed some of his lands, including Wild Woods, because in 1885 he was still making payments to his more fortunate neighbor Stephen Duncan, Jr., who held a mortgage on that Mississippi plantation.[10]

Stephen Duncan is worth some further comment. He was a physician from Pennsylvania who became an extremely successful planter and businessman. By 1851 Duncan owned six cotton plantations, two sugar plantations, and 1,041 slaves. In 1856 Hampton III owed Duncan $26,360 in notes.[11] By remaining loyal to the Union, Duncan managed to survive the war with his wealth, much to the chagrin of his neighbor Hampton. That chagrin notwithstanding, Stephen Duncan, Jr., heir to his father's fortunes, handled Hampton's postwar debts in a manner that enabled the bankrupt general to continue as a planter after declaring financial bankruptcy in 1868. Duncan leased the property back to Hampton, who was obligated to make annual payments that, when completed, would result in regaining ownership.[12]

As a young man, Wade Hampton III worked with his family in South Carolina and along the Mississippi as a planter. Influenced by the optimism of the cotton South, he bought 3,250 acres from Frederick G. Turnbull in Washington County, Mississippi, and divided this purchase into two plantations: Wild Woods and Bayou Place. Wild Woods—on the shore of Lake Washington—became his Mississippi home. In 1845 Hampton purchased another tract from Turnbull; this became an addition to Bayou Place. Also in 1845 the young Hampton joined his father and brother Kit in buying 2,300 acres in Cashiers Valley, North Carolina. This cool mountain retreat, where the Hamptons built a hunting lodge and several cottages, became a favorite spot for hunting, fishing, and relaxation.[13]

Understanding Wade Hampton III as a sportsman is important to understanding his career. Early writers on the Civil War probably made too much of the Southern soldiers having been prepared for war by their outdoor experiences, because that argument belittles the similar experiences of the Union soldiers, especially those from the West. Nevertheless, in the case of Hampton the argument holds true. Much of his superb skill as a leader of cavalry came from his earlier-acquired skills as a hunter on horseback. A writer in *Harper's New Monthly* in October 1855 commented, "The planter of the South, more than the citizen of any other section of the union, indulges in the manly excitement of the chase; they are, without exception, excellent horsemen, and have a thorough knowledge of woodcraft."[14] Hampton had considerable access to unpopulated lands. He had been well trained by his father and his grandfather, both of whom were excellent sportsmen. He also owned splendid horses, and he had the leisure time to use them. The most adventuresome of the hunts were for bear, especially in Mississippi. There were dogs specially bred for hunting bear. Hampton used steamboats and barges to move his hunting parties deep into the Mississippi swamps. The horses followed the dogs until a bear was treed, and then came the kill. Hampton's favorite weapon for killing the bear was the long knife. One can scarcely imagine the excitement of doing in the ferocious animal at close enough quarters for the use of a knife, notwithstanding its length. Theodore Roosevelt in *The Wilderness Hunter* said that Hampton killed eighty bear with the long knife. One part of the Hampton holdings along Lake Washington in Mississippi was known as "Bear Garden." While Roosevelt's number may be exaggerated, Hampton was without question an excellent and fearless hunter.[15]

Hampton's correspondence shows the great importance he placed on hunting and fishing. In the winter of 1859 he reported to his sister that he had caught forty trout in two outings of about an hour each.[16] In 1860 he wrote to Alexander Wilson (presumably a caretaker) at Cashiers, North Carolina, to instruct him to put trout in a spring for spawning and then put the eggs in running water for hatching. He asked Wilson to get two to four dozen fish to be sent to Columbia.[17] All of this activity contributed to his being a powerful man: six feet tall, barrel-chested, with blue eyes and light brown hair.[18] He had a thick head of brown hair, turning white with age. He wore a thick mustache and muttonchop beard. His demeanor was one of aristocracy, yet strikingly plain and unforced.

At the death of Wade Hampton I the Houmas estate went to the general's widow, Mary Cantey Hampton, and to the two surviving daughters, Caroline Hampton Preston and Susan Hampton, soon to be married to John L. Manning. In 1840 the Prestons moved to Mississippi to manage their lands and those belonging to the general's widow. In 1848 Mary Cantey Hampton deeded her share of Houmas to the Prestons. In the same year the Prestons built the impressive Houmas mansion. A decade later they sold their part of Houmas for $1.5 million.[19]

In 1846 the Prestons decided to travel to Europe, and they invited Wade and Margaret to accompany them. Margaret declined because of pregnancy; Wade went for a memorable experience. They took with them a letter of introduction to the Duke of Wellington, and they were indeed entertained by Lady Wellington and other notables. Young Hampton especially enjoyed a visit to the royal stables at Hampton Court, the original home of his grandfather's famous horse Monarch. He also visited Blenheim, the estate of the Duke of Marlborough, and Chatsworth, the home of the Duke of Devonshire.

When he visited the House of Commons he heard speeches by Disraeli and Lord John Russell.[20] He invited a number of his titled hosts to visit his Mississippi estates for hunting. Within months the English friends made the return visit, and they enjoyed the hunting immensely.[21]

On June 27, 1852, Margaret Preston Hampton died, leaving her husband with four children: Wade IV, age twelve; Preston, age nine; Sally, age seven; and Harriet, age four. Hampton buried her in the family plot in the Trinity churchyard. His unmarried sisters, living at Millwood, took charge of the rearing of his children. Wade III divided his time between Millwood and the Mississippi plantations.[22]

In 1852 Hampton, thirty-four years old, began his political career by entering the South Carolina House of Representatives to represent Richland County.[23] He served with John S. Preston and John L. Manning,[24] both related to Hampton by marriage. Preston had returned from Mississippi in 1848. Manning was elected governor in December 1852.

Two issues dominated South Carolina politics in the decade of the 1850s: slavery and the perceived threats to that "peculiar institution" and, closely related, the possibilities of seceding from the federal union. The tone of political discussion had changed significantly and tragically in the two decades from the 1830s to the 1850s. In the early 1830s, the two factions were the Nullifiers and the Unionists; the former wanted to nullify tariff legislation, and the latter wished to work out difficulties by more traditional methods. In the 1850s the political leadership had "calculated the value of the union,"[25] and many generally concluded that its value could be sacrificed for the good of South Carolina. Consequently the state in the 1850s was divided between those who supported secession of South Carolina alone and those who supported secession only in cooperation with other Southern states. Both father and son Hamptons were cooperationists, that is, they believed secession to be legal, but it was a remedy to be approached with considerable caution. Benjamin F. Perry, a leading voice for the cooperationists, wrote that the largest planters, including Wade Hampton II, did not urge secession. Specifically, "Colonel Hampton . . . very decidedly opposed any rash or precipitate action." Perry noted the irony in the fact that "others owning two or three Negroes or none at all have urged the good people of South Carolina every week to secession in defence of slavery."[26]

Slavery was obviously the great issue of this age, and students of Hampton are driven to question what this representative of South Carolina thought about the peculiar institution. Much to the frustration of later generations, the paucity of extant personal papers leaves us with only speculative conclusions. He was born into one of the great slave-holding families, and it is likely that he accepted slavery as a given. It is also likely that he was, through the influence of his father, accustomed to humane treatment of slaves, an ideal of the slave-holding aristocracy. While there are no written records of his philosophical stance, one can conclude from his actions that Hampton was, as in all matters, a moderate on the issue of slavery. His role in the legislature certainly points to this conclusion, as does his attitude toward secession. His attitude toward freed blacks after the war certainly indicates that he did not have the deep-seated fear and hatred that was characteristic of many of his fellow South Carolinians.

Wade Hampton III's record as a member of the South Carolina General Assembly was not especially distinguished (one suspects that this service was not his highest priority), but the record does indicate that he was no fire-eater; he was instead a moderate whose primary interest was in the progress and stability of business. His first measure was to recommend the incorporation of the Exchange Bank in Columbia. Later in the same session he introduced a bill to authorize the South Carolina Railroad to build a bridge over the Congaree River. Hampton served on the Committee on Federal Relations and the Committee on Agriculture. In December 1852 he voted to increase the appropriations for public schools.[27] The legislature elected the third Wade Hampton to the South Carolina College Board of Trustees, carrying on another family tradition. In the following year Hampton sent a check to President James H. Thornwell of South Carolina College to establish a scholarship for a promising student in financial need.[28] In the session of 1853 he supported the incorporation of the Columbia and Hamburg Railroad, the incorporation of the Columbia Iron Manufacturing Co., and the construction of a hospital for the insane in the vicinity of Columbia.[29] Hampton retained a special interest in the asylum for many years. In 1854 he introduced a bill to incorporate the Southern Mutual Life Insurance Co. The Committee on Federal Relations, chaired by Edward McCrady, considered a measure to have presidential electors elected by the people rather than by the general assembly. When the committee reported this bill, Hampton voted for its passage, a relatively progressive measure. The bill failed to pass.[30] Hampton was by now chairing the Committee on the Lunatic Asylum. In 1856 he became a member of the Ways and Means Committee, a sure sign of his acquiring more influence. He voted for a new edition of the Seaman's Act, to incarcerate free black merchant seamen for the duration of their ships' stay in the Charleston harbor. This act brought down on this state the opprobrium of the outside world. Apparently, this was a dark side of slavery that Hampton accepted. In 1856 Hampton became a member of the Joint Committee on the New Capitol Building. He presented a resolution that passed to authorize the appropriation of ten thousand dollars for removing obstructions in the Congaree and Santee rivers from Granby to the mouth of the Santee.[31] Hampton was elected to the South Carolina Senate in 1858. In the upper house he served on the Committee on Federal Relations, Committee on the Legislature, and the Committee on the New Capitol. He resigned from the Senate in 1861 because of his military service.[32]

The most important issue in which Hampton became embroiled in his legislative experience was the debate over the possibility of reopening the Atlantic slave trade, a traffic outlawed by Congress in 1808. Leonidas W. Spratt of Charleston in 1852 launched a movement to reopen the African slave trade, the primary motive being to make available labor for the expanding cotton economy of the Southwest (Alabama, Mississippi, and Louisiana). In the light of the growing antislavery movement, such a measure would inevitably have been extremely inflammatory. In 1856 Gov. James H. Adams in his message to the legislature endorsed reopening the trade. Adams reasoned that since slavery was a blessing the slave trade could not be evil. It would be desirable for all whites to own slaves, thereby giving even the poorest white a stake in the institution. Since the South was not benefiting by white immigration, there should be another way for this region to control its labor supply.[33] Speaker Thomas Y. Simon introduced a resolution condemning the move to reopen the slave trade as giving "neither repose or security to the institutions of the South but must tend to distract and divide the counsels of our state and to alienate from her [the] support and sympathies [of] her sister states."[34] The controversy concerning the reopening of the slave trade lasted for much of the decade of the 1850s. It is difficult to judge how widespread was the support for this obviously radical measure. William C. Preston thought that few people favored actually reopening the slave trade, but most were afraid to voice their opinions.[35] To an extent Preston was correct, in that fire-eaters had successfully propagandized the state.

Fortunately there were prominent opponents to reopening the slave trade. The Reverend James Henley Thornwell, a leading Presbyterian minister, for a time president of South Carolina College, and one of the most eloquent defenders of the institution of slavery, opposed renewing the African slave trade and expressed to the governor that such a measure would "dehumanize the domestic quality of slavery."[36]

Hampton received strong encouragement to oppose the measure from his former professor and prominent intellectual of this era, Francis Lieber, who had moved on to a position at Columbia College (later Columbia University). In a letter to his former student, Lieber wrote, "Depend upon it, my friend, the truest, most radical argument it is that African slave trade is a godless, unchristian crime and infamy, the blot of our race, and renewing it would be a high-handed rebellion against civilization." He urged Hampton to "do what you can in your sphere and your line to arrest this slur on humanity."[37]

It was on the issue of reopening the slave trade that Hampton made his most significant stand to that date, and he was constant in his position. In 1854 Hampton stated for the *New Orleans Bulletin*:

We take pleasure in distinctly and emphatically reiterating the statements we have made on previous occasions, that were the question of reopening the slave trade left exclusively to the decisions of the slaveholders it would be voted down by an overwhelming majority. . . . Yet the editorials of the *Mercury* have been reproduced in most of the Free Soil and abolition journals of the North, and heralded to their readers as a full and fair expression of Southern sentiment! Nothing could be more contrary to the will and wishes of our people. We feel entirely sure that not a precinct, even in Louisiana, would sustain it.[38]

Robert Barnwell Rhett of the *Charleston Mercury* was one of the most outspoken advocates of reopening the slave trade.

On December 10, 1859, Hampton addressed the South Carolina Senate on this issue. He described his opposition to the reopening of the slave trade as "unalterable and uncompromising." He saw this measure as "fraught with greater danger to the South than any other that has ever been proposed." He was specifically opposing a resolution presented by Sen. Edward B. Bryon of St. John's Colleton, who had argued that the acts of Congress forbidding the slave trade were unconstitutional. The minority opinion of the Committee on Federal Relations supported the opinions of the lowcountry senator. Hampton argued that the congressional acts were within the spirit of the Constitution. He pointed out that the framers of the Constitution expected just such a law to be enacted as soon as possible. This was a compromise to which the South had agreed. The Northern half of the compromise agreed to allow the trade to be legal until 1808. Hampton informed the Senate that in the Constitutional Convention both South Carolina and Georgia initially refused to agree to a constitution that prohibited the slave trade. Without the compromise the constitution making could have been wrecked. "But the danger was averted. Wise and better counsel prevailed then, as I trust in God they may now." Charles Cotesworth Pinckney represented South Carolina on the committee that produced the compromise. Hampton quoted John C. Calhoun, who in a speech concerning the Treaty of Washington stated his opinion that closing the slave trade was both right and expedient. Calhoun at one point referred to the slave trade as "that odious traffic." The resolution of the Committee on Federal Relations, which Hampton supported, stated: "Resolved, that it is impracticable to reopen the slave trade, all agitation on this subject is unwise, inexpedient, and impolitic." Further in the resolution there is a reference to the proposition as being absurd. Hampton mentioned those Southerners who advocated carrying on the trade in slaves illicitly as being "the worst enemies the South has to contend with." He said that he had less sympathy for those Southerners who were appealing to a "higher law" of greed than to those Northerners who were appealing to a higher law against slavery. At least the Northerners were arguing on the basis of virtue, mistaken or not. The advocates for an illicit trade in slaves were motivated by greed alone. Hampton recognized that some were pushing for the reopening of the slave trade as a means of speeding up the division of the Union. In words almost Lincolnesque, Hampton advocated preserving the Union, because of "hallowed association consecrated by the blood of patriots." He also argued that the South could better defeat the abolitionists by staying within the Union and under the federal constitution. Near the end of his speech Hampton in a rather retrospective mood commented with obvious sadness that he despaired of the Union unless the hostility in both the North and the South abated. He spoke eloquently of the danger of hastily destroying the Union, predicting that building another would be difficult. Hampton had proposed that the Committee on Federal Relations recommend a resolution, which the committee did not pass, condemning the reopening of the slave trade, characterizing that trade as "cruel and inhuman." He spoke of the impossibility that "the public voices of Christendom, which have so loudly, unitedly, and justly stigmatized this traffic as unholy, could be silenced, or that the still small voice, which is continually speaking to our hearts, could be hushed."[39]

The move to reopen the slave trade went nowhere, but it is an interesting insight into the spirit of the times. While Hampton never condemned slavery per se, he did evince a remarkable understanding of political realities and a significant understanding of an ugly side of the peculiar institution. There was an interesting review of the debate in *Debow's Review* (New Orleans). The writer stated that some believed that the slave trade could only be reopened by the establishment of a Southern confederacy. Yet, the recent Southern Commercial Convention did not support reopening the trade. The writer did not believe that even a Southern nation would begin the slave traffic again.[40] He was of course prescient.

The general tone of Hampton's service in the Senate was like that of his service in the House of Representatives. He normally represented the interests of business and commerce, especially the business of his constituents. He presented bills to pay R. W. Gibbes for printing state materials. He presented a petition from Edward B. Heyward seeking a charter for Garner's Ferry. The one important issue that gives an insight to a progressive Hampton was that of reopening the slave trade. At one point the Senate considered a resolution condemning Congress for declaring the slave trade piracy. Hampton moved that the resolution be tabled, and his motion passed.[41]

In addition to his political involvements, these were important years in Hampton's personal life. The former governor and senator, Calhoun protégé, and nullifier George McDuffie died in 1851, leaving a daughter, Mary Singleton McDuffie, who then went to live with her maternal grandfather, Col. Richard Singleton. Singleton died in 1852, and Mary then went to live with her aunt, Mrs. John Coles Singleton, who lived at Albemarle on the outskirts of Columbia. In 1853 Mary's uncle Matthew Singleton of Kensington died, leaving no adult male to manage the family affairs. Col. Wade Hampton suggested that Wade III assist Mary with the management of her business affairs. In March 1856 the young Wade Hampton wrote to "Miss Mary" to advise her on the disposition of the slaves she had inherited. He indicated that he could arrange the sale of up to one hundred slaves through the market in New Orleans, advising her to keep the others for a later and more favorable market. He expected to get seventy-five thousand dollars for the one hundred slaves, adding that if she sold the slaves on credit she could expect an interest of 8 percent on a note of five years.[42] The relationship between the wealthy and attractive widower and the attractive young woman eventually went beyond business. On Valentine's Day, 1857, Hampton wrote this verse for his young advisee:

> Ah me! Will she listen today and believe
> In the notes of their (birds) musical letter?
> Will her smile come to bless? Or must I confess
> To the wish—that I never had met her.[43]

She succumbed to his charm, and Hampton began the next stage of his career. They married on January 27, 1858, at Albemarle. She was twenty-eight and he forty. After a honeymoon at Kensington, Hampton took his bride to his Mississippi plantations. When they arrived in New Orleans, they learned of the death of Wade Hampton II. The younger Hampton was deeply moved by the death of his father; the family responsibility now passed to him. George McDuffie, the first child of Mary and Wade Hampton, was born at Millwood in January 1859. Wade then began construction of a home for his family. This white house with the requisite columns became known as Diamond Hill, located in what later became Forest Hills in Columbia. They lived at Millwood until the new house was finished. The Hamptons occupied Diamond Hill in the winter of 1859–1860. Benjamin F. Perry, the outspoken unionist and friend of the Hamptons, visited at the new house in January 1860. Perry later remembered the house as having the finest library in the state and Wade Hampton III as a "gentleman of great literary taste and scholarship."[44]

The Mississippi lands were the core of Hampton's business ventures. There, but for the gods of war, he could have continued building the family fortunes, as his acquisition of additional lands involved him in taking on debts that eventually sank him. When one links those debts to the ones he acquired with his father's estate in 1858, the financial doom caused by the war becomes even more understandable. Even in the 1850s there were indications that Hampton was over his head in debt. The Bank of the State of South Carolina sent a notice to John L. Manning that a note drawn by Hampton and endorsed by Manning, John S. Preston, and Mary Cantey Hampton was in arrears.[45] Writers have often referred to Hampton as being one of the richest of Southern planters before the war. James M. McPherson in his *Battle Cry of*

Freedom indicated Hampton as "reputed to be the richest planter in the South."[46] Hampton's debts likely make that not quite true. The 1850 Slave Schedule for Richland County, his South Carolina home, indicated that Wade III owned 8 slaves. The 1860 schedule for the same county indicated that he owned 30 slaves. The 1850 Slave Schedules for Mississippi do not show any slaves possessed by Hampton III. The 1860 Slave Schedule for Issaquena County, Mississippi, indicated Hampton's owning 249 slaves. Regretfully, the 1860 slave schedule for Washington County is not extant, but in a letter written in 1877, Hampton indicated that in 1860 he owned twelve thousand acres and 1,000 slaves in Mississippi. The 1860 Schedule for Issaquena County had Hampton's neighbor Stephen Duncan owning 706 slaves in that county, and he possessed vast wealth in mortgages on other properties.[47] The Mississippi land in 1860 was worth from fifty dollars to five hundred dollars per acre. Hampton harvested about 4,700 bales of cotton in 1861, and all of it was lost in the war.

In January 1860 Hampton received a letter from an English friend, T. W. Probyn, who had visited Hampton in America. This remarkable letter expressed thoughts that had great significance for Hampton and his culture. Probyn was saddened by the developments in the United States. He thought that the South was mistaken in its adamant defense of slavery. He hoped that the South, for which he had obvious affection, would change of its own accord, to mollify the peculiar institution. He argued that slavery

> cannot in the days in which we live remain unaltered as a permanent institu-
> tion. Look at Russia, her intelligent sovereign and her ablest statesmen . . .
> feel that serfdom must fall, and despite the many difficulties and dangers
> attending the change they are wisely undertaking it. The world moves on and
> those who do not progress with it are crushed by it. You cannot do all at once,
> but for your own sakes do something in time, and do it of your own free will,
> and you will be supported by all the intelligence and worth of the world and
> by the friendly gratitude of the gentle affectionate Black Race who have been
> so greatly wronged by us white men.[48]

One can hardly imagine a more ominous statement, pregnant with genuine wisdom and damning for the future of Hampton's culture. Hampton's fellow citizens would have considered this letter extremely inflammatory. South Carolina and the rest of the slave-holding South were indeed under siege, defending an institution against all change when even backward Russia was bending to the forces of history and thereby saving itself from the destruction of revolution, if only for a generation.

The Hamptons were no ordinary South Carolinians, not even ordinary slaveholders. The family entertained ideas that would have been considered heretical in the homes of their neighbors. The venerable historian T. Harry

Williams wrote of the South of this time, "most Southerners refused even to view slavery as a discussible question or to consider its relation to their or man's future."[49]

Wade's brother Frank married a New York beauty named Sally Baxter, who injected and reflected thinking not always typical of that era and locale. Sally was so remarkable that none other than William Makepeace Thackeray had come to admire her as a young girl. They began a correspondence that continued when Thackeray returned to England and Sally moved to South Carolina. Henry Adams commented in his *Education of Henry Adams* that Thackeray grieved woefully when news came of the death of Sally Baxter Hampton in 1862 (at Millwood of tuberculosis).[50] Sally both loved and was repelled by her new environment.[51] She obviously loved her husband, Frank— he survived her by less than a year; he was killed at the Battle of Brandy Station in June 1863. She also loved and admired the rest of the family. In a letter to her father she described Wade Hampton as "the soul of kindness to me and is withal so charming, so lovable that I can't say too much in his praise. He has, in common with them all, singularly unpretending manners and this joined to perfect ease and familiarity with the world, gives him at first the appearance of indifference. But his constant thoughtfulness of others and forgetfulness of self, this thorough goodness of heart and purity of mind warms you in a moment." Wade III became the godfather of Frank and Sally's son, Franky.[52] Sally wrote to her father in New York about slavery, "Anybody who stops to investigate can't but see how utterly unpracticable to the Southern mind is any idea of compromise, and how Northern fanaticism on this subject is to be moderated Heaven alone knows."[53]

In addition to Thackeray, Sally and Frank enjoyed the friendship of unusually interesting people. Dr. and Mrs. Samuel Gridley (Julia) Howe of Boston, who met Sally and Frank in Cuba (Julia Howe later recalled, "We became friends at once"), visited the Hamptons and stayed in the home of Wade Hampton III in 1859. Mrs. Howe would later write "The Battle Hymn of the Republic."[54] Both she and her physician husband were abolitionists. Dr. Howe was one of several prominent Northerners who backed John Brown in his attempt to incite a slave insurrection at Harpers Ferry.

Sally was indeed capable of standing apart and judging what was happening about her. She wrote in December 1860, "I for one don't dare look into the abyss of horror which opens before us. Sure no country ever before contained the elements for more utter anarchy." She touchingly quoted Coleridge, "And to be wroth with one we loved—Doth work like madness in the brain." She stated her own rather difficult but thoughtful position by concluding, "I am no Southerner heaven knows and at heart if not an abolitionist at least antislavery but just concede that the tone of the South has been most calm—manly and decided. They act with a strong feeling of patriotism and desire for justice to their country but at heart with as ardent a regret for the dissolution of the union as I have." In her most moving reflection on the crisis before her, she said, "Carolina women say they are proud to give sons and husbands to defend their country—Alas! I have no country to defend for the country is dead."[55] In the days just prior to the Secession Convention, members of the legislature often gathered at the Hampton home for relaxation and conversation. Sally gathered that they were sad at the thought of disunion and that they were aware that they might be moving toward self-destruction.[56] She understood that Wade Hampton believed that secession was legal but unwarranted at that time.[57]

The insights into the Hampton family gained from the letters of Sally Baxter Hampton illustrate that this was indeed no ordinary family. Doubts about the Southern cause were being expressed in the family of the man who became the state's most prominent Confederate officer. One must remember that even unionists far more outspoken than Hampton, who was not a unionist in the strictest sense, went with their state when secession was a fact, for example, B. F. Perry and James Louis Petigru. The society Sally had come to love and fret about would soon be in devastation, although she did not live to see it.

Other ominous issues regarding Hampton's future raised their heads in this decade. The editor of the *Daily South Carolinian* asked why South Carolina as an agricultural state had done so little for agricultural education. "Why has she no professor of agriculture in her college, no school of agriculture within her limits?" He pointed out that South Carolina College was a classical institution and most of her graduates became planters.[58] In 1855 one George Tillman, whose younger brother Benjamin later conquered the Hampton culture, spoke in the legislature in support of allowing the popular vote to select presidential electors (a measure Hampton supported). He spoke of the state's leadership as "an odious, cunning tyrannical, intriguing oligarchy. Yes, sir, an oligarchy, for I will not disgrace the English language by calling it an aristocracy. Which I can at least respect in a proper way."[59] Hampton's fortunes became the victims of such forces.

THREE

Of Arms and the Man

The decade of the 1850s was near the end of the world for the aristocratic rice
and cotton planter–slaveholders such as Wade Hampton.[1] The critical issues
which ultimately led to the Civil War were all there in the entire decade, but
it is difficult to say when the war became inevitable. One should recall the letter sent to Hampton by his English friend T. W. Probyn in 1860. Even at that
late date, if backward Russia could address its serf problem, surely the South
in the New World could avoid catastrophe by adjusting to change, even modestly, and that was all Lincoln asked.

While the radical fire-eaters neither left the state nor their argument for
unilateral secession, they did not, in the decade of the 1850s, enjoy a continu-
ous rise to power. The radicals led by Robert Barnwell Rhett and Francis W.
Pickens were rebuffed in their efforts to initiate secession over the Compromise of 1850. Moderates dominated the convention, which met in Nashville to
consider a Southern response to the compromise. South Carolinians favoring
secession only in cooperation with other Southern states, the cooperationists,
joined forces with South Carolina unionists, who favored working out the
South's problems within the Union. Together these two factions scored a
significant victory over the fire-eaters in the canvass of October 1851, the election of delegates to represent the state in the forthcoming Southern Convention to be held in Montgomery, Alabama, the following January.[2] In this
political contest, Wade Hampton II joined forces with the likes of A. P. Butler,
Langdon Cheves, James L. Orr, B. F. Perry, and John S. Preston.[3] At least for
a time secession was a dead issue. It is important to be aware, however, that
even the Unionists and cooperationists were united in defending slavery. Benjamin F. Perry, surely one of the most articulate Unionists, wrote in an article
titled "Disunion," published in the *Charleston Courier*, August 20, 1860, "It
may be that I am mistaken in supposing slavery to be out of reach of the assault
of its foes, and if so I will be as ready as any one to defend it at the sacrifice of
the union itself, as much as I value the union."[4]

It is difficult to say precisely where Wade Hampton III stood relative to
these issues. He was not yet the leader he was to become. Clearly he was not a
radical fire-eater. His speeches pertaining to the reopening of the slave trade

indicated that he was at least inclined toward being a unionist. B. F. Perry, who knew Hampton well, said, "He was a union man till his beloved state seceded."[5] He surely followed his father's lead in representing the conservative, stable, responsible interests of the state. As for slavery, Hampton was a moderate in his beliefs, and in a time of hardening attitudes, that was of some real significance. He was at least questioning the economic value of slavery.[6] His speeches against the reopening of the slave trade indicated that he saw part of slavery—the African slave trade—as cruel and inhumane. Again, that position was not unimportant for a major slaveholder. At that time any questioning of the peculiar institution was potentially treasonous.

The calm following the Compromise of 1850 was shattered by several events. The congressional debates over the Kansas-Nebraska Bill introduced by Sen. Stephen A. Douglas broke the calm in 1854. In 1856 Rep. Preston Brooks of Edgefield, South Carolina, beat Sen. Charles Sumner of Massachusetts with his walking cane in the U.S. Senate chamber until the senator was senseless. That incident demonstrated the depth to which the sectional split had sunk. Still, apparently there was hope. In 1857 the House of Representatives elected South Carolina's James L. Orr as Speaker.

The continuing and central problem was slavery, and even unionists and cooperationists were not willing to bend in their defense of the peculiar institution. The national debate over slavery reached a new level of crisis in 1859 with John Brown's raid at Harper's Ferry, Virginia. That attempt at inciting a slave insurrection and the backing it received in the North aroused the fears that had haunted the white South since the beginning of slavery. White Southerners had dreaded the possibilities of slaves turning on their masters, and here was an open attempt supported by some vocal elements in the North. The South obviously overreacted, but that judgment is with the benefit of hindsight.

The story of the Democratic Convention in Charleston in 1860 and the uncompromising forces that pulled it apart and thereby ensured the election of the Republican Abraham Lincoln has been told and retold enough without further repetition here. Hampton spent much of this time at his Mississippi plantations, playing almost no role in these events. On December 20, 1860, South Carolina seceded, and an era ended. Wade Hampton III had not been a part of the furor leading to secession, and he did not respond to the new Republic of South Carolina with great enthusiasm. Sally Hampton reported to a New York relative on January 11, 1861, "Wade Hampton for instance reprobates most strongly the firing on the *Star of the West* and is entirely disgusted with the manner in which matters are conducted down there."[7]

Hampton spent much of the time in the winter of 1860–1861 at his Mississippi plantations. This was a good time for those Hampton enterprises: the crops were good, and the prices were also good. Part of the tragedy for the

Hamptons was in the fate of those Mississippi crops. When the war began there was an accumulation of 4,700 bales of cotton on Hampton's Mississippi plantations, worth about $1.2 million in Union currency. Hampton offered the cotton to the new Southern government with the suggestion that it be shipped to Europe and used there to purchase arms.[8] Nothing was done, perhaps because of bureaucratic apathy, but it is possible that the reluctance to accept Hampton's offer might have been a result of the belief held by some that if the South withheld its cotton from Europe those economies would soon be on their knees, thereby assuring intervention on behalf of the Confederacy. The entire crop of 1861 was lost to the Hamptons; much of it destroyed to prevent its falling into the hands of the enemy. That loss plus the others of the war years when matched against the mortgages contracted a few years earlier led to financial ruin. Many of the major planters along the Mississippi River opposed secession because they feared the loss of the prosperity so prevalent just before the war. Hampton's nearest Mississippi neighbors, the Stephen Duncans, left the seceding South in disgust and returned to their native North. They returned after the war and remained wealthy people.[9]

All of this notwithstanding, Hampton went with his native state and became its most prominent Confederate. That loyalty to state over a national loyalty was part of the spirit of the times. The significant thing with Hampton was his absolute dedication to the cause once the decision was made. Hampton went to Montgomery, Alabama, the capital of the new Confederacy, where he conferred with the Confederate secretary of war, Leroy P. Walker, and with President Jefferson Davis. He took with him letters of introduction from the governor of South Carolina, Francis W. Pickens, and from Gen. P. G. T. Beauregard in command of the port of Charleston. Hampton offered his services for the cause. He reported to his sister, "The Secretary of War says he will do all in his power to assist me and the President is very friendly." He summarized his intentions, "I trust that I may yet have the opportunity of proving that I can do the state some service. I want a place where I can do real hard work; not one where the only duty is to wear a uniform. Send my sash to Mary."[10] He got his wish in full.

Hampton returned to South Carolina and set out to recruit and equip the Hampton Legion. Interestingly President Davis authorized Hampton to have his men sign up for twelve months. Visions of a short war proved to be a burden for both the Union and the Confederacy. Governor Pickens commissioned Hampton a colonel. Presumably to assist him with his own lack of military training, Hampton made B. J. Johnson, commander of the Washington Light Infantry Company of Charleston, lieutenant colonel and second-in-command of the legion. Johnson's Light Infantry became a part of the Hampton Legion.[11] The Legion began as a part of the state militia and then joined the Confederate service. President Jefferson Davis submitted to the Confederate Congress the recommendation that Hampton be appointed colonel in the provisional army of the Confederacy. He was to rank from July 12, 1861.[12]

While recruiting the legion, Hampton visited B. F. Perry for a time and secured the support of that outspoken Unionist, also then throwing his lot in with the state. Perry encouraged the men of his community to join the Legion. In a speech Perry proclaimed, "Hampton will make a spirited and wise commander in battle, but a kind and protecting father to his Legion"; Perry's son joined the Legion.[13]

The Hampton Legion was formally mustered into active service on June 12, 1861, in Columbia. It consisted of six companies of infantry, four companies of cavalry, and a battery of artillery. Hampton bought six field guns and other equipment at his own expense.[14] The infantry units included the Columbia Zouaves (presumably with the colorful uniforms those units wore in the early part of the war); the Edgefield Hussars, commanded by Capt. Matthew Calbraith Butler, who would be a Hampton colleague for many years in the military and in politics; and the Washington Artillery and the Washington Light Infantry, both of Charleston. The Washington Artillery was at first commanded by the West Point–trained Stephen D. Lee, who later became the Confederacy's youngest lieutenant general. It soon became known as Hart's Battery, commanded by James F. Hart. There were also an impressive number of black servants who assisted their aristocratic masters in preparing food, cleaning up, and other tasks. Hampton's body servant was Kit Goodwyn, whose loyalty lasted long after the war.

There was much excitement about the Hampton Legion. The ladies of Charleston made a flag for the legion, using a silk dress given by a member of the Hampton family. The design on the flag was a circle of oak leaves encircling "Hampton Legion." After the war the flag, "tattered, stained, and bullet-riddled," was returned to one of the makers.[15] A class of young girls in Columbia, none over seventeen, presented a concert in the summer of 1861 to raise funds for the Hampton Legion. The participants included Susan Preston, daughter of Wade III's Aunt Caroline Hampton and John S. Preston; Annie Hampton, daughter of Christopher Hampton, brother of Wade III; and Sallie Hampton, daughter of Wade III. They succeeded in raising a total of $150 in silver, which was spent on a package sent to the Legion after the Battle of Manassas.[16] In September 1861 the Black Oak Soldiers Relief Association recorded that they had made a total of 399 overcoats for the legion.[17] In that same month a society in Eutawville reported having accumulated "a large number of pantaloons for Hampton's Legion."[18]

Hampton's son Preston, having served briefly in Charleston at the siege of Fort Sumter, joined the Legion in Columbia. Wade IV became an aide on the staff of Gen. Joseph E. Johnston. Brother Frank became an officer in the cavalry of the Legion. The family was fully committed.

The legion, pulled together as a unit in its initial training at Camp Hampton near Columbia, was indeed a corps d'elite, but it did not long remain intact. Units of this makeup were not suited for modern warfare. Not long after the First Battle of Manassas the legion was separated and assigned to larger units.[19] Although the legion did not survive long as a unit, its personnel achieved real distinction in the war. Hampton became one of the three Confederate lieutenant generals without West Point training. The other two were Nathan Bedford Forrest and Richard Taylor, the son of the late President Zachary Taylor. M. C. Butler became a major general. Three of the Hampton Legion officers became brigadier generals: James Conner, Martin Gary, and T. M. Logan.[20]

For several months Hampton remained a member of the South Carolina Senate, perhaps an indication of his faith in a short war. Generally, however, he tended to be more of a realist. On October 8, 1861, well after the Battle of Manassas, Hampton submitted his letter of resignation to the president of the Senate: "As my duties as an officer of the army may render it impossible for me to discharge those of a State Senator, I beg to tender my resignation as Senator from Richland County."[21]

Apparently Gen. Pierre Gustave T. Beauregard offered Hampton the position as aide, but the commander of the legion understandably preferred to have a command of his own. He wrote Beauregard to decline the role as aide and to request that the legion be assigned to the Creole general's command. He assured Beauregard that the men of the legion, although inexperienced, would be worthy of their assignment.[22]

There was not much time between their initial training and actual combat service. On June 24, 1861, the Legion left Columbia for the Virginia front. On July 19 the legion of six hundred men left Richmond for Manassas, where General Beauregard, with about twenty thousand troops, guarded the rail junction. Union general Irvin McDowell with about thirty-five thousand troops threatened from the north. There were another eleven thousand Confederates in the Shenandoah Valley under the command of Gen. Joseph E. Johnston. The Union plan was for the fifteen thousand Federal troops at Harper's Ferry under the command of Gen. Robert Patterson to keep the Valley Confederates sufficiently occupied to prevent their reinforcing Beauregard's force. Lincoln ordered McDowell to move with his admittedly green troops against the equally green Rebels—or so Lincoln reasoned. The Confederate intelligence was equal to the task of being quite aware of the Union plans. On July 18 and 19 Johnston slipped away from the Union troops in the Valley and entrained for Manassas. McDowell's force had begun moving southward on July 16. The battle began on July 21 when Union troops attempted to turn the Confederate left by crossing Bull Run two miles upriver from the turnpike bridge. A South Carolinian, Col. Shanks Evans, learned of the flanking Yankees and moved to his left to meet them and hold them off until other Rebel forces could come up.[23]

The Hampton Legion participated in the midst of this first significant battle. They detrained at Manassas after firing had begun. Hampton led his men to the Robinson House on the northern side of the battlefield and then to a stonewall along the Warrenton Pike, which was the main north-south road crossing the stone bridge over Bull Run. Most of Johnston's troops had arrived from the Valley. The brigades of Gen. Bernard Bee (also of South Carolina) and Col. Francis S. Bartow, from Johnston's Valley force, reinforced Evans on the Rebel left. Even so, the Confederates were soon forced back by the Union onslaught. The Confederate retreat could have become a rout save the defensive positions of Gen. Thomas Jackson (thereafter Stonewall Jackson) and the Hampton Legion, which faced the Union brigade commanded by Col. Erasmus D. Keyes. The legion suffered 121 casualties, but they fought furiously and stopped Keyes, who moved off and took no other part in the engagement. At one time the legion was surrounded on three sides. Bee and Bartow urged Hampton to pull back. It was likely that a mixture of inexperience and determination kept the legion forward longer than they should have been. Lt. Col. B. J. Johnston, Hampton's second-in-command, was killed. The legion pulled back to the brow of Henry Hill, the base of the Confederate's strongest defense, where Hampton reformed his troops in a ravine. The Union troops made a number of brave but piecemeal assaults. Confederate counterattacks finally broke the Union left, and the Rebels rolled forward. Hampton joined in the general attack, but he was wounded, and the command of the legion passed to Capt. James Conner. The legion followed up on the victory by charging two miles beyond the stone bridge in the center of the battlefield. The Confederate advance then halted. The victors were almost as disorganized as the fleeing Yankees.[24] Hampton, receiving a not-very-serious wound to his head, deeply regretted having to miss the final assault.

Hampton's reputation was beginning to soar. Douglas Southall Freeman, in his summary of Hampton's role in the Battle of Manassas, wrote, "There was more of potential military excellence about him than his superiors at the moment realized."[25] Gen. Joseph E. Johnston in his memoirs written after the war praised Hampton's conduct in this battle, particularly citing his "courage and admirable soldiership."[26] The still-green legion had played a pivotal role in a major battle. Both President Davis and General Beauregard were high in their praise of Hampton's role in the Confederate victory.[27]

The troops in Hampton's command developed a great devotion for their leader. Hampton's sister wrote, "His men are perfectly devoted to him and well they may be, for . . . he is so noble, so good, and such a brave heart and yet so gentle and precious."[28] Although a sister's letter of praise is hardly an objective source, there is much truth in her judgment. Maj. T. G. Barker, who served as adjutant for the Hampton Legion, wrote, "I do not believe any officer in the Southern Army received such deep and loving personal devotion from his soldiers and officers as General Hampton seemed to compel by his irresistible charm of character. No commanding officer was more implicitly trusted by his men in battle or on the march."[29] Hampton proved to be an able military leader; yet he was essentially a gentle man with little of the bombast of the more colorful leaders around him, notably Jeb Stuart.

His greatest fame came as a cavalry commander, but certain aspects of his military talents were apparent before he commanded cavalry. An essential quality for any officer leading ground or mounted troops is that of surveying the terrain and quickly understanding where the advantageous positions are, usually the high ground. In Hampton this seemed to be an innate quality, perhaps coming from his love for the outdoors and his experience as an outdoorsman, but it was probably more innate than acquired. His colleague M. C. Butler wrote of him, "General Hampton appeared possessed of almost an instinctive topographical talent. He could take in the strong strategic points in the field of his operations with an accuracy of judgment that was surprising to his comrades."[30] Hampton was also unfailingly brave and considerate of his men. All of his talents as a military leader were not apparent in the first battle; they came with experience. But it is significant that he played a major role in the first battle.

After Manassas the Confederate army, faced with the necessity of recouping its strength, established headquarters in the vicinity of Fairfax Courthouse, between Manassas and Washington. In late October the Confederate commanding general, Joseph E. Johnston, moved to a line based on Centreville, a position less easily turned.[31] Immediately after the Battle of Manassas the legion was badly depleted. Hampton wrote to his friend William Porcher Miles, a member of the Confederate Congress and chairman of the House Committee on the Military, that the strength of his infantry was down to 226, largely because of illness.[32] In October 1861 Colonel Hampton was in command of the Fourth Brigade of Infantry, First Division, commanded by Maj. Gen. Earl Van Dorn. The brigade included the Hampton Legion. In November Hampton was transferred to the Third Division, commanded by Maj. Gen. James Longstreet.[33] Hampton's brigade now defended a position on the Occoquan River east of Manassas. The brigade dug a line of rifle pits, which Hampton considered to be inadequate for the defense of his position. He was severely limited by a lack of equipment.[34]

Hampton was not loath to try political influence to get his way. In December 1861, probably moved by the Union victory at Port Royal, he again wrote to Congressman Miles, this time to ask him to urge the secretary of war to transfer Hampton and his men to South Carolina to participate in the defense of their home state. The colonel assured the congressman that he had no desire to depart Virginia if a battle was pending.[35]

Colonel Hampton seemed to relish his military role. On December 20 he reported to his immediate superior, Gen. W. H. C. Whiting, that his troops had engaged in a skirmish with a body of enemy cavalry, and the enemy had retreated. The colonel wanted more action. He asked for permission to lay a trap for Yankee units coming to Pohicks Church: "There is no chance for a fight here, so we will have to look up one."[36] It is not known whether Hampton set his trap.

In all of this Hampton evinced a remarkable optimism. In January 1862 he wrote to his sister that he expected the major European countries to recognize the Confederacy as soon as the Southern ministers reached their destinations (presumably referring to James Mason and John Slidell, who were captured and then released in the HMS *Trent* incident). He assured her: "Our affairs are prospering and God seems to bless our efforts. I look to the breaking up of the Yankee government and it will be a blessing to mankind, when this occurs."[37]

After further reorganization in early 1862 Hampton was commanding a brigade consisting of the Fourteenth Georgia Infantry, the Nineteenth Georgia Infantry, the Sixteenth North Carolina Infantry, and the Hampton Legion. The appropriate rank for a commander of a brigade was brigadier general. Accordingly Gen. Joseph E. Johnston recommended that promotion in February 1862.[38] To the exasperation of Johnston and Hampton, the promotion was a long time in coming through.

The enlistment terms for the South Carolinians in the Hampton Legion were to expire on April 15, 1862. Hampton was confident that nearly all would extend their service. In special circumstances (including connections of friendships) the colonel secured early discharges. Hampton asked his sister to notify Dr. D. H. Trezevant and Dr. James Henley Thornwell that he had obtained discharges for both of their sons, but both refused to leave.[39] Sadly, both were to die in service.

Fearing a flanking move by the much larger Union army now being molded by Gen. George McClellan, the ever-cautious General Johnston decided to pull back again, this time to a line along the Rappahannock River. Hampton's brigade defended one of the more advanced positions on the Occoquan, being responsible for about twelve miles of the Confederate front. He had one regiment at Wolf River Shoals, one regiment at Davis Ford, and one in the Occoquan Valley.[40] His withdrawal was consequently difficult, and Union forces were watching the Rebels by the use of hot-air balloons. The move took place on March 8, 1862. After the move President Davis was aggrieved to learn that great quantities of supplies were destroyed or abandoned. Subsequently Secretary of War Judah P. Benjamin inquired of the truth of the reports. Hampton reported to his immediate superior, Gen. W. H. C. Whiting, that for lack of adequate transportation he had to lose some materials,

but much of it private, not government property, a point that especially bothered Hampton, believing that such a loss was an unfair burden to common
soldiers. General Whiting reported that Hampton had conducted the move
"with consummate judgment, precision, and skill."[41] General Johnston
deeply resented what he considered to be needless interference from civilian
authorities. Hampton was himself not above resenting those authorities
above him.

In mid-March 1861 General McClellan began a great flanking movement
by embarking his troops to Fortress Monroe at the southern tip of the peninsula formed by the York River to the north and the James River to the south.
The Union army had never yielded control of this fort to the Rebels. Ultimately, McClellan had approximately 121,500 men on this eastern approach
to Richmond. The Union army was supplied by the navy and amply so. It fell
to Maj. Gen. John Magruder to hold off the Union assault until General
Johnston could move his army to protect the Confederate capital from this
new threat. Magruder, with 17,000 men and a gift for theatrics, succeeded in
making McClellan believe that he faced a much larger force. The ever-cautious Union commander began a siege operation.

Johnston pulled his army from its position between Richmond and Washington and moved to the peninsula in the first days of April 1862. Magruder
had held a line based on Yorktown and watched McClellan preparing for a
siege with an abundance of heavy artillery. Johnston's army first moved to the
Yorktown line, but on May 4, in order to avoid being battered by the siege
guns, they pulled back to the vicinity of Williamsburg. Colonel Hampton
played a role in this action. Gen. D. H. Hill reported that during the move,
"The Yankee cavalry made its appearance, but after a charge by Hampton,
remained quiet."[42]

At this time Hampton, who was still a colonel, commanded a brigade in
Brig. Gen. W. H. C. Whiting's division on the left of the Confederate line.[43]
Hampton's next action was to oppose a Union amphibious landing to flank the
Confederate line. Federal transports ferried troops to the south bank of the
York River near the head of that waterway, landing below Eltham. General
Whiting received orders to stymie this attempt to turn the Confederate left
flank. He ordered the brigades of Gen. John Bell Hood and that of Colonel
Hampton to attack the enemy already on land.[44] The brigades of Hood on the
left and Hampton on the right assaulted a Union force of between fourteen
and sixteen regiments of infantry and one battery of artillery. Hampton at one
point turned back a Yankee attempt on his flank. In this action the Hampton
Legion was functioning as a regiment under the command of Lt. Col. J. B.
Griffin. The Rebels drove their opponents through a heavy forest to the shore,
where the Union gunboats provided a protective cover. The attempt to
outflank the Confederates had failed.[45] The Hampton brigade suffered no

deaths and four wounded.[46] General Johnston was pleased with the leadership of Hampton in this action, and he again recommended to President Davis that the brigade commander be promoted to brigadier general.[47] On the recommendation of President Davis the Confederate Congress confirmed Hampton's promotion to brigadier general to date from May 23, 1862.[48]

After the battle along the York River, Hampton wrote to his sister, "McClellan seems in no hurry to follow up and we will have everything ready for his reception. If we whip him here and I have no doubt but we shall, we will have every prospect for peace. . . . I have the most vindictive feelings toward the whole Yankee race."[49] A few days later he wrote to his sister, "it may please God to take me. . . . I have done my duty as a soldier and none of my name need be ashamed of me."[50] His attitudes of vengeance and fatalism steeled him for a long, arduous service.

Johnston continued his withdrawal to a line about seven miles east of Richmond, and there he made his stand. By the end of May, McClellan had his army astraddle the Chickahominy River, which flows from the north of Richmond in a southeasterly direction, at times almost in the middle of the peninsula before turning south to empty into the James River. As a result of recent rains the river was overflowing its banks. Johnston chose this time for his major counterattack. The Confederates launched an assault on the Union left south of the river. Largely because of faulty communications, the attack was mismanaged. This engagement, known as the Battle of Seven Pines, was indecisive. The attacking force is usually more vulnerable than the defenders, and this was the case in this battle at the outskirts of Richmond. The Southerners suffered one thousand more casualties than the Northerners. One of the casualties was Gen. Joseph E. Johnston, wounded on May 31, 1861.

Brigadier General Hampton played a major role in the Battle of Seven Pines. Gen. Gustavus W. Smith, commanding the Rebel left wing, ordered Hampton's brigade to advance on the Union right. Johnston Pettigrew, also of South Carolina, commanded another brigade in the assault. In the initial advance Hampton's brigade drove the enemy some distance through thick forest. Then to their surprise they found themselves subjected to enfilade fire from elements of the Union II Corps, commanded by Brig. Gen. Edwin V. Sumner. The Yankees had moved to Hampton's left flank and were firing from a ditch at the advancing Southerners. The result was slaughter. Half of Hampton's men who were engaged became casualties; 45 were killed and 284 were wounded.[51] Three brigades were involved in this particular attack; all three brigade commanders were hit. One commander, Robert Hatton, was killed. Pettigrew was wounded, presumed dead, but captured, to be exchanged later.[52] Hampton was wounded in his foot. He remained on his horse while Surgeon E. S. Gaillard, medical director of General Smith's command, extracted a minié ball from the general's foot. All the while they were under fire from

Union forces. The surgeon's horse was shot from under him just before he operated on Hampton's foot, and shortly after the operation, the surgeon was wounded in his right arm. That limb was amputated. Such was the chaos of the battle.[53] The battle ended without a clear victory for either side.

On June 1, 1862, Gen. Robert E. Lee succeeded Joseph E. Johnston in command of what became known as the Army of Northern Virginia. The new commander received glowing reports of Hampton's performance. When General Smith submitted his official report of the battle he commented, "Wade Hampton was seriously wounded but was able to keep his horse and refused to leave the field. . . . General Hampton, on this as on many previous occasions, was remarkable for his coolness, promptness, and decided practical ability as a leader of men in difficult and dangerous circumstances. In these high characteristics of a general he has few equals and perhaps no superior."[54] This was indeed high praise for the non–West Point graduate. Two of the compliments were especially significant: coolness under fire and practical ability. Hampton often rushed before his men into the heat of battle with little apparent concern for his own safety, and he seemed to exercise an instinctive understanding of the tactical situations.

Hampton's wound was serious enough for him to go to Richmond and then to Columbia for convalescence.[55] He received a hero's welcome in South Carolina, where Governor Pickens's wife gave a reception in the general's honor. When Hampton entered the reception, leaning on crutches, Mrs. Pickens took the crutches away and placed Hampton's hand on her shoulder, saying, "This is the way to greet heroes." Mrs. Chesnut commented on the occasion that Hampton was thoroughly embarrassed. "He is a simple-mannered man, you know, and does not want to be made much of by women. . . . He looked as if he wished they would leave him alone." When Hampton was asked for his opinion of the progress of the war, he replied, "If we mean to play at war, as we play a game of chess, West Point tactics prevailing, we are sure to lose the game. They have every advantage. They can lose pawns ad infinitum, to the end of time and never feel it. We will be throwing away all that we had hoped so much from—Southern hot-head dash, reckless gallantry, spirit of adventure, readiness to lead forlorn hopes."[56]

When Hampton returned to duty he found that the remains of his brigade had been divided to replenish other units. Hampton was assigned command of a brigade in the Army of the Valley, under the command of Gen. Stonewall Jackson. The Valley Army had just conducted one of the most remarkable campaigns in the entire Civil War, moving quickly from one contest to another and defeating the enemy piecemeal, thereby tying up a much larger Union force in the Shenandoah Valley and preventing their reinforcing McClellan on the peninsula. Hampton joined Jackson's force when they reached the peninsula.

Then came General Lee's first major battle. At this time most of the Army of the Potomac, about 125,000, was on the south side of the Chickahominy River. Only the Fifth Corps, commanded by Maj. Gen. Fitz-John Porter, was north of the Chickahominy. The Fifth Corps was responsible for the security of the Union supply base at White House on the Pamunkey, one of the head-waters of the York River. General Lee decided to take advantage of this division of the enemy's forces by striking at Porter's corps while they were at least somewhat detached from the main body. The result was the Seven Days Battle, June 25–July 1, 1862, a tragically costly and still indecisive contest. The basic failing on the Confederate side was that Lee had not yet cemented his command into a smoothly operating entity. Lee left Magruder with about twenty-two thousand men to face off the main enemy force of seventy-one thousand while he sent the divisions under the command of Major Generals A. P. Hill, James Longstreet, and D. H. Hill north to join Jackson's army when they arrived from the Valley in a coordinated attack across the Chickahominy. The catch was in two weaknesses: the weariness of Jackson, having just fought the brilliant Valley campaign, and ineffective coordination. In the afternoon of June 26 A. P. Hill crossed the Chickahominy and attacked Porter's troops, who were in a well-defended position on a high bank behind Beaver Dam Creek; he received no help from other Rebel units, although Jackson's troops were only two and a half miles away.

Even though Porter had succeeded in fighting off the Southern attack and had inflicted terrible losses on the attackers, McClellan decided to order Porter to move the supply base from White House on the Pamunkey River to Harrison's Landing on the James River. His thinking on this was sound, but the Union was indeed vulnerable in making such a move in the face of an aggressive enemy as that commanded by R. E. Lee. Again poor coordination inhibited the Confederates in their attempt to seize the advantage of this situation. As Porter's troops withdrew on June 27 it was again A. P. Hill's division that led in the assault at Gaine's Mill. Hill received help from Longstreet and D. H. Hill, but Jackson's forces were again late in getting to the scene of action. Late in the day on June 27 Porter succeeded in crossing the Chickahominy; thus the Union soldiers were no longer divided. On June 28 McClellan moved his unified army toward the James River. On June 29 Magruder led an attack on the retreating Union army at Savage's Station. After a sharp fight the Federals broke off the engagement and continued their move toward the James. On the night of the twenty-ninth Jackson moved his troops across the Chickahominy. It was Jackson's duty to hit the rear of the Union column.[57]

Lee ordered Jackson to "pursue the enemy on the road he has taken." On the morning of June 30 Hampton led the column approaching White Oak Swamp. McClellan's army was on the southern side of the swamp. The problem was how to get through this obstacle and hit the enemy. The forces of Magruder and Huger were to attack the Federals' right flank. Longstreet and A. P. Hill were to move around the Union army and block their retreat. This was indeed a grand attempt to destroy the Union army. The plan, although it was poorly executed, was typical of Lee's daring tactics. On Monday, June 30, Lee ordered an attack on the Northerners in what became known as the Battle of White Oak Swamp. Longstreet and A. P. Hill attacked the Union right flank; they expected Jackson to hit the Union rear. Jackson found a partially destroyed bridge, and he attempted to send the Second Virginia Cavalry under the command of Col. Thomas T. Munford over, but they were stopped by Union fire. Jackson was then apparently content to engage in desultory fire from the edge of the swamp. At this time Hampton and his son Wade IV, who had joined his father as an aide (the role in which he served Joseph E. Johnston until the latter's wound in the Battle of Seven Pines), did some reconnoitering. They found a possible passage through the swamp, an opening, "not at all boggy," a ford over a stream with a hard, sandy bottom. The Federals apparently were not aware of this passage to their rear. The two Hamptons could see the rear of the Union position from across the stream. Hampton excitedly reported this opportunity to General Jackson. To Hampton's surprise and dismay, Jackson "drew his cap down on his eyes which were closed, and after listening to me for some minutes, he rose without speaking. . . . That was all."[58] Thus Jackson apparently let a golden opportunity slip by. The most logical explanation for this lapse in the otherwise brilliant and aggressive Jackson is that he was extremely tired and needed rest from the rigors of the Valley campaign and from the move from the Valley to the peninsula.

There was yet one more act in this fateful drama. On July 1 McClellan had his army in a well-defended position on Malvern Hill, just north of the new base at Harrison's Landing. Lee ordered a major attack, which resulted in great losses to the attackers. Jackson's men fought valiantly, but Hampton was held in reserve, taking no part in the battle. General Lee lost five thousand dead and wounded at Malvern Hill.

General Lee, recognizing the agonizing failures of the Seven Days Campaign, reorganized the Army of Northern Virginia into two corps, one commanded by Longstreet and the other by Jackson. As a part of this reorganization, Hampton on July 26, 1862, received orders to report for duty in the Cavalry Division of the Army of Northern Virginia,[59] commanded by the flamboyant Maj. Gen. J. E. B. Stuart. Significantly, Hampton was then a brigadier general. The long delay in getting the rank appropriate for a brigade commander was offensive to Hampton. He was on occasion jealous of the West Point graduates and especially West Point graduates who were Virginians. General Johnston, in a letter of May 25, 1862, indicated that he had heard that Hampton had declined a promotion,[60] presumably from pique. It is not clear what finally moved the bureaucracy, but Hampton received his promotion. In a letter dated June 11, 1862, General Lee referred to Hampton as brigadier general.[61] General Hampton was ordered to command the First Cavalry Brigade, consisting of the Cobb Legion, commanded by Col. P. McB. Young; the Second South Carolina, commanded by Col. M. C. Butler; the Jeff Davis Legion, commanded by Col. William Martin; the Phillips Legion, commanded by Col. William Rich; the Tenth Virginia, commanded by Col. J. Lucius Davis; and the Horse Battery, commanded by Capt. J. F. Hart. At this time Col. W. H. F. Lee, the son of R. E. Lee and known as Rooney Lee, commanded the Ninth Virginia Cavalry in the Second Brigade commanded by Brig. Gen. Fitzhugh Lee, the nephew of General Lee.[62]

Events again forced the Confederates to make a major shift in positions. General Lee learned that the Federals were assembling a large force under the command of Maj. Gen. John Pope in the area around Washington. Lee therefore moved General Jackson with a force of eleven thousand men to the north of Richmond to watch General Pope, while he and the remainder of the Rebel army watched McClellan on the eastern side of Richmond. Convinced that McClellan posed little threat, in mid-August Lee ordered Longstreet and the major part of the Army of Northern Virginia to join Jackson. General Lee left Gen. Gustavus W. Smith with the remainder of the Confederate army to guard against any threat from McClellan. Hampton and his brigade of cavalry remained with Smith with instructions to keep scouts out to gain intelligence of Union movements in this region.[63] Hampton had not yet earned the reputation as an extremely effective cavalry leader. There was nothing negative; he was still untried in this role, and that is probably why he was assigned to the less-important role of scouting the not-very-threatening McClellan, while Fitz Lee and his brigade were to the north of Richmond, involved in the preliminaries leading to the defeat of General Pope in the Second Battle of Manassas, August 29–30, 1862.

Hampton did indeed scout the moves of McClellan. On August 5 units of cavalry found that the Federals were moving from Westover to Malvern Hill, the site of the earlier battle. Confederate infantry drove the bluecoats from Malvern Hill while, as General Lee later reported, Hampton's brigade kept the enemy troops from threatening adventures.[64] There were other minor skirmishes involved in the duties of scouting. Hampton's scouts later gained considerable fame for themselves and for their commander. Lee, learning that much of McClellan's army would move north to reinforce General Pope, urged President Jefferson Davis, who was often involved in directing troop movements, to order the removal of the divisions of Layfayette McLaws and D. H. Hill and Hampton's cavalry brigade to join the main body of the Army of Northern Virginia to the north of Richmond.[65] General Lee also took steps to strengthen Hampton by asking the secretary of war to add the Second

North Carolina Cavalry regiment, a unit Lee believed was not needed in North Carolina, to Hampton's brigade.[66]

Hampton would earn his greatest military fame as a cavalry commander. This makes advisable some consideration of the role of cavalry in the Civil War. The development of rifled weapons and the resulting increase in accuracy of infantry firepower made a fundamental change in the best use of cavalry. Cavalry in frontal assaults became so costly in casualties as to make that Napoleonic tactic outdated. In the Napoleonic era, cavalry often played a devastating role in charging infantry, who attempted to protect themselves by forming "squares" of infantrymen armed with long bayonets, barriers which were difficult for horsemen to break up. Rifled weapons enabled infantrymen to shoot cavalry horses and their men as elevated targets long before they could reach the defensive lines. Cavalry therefore became most proficient in roles in which speed was an important factor. Horsemen became effective at scouting, hence the sobriquet "eyes and ears of the army." The role of reconnaissance and counterreconnaissance (seeking information about the enemy and denying information to the enemy) became the most important function of Civil War cavalry. Cavalry often screened the movements of the main body either in advance or retreat.[67] Cavalry on occasion functioned as mounted infantry; armed with light rifles they would move rapidly to a new position, dismount, and act as infantrymen; then move again when it was advantageous to do so. Their advantage in this role was speed, allowing them to change quickly from one position to another. Still, cavalry did on occasion attack enemy units, firing pistols first and then using sabers, usually attacking enemy cavalry or small groups of infantry in this fashion. Civil War cavalry were especially effective in conducting raids behind enemy lines to disrupt lines of communication and supplies. The raids of Nathan Bedford Forrest behind the lines of General Sherman in Georgia and Tennessee were effective in delaying the Union advance for months. Hampton would be involved in a number of raids, some of which were spectacular. He starred in all cavalry roles, most dramatically in attacking with sabers drawn, actually killing a number of enemy with his saber. In the use of the saber Hampton was unusual. Many of his colleagues in the cavalry service thought that the saber was outdated. The Confederate partisan fighter John Singleton Mosby even stopped his men from carrying sabers, and the Union general James H. Wilson found the saber to be of little value. There were only a few engagements in which the saber figured prominently, and Hampton was a participant in each. One was at Brandy Station just before the Gettysburg campaign, and the other was on the third day of the Battle of Gettysburg. On that fateful third day Gen. George A. Custer led the Fifth Michigan Cavalry in a column attack on Hampton's approaching column, both sides with sabers drawn. The result when the two collided was "a crash like the falling of timbers. . . . So sudden and violent was the collision that many of the horses were turned over end and crushed their riders beneath them."[68] This was the last major war in which mounted cavalry played a significant role, and Hampton had a major part in the drama.

Brigadier General Hampton joined Maj. Gen. Jeb Stuart north of Richmond prior to the invasion of Maryland culminating in the Battle of Sharpsburg (Antietam), September 17, 1862. Stuart reported that Hampton's brigade had joined him just prior to their crossing the Potomac on September 5. The flamboyant commander moved with his two brigades, one commanded by Hampton and the other by Fitzhugh Lee. The Hampton brigade had been augmented by the addition of the First North Carolina Cavalry. Lt. Col. Frank Hampton, brother of Wade, was second in command of the Second South Carolina Regiment.[69]

There were a number of brief skirmishes prior to the main battle. Enemy cavalry engaged the Hampton brigade at Poolesville on September 6, 1862. The Northern cavalry were turned back.[70] The Confederate Army moved as far north as Frederick, Maryland. When Lee realized that there was a Union force of almost twelve thousand at Harper's Ferry, he divided his army and sent Jackson and part of the Rebel army to seize that possible threat to the Southern line of communications, therefore making the Confederate army vulnerable. McClellan learned of this weakness when a Yankee private discovered a copy of Lee's orders directing the division of the army. The Army of the Potomac then surprised Lee by their speed in pushing west to attack the invaders piecemeal. Lee quickly began concentrating his army along Antietam Creek near Sharpsburg. Stuart's cavalry became the rearguard, protecting the main body as it moved westward. Hampton's brigade fought a sharp skirmish on the outskirts of Frederick and then retired. That was repeated again and again as the cavalry sought to gain time for the main body of the army by delaying the Union advance. Stuart's troops fought a delaying action at the Catoctin Mountain Range, where the cavalrymen dismounted and fought as sharpshooters. Hampton's Blakely guns fired into the approaching Union columns. The Rebels then retired to Middleton and then to the South Mountain Range.[71]

Preston Hampton was accompanying his father as his aide. After they entered Maryland in a brisk action near Burkittsville, the father, about to charge into action, snatched off his coat and threw it to his son, shouting, "Take care of my overcoat, Preston." The father drew his saber and rode into the fight. The son flung the coat into a fence corner and exclaimed, "I've come to Maryland to fight Yankees, and not to carry father's coat."[72] The son was of the same mettle as his father.

During these delaying actions, the Union force at Harper's Ferry surrendered to Jackson, and Lee ordered the victorious Rebels to move quickly to Sharpsburg to join the main army before the Army of the Potomac arrived.

During the actual Battle of Antietam, on September 17, Stuart's cavalry helped protect the Confederate left from Union encirclement, and the cavalry batteries fired on the Union right. Hampton did not play a major role in this great battle. The cavalry's role was in protecting the Confederate army as it moved to its position west of Antietam, and after the battle the cavalry provided the necessary protection for the Army of Northern Virginia to move back across the Potomac into Virginia.

In the fall and winter of 1862 the brigades of Hampton and Fitz Lee alternated in outpost duty. From time to time they raided enemy supply lines, and they guarded the Confederate railroads.[73] The most significant of these raids encompassed Chambersburg, Pennsylvania. On October 6 Stuart gathered six hundred select cavalrymen and prepared them for a daring raid into enemy territory. Hampton was second in command. They crossed the Potomac near Hedgesville and pushed north near Hagerstown. Butler's men captured a few Union stragglers from General Cox's division, which had just passed on the National Turnpike. The Rebel raiders pushed northward essentially undetected. On the evening of October 10 they reached Chambersburg. City officials were told to surrender or suffer a cannonade, which would begin in thirty minutes. Stuart's remarkable artillery commander, Maj. John Pelham, accompanied the raiding party, and Pelham had his artillery trained on the town of Chambersburg. The city yielded without a struggle. Stuart named Hampton the military governor of Chambersburg. The raiders took what supplies they could carry and then destroyed a military warehouse. They abandoned Chambersburg on October 11, the town having suffered little damage. The Rebels then moved on to Cashtown about seven miles from Gettysburg. They crossed the Potomac back into Virginia, having two men captured and one wounded.[74] Stuart gloried in this kind of action. Although Hampton did not seem to take as much pleasure as Stuart in such high military drama, he was quite effective in participating in these daring expeditions. In time he led his share of such adventurous raids.

Hampton had performed well in the Antietam campaign, but he did not receive from his Virginia superiors the recognition he felt that he deserved. J. E. B. Stuart failed to compliment Hampton warmly, and Hampton thought that Gen. R. E. Lee himself had not given him the proper recognition. General Lee had indicated in his report that Hampton had retired from Martinsburg and thereby allowed the Union general Pleasonton to occupy the town. Hampton wrote to General Stuart to correct Lee's statement, indicating that Gen. Fitzhugh Lee's sentinels had failed to report any enemy advance. "The enemy did not advance over any road under my supervision."[75] Hampton could be rather prickly, and he was capable of jealousy of the Virginia West Point clique. He was especially resentful of Fitz Lee. Hampton wrote to his sister, "He [Stuart] has always given us the hardest work to perform and the worst places to camp at."[76] It is of course entirely possible that Hampton's irritation with the Virginia West Point clique was well founded. All of this notwithstanding, Hampton obviously earned the trust of both Stuart and Lee. It is not surprising that this planter without military training had to earn their trust; trust was not assumed.

The Confederate cavalry underwent a reorganization in the fall of 1862, resulting in a cavalry division of four brigades, the first commanded by Brigadier General Hampton, the second by Brig. Gen. Fitzhugh Lee, the third by Brig. Gen. W. H. F. "Rooney" Lee, and the fourth by Brig. Gen. W. E. "Grumble" Jones. The horse artillery was under the command of Maj. John Pelham, by then known as the Gallant John Pelham.[77]

In the late fall and early winter of 1862–1863, the Army of Northern Virginia was headquartered in the vicinity of Fredericksburg, Virginia. Gen. Ambrose Burnside, then the commander of the Army of the Potomac, began massing his forces to the north of the Rappahannock River. Stuart's cavalry made a number of highly successful raids behind the enemy lines before and after the Battle of Fredericksburg, and Hampton led many of these actions. On November 27 Hampton led 128 men across the Rappahannock, attacking the enemy to the north of Falmouth and capturing one hundred horses and 95 officers and men.[78] On December 10 Hampton led 520 men on a raid on the Union supply depot at Dumfries, netting 50 prisoners and seventeen supply wagons.[79]

On December 13 Burnside made his disastrous attack on the Confederate positions just beyond the town of Fredericksburg. The high casualty rate among the attackers against the well-fortified Confederate defenses demonstrated the hazards of such frontal charges. The cavalry played no important role in the actual battle. The horsemen were of value only in scouting, raiding, and protecting the flanks of the infantry lines. The Union soldiers pulled back across the Rappahannock River and licked their wounds.

The Rebel raids continued. Just before Christmas, 1862, Confederate scouts learned that a large number of sutler wagons were headed southward to the headquarters of the Army of the Potomac, presumably bringing supplies, including items that would make Christmas special for an already well-supplied army. Hampton gathered a force of cavalry and crossed the Rappahannock late in the evening. They bivouacked and early the next morning headed for Dumfries. Hampton had M. C. Butler lead his regiment in an attack on Dumfries, catching their opponents still asleep. Hampton led the other troopers on an attack on the road north of Dumfries. They carried off a wide variety of goods, including shoes, hats, underwear, and food; and they destroyed what could not be carted away.[80] Hampton wrote to his sister that General Lee had complimented him on his success. He also reported, "I have been drinking Burnside's champagne and find it very good."[81]

The raids continued fast and furiously, but they were not all equally successful. On December 26, 1863, General Stuart led 1,800 men on a raid toward the Occoquan. This time Stuart found Dumfries too well protected to be assaulted by cavalry. Rooney Lee, Hampton, and Fitz Lee led their units in supposedly coordinated but detached movements. There was more than the usual confusion among the Rebel raiders. Still, the raiders captured 200 prisoners, 200 horses, 20 wagons, and miscellaneous loot.[82] Hence, even the less successful raids were productive. General Lee expressed his appreciation of the obvious skill of the South Carolinian, writing in a letter to Stuart: "The manner in which General Hampton placed and executed his expedition reflects great credit upon himself, officers, and men."[83] The politically astute Hampton sent two Union guidons captured north of the Rappahannock to Secretary of War J. A. Seddon, who displayed them in his office.[84] Perhaps to counter the frequent infantry criticism that cavalry had it too easy, General Lee issued a general order to announce some of the successes of the cavalry of the Army of Northern Virginia. According to this announcement, Stuart's men had, in the month of December 1862, captured a total of 420 men and a number of officers and 545 supply wagons.[85]

As yet another bit of evidence that Hampton increasingly impressed General Lee, the commanding general offered the South Carolinian command of the brigade that had been under Maxcy Gregg, who had been killed in the Battle of Fredericksburg. Hampton preferred staying with the cavalry, where he was indeed at his best. President Davis suggested that Hampton might command the cavalry in North Carolina, but General Lee could not spare this gifted leader.[86]

This increasing recognition notwithstanding, Hampton disliked Stuart and continued to be suspicious of the Virginia West Pointers. Hampton wrote to Mary Fisher in January 1863: "All my time and correspondence of late have been taken up in quarreling with Stuart, who keeps me here doing all the hard work, while the Virginia brigades are quietly doing nothing. . . . Unless General Lee, to whom I have appealed, interferes, Stuart will certainly have my brigade out of the field before very long."[87] It is significant that others not included in Stuart's clique also expressed resentment of the flamboyant Stuart. The Georgian T. R. Cobb, who had recruited the Cobb Legion, wrote to his wife after Stuart had ridden around McClellan's army on the peninsula, "In other words we were doing the dirty work and the gentlemen doing nothing were placed . . . where éclat and honor were to be obtained."[88]

Hampton's letters to his sister reflect interesting feelings from this aristocratic planter-turned-soldier. He revealed something of the experience of riding literally into harm's way: "The Yankees stood at first and I rode into the midst of them. The first two blows I struck brought down a man each time. The poor devil had his skull fractured frightfully. . . . I have been in 43 fights and yet the hand of God has saved me in all of them." He then stated, "I am sick of the horror of war,"[89] assuring her of his humanity in the midst of barbarity.

After the Battle of Fredericksburg, the two armies went into the winter season of less activity, facing each other across the Rappahannock River. Fitzhugh Lee's brigade did picket duty along the Rappahannock above the mouth of the Rapidan, and Rooney Lee's brigade did the same near Port Royal. Hampton took his brigade to the south of Virginia to seek a new supply of horses.[90] The assignment of seeking fresh mounts revealed a problem of staggering importance to the Rebel cavalry. On February 6, 1863, a detachment of Union troops attempted to destroy a bridge at Kelly's Mill. Hampton's brigade drove off the enemy, but they could not continue the pursuit "because of the condition of the horses."[91] The process of "recruiting" horses, which took several months, was of immense importance; maintaining an ample supply of able mounts was an increasingly difficult problem for the Confederate cavalry. As the war wore on, the Southern supply of good horses dwindled alarmingly. One reason for Lee's daring to invade Pennsylvania in June 1863 was the hope of confiscating enough horses to bring the cavalry back to the comparative supremacy it had enjoyed in the early months of warfare. General Stuart was subjected to much criticism for his dramatic raids because those adventures often took a toll in horseflesh that made the value of the captured booty at least questionable.

In the spring of 1863, the problem in maintaining the quality of mounts was especially bad for Southerners because Northerners were reorganizing and re-equipping their cavalry. After reorganization, the Army of the Potomac had four full divisions of cavalry, all serving under Maj. Gen. George M. Stoneman. Each brigade contained one regiment of mounted rifles, armed with Spencer repeating rifles. The supply of horses for the Union cavalry appeared to the Southerners to be inexhaustible,[92] and the Union leaders knew the condition of the Southern army's horses. General Stoneman reported to his superior that Hampton had crossed the Rappahannock with "horses very tired, so said."[93] Maj. Gen. Daniel Butterfield reported, "Enemy's artillery horses said not to be able to move their guns."[94] For all of this concern, which was real, General Lee managed to move many guns toward Gettysburg the following June.

There was not much activity in the first two months of Hampton's absence from the Virginia front. One brief engagement had tragic results for Stuart's cavalry. On March 17 Pleasonton's cavalry again attacked at Kelly's Ford. They were repulsed, but not before they had killed the "Gallant Pelham." Stonewall Jackson was supposed to have said at Fredericksburg, "With a Pelham on each flank, I could vanquish the world."[95] The Battle of Kelly's Ford, the first cavalry victory for the cavalry of the Army of the Potomac, was startling evidence of the shifting balance in supremacy.[96]

Then in the first days of May, the Army of Northern Virginia won the stunning victory of the Battle of Chancellorsville in which Lee divided his forces before a larger army and used the brilliant tactician Jackson to execute an envelopment of the Union right flank. Jackson himself was the victim of one of those all-too-frequent confusions of combat—his own troops shot him while he was returning from a reconnaissance. Hampton played no part in this battle.

By early June Hampton was back on duty along the Rappahannock.[97] At this time General Lee was making preparations for the invasion of Maryland and Pennsylvania, and the Federals were recouping from Chancellorsville. The Union cavalry made a significant turn for the better, an ominous turn for Hampton and his compatriots. On May 22, 1863, Brig. Gen. Alfred Pleasonton replaced General Stoneman as the commander of the Union cavalry corps.[98] The advantage the Confederate cavalry had enjoyed in the early part of the war evaporated in the summer of 1863. This is not to say that there were no more victories for the Rebel cavalry, but there was no more enduring supremacy.

All of this notwithstanding, the Army of Northern Virginia, after the Battle of Chancellorsville, was supremely confident of its own strength. That confidence was soon severely tested in the greatest cavalry battle of the war. On June 8, 1863, General Stuart conducted an impressive review of his cavalry for the commanding general. General Lee watched as ten thousand men passed in review. The next day Stuart's men were to begin their screening of the Rebel move into the Shenandoah Valley, the first step toward the invasion of the North. Early on the next morning, June 9, Stuart suffered an almost devastating surprise when two detachments of Union cavalry and infantry crossed the Rappahannock at two fords. Gen. John Buford led one force across Beverly Ford, and Gen. David M. Gregg led another across Kelly's Ford to the southeast. They were supposed to cross the river at dawn, converge at Brandy Station and move toward Culpeper. The Confederates were surprised, but they remained poised, and they reacted quite well.

Hampton led four regiments into the fight, literally following the sound of firing. Capt. J. F. Hart, commanding Hampton's artillery, played a major role in preventing disaster when he quickly wheeled two of his guns into position and began firing on the attackers. Parts of Hampton's brigade were involved in the fighting at both Kelly's Ford and at Beverly Ford. As often happened, Hampton had some of his men dismounted, fighting as sharpshooters. While heavily engaged to his front, Hampton was surprised to find enemy to his rear. These were the enemy cavalry who had crossed at Kelly's Ford without opposition. In a true test of soldiering, Hampton and others turned to face in another direction. The arrival of Confederate infantry reinforcements made the Federals decide to withdraw.

The Battle of Brandy Station was a cavalry fight of the most dramatic nature. There were men fighting on horseback, using sabers, pistols, and rifles; others fighting dismounted; and the horse artillery played a major part. It is significant that the arrival of infantry in large numbers brought it all to an end. It was a day of surprise, confusion, and tragedy. At one point Rebel artillery, bewildered by the confusion of fighting on several fronts, opened fire on Hampton's column. And, saddest of all for Hampton, his younger brother Frank Hampton, serving in the regiment commanded by M. C. Butler, was mortally wounded while trying to fight off an attacking Union column. General Hampton reported rather stoically, "Among the killed I regret to announce the name of Lieut. Col. Frank Hampton, Second South Carolina Regiment, a brave and gallant officer, . . . who fell while gallantly leading his men in the dashing charge made by his regiment." Hampton's report bristled with resentment for General Stuart. He complained that Stuart had ordered the Second South Carolina Regiment to change its position from protecting Brandy Station—which gave its name to this battle—without informing Hampton. Years later he commented to Maj. Henry McClellan, who had been Stuart's assistant adjutant general, "Stuart managed badly that day." Col. M. C. Butler suffered a severe wound that resulted in the loss of a leg. Gen. Robert E. Lee arrived on the scene to see his son, Brig. Gen. Rooney Lee, carried off the field wounded. Both returned to action after a time. (Rooney Lee was captured while recovering, and he remained a prisoner for several months before being exchanged.) Stuart succeeded in driving off the enemy, but it was a narrow escape from defeat.[99]

As the Army of Northern Virginia began its move northward, General Lee ordered Stuart to cover the flanks. Lee often gave orders that allowed considerable discretion on the part of the commanders on the scene, a method of exercising command that depended on smart and responsible subordinates, since the poor communications of the time made corrections in the process of battle very difficult. Stuart's exercise of discretion in the Gettysburg campaign set off controversies that have extended more than a century. In the initial stages of the campaign, the brigades of Hampton and "Grumble" Jones guarded the line along the Rappahannock, shielding the movements of A. P. Hill's corps. By June 15 a division of Ewell's corps of the Confederate army was crossing the Potomac. There were a number of skirmishes between the opposing cavalry units as the Rebel army slid into the Shenandoah Valley and then moved north to enter Maryland and Pennsylvania. Lee ordered Stuart to take three of his brigades, cross the Potomac, guard Ewell's flank, and gather food and forage. Lee expected Stuart to guard the Confederate right as they moved through the Shenandoah and Cumberland valleys. Hampton, Brig. Gen. "Grumble" Jones, Brig. Gen. Beverly Robertson, Col. Thomas T. Munford (commanding in the absence of Fitzhugh Lee, who was recovering from an illness), and Col. John Chambliss (commanding in the absence of Rooney Lee, wounded and later captured) commanded Stuart's five brigades. Stuart left the brigades commanded by Jones and Robertson with the main body of the army. Those two cavalry brigades were instructed to guard the gaps in the Blue Ridge chain, west of which Lee's army marched northward. General Lee ordered Stuart to take his remaining three brigades and move into Maryland on Gen. Richard Ewell's right, guard his movement, keep him informed, and collect supplies from the enemy.[100]

Because of the resourceful Maj. John S. Mosby and his band of rangers, Stuart was actually well informed of the movements of the Army of the Potomac. Mosby informed Stuart that the Union units were so separated that the wily Confederate cavalry could easily pass between them undetected. This was too much for the flamboyant Stuart to resist. Stuart considered his ultimate destination to be York, Pennsylvania, where he expected to meet Ewell's troops, but he chose a circuitous route of approaching both Washington and Baltimore and thereby causing consternation in those major Union cities. He would also have the opportunity to damage communications between those cities and the Union forces, and with it all gather supplies by raiding Union depots and supply trains. They actually passed within a few miles of Washington, and the Union consternation was real, but General Stuart was failing in the important task of keeping his commanding general informed of enemy movements.[101] General Lee was not kept informed of the precise location and movements of the Army of the Potomac, and this was the most important role of cavalry in this campaign.

Elements of Lee's army actually moved ahead of the cavalry. On June 27 Stuart and his troops crossed the Potomac at Rowser's Ford. By that same day both Hill's and Longstreet's corps were concentrated in the vicinity of Chambersburg, Pennsylvania.[102] Significantly, on June 28 Maj. Gen. George Meade replaced Maj. Gen. Joe Hooker in command of the Union army. The Confederates now faced a more able opponent. Late on the same day, Lee learned from a paid spy that the Army of the Potomac was headed in the direction of South Mountain from whence they could threaten the Confederate supply line. This was of course information that should properly have come from General Stuart, but that colorful cavalier was seventy miles away near Rockville, Maryland, eight miles from Washington, and much of Meade's army was between the Confederate cavalry and its army. Stuart was indeed passing around the enemy, but to what profit?

The Rebel cavalry proved to be a genuine nuisance to the Federals. On June 28 Stuart captured a supply train near Rockville, Maryland; he destroyed some supplies and took with him 125 wagons. That impedimenta slowed down Stuart's progress, and this was one reason for his tardy arrival at Gettysburg.[103] There were occasional brushes with enemy cavalry, but the Rebel cavalry made their circuit with relatively little damage to themselves, and they did hurt the Union war effort, although not enough to have influenced the forthcoming great battle. On June 29 Fitz Lee, again with his men, and his brigade tore up the tracks of the Baltimore and Ohio Railroad and cut the telegraph line in Hood's Mill. Such damage could be repaired with little delay.

Stuart became engaged with the enemy as he entered Pennsylvania. On June 30, just as the two principal armies were beginning to converge on Gettysburg, Stuart's leading elements approached Hanover, Pennsylvania, almost due east of Gettysburg. Chambliss's brigade came upon a column of Gen. Judson Kilpatrick's cavalry. At this time Hampton's brigade was escorting the supply train and the artillery, well back in the Confederate column. After a brief skirmish Stuart decided to avoid a major battle in that location. To protect his wagon train and to avoid a battle, Stuart led his troops eastward, thereby causing even more delay in joining the main body.[104] Stuart's move eastward caused Kilpatrick to misread the situation. The Union cavalry then moved directly northward, passing west of Stuart's route. The result of these moves was that both the Union and Confederate cavalry wasted July 1, the first day of the epic battle.

Lee's headquarters were by now in Cashtown, about seven miles west of Gettysburg. Stuart, now realizing the urgency of his situation, pushed his men to exhaustion, reaching Dover to the east of Gettysburg on July 1. The Confederate army was therefore still without the best of their cavalry cover. Stuart sent Maj. Andrew R. Venable to locate Gen. Jubal Early, who was of course busily engaged at Gettysburg. It was not until 1:00 A.M. on July 2 that Stuart learned of the location of his commanding general. He was to miss more than half of the battle. Upon establishing contact with his cavalry commander, Lee ordered him to position his men on the Confederate left. Late on July 2 Stuart assumed his position.[105]

Hampton saw limited action almost immediately. On July 2 the Union general Kilpatrick received orders to proceed from Gettysburg toward Abbottstown (east northeast of Gettysburg) to prevent the Confederates from executing a flanking movement from the northern side.[106] As Stuart was moving to take his position on the Rebel left he learned that enemy cavalry was moving toward Hunterstown (north-northwest of Gettysburg). He then ordered Hampton to hold the enemy in check at Hunterstown. Quite logically the high drama of these events spun off some interesting stories. According to one story, as the Rebel troopers moved to Hunterstown someone shot at Hampton. The general then rode in the direction of the shot. He found a Northern cavalryman armed with a Spencer repeating rifle, huddled in a thicket. The two foes exchanged shots, Hampton firing his pistol; both missed. In the next attempt the Yankee's rifle fouled, whereupon the Northerner raised his hand as if to ask for a pause in the duel. The chivalrous general waited for the opponent to clear his weapon. When the Yankee raised his rifle for another try, Hampton fired his pistol and hit his opponent's wrist. The Northerner then ran away.[107] Perhaps apocryphal, it is representative of the chivalric ideal of the time. The skirmishes on July 2 resulted in a standoff.

The real cavalry fight came on the third day of Gettysburg. Early on the morning of July 3 Hampton received orders to pass through Hunterstown and get on the enemy's right flank. General Lee wanted his cavalry to be in a position to assist in achieving a complete victory in the event that Pickett's charge succeeded. The Confederate cavalry were to add a measure of success "by spreading confusion in the Union rear and rounding up fleeing soldiers."[108] As Hampton approached Hunterstown he met Cobb's Legion, which the Northern cavalry had pushed out of the town. Hampton put Cobb's Legion in a defensive line and called up other units, including Fitz Lee's brigade. Together they repelled a charge by the Sixth Michigan Cavalry led by Gen. George Armstrong Custer. When Hampton rode back to check with Stuart, Fitz Lee ordered a charge in pursuit of the repulsed Union horsemen. Hampton returned to find the assault under way. He at first countermanded Lee's order, but quickly realized that it was too late. At first the Confederates drove the Federals, but eventually the attacking units found themselves confronted by massive Union reserves, located on the edge of woods with sharpshooters out front. General Custer again led the Union counterattack, and Hampton led a countercharge that resulted in hand-to-hand fighting with pistols and sabers. When the opposing charges met, horse and men tumbled head over heels, crushing men beneath. There was a deafening sound of gunfire, shouts and screams of agony.[109] Hampton realized that his troopers had advanced too far to be properly supported, and he tried to get them to fall back. Other Confederates saw Hampton in the advanced position and assumed that he wanted a general attack, and they came forward, but not before Hampton found himself surrounded by Yankee cavalry. One Northerner struck Hampton's head with a saber, resulting in a cut, but not as deep as it might have been because of the cushioning effect of a slouch hat and thick hair. Several Confederate horsemen rushed to defend the general. One shouted, "General, General, they are too many; for God's sake leap your horse over the fence." Hampton did just that, but as he tried to get away he took a bullet wound in his side. Col. Lawrence Baker assumed command as Hampton fell wounded.[110] This ended Hampton's role in the Battle of Gettysburg.

In retrospect Hampton charged Fitzhugh Lee with rashness in prematurely ordering the attack on July 3. Both generals—Stuart and R. E. Lee—tried to placate Hampton and Fitz Lee.[111] Hampton harbored his resentment of Fitz Lee for many years. In his report on the Gettysburg campaign, General Lee wrote, "Brigadier General Hampton was seriously wounded while acting with his accustomed gallantry."[112]

It is interesting that on the night of July 3, after the failure of Pickett's charge and the virtual end of the battle, Colonel Black with the First South Carolina Cavalry fought off Yankee cavalry trying to come around the Confederate right.[113] This was the proper role for cavalry in a pitched battle, to protect the flanks of the main body.

In Lee's retreat back to Virginia, his cavalry played the proper role of screening. Stuart did a creditable job of fending off the pursuing Yankees. Hampton rode in an ambulance. It was undoubtedly an agonizing journey as Brig. Gen. John D. Imboden's cavalry escorted the long train of supplies and wounded. His men heard the wounded crying, "O God! Why can't I die?" and "My God! Will no one have mercy and kill me?"[114] Hampton left no record of his agonies on the retreat.

In the retreat to Virginia, General Lee ordered Stuart to use the brigades of Hampton and Fitz Lee in guarding the flanks and rear of Imboden's seventeen-mile-long column. They pushed toward Williamsport, Maryland, where they expected to cross the Potomac. By July 12 General Lee had his army in a well-fortified position north of the Potomac in the vicinity of Falling Waters and Williamsport. General Lee apparently hoped that General Meade would make a major attack there and give the Confederates the opportunity to even the score from Gettysburg, but it was not to be. On July 14 the Army of Northern Virginia completed its crossing to the southern side of the Potomac.[115] The Hampton brigade in the Gettysburg campaign lost 60 killed and 256 wounded, the heaviest casualties of any of the cavalry brigades.[116] The Gettysburg campaign was over. Historians have tended to call this the high-water mark of the Confederacy, implying that ebb tide followed. There was, however, plenty of fight left in the Confederate forces, especially in the Army of Northern Virginia.

FOUR

The Abyss of Horror

Hampton and Gen. John B. Hood, who was also wounded, went first to Staunton, Virginia, for medical care.[1] Hampton then went on to Charlottesville for further convalescence. He wrote to Sen. Louis T. Wigfall on July 15, 1863, "I have been handled pretty roughly, having received two saber cuts on the head—one of which cut through the table of my skull—and a shrapnel wound in my body, which is there yet. But I am doing well and hope in a few days to be able to go home. Suppose you meet me at Gordonsville as I pass."[2] He soon returned to his home in Columbia, where he remained until the beginning of November.

Then came time for reflection. On August 13, 1863, while convalescing in Columbia, Hampton wrote his official report on his role in the Gettysburg campaign. It was all in all a dispassionate accounting of dramatic events.[3] In a letter to Gen. Joseph E. Johnston, written a month after the battle, the wounded veteran of Gettysburg was less restrained. He characterized the campaign as "a complete failure." He commented that Gen. R. E. Lee had used "unimaginative tactics." Further, "The position of the Yankees was the strongest I ever saw and it was vain to attack it. . . . We let Meade choose his position and we attacked."[4] Few historians would argue with that appraisal.

Hampton found his family deeply involved in war efforts on the home front. His sister Kate served as president of the Soldiers Relief Association, the group responsible for founding and operating the Wayside Hospital at the railroad station in Columbia. This hospital provided much-needed and valuable care for wounded soldiers en route from the battlefields to their homes and hospitals located in the interior of the Confederacy. The suffering of wounded men subjected to delays in the rather primitive and inefficient railroads were alleviated by the care of the women of Columbia. Hampton's daughter Sally and his cousin Susan Hampton Preston had been among the founders and remained workers at Wayside Hospital. Hampton's step-grandmother, Mrs. Wade Hampton I, unable to do active nursing because of her advanced age, was a generous donor to the cause.[5]

Hampton found the state to be badly divided in its support of the war effort. The Charleston *Mercury* was harshly critical of the leadership of

Jefferson Davis. Some argued that the ones who were most anxious to have the state secede were the least involved in the actual war. Benjamin F. Perry, who had been a unionist until secession was a fact, wrote in his journal, "There is a great want of patriots in the country, and especially among the leading secessionists. They ought all go into the war, but all are at home. Rhett, Colcock, Magrath, Hayne, Gist, Pickens, Chesnut, Orr . . . and hundreds of others who inaugurated this revolution are all at home or in some civil office and not in the army where they ought to be."[6] Perry's son had joined the Hampton Legion with the blessings of his father. It is significant that Hampton, who was often critical of General Stuart and occasionally critical of General Lee, remained loyal to President Davis to the end. He must have been discouraged by what he saw on the home front.

While Hampton was recovering in Columbia, General Lee acted on the advice of General Stuart and reorganized the cavalry of the Army of Northern Virginia. In the new cavalry, there were seven brigades, each commanded by a brigadier general, and these brigades were grouped in two divisions, each commanded by a major general. One was the newly promoted Hampton, and the other Fitzhugh Lee. In securing the promotion to major general for Hampton, General Lee wrote that the promotion was earned by both service and gallantry.[7] President Davis asked the Confederate Congress to approve Hampton's promotion to major general, to date from August 3, 1863. Congress gave its approval.[8] The date was significant in that it meant that he was senior to Fitz Lee and Nathan Bedford Forrest. The First Division, commanded by Major General Hampton, consisted of three brigades: the Jones Brigade, commanded by Brig. Gen. W. E. Jones; the Baker Brigade, commanded by Brig. Gen. Lawrence S. Baker; and the Butler Brigade, commanded by Brig. Gen. M. C. Butler.[9]

The Hampton Brigade was of course active while their commander was convalescing. Col. Lawrence Baker commanded in Hampton's absence until he was also wounded at an engagement at the second battle at Brandy Station on August 1, 1863. When the enemy cavalry crossed the Rappahannock River on July 31, Baker led his brigade in retarding the Union advance until Confederate infantry could come up on the following day and drive the enemy back. The command then went to Col. Pierce Manning Butler Young. The Division's action at Brandy Station drew special praise from both General Lee and General Stuart.[10] In early September General Meade began to move the Army of the Potomac into a position north of the Rapidan River. Stuart's cavalry was assigned picket duty, the Hampton division on the left and the Fitz Lee division on the right. As the two opposing armies jockeyed for position, there were several cavalry engagements. Stuart led the Hampton division in the most significant of these, the battle known as the Buckland Races, October 19, in which the Confederates routed the

Union cavalry led by Gen. Judson Kilpatrick (known as "Kilcavalry"). The Hampton division performed well. Meade then went into winter quarters at Culpeper Courthouse.[11]

On October 31, 1863, there was still another adjustment in the organizational structure. The Hampton division then consisted of three brigades: Gordon's brigade, commanded by Col. James B. Gordon; Young's brigade, commanded by Col. Pierce Manning Butler Young; and Rosser's brigade, commanded by Col. Thomas Lafayette Rosser.[12]

On November 3, 1863, Hampton, having sufficiently recovered, reported for duty,[13] although he still suffered some from his wounds. He wrote to his sister that he was quite strong, but his hip hurt on occasion, especially when he mounted his horse or when he rode long distances.[14] But he wasted no time in getting back into action. On the night of November 17, he took five hundred men and crossed the Rapidan at Ely's Ford, entering enemy territory and striking part of the Eighteenth Pennsylvania Cavalry. With the loss of only one man, Hampton's troopers captured one hundred horses and mules and several wagons and then withdrew by way of Germana Ford.[15]

Then came more action and more frustration. On November 26 General Lee, learning that General Meade was moving his army toward Orange Courthouse, shifted his army eastward to block the advance. Hampton's cavalry encountered the enemy near New Hope Church and thereby played a part in checking the enemy's movement. Lee then moved his army into a line west of Mine Run, where he formed a solid front to ward off a Union advance. Meade's army dug in opposite the Confederates. Hampton attempted to penetrate the rear of the enemy, but he was recalled because of a report that the Yankees were moving around the Confederate right.[16] In the ensuing Battle of Mine Run, General Stuart improperly interfered with Hampton's command. Stuart, who should have supervised the movement of his troops by working through their immediate commanders, instead rushed forward and seized command of the first brigade he found, and when another brigade came forward he seized control of that one also.[17] Hampton later wrote in his report that he did not know the whereabouts of his men. His resentment of Stuart was often justifiable.[18] For all of this, the Mine Run Campaign was indecisive; both armies withdrew to their previous positions. To add more fuel to the ill feeling, Stuart was campaigning for the formation of a cavalry corps complete with a third division, which Rooney Lee would command, and promotion to lieutenant general for himself. To form the third division he would remove one brigade from Hampton's command.[19]

General Stuart's political campaign for command of a corps was partially successful. At the beginning of the year 1864, the newly formed Cavalry Corps of the Army of Northern Virginia consisted of two divisions, one commanded by Hampton and the other commanded by Gen. Fitzhugh Lee. Hampton's division had 297 officers and 3,931 men.[20] Stuart did not gain promotion to lieutenant general.

In the winter of 1863–1864, the logistical problems pertaining to the condition and supply of horses became an obsession with Hampton. In the Confederate service the cavalrymen furnished their own horses. The government paid the horseman forty cents per day for the use of the horse. Each trooper was responsible for replacing any horse lost to combat or illness. The troopers found it easier to find replacements by returning to their home areas. If a man from the Deep South lost his horse, his wish was to return home to "recruit" a replacement, and this could take a month. Another way of securing replacements was to seize Yankee mounts by raiding or by conquest in battle. Obviously commanders could not allow every man without a mount to take a month off to return home. Some of the dismounted served temporarily as infantrymen. In September 1863, 14 percent of Stuart's men were without mounts. Shortage of food for the horses was another serious problem. The areas around the armies in Virginia were soon depleted of forage, and the Confederate railroads were never up to the needs of the armies. As the war wore on, the railroads deteriorated more and more. All of this meant that the Confederate cavalry was weakening just as the Union cavalry was coming to full strength in numbers and quality. While the Union horses were subsisting on about ten pounds of grain a day, the Confederate horses were getting about five pounds per day. They were often hungry enough to eat the bark from trees. General Stuart himself lost six horses in six months, to illness, wounds, or overexertion.[21] Hampton's official letters from this time on are replete with concerns about the condition of his horses.

Hampton's problems concerning mounts were more severe, because two of his brigades were from Alabama, the Carolinas, Georgia, and Mississippi. The distances from their homes made it especially difficult for these men to keep themselves mounted. As a possible solution to this problem Hampton wrote to General Lee to suggest that two of his brigades be sent to the Roanoke River near Weldon, North Carolina, "where forage is abundant and where they will have an opportunity not only of procuring fresh horses, but also of doing good service by protecting a valuable portion of our country." Hampton also told General Lee that he understood that there were four regiments and several independent companies of cavalry in South Carolina. He suggested the possibility that two of his brigades in Virginia be sent to South Carolina in exchange for those fresh units. "If the horses are kept here this winter on short forage, these brigades will not be in condition for active service, nor will they ever be able to fill up their ranks." He also suggested that he be sent to Mississippi for recruiting. Gen. Joseph E. Johnston had asked for him. Writing "It would give me great pleasure to join him," he reminded General Lee that he knew Mississippi well.[22]

Hampton even had personal reasons for his interest in serving in Mississippi. He had known for some time that the Yankees had seized his plantations along the Mississippi. He was also bitterly aware that the owner of a neighboring Mississippi plantation, the native Pennsylvanian Dr. Stephen Duncan, had proven to be a unionist and had been compensated by the Union government for the destruction of his cotton and gin. Hampton wrote to his sister, "Duncan should be sent away, for I regard him as a contemptible traitor."[23] This Duncan and his son played a significant role in Hampton's postwar bankruptcy and partial recovery, a role that caused Hampton to form a more favorable opinion of the Duncans.

General Johnston had indeed requested that Hampton be transferred to his command, having written to President Davis pointing out that Hampton was intimately acquainted with the area along the Mississippi.[24] It is interesting that Wade Hampton IV again served as aide-de-camp to General Johnston, who was commanding general of the Department of Tennessee.[25] The president replied simply that "Gen. Hampton cannot be spared."[26] Hampton's reputation was such that even Gen. James Longstreet, who was at this time on detached duty in Tennessee, wrote to request him for his cavalry commander.[27] The Confederate authorities decided that Hampton's services were most needed by the Army of Northern Virginia. The refusal of requests for Hampton's services in the west was a part of the general neglect of the western army by the Richmond government.[28]

Hampton continued his pleas for help in improving the condition of his horses. On February 12, 1864, he wrote to General Lee, "The last fruitless expedition did my horses much harm." He reported that many of his men could not be mounted. "I was therefore very unwilling to take my reduced and worn-out command on a march, unless there was an actual necessity for my doing so."[29] When one considers the friction between Hampton and his West Point–trained superior officers, it is remarkable that they were patient with this talented amateur who went around the chain of command to write letters to the commanding general and, more, that he was willing to say what kind of expeditions he was willing to undertake. Traditionally, the true soldier obeys orders without question: "Ours is not to question why." General Lee's first reply to Hampton's request was a denial. Lee reasoned that the forage in the Roanoke area was not good because of damage done by a recent flood. Lee had asked the Confederate government to transfer the underused cavalry in South Carolina to the Virginia front, but the generals in that state objected.[30] On February 1, 1864, Hampton wrote to General Stuart's adjutant that his supply of forage was almost exhausted. "Only one shipment came last week, and none is expected until next Tuesday." Part of Hampton's command had no forage. Within the last twelve months Hampton's command had acquired a total of two thousand horses, and, at the time of his letter, less than five hundred men could be mounted.[31] On February 13 Hampton wrote to Secretary of War James A. Seddon, specifically asking that the Butler Brigade, then commanded by Col. P. M. B. Young while Butler was recovering from his wound at Brandy Station, be transferred to South Carolina for recruiting. Two-thirds of this brigade was dismounted. The letter to Secretary Seddon was properly routed through the chain of command. Stuart in his endorsement objected to any weakening of his command, and General Lee insisted that any units sent to the Deep South be replaced with fresh troops.[32]

General Lee, on at least one occasion, expressed genuine irritation with Hampton's complaints and lack of respect for the normal chain of command. When Stuart removed one brigade from Hampton's command and transferred it to Fitz Lee's division, the South Carolinian complained to Gen. Robert E. Lee, who replied curtly, "I would not care if you went back to South Carolina with your whole division."[33] Hampton was stung by that response. Fortunately, time healed these wounds.

Despite Hampton's almost obsessive concern with worn-out horses and dismounted troopers, he could on occasion be remarkably optimistic. He wrote to his sister, "If we can only win the first great battle of the campaign I hope that we can see the beginning of the end. . . . We are in better condition and in higher hopes than we have ever been & I do trust that God will grant us peace."[34]

In the midst of these negotiations about the care of mounts, Union general Philip Sheridan, recently transferred from the west to command the cavalry of the Army of the Potomac, launched a dramatic raid that was intended to break into Richmond, free Union prisoners held in Libby Prison, and possibly kill Jefferson Davis and his associates. Beginning on February 28 General Custer led a diversionary raid toward Charlottesville and succeeded in drawing Stuart off in that direction.[35] On February 29 Hampton learned from his scouts that the cavalry under the command of Gen. Judson Kilpatrick was moving. Kilpatrick left on this raid with 2,375 men and one battery of horse artillery (six pieces). Hampton gathered his men and moved toward Hanover Courthouse. The Federals planned for Kilpatrick to make a dash straight for Richmond while Col. Ulric Dahlgren (son of John A. B. Dahlgren, chief of the U.S. Naval Bureau of Ordnance and inventor of the Dahlgren gun) took a smaller unit of cavalry of 460 men and approached Richmond from the west. The two were to make a surprise and coordinated attack on the Southern capital. Hampton found the troopers under Kilpatrick camped near Atlee's Station about ten miles north of Richmond. The Confederates watched the Union campfires and waited for their opportunity. Hampton led an attack that surprised the surprisers, overrunning the Union camp, taking 133 prisoners, and capturing wagons and supplies, including fifty-five guns. Kilpatrick led the remnants down the peninsula to the Union lines around Williamsburg.[36]

Meanwhile, things went awry for Colonel Dahlgren, who became separated from his unit. Confederate militia killed Dahlgren and captured between 70 and 80 of the Union troopers. The remnant of this command rejoined Kilpatrick at Tunstall's Station. It is interesting that Union general Meade in his official report referred to Hampton's attack on Kilpatrick as "some slight and insignificant skirmishing." Yet Meade wrote that Kilpatrick "withdrew his command and hurriedly made his way to Williamsburg."[37]

Subsequent to the Kilpatrick-Dahlgren raid, Gen. R. E. Lee sent to Major General Meade copies of papers purportedly found on the body of Dahlgren, directing him to murder President Davis and his cabinet. Meade replied, denying the authenticity of the papers.[38] The papers were believed in the Confederacy and became more fuel for the furor of war.[39]

During the excitement of the Kilpatrick-Dahlgren raid Hampton apparently learned that he was to get his wish to send two of the veteran regiments to the Deep South to be replaced by fresh units. On March 6 Hampton wrote to General Stuart, "I have not availed myself of my leave of absence, as the weather has not been favorable for the movement of troops, and if my presence here is longer necessary I will cheerfully forego my visit home."[40] General Lee's headquarters issued the formal orders on March 18, 1864. The first and second regiments of South Carolina cavalry were to move to South Carolina and there report to General Beauregard. The horses were to move by the highways; the dismounted troopers and baggage were to go by rail. The orders provided for replacements to report to the Virginia command. The Fourth South Carolina Cavalry under the command of Col. B. H. Rutledge, the Fifth South Carolina Regiment under the command of Col. John Donovant, the Sixth South Carolina Regiment under the command of Col. Hugh Aiken, the Seventh Georgia Cavalry, and three remaining companies of the Twentieth Georgia Regiment were to proceed to the Virginia front. The South Carolina regiments were to be folded into a brigade commanded by Gen. M. C. Butler.[41] Hampton then returned to his home state. On April 1 he wrote to Beauregard's headquarters, the command for the replacement troops, to request that the South Carolina regiments slated to go to Virginia rendezvous in Columbia. Hampton was responsible for the exchange of regiments and for readying the fresh troops for service in Virginia.[42]

Hampton found the fresh troopers to be poorly equipped. Presumably he exerted his best efforts to correct those deficiencies. He also ran into some local opposition, as there was a political move to keep the Rutledge regiment in South Carolina. Hampton wrote to Richmond to forestall that effort, arguing that these troops were needed more in Virginia. His arguments were successful. General Butler was sufficiently recovered to assist in the transfer of these units to the front.[43]

Hampton's time at home was not all work. The newspaper the *South Carolinian* reported a huge barbecue for the general. The event took place on the grounds of the Lunatic Asylum, where the hosts served 3,500 pounds of meat on long tables. "Amid stained battle flags there were jaunty banners proclaiming 'Welcome Home,' 'Go Forth To Honor and Victory,' 'Trust in God and Keep Your Powder Dry.'" Hampton addressed the gathering. One of the other speakers was the minister of Columbia's First Presbyterian Church, Dr. Benjamin M. Palmer, who in referring to slavery told his audience, "I believe, as I believe the fact of my being, that the only hope of republican institutions on this continent is to be found in the perpetuation of that institution [slavery] which has been made the occasion for war."[44]

The *South Carolinian* proclaimed Columbia to be "the liveliest place in the Confederacy. The ladies are all agog over the soldiers; private parties, soirees and sociables are the rage." Still, all was not pleasant on the home front. In its desperate need for soldiers the Confederacy had approved the recruiting for Southern service the foreign-born Union troops who were prisoners in Southern camps. The rationale was that these men were drafted against their wills. The First Foreign Battalion—mostly Irish and French born—were to be trained in Columbia. They proved to be an unruly lot. Columbians complained about a rash of robberies and believed that these former Union troops were the culprits. Some parties even broke into General Hampton's home, stole jewelry and left a bit of graffiti, for example, "Hang Hampton." The foreigners were the obvious suspects.[45]

The veteran cavalry units' return to Columbia elicited some moving observations. Sophia Lovell Cheves Haskell wrote in her diary that the veterans "look very proud & their spirit is high. They say just give them some new recruits and a few fresh horses & they are ready and eager for another campaign in Virginia, but I can hardly look at them without tears in my eyes, to think of their full ranks and nice uniforms & bright faces when they first went off and now to see them with only between 200 and 300 men and they are miserably clothed with their poor frames of horses and skins burnt the color of mahogany. Oh! It is pitiful to look up and down the line and miss three fourths of their faces, young boyish faces, so full of ardent hope and life, but the spirit is higher than ever and the faces have that look on them that shows they are men to do or die."[46]

In making preparations for returning to action, Hampton requested the colonels in command of the First and Second South Carolina Regiments of Cavalry, the two units being left in their home state, to detach ten men each for service as scouts. This was the most dramatic and daring part of Hampton's military experience, in that these scouts were frequently behind enemy lines, often in Union uniforms, gathering intelligence for the use of Rebel cavalry. If the scouts were caught they were often considered spies and subjected to the possibility of death by hanging. Hampton's request for these men included an interesting statement that they did not have to have mounts, "as they can soon mount themselves in the lines of the enemy."[47] It was normal that he secured these scouts from veteran regiments. Scouting was attractive service to only the most adventurous of men.

When Hampton returned to the Virginia front on May 2, 1864, General Stuart had had his way in forming three divisions in his cavalry corps; the first division commanded by Hampton, the second by Fitzhugh Lee, and the third by W. H. F. "Rooney" Lee, the son of Gen R. E. Lee. Hampton's division consisted of three brigades: one commanded by Brig. Gen. M. B. Young, another by Brig. Gen. Thomas L. Rosser, and the third by Brig. Gen. M. C. Butler, now returned minus a leg to duty from convalescence.[48]

On March 9, 1864, President Lincoln promoted Ulysses S. Grant to the rank of lieutenant general and made him commander of all of the Union's land forces. Grant had made his reputation as an effective fighter by his victories in the West, especially at Vicksburg and Chattanooga. The newly appointed commanding general decided to make his headquarters with General Meade's Army of the Potomac. This meant that Grant directly ordered the movements of the Army of the Potomac and indirectly ordered the movements of General Sherman's army in the western theater. On May 5–6 Grant launched the Union army on a move intended to flank the Rebel right and move directly on Richmond. General Lee anticipated the move and ordered his own flanking movements. The result was the bloody Battle of the Wilderness, in which the Union forces lost 17,500 casualties and the Confederates lost 10,500. Although stymied in this move, Grant did not retreat, but instead attempted another flanking attack. The Federals tried to pass the Confederate right, and the result was a foot race. General Lee ordered Gen. R. H. Anderson in command of the First Corps to move to Spotsylvania and block the Union advance. Hampton's men cut trees to obstruct the roads and slow the Union advance.[49] Lee's troops got in position and faced the Union attack in the Battle of Spotsylvania, May 8–19, 1864. The Rebel cavalry was relatively unimportant in these closely fought engagements.[50] The cavalry performed picket duty, scouted the enemy movement to keep the Rebel command informed, and sought to protect Richmond and the supply lines from Union raids.

In the midst of these momentous infantry battles, there was an equally momentous turn of events for the opposing cavalry corps. Gen. Philip Sheridan, now commanding the unified cavalry corps of the Army of the Potomac, was anxious to take on the fabled Rebel cavalry of J. E. B. Stuart. General Grant allowed Sheridan to unleash his forces for a raid pointed directly at Richmond. This allowed Sheridan to lead ten thousand Union cavalry southward in a bold challenge to Stuart. The latter chased the Federals with only half of his troopers, leaving the others to perform scouting duties for the Southern army then engaged at Spotsylvania. The Northern cavalry reached Beaver Dam Station, the advanced supply base for the Army of Northern Virginia, and they destroyed enormous quantities of supplies, badly needed by the Rebels. On May 10 the Union cavalry destroyed two locomotives, one hundred rail cars, and ten miles of track on the Virginia Central Railroad, and they then headed for Richmond. This was indeed a major raid. General Stuart finally faced the attackers at Yellow Tavern, six miles from Richmond. After a hard-fought battle the Union attack was blunted, but not before one of the Union cavalrymen shot Stuart with a .44 caliber pistol. Sheridan's force moved on to the outskirts of Richmond, made an ineffectual attack, and were repulsed. The colorful and effective cavalier Stuart died May 12.[51] By May 25 Sheridan was back within the Union lines.[52]

General Hampton was then the ranking cavalry officer in the Army of Northern Virginia. Nevertheless, General Lee waited for several months before officially appointing Hampton as the commander of his cavalry corps. While it is not known precisely why General Lee hesitated, one can assume that Hampton as a non–West Point trained officer had again to prove himself. It is also likely that General Lee was aware of the jealousy between Hampton and Fitzhugh Lee and was loath to name one over the other. The troopers, however, already had confidence in Hampton's abilities. One cavalryman wrote, "Under Stuart stampedes were frequent, with Hampton they were unknown."[53] This statement captures the essence of Hampton's leadership. He was not flamboyant, but steady, unflappable, and completely courageous. He was a quick student of the military terrain, able in the heat of battle to understand the lay of the land and act accordingly. D. S. Freeman, the astute student of Lee's lieutenants, wrote of Hampton in this stage of his career, "In combat he was the peer if he was not the superior of Fitz Lee, though Hampton was not as resourceful in finding provender for the horses."[54] For several months after Stuart's death, the three cavalry divisions reported separately to the commanding general.

Within days after Stuart's death Hampton was engaged in the Spotsylvania campaign. After another Union assault on the Bloody Angle had failed on May 18, it became apparent that Grant would again shift to his left. General Ewell secured from General Lee permission to meet this Union move with a flank attack. Hampton's division covered the Ewell attack, which, however, did not go as planned. Hampton, with the use of his horse artillery, assisted significantly in holding the enemy off until nightfall, thereby avoiding a complete failure.[55]

After the Battle of Spotsylvania Grant continued moving to the east to flank the Southern army. On May 27 the leading troops of the Union army crossed the Pamunkey River in the vicinity of Hanovertown. On the afternoon of May 28 Hampton and Fitzhugh Lee and their men opposed General Sheridan at Hawe's Shop. General Lee ordered Hampton to make a forced reconnaissance to determine the enemy's strength and movements, and Hampton used the men recently arrived from South Carolina. The newcomers fought dismounted as infantrymen, and they acquitted themselves well—so well that Hampton himself had to lead them out of the fight. This fight helped delay the Union advance, and it proved that Union infantry were following the cavalry south of the Pamunkey River.[56] General Lee then moved to his next defensive position. The Southerners again faced the Northerners with an entrenched defense at Cold Harbor. On June 3 Grant ordered a frontal assault, which resulted in the disastrous loss of 7,000 Union soldiers in one day. The Confederates lost fewer than 1,500.[57]

The Union cavalry had advantages now that would endure to the war's end. Sheridan had in his command about 15,000 men, all well mounted. His men were armed for the most part with Spencer breech-loaded rifles firing metallic cartridges. The opposing Confederate cavalry consisted of about 7,000 men, not as well mounted and armed with muzzle-loaded rifles firing paper cartridges.[58] Still, the Rebel spirits were high, and the condition of the horses was improved because of the steps taken that spring.

Shortly after Grant's disastrous assault on the Rebels at Cold Harbor, the Union commander launched an operation intended to damage the Southern supply lines and perhaps draw Lee's army out of their trenches. Gen. David Hunter with the Union army in the Shenandoah was to move up the valley, destroying the sources of Rebel supplies, cross the Blue Ridge, and destroy the supply base at Lynchburg. Meanwhile, Sheridan was to take a force and move west from the Army of the Potomac, destroy the railroads from that direction, and link up with Hunter. General Lee sent Gen. Jubal Early with Jackson's old corps to confront Hunter. Early's arrival stopped Hunter's efforts short of destroying Lynchburg.[59] On June 7 Sheridan crossed the Pamunkey with about 9,000 men and six batteries and headed westward. Hampton, surmising that the Federals were striking toward Gordonsville and Charlottesville, took his and Fitzhugh Lee's divisions (about 4,700 men and three batteries) in pursuit. Rooney Lee's division remained with the main army. By June 10 Hampton's division was beyond Sheridan. The Confederates camped at Green Spring Valley, three miles beyond Trevilion Station. Sheridan was bivouacked at Buck Childs, three miles east of Trevilion Station. That same night Fitzhugh Lee's division camped near Louisa Courthouse. Hampton planned a coordinated attack from two directions. Both divisions attacked, but one unit of the enemy, led by General Custer, eluded Fitz Lee and approached the rear of Hampton. The Hampton division had to form another line, which succeeded in repulsing Custer's attack. The Confederates counterattacked with such success that they captured

Custer's headquarters wagon. Hampton put his troopers in a strong defensive position along a railroad embankment, which Sheridan's men attacked. Fitz Lee's troops struck the Federals on their flank with considerable success. Sheridan disengaged on June 12 and moved back toward the Army of the Potomac. While the Northern cavalry had destroyed some trackage and supplies, Early at Lynchburg and Hampton at Trevilion Station had stymied Grant's plan. Hampton followed Sheridan on his retreat all the way to White House on the Pamunkey, east of Richmond. There were several skirmishes along the way, most important with Gregg's cavalry at Charles City Courthouse.[60] Hampton realized that White House was a major supply depot for the Union army and that it was too well defended for him to mount an assault without reinforcements. He sent a dispatch to General Bragg, asking him to relay the message to General Lee, to urge the Confederate command to send one infantry brigade to assist Hampton's cavalry in seizing White House.[61] The Confederate command could not comply.

By mid-June 1864, General Grant had moved his army south of the James River; he began the long siege of Petersburg. When the Union army first reached the position east of Petersburg they could easily have taken that Rebel city; it was only weakly defended by troops under the command of General Beauregard. But the Union attacks were uncoordinated and ineffective, and the Confederates were determined and lucky.[62] General Lee moved his troops into defensive lines, essentially east of Petersburg. Lee ordered Hampton to move his command to the right of the Army of Northern Virginia. It then became Hampton's primary responsibility to anchor the Confederate right and to protect the railroads that brought supplies from the south to Richmond and Petersburg. Lee instructed Hampton to "Keep yourself thoroughly advised of his [the enemy's] movements and intentions as far as practicable."[63] Much of the conflict in the remaining months of the siege of Petersburg—and that means the remaining months of the Confederacy—had to do with Union attempts to pass the Rebel's right flank and cut the lines of supply to the Southern capital. There were occasional frontal attacks on the opposing defensive lines, but the real and finally telling attempts were on the Confederate right flank, and this was where Hampton played his leading and best role in the final act of the Southern tragedy.

As Hampton assumed these heavy responsibilities, the commanding general developed a greater and greater appreciation for this talented amateur soldier. On June 24 the Union forces advanced and entrenched themselves at Nance's Shop, south of Petersburg. The Confederates under Hampton counterattacked and drove the enemy from their new position. In his report of this engagement, General Lee wrote, "Great credit is due to General Hampton and his command for their handsome success."[64]

The vulnerability of the Confederate supply lines was demonstrated by a series of Union raids on the major lifelines of the Confederate capital. Beginning on June 22 Maj. Gen. James H. Wilson led a raid with about five thousand Union cavalrymen and twelve guns to Reams Station on the Weldon Railroad, the main supply line from the south, where they wrecked the tracks and then rode south and westward and struck the Southside Railroad (Petersburg to Lynchburg) at Ford's Station. On the next day Gen. August Kautz led a detachment from Wilson's command on another raid to the Burkeville Junction of the Southside and the Richmond and Danville Railroad. Kautz then pushed on to the railroad bridge over the Roanoke River. Failing to destroy that bridge, he moved to return to General Wilson. The Union cavalrymen then went eastward to the Stony Creek Station, where they ran into the Rebel cavalry under the command of Gen. John R. Chambliss, part of Hampton's command. On June 27 General Lee had instructed Hampton to move to Stony Creek to intercept the Union cavalry returning from those dangerous raids.[65] When General Meade ordered Wilson to undertake this raid he thought that Hampton and his men were still at White House. He assured Wilson, "Sheridan will keep Hampton occupied."[66] Wilson replied to General Meade, "If Sheridan will look after Hampton, I apprehend no difficulty."[67] Sheridan fell short of these expectations; Hampton reached Stony Creek on June 28 and immediately dispatched scouts to locate the enemy. They found that Wilson's command was approaching Reams' Station. Hampton asked General Lee to order Fitzhugh Lee to join in this engagement, and the general complied. Fitzhugh Lee's division took a blocking position near Reams Station. Hampton used Butler's brigade in enveloping the enemy's rear while Hampton himself directed a frontal attack. Wilson's cavalry suffered a severe defeat and only narrowly escaped being annihilated. The Rebels captured 1,306 prisoners and four cannon. Hampton stated in his report that only the lack of coordination with Gen. Fitzhugh Lee allowed the remnant of the enemy to escape capture.[68]

On July 4, 1864, Hampton wrote a telling letter to his sister. He recounted to her that his men had been engaged for twenty-five days in pursuit and conflict with the enemy, sometimes going for days without food and sometimes riding all night. "We have captured, wounded or killed nearly 5,000; whipping them in every fight."[69] His spirits were obviously high in this period soon after the death of Stuart.

Several incidents in this time indicated the rising reputation of Hampton as a superb cavalry leader. The Ninth Virginia Cavalry Regiment captured two standards from the enemy and then gave them to Hampton as a personal gift. When Hampton asked the authorities whether he was permitted to retain them, he learned that the standards must be forwarded to the War Department. General Lee suggested that the War Department give them to

Hampton as a "worthy compliment to a gallant officer and meritorious patriot."[70] Gen. John B. Hood, only two days after assuming command of the Confederate army before Atlanta, wrote to the secretary of war to request that Gen. Wade Hampton be reassigned to his army. "If a lieutenant general is to be appointed and sent to me, I know of no one that I would prefer to Major General Hampton or S. D. Lee [another South Carolinian]."[71] Recognition of Hampton's abilities came not only from his superiors but also from those who served with him. Edward Wells, who knew Hampton as a soldier, wrote that the general seemed to know every private and every horse, often asking why a trooper was not riding his regular mount.[72] U. R. Brooks, who also knew Hampton as a soldier, wrote that the general was an inspiration to those around him. Once, in a battle, a thoroughly rattled officer rode up to Hampton and said, "General, I am not equal to the task. I have turned my regiment over to the next in command." Hampton replied, "Colonel, you are a gentleman, and you have heavy responsibilities. Now, return to your command and be what almighty God has made you—a man."[73] Whether this is a completely accurate quotation of General Hampton's, it is indeed a remarkable statement of the Southern gentleman's creed. The ultimate recognition came when General Lee named Hampton the commanding officer of the Cavalry Corps of the Army of Northern Virginia on August 11, 1864.[74] On July 2, 1864, General Lee had written to President Davis to recommend that Hampton be named the commander of the Cavalry Corps, stating rather revealingly that Hampton "had displayed both energy and good conduct, and although I had feared he might not have that energy and endurance so necessary in a cavalry commander, and so eminently possessed by General Stuart . . . I request authority to place him in command."[75] With all the recognition of Hampton's qualities as a leader, he was also reputed to be an excellent horseman. One observer wrote, "He sat while on the gallop with rare ease, scarcely a swing being noticeable, despite the rapid pace."[76]

In an attempt to save the Shenandoah Valley and threaten Washington so much that Union forces before Petersburg would be weakened by shifting forces to the Union capital, General Lee had Gen. Jubal Early, with fifteen thousand troops, sweep northward down the valley and across the Potomac on July 6. On July 9 Early was only five miles from Washington, but he was not strong enough to carry those formidable defenses. As the Rebel force withdrew into Virginia, General Lee sought to reinforce the Confederate forces in the vicinity of the Blue Ridge.[77] On August 7 General Lee sent Lt. Gen. Richard H. Anderson with Kershaw's division to Culpeper, just east of the Blue Ridge Mountains. From there Anderson could move into the Shenandoah Valley if needed. On August 11 Lee ordered Hampton to take one division and move to Culpeper to reinforce Anderson and to help form a threat to any enemy movement into Shenandoah Valley. Lee hoped by keeping a visible force in the area to force the enemy to drain forces from the Army of the Potomac to defend Washington.[78] Three days later General Lee was forced by circumstances to change his plans. Gen. David Gregg was threatening the Confederate flank, and Lee ordered Hampton to halt his command and return to the Richmond area.[79]

On August 18, 1864, with their relentless pressure on the dwindling Confederates, Union forces succeeded in seizing a foothold at Globe Tavern on Weldon Railroad, the major supply route connecting Petersburg and Richmond with Wilmington, North Carolina. There ensued a number of engagements as the Rebels sought to regain control of this artery. Hampton's cavalry, especially the brigade commanded by Brigadier General Butler, fought a major battle on August 25, which resulted in the Southerners regaining Reams Station. In this battle Hampton's cavalry conducted an attack on hastily constructed Union breastworks, a rare feat for Civil War cavalry. The Rebels succeeded in breaching the Union line, in large part because of coordination with the infantry under the command of Gen. A. P. Hill. The difficulty of battlefield communications in this war made success in coordinated attacks unusual enough to merit special comment. In his report on this Battle of Reams Station, General Lee wrote that General Hampton had played a major role in the success of the day.[80] The Federals, however, had permanently interdicted the Weldon line. Thereafter, the Confederates used wagons to haul goods from the northern terminus of the Weldon Railroad at Stony Creek over the back roads of Dinwiddie County to the Boydton Plank Road and into the bases at Petersburg. Maintaining the Confederate stronghold became increasingly difficult.[81]

It is interesting that fellow South Carolinian and Harvard-educated Mart Gary, who became one of Hampton's major political antagonists, had become a brigadier general in command of a brigade that originated in the Hampton Legion. Gary had remolded his unit into a highly mobile, mounted infantry unit. The Gary Brigade assisted Hampton in the fights along the Weldon line.[82]

General Hampton could on occasion be harsh. On August 27 Union general David Gregg sent a message across the line, using a flag of truce, asking permission to bury the Union soldiers killed in the Reams Station action. Hampton denied the request, stating, "the dead will be buried and the wounded cared for."[83] In the midst of all these deaths, there was a rumor that Hampton himself had been killed. He wrote to his sister that the rumors were in error.[84]

The fall of 1864 brought Hampton an opportunity to out-Stuart Stuart. In early September Hampton's scouts, especially one Texan sergeant, George B. Shadburne, brought word from behind enemy lines that the Federals had gathered about three thousand cattle near Coggins Point on the James River, not far from City Point, the main supply base for the Army of the Potomac. Shadburne also learned that General Grant had sent General Sheridan, the most able of the Union cavalry commanders, to the Shenandoah Valley to wreak such destruction there as to deprive General Lee of supplies from that source. The scouts informed General Hampton of the locations of the enemy troops around the cattle. It was of course significant that Sheridan's able leadership was to be absent. The opportunity of raiding to secure such a supply of food for the hungry Rebels was irresistible.

Shadburne was the most competent of Hampton's scouts, many of whom had been recruited by the general himself. Typically the scouts had been coon hunters, bear trackers, deer stalkers, or simply excellent woodsmen. Hampton characterized Shadburne as "a handsome young fellow, with large, soft mild eyes; but as soon as a fight began he was instantly transformed into the dashing cavalier, his whole soul seemed to be in the battle, and his black eyes blazed like fire. Armed with at least two pistols, and often with three, he would dash through the enemy firing with rapidity and precision." Shadburne gained some information from one Molly Tatum, a Rebel loyalist sympathizer living behind the Union lines. He also learned that General Grant was to be away for a time.[85]

This was the opportunity for the "Great Beefsteak Raid." Hampton first secured permission from Gen. R. E. Lee for the daring raid, and he then gathered a body of troops, including Gen. Rooney Lee's brigade, the brigades of Gen. Thomas Lafayette Rosser and Gen. Jimmy Dearing, and smaller units selected from other brigades. The raiders bivouacked the night of September 14 well behind some of the Union troops. The next morning they moved to Cook's Bridge, a bridge partially dismantled, over the Blackwater River. Hampton had his engineers rebuild the bridge enough for their crossing. He chose this route because he assumed that the Federals would not expect a raid across the river with a destroyed bridge. His assumption was strategically accurate. On the night of September 15, General Lee conducted a demonstration to distract the Union command's attention from the cow pens. The Confederates approached their bovine objective by dividing into three prongs, Rooney Lee leading the prong to the northwest of the objective, Jimmy Dearing leading the prong to the northeast of the objective, and Rosser leading the center of the trident attack straight for the cow pens at Coggins Point in the vicinity of Sycamore Church. Rooney Lee's division went to the Union camp near Prince George Courthouse with the plan of blocking any interference from the west of the main objective. Dearing's troopers went to Cocke's Mill with the plan of blocking any interference from the east. The three-pronged attack was amazingly well coordinated. Rosser attacked at 5:00 A.M., killing or capturing the videttes and overpowering the

120 men directly caring for the cattle. Hampton accompanied Rosser. Generals Rooney Lee and Dearing from their opposite positions covered the Confederate withdrawal. The enemy made a counterattack, which General Rosser withstood. Rosser's men had to overcome the First Cavalry Regiment of the District of Columbia. The entire attack was in the dark of night, which made the success of the Confederates impressive because of the difficulty of coordination. Darkness also assisted their attempt for surprise. Hampton's force came back into the Confederate line with 2,486 cows, 304 prisoners, and eleven wagons. Rooney Lee's men brought up the rear and fought several rearguard actions. Brig. Gen. Henry Davies led a Union force in an attempt at intercepting the captured herd. In the Great Beefsteak Raid, the Southerners lost 10 men killed, 47 wounded, and 4 missing. One scout, Sergeant McCalla, was among those killed. Shadburne himself served as a guide for the raid.[86]

The Great Beefsteak Raid was of course an astounding success. It provided a much-needed boost to Southern morale. The Northern press was extremely critical of General Meade for permitting such a humiliation. President Lincoln was reported to have commented, "It was the slickest piece of cattle-stealing I ever heard of."[87]

The raid was made possible by astute and courageous scouts. The exploits of scouting easily slipped from military control to something like free enterprise. Warfare has normally been attended by some degree of uncontrolled activity, not strictly military in nature, but based on violence or threats of violence. Nonmilitary types who sought scavengerlike to take advantage of the absence of civil or military control in the war zone usually followed the opposing Civil War armies. People living in the vicinity of the fighting were subjected to foraging by the armies and robberies by riff-raff who followed in the wake of the organized violence. The Confederate government became concerned about people posing as raiders seeking their own profit. In October 1864 the Richmond authorities issued instructions to the division commanders of the Army of Northern Virginia to watch out for "people pretending to be Confederate scouts." These people were operating behind the enemy lines, where they committed robberies and would "mistreat Federal deserters." Division commanders were ordered to arrest scouts who were not authorized by the cavalry commander.[88] It was logical that the commander of the cavalry corps should be in charge of the scouts since their prime function was intelligence, a cavalry-related responsibility.

The Union pressure was indeed relentless. On September 27–28 Union forces attacked part of Hampton's cavalry west of the Weldon Railroad. The Rebels counterattacked with a combination of cavalry and infantry, and the enemy was repulsed; but each attack wore the Southerners down a bit more.[89] General Hampton was quite aware of the political importance of the warfare just prior to the Union presidential election coming up in November. Lincoln faced opposition from the Democratic Party's nominee, George B. McClellan. Southerners hoped that a victory for McClellan would lead to peace. Hampton assumed that General Grant would make special efforts for victory in this strategically important time. He wrote to his sister, "If Hood gains a great success in Georgia and we can defeat Grant here, we may hope for peace."[90]

On October 27 two Union corps made a poorly coordinated attack in the vicinity of Burgess Mill. This battle was almost identical to the Battle of Five Forks five months later, the Union victory that led directly to Appomattox. The purpose of the Union attack was the Southside Railroad connecting Petersburg and Lynchburg, a supply line so valuable that its severance would almost assure the necessity of the withdrawal of the Army of Northern Virginia from its stronghold around the Confederate capital. The Union victory at Five Forks on April 1, 1865, cut off Lee's retreat to Danville and forced him to move toward Farmville, near Appomattox. Hampton's resistance in October was sufficient to delay the ultimate Union victory. Grant had Gen. Ben Butler make a diversionary move north of the James River while the much more effective Gen. Winfield Scott Hancock led the major assault, using the Second, Fifth, and Ninth Corps of Union infantry and the cavalry under Gen. David Gregg. Hancock with the Second Corps moved down the Vaughn Road while Gregg sought to turn the Confederate right. The Union attack on the morning of October 27 drove in Hampton's pickets. Butler's men reinforced the pickets and became engaged with the attacking infantry. The Fifth and Ninth Corps were on the Union right, and they faced fortified Southern positions. This is significant because Hampton sent word to Gen. James C. Dearing to bring his brigade from the trenches to the north to assist General Butler in repelling the attack. Gen. A. P. Hill, not wanting to weaken the lines while under threat from a frontal attack, refused to allow Dearing to move his men. Hill sent word of this decision to Hampton by an officer who was captured by Union soldiers before he could find Hampton. Consequently Hampton did not know that he was not to receive the reinforcements from Dearing. The embattled Hampton realized that he was threatened from his rear and changed fronts just in time. Meanwhile, General Hill released an infantry unit under Gen. Henry Heth to assist the Rebel cavalry. Presently, General Hancock found himself being counterattacked from several sides by the cavalry under Gen. Rooney Lee, by Butler's troopers, and by Confederate infantry.[91]

In this successful turning back of the Union assault, Hampton suffered a personal tragedy of epic proportions. In his official report Hampton wrote, "In this charge, while leading the men and cheering them by his words and example, Lieutenant Thomas Preston Hampton, aide-de-camp, fell mortally wounded, and Lieutenant Wade Hampton, who was acting on my staff, received a severe wound."[92] Preston was an aide to his father, and Wade, who had been on the staff of Gen. Joseph E. Johnston until the general was relieved before Atlanta, was temporarily serving with his father. Preston excitedly rode to encourage the Rebel attack and was felled by a Yankee bullet in his groin. Young Wade rode to his brother's assistance, and he, too, was wounded. The general rode to where Preston had fallen, dismounted, quickly realized that the wound was fatal, and held the dying son in his arms: "My son, my son!" He kissed Preston and released him to an attending surgeon, Dr. B. W. Taylor. The doctor also took care of Wade, whose wound seemed to be less than mortal. Presently, the general remounted his horse and returned to directing artillery fire in the concluding phase of the Battle of Burgess Mill. This pathos-laden scene evoked emotion from the father not unlike that of King David's "O my son Absalom, my son, my son Absalom! Would God I had died for thee, O Absalom, my son, my son!"[93] Still, the general returned to his duties when he realized that there was nothing more that he could do. Mary Boykin Chesnut described Preston Hampton as a beautiful young man. She quoted an admiring girl's description of the young Hampton as having "the figure of Hercules, the face of Apollo."[94] Such was the fate of much of the flower of the South's manhood. Capt. J. F. Hart, commander of the horse artillery that had begun the war as the Washington Artillery in the Hampton Legion, lost a leg in this battle. The next day the Rebels drove the Federals back to their lines.[95]

There is no question that, notwithstanding his stoic and militarily correct behavior immediately after Preston was fatally wounded, Hampton grieved sorely for his son. Three years after the battle Hampton wrote to Gen. R. E. Lee, "But even after the lapse of three years, I fear to trust myself to speak of that brave boy, who stood by my side in more than seventy fights." The sad father commented to General Lee that Preston's friends and colleagues spoke of his having "that almost womanly tenderness which marked his intercourse with his friends and to that courage which even among men where the possession of that quality was the rule and not the exception made him conspicuous on the battlefield. The highest praise that can be given to the soldier as it is the highest that can be bestowed on anyone is to say that he did his duty."[96]

Mrs. Wade Hampton came to the Virginia front to comfort her grieving husband. They stayed in a cottage near Petersburg. Hampton wrote to his sister, "God only knows how much I need comfort for my heart is sorely bruised. It cries out for my beautiful boy all the time, and I cannot become resigned to his loss, but I pray that God has taken him to His eternal rest."[97] Mary was still there in early December. Hampton had to leave her to engage the enemy, presumably the raid of December 7. During that battle the Yankees came within three miles of the Hamptons' cottage. General Lee sent for Mrs. Hampton and kept her informed of her husband's whereabouts.[98]

The Battle of Five Forks in the spring of 1865 was Burgess Mill revisited, and that time the Yankees won. General Lee reported to President Davis, "Our cavalry at Burgess Mill I think saved the day."[99] Lee wrote to Hampton after the war, "If you had been there with all of your cavalry the results of Five Forks would have been different."[100]

The Battle of Burgess Mill was the last major Union attempt to flank the Confederates in the fall campaign. It is interesting that most of the cavalry-men in this battle fought dismounted. Hampton had completed a line of breastworks that were manned by dismounted cavalrymen. The troopers, commanded by General Dearing, whose aid Hampton had sought, were also manning trenches as infantrymen.[101]

On December 7, 1864, Gen. Gouverneur K. Warren, leading the U.S. Fifth Army Corps, reinforced by other units and accompanied by Gregg's cavalry, conducted a raid down the Weldon Railroad. Again the purpose was to isolate Petersburg and Richmond. Gen. A. P. Hill's infantry and Hamp-ton's cavalry succeeded in turning the Federals back. Hampton possessed a remarkable ability to read the intentions of the enemy. He moved his troops to get ahead of the Yankees, putting them in a defensive line near the village of Hickford. The Federals were indeed turned back, but not before they had destroyed several miles of track on the Weldon Railroad. This blow was not fatal to the Confederates.[102]

Mary Hampton was still with her husband in early January 1865. Hamp-ton, obviously in better spirits, wrote to his sister, "Mary grows fat" with her life in Virginia.[103]

Historians in looking back at the flow of events of this time too easily read in an inevitability of defeat that was not at all clear to those on the scene. In late 1864 one of the Confederacy's most able bureaucrats, Josiah Gorgas, head of the Ordnance Bureau, was making plans for improvements in South-ern arms. Gorgas asked Hampton to nominate one or two men who could go abroad to advise in the purchase of advanced weapons suitable for the cav-alry.[104] The prospect of buying arms in Europe must have been tantalizing to the command, which often had to depend on the enemy for arms of any kind. In November 1864, Hampton sent word to the famous ranger John S. Mosby, asking that he make special efforts to capture arms, especially carbines, from the enemy or from citizens who may possess them. "Many of our men are without cavalry arms, and many have no arms at all."[105]

Despite these hardships and despite the progress of the Union army in Georgia, Hampton himself remained confident that with the proper effort South Carolina could withstand the onslaught of General Sherman. He wrote his sister, "If all men in the country will defend the place [South Carolina] the Yankees never will get it."[106] Hampton had written to the governor of South Carolina, "I wish that I could be there, for I should like to strike one blow on the soil of my own state."[107] He would get his chance, but with so little in the way of resources as to be almost helpless.

By this time the course of the war had taken drastic turns. Sherman had taken Atlanta, Lincoln had won reelection, Savannah had fallen to Sherman, and General Hood had suffered catastrophic defeat at Nashville. In Virginia General Sheridan had devastated the Shenandoah Valley and thereby contributed to the further isolation of Lee's army from sources of supply. In Hampton's own command more than 20 percent of his men were without horses of any kind, healthy or sick.[108]

General Sherman's success in Georgia and the likelihood that his army would eventually work its way into Virginia and link up there with the Army of the Potomac made General Lee consider sending part of his army to join in the defense of the Carolinas. Even the Union high command anticipated such a move. In late November 1864, General Grant reported to General Meade the possibility that General Hampton had already gone with part of his troops to Georgia.[109] Although Hampton was still in Virginia, he and Lee were indeed taking steps to strengthen the opposition to Sherman. On November 24 Hampton ordered those troopers who were in Georgia, presumably seeking mounts, to report for duty first at Augusta, Georgia, and then at Columbia, South Carolina.[110] General Lee's willingness to divide his army even further was a measure of his sense of desperation. In early December 1864, he sent Colonel Young's brigade without their horses to Georgia and South Carolina.[111] These troops went without their horses because the commanders were confident that they could be remounted in their home states. Gen. Fitzhugh Lee's command was already serving with Gen. Jubal Early in the Valley. The strength of the cavalry directly serving the Army of Northern Virginia on January 10, 1865, was 5,477 men and 323 officers. These troops under the immediate control of Hampton consisted of part of Butler's division, W. H. F. Lee's division, and the horse artillery.[112] The brigade of Col. Pierce Manning Butler Young (of Butler's division) was already in South Carolina, and General Lee was considering sending the rest of Butler's force southward.[113] There were several reasons for sending part of the cavalry to South Carolina, the most obvious being to confront General Sherman. The Confederate leadership understood that if Sherman's army linked with Meade's army all hope was gone. Then there was the always-present concern for recruiting fresh horses. It is significant that Young's men left their mounts in Virginia. Also, the troops from Georgia and South Carolina serving in Virginia became restive when they realized that their home states were being overrun by what appeared to be a ruthless enemy. A committee representing Hart's Battery, which had served with Hampton from the beginning of the war, presented a resolution asking General Hampton to use his influence to get them transferred with him. General Lee did not think that he could spare them. They did, however, go south in time to participate in the Battle of Bentonville in March 1865.[114]

On January 19 General Lee began to strengthen the southern front when his headquarters issued orders for General Butler to move his men from Virginia to South Carolina, where they were to report to Lt. Gen. William J. Hardee. General Lee assumed that these men would serve in South Carolina during the winter and return to Virginia for the spring and summer campaign. Lee also decided to send Hampton "to aid in mounting the men in South Carolina and placing them in the field." The nebulous nature of this order placed Hampton in an awkward position. He was returning to his home state, where he obviously wanted to play a significant role in defense. This could be the classic defense of hearth and home. Yet he came to South Carolina with no troops under his command. When he did acquire a command, it was so late and the situation so hopeless that the frustration must have been almost unbearable. Hampton's military role in his home state was the most disappointing in his otherwise amazingly successful service. He regained some of his accustomed glory in North Carolina just as the war ended. General Lee had asked that the Confederate government collect horses that the men could purchase at reasonable prices. These moves left only one cavalry division with the Army of Northern Virginia in the Richmond-Petersburg area, the division commanded by General Lee's son Rooney.[115] In late February the division commanded by Fitzhugh Lee rejoined the main army before Petersburg.[116]

For a soldier to continue fighting with vigor there must necessarily be some measure of hope. Hampton had that quality of soldiering until the end. A short time before he left the Virginia front he wrote to his sister: "I am going to see if I can do anything for my state, as General Lee thinks that I can do good there."[117] On January 20, as he was about to take a train southward, Hampton wrote to his friend Sen. Louis T. Wigfall, "We are passing through a fiery ordeal but if we 'quit ourselves like men we must be successful. I do not allow myself to contemplate any other than a successful issue to our struggle."[118] To understand this attitude at this stage of the war it is well to recall that Jefferson Davis and those under his influence believed that they were involved in a struggle for independence much like that conducted by George Washington, and that meant that the goal could be simply to fight until the enemy tired of the cost of the conflict. In that frame of mind, just maintaining an army in being might be enough for eventual triumph for the cause.

General Sherman, having taken Savannah, Georgia, in December 1864, made his plan to conquer South Carolina, where secession had begun. He intended to confuse the Confederates as to his intentions, whether his next conquest would be Augusta or Charleston. On February 1, 1865, Sherman's army, consisting of the Army of the Cumberland, the Army of Tennessee, and the Army of Ohio, numbering approximately sixty thousand men, left Savannah to invade South Carolina. His purposes were twofold: to continue destroying the resources that supported the Confederate war effort and eventually to join with Grant in the final defeat of Lee's army in Virginia.[119]

Thus began the last act of South Carolina's part in the Confederate revolution. The right wing of General Sherman's army was under the command of Maj. Gen. O. O. Howard—the "Christian General" who would later be in charge of the Freedmen's Bureau. It was this wing that would take and occupy Columbia. Maj. Gen. Francis P. Blair, Jr., commanded the Seventeenth Corps within the right wing. (Blair will be the Democratic nominee for vice president in 1868, and Hampton will be one of his boosters.) The Federals moved into South Carolina in two prongs, one apparently aiming for Augusta and the other for Charleston. These moves succeeded in preventing the Southern forces from concentrating. Not only was there a failure to concentrate forces, a fundamental factor in military tactics, but the Rebels also waited until too late to prepare defenses of South Carolina's capital city, which indeed had real significance for the Confederacy.[120]

The Confederate leadership mismanaged their defensive forces in South Carolina. Columbia had manufacturing firms that produced clothing for uniforms, gunpowder, medicines, rifles, shells, cannon, swords, and shoes.[121] The situation in Columbia was made worse by the movement of people and goods from Charleston to the capital city, presumably for safety from Sherman's expected taking of the port city. Gen. P. G. T. Beauregard in command of the Southern forces in South Carolina divided his troops to defend the several possible avenues of approach for Sherman's army, and that meant trying to defend Charleston, Branchville, and Augusta. Such a division of forces in the face of a superior enemy was of course a cardinal tactical sin. When Beauregard decided on February 14 to evacuate Charleston, he found that it was too late to move the troops to Columbia, that way being blocked by Union forces. He had therefore to send those men northwesterly toward Chester, thereby depriving Columbia of some possible defensive forces.[122] Only on February 6 did Beauregard send word from Augusta to his subordinates in Columbia to start preparing defensive positions.[123] The next day, February 7, General Beauregard ordered Hampton to assume command of the cavalry divisions under Generals Butler and Young.[124]

There was genuine confusion about whether Hampton had troops to command before the night of February 16, the eve of Sherman's actual taking of Columbia. Hampton himself did not believe that he had troops directly under his command. The best apparent explanation has to do with who outranked whom. Butler's brigade had been ordered to report to Lt. Gen. William J. Hardee, who obviously ranked Hampton. Beauregard indicated to General

Hardee in a report dated February 11, "Hampton having no troops yet to operate with I have placed him in command of this city [Columbia] and vicinity."[125] This was several days after Hampton had been assigned command of Butler's and Young's divisions. A letter from Beauregard to Gen. R. E. Lee on February 12 helps in understanding the situation. Beauregard recommended that General Hampton be promoted to lieutenant general to command all the cavalry in the Department of South Carolina, Georgia, and Florida. The commanding general of that department commented, "Major General Wheeler, who ranks [Hampton] only a few days, is a modest, zealous, gallant, and indefatigable officer, but he cannot properly control and direct successfully so large a corps of cavalry."[126] Beauregard thereby damned Wheeler by faint praise and recommended Hampton as the more able commander. This explains why Hampton knew nothing about the efforts for his promotion until he received the letter from President Davis. Hampton had only limited respect for Wheeler. Late in life Hampton wrote to a friend, "Wheeler never was a lieutenant general though he has signed himself as such."[127]

Hampton worked to achieve a defense of Columbia, but it was late. It is interesting that Hampton tried to work with Capt. Garnett McMillen, who was in charge of "sub terra defenses," in placing what later became known as land mines on a causeway eleven miles below Columbia. Such measures by Confederates earlier in the war evoked from Union leaders charges of inhumane tactics. But the rush of events and shortage of transportation prevented this defensive measure.[128] General Hampton learned from Union prisoners on February 14 that Sherman was moving on Columbia, and he so informed General Beauregard.[129] Beauregard was at last convinced that he should concentrate troops for the defense of Columbia. He instructed Hampton "to order in my name" General Wheeler to concentrate his troops to defend Columbia.[130] The stipulation "in my name" was necessitated by Wheeler's rank. Beauregard tried to move troops from Augusta to Columbia to be under the command of Generals Carter Stevenson and Hampton. Beauregard hoped that the defenders could hold on a line along the Congaree Creek, four miles below Columbia. General Butler was to hold a line along the Saluda River. By this time, however, even Beauregard knew that Stevenson was being flanked by the approaching Union army.[131]

At about 8:00 P.M. on February 16, the day before Sherman's army occupied Hampton's hometown (and burned his family homes), Wade Hampton, apparently unaware of his nomination for promotion, received news of his promotion to the rank of lieutenant general and orders placing him in command of Confederate cavalry in South Carolina. Two days previously, on February 14, 1865, President Davis had recommended that the Confederate Congress approve promotion of Hampton to the rank of lieutenant general.[132] Davis wrote to the new lieutenant general, "You will understand it was an expression of my appreciation of your past services and confidence in your ability and future usefulness."[133] Despite the fact that this promotion came late in the war, it had (and has) real significance. Wade Hampton was one of only three men who had not been trained at West Point to reach the rank of lieutenant general in the Confederate service (the others being Nathan Bedford Forrest and Richard Taylor). J. E. B. Stuart died at the rank of major general. One can assume that Hampton found real satisfaction in this recognition.

By the night of February 15, Federals were within four miles of Columbia. On the next day Beauregard reported to General Lee, who was now in command of all Confederate forces, that he had about twenty thousand men stretched along a 240-mile line from Augusta to Charleston. He knew that a successful defense of Columbia was doubtful. On the evening of February 15 and during the next day, the Rebels fired on the enemy across the river. The Confederate defenders retreated across the Congaree River Bridge and burned it. On February 16 General Sherman ordered General Howard to have his men cross the Saluda and Broad Rivers, enter Columbia from the northwest, destroy public structures, railroads, and manufacturing establishments, but save private dwellings.[134]

Professor Marion Lucas, the best authority on the taking and burning of Columbia, believes that the Confederate leaders, most notably General Beauregard, were paralyzed by defeatism. As the defending troops streamed into the city, Columbia descended into chaos. Some of Major General Wheeler's troops took advantage of the confusion to engage in looting. General Hampton attempted to stop these outrages, but to no avail. Hampton's wife took a train out of the city. Authorities tried to remove government stores before the Yankees came, but the efforts came too late and with terrible mismanagement. The losses were immense for a cause sadly lacking in resources. On February 14 Beauregard had instructed Hampton to have Columbia's large supply of cotton removed from the city and burned to prevent its falling into Union hands. Again, the confusion of those days prevented the execution of the orders. Most of the cotton was moved into the streets, presumably for burning. Hampton wisely advised Beauregard to refrain from ordering the cotton to be burned, for fear that the fire would spread through the city. Hampton reasoned that Sherman could not possibly move the cotton; the railroads were being destroyed. The Confederate leaders had to leave most of the cotton in the middle of the streets. Their main efforts were to remove or destroy military and logistically valuable goods and to evacuate the city. Beauregard agreed, and on the morning of February 17 Hampton issued the order that the cotton not be burned. In the incredible confusion of that day, some of the cotton was fired anyway. The confusion of a panic-stricken city made the effective execution of orders difficult.

The post commander of Columbia having already fled the city, Hampton assumed command on the morning of February 17, and, realizing the futility of further resistance, he ordered Maj. Gen. Carter Stevenson to withdraw from his defensive position east of the Congaree and move toward Winnsboro with Wheeler's cavalry covering. He also ordered General Butler, who was in a position at Granby, south of the city, to move around Columbia and rendezvous with Stevenson at Winnsboro.

Columbia fell without a real struggle; the struggle came afterward. Mayor Thomas Jefferson Goodwyn went with several colleagues to surrender the city to the conquering army. He asked that General Sherman protect the citizens and their private property. Later the general gave that assurance.[135] The last of the defenders evacuated and the Union troops moved in. General Hampton moved north to Killian Station about ten miles from Columbia and spent the night of February 17 there. He surely saw the glow of the burning of his city, including the several fine Hampton homes.[136] Emma LeConte, the young daughter of the scientist of South Carolina College and effective producer of explosives for the Confederate government, recorded events in her diary. At 7:00 P.M. on the night of February 17, she observed from her home on the college campus that "On one side the sky was illuminated by the burning of General Hampton's residence a few miles off in the country."[137]

Despite the catastrophe of the first day in his new command, Hampton was back in an aggressive mood the next day. He proposed to General Beauregard that the troops from Charleston be sent to Camden, from which an attack could be launched on the Seventh Corps while it was separated from the main body of the Union army. Hampton reasoned that while this body of Federals was moving in a rough and unknown (to them) territory, they were vulnerable to attack by a smaller unit of Confederates who knew the area. Specifically he proposed to concentrate Rebel troops at the crossings of the Wateree Swamp.[138] The classically educated Hampton was probably remembering the Greek opposition to the Persian invasion at Thermopylae in 480 B.C.

Beauregard was by this time too much in the paralysis of defeat to engage in such a daring counterattack. On February 21 Beauregard accepted Hampton's advice and allowed the cavalry commander to have General Butler operate with his men on the flanks and rear of the advancing Union army.[139] Hampton's troops succeeded in harassing the movements of Sherman's army. General Sherman himself reported that he had dispatched a cavalry unit under the command of Captain Duncan with orders to interrupt the railroad from Charleston to Florence, but that unit was repulsed by General Butler's division.[140] On February 19 troops under the command of Hampton attacked elements of the Fifteenth Corps, which had just crossed the Wateree River. This time the Confederates were repulsed.[141] Still, the Yankees were meeting at least some resistance. There is little doubt that Beauregard was not acting with a sense of military aggressiveness equal to that of Hampton, but in a letter to President Davis he engaged in what appears now to have been a flight of fantasy. He proposed to the Confederate president that the Rebel high command concentrate thirty-five thousand men at Salisbury, give Sherman battle there, move on and crush Grant, and then march into Washington and "dictate peace" terms.[142] Beauregard was not that imaginative "on the ground."

In the midst of barbarity there were interesting acts of humanity. According to Union reports, on February 21 the Second Division of the U.S. Twentieth Corps approached Winnsboro, South Carolina. From a distance of about two miles the Union troops saw heavy smoke from the town. They rushed into Winnsboro and assisted in stopping the fire. Only one square burned. The reporting Union officer recorded, "Winnsborough is a pretty town of about 2,500 population, the seat of justice for Fairfield County." The Union officers found that General Hampton had left a note pledging his word that any Union men left in the town as safeguards after the main body had moved on would be protected from arrest or injury by any Confederates later entering the town. The Federals left two soldiers to protect the town from the looting that usually accompanies the chaos of a war zone. Men of Butler's cavalry entered Winnsboro on the next day, and they showed the Yankee soldiers every possible courtesy. When the two guards left town to rejoin their unit, the townspeople gathered to express their appreciation.[143]

On February 22 Gen. Robert E. Lee, as commander of all Confederate forces, ordered Gen. Joseph E. Johnston to assume command of the Army of Tennessee and all troops in South Carolina, Georgia, and Florida. General Beauregard was ordered to report to Johnston for assignment.[144] This was an action President Davis must have found to be a painful necessity. Davis had relieved the cautious Johnston in the last days before the fall of Atlanta and replaced him with Gen. John Bell Hood, who proved to be more aggressive, but less wise than Johnston. Under Hood, the Army of Tennessee had virtually disintegrated with the Battle of Nashville in December 1864. In these waning days of the war, General Johnston ably pulled the army together for a surprising but futile last struggle. Hampton was a major player in this finale. Lee ordered Johnston "to concentrate all forces and drive back Sherman."[145] Concentration was of course the proper action in this situation.

The burning of Columbia ignited a controversy that has endured for almost a century and a half. Professor Lucas in his fine study concluded that the burning was "an accident of war." Lucas found fault with most of the main characters: the governor, the mayor, General Sherman, and the Confederate military commanders, including General Hampton, who waited too late to take the appropriate precautions, such as removing the highly combustible supplies of cotton and the equally volatile and plentiful supplies of whiskey; their confused orders to burn and then not to burn the cotton; the intentional burning of some buildings and supplies to prevent their falling into enemy hands; and the uncontrolled activities of released Union prisoners of war and vandals, who took advantage of the confusion.[146] Hampton from time to time for the rest of his life defended his own role and condemned that of General Sherman. One element of blame for the Union general is inescapable: a commanding general is responsible for the actions of his command, and some Union soldiers undeniably participated in the burning of Columbia. General Sherman was clearly unequivocal in his official report: "I decline on the part of my army any agency in this fire, but, on the contrary, claim we saved what of Columbia remains unconsumed, and without hesitation, I charge General Wade Hampton with having burned his own city, not from a malicious intent . . . , but from folly and want of sense, in filling it with lint, cotton, and tinder." Sherman assumed that Hampton's men had actually fired the cotton in the streets and that fire was blown by high winds to the destruction of about one-third of the city.[147] Sherman's report lacked in veracity, but more important, he did not understand the circumstances gripping Columbia in the final hours before its fall. In his memoirs General Sherman wrote, "In my official report of this conflagration, I distinctly charged it to General Wade Hampton, and I confess I did so pointedly, to shake the faith of his people in him, for he was in my opinion boastful, and professed to be the special champion of South Carolina."[148]

Then came the last events in South Carolina's war. By February 21 the main body of the Union army had moved to Winnsboro. General Kilpatrick's cavalry occupied Lancaster. On March 2 the leading elements of the Twentieth Corps, commanded by Maj. Gen. Henry Slocum, was in Chesterfield, having skirmished with Butler's cavalrymen. In Cheraw the Federals found and destroyed a significant store of Confederate supplies sent there from Charleston. By March 9 the leading elements were approaching Fayetteville, North Carolina.[149]

In the movement of Union troops from Columbia, Sherman again succeeded in confusing the Confederates. On February 25 Hampton sent word to General Beauregard that the Federals seemed to be advancing toward Charlotte. General Hampton proposed that the Southerners take a defensive position in the vicinity of Fort Mill.[150] The Union move to Winnsboro logically made Hampton assume a further move in that direction. Instead, the Federals wheeled to their right and advanced more directly northward.

As the two opposing armies groped northward there occurred an interesting incident. On February 24 General Sherman wrote to General Hampton that he had learned that several Union foragers had been killed. Attached to the bodies was a note, "Death to foragers." There was also an incident involving a lieutenant and seven enlisted men near Chesterfield and another of twenty men near Festerville. Sherman indicated that he had ordered a similar number of prisoners in Union hands "to be disposed of in a like manner." Sherman argued that the right to forage was as old as history. "Personally I regret the bitter feelings engendered by this war, but they were to be expected, and I simply allege that those who struck the first blow and made war inevitable ought not, in fairness, to reproach us for the natural consequences. I merely assert our war right to forage and my resolve to protect my foragers to the extent of life for life."[151] On February 27 Hampton replied to Sherman, "I assure you that for every soldier of mine 'murdered' by yours, I shall have executed two of yours, giving preferences to any officers who may be in our hands." Hampton indicated that he had not authorized the killing of foragers, but he had ordered his men to kill any Yankees caught setting fire to houses they had plundered. "May I ask if you enumerate among these [war rights] the right to fire upon a defenseless city without notice, to burn that city to the ground after it had been surrendered . . . , to fire the dwelling houses of citizens after robbing them and to perpetuate even darker crimes than these."[152] Since there is no evidence of either general executing prisoners, the incident must have died there. Both sides held enough prisoners that such threats had terrible possibilities. When one considers what Hampton had suffered by this time, the death of a brother, a son, and other relatives and friends, the loss of his home and fortune, and multiple wounds to himself, the heat of his reply is understandable. Apparently Hampton's reply was also effective in protecting the lives of Confederate prisoners.

Gen. Joseph E. Johnston was attempting to pull together his scattered command in Fayetteville. Lt. Gen. William J. Hardee, who had faced Sherman since Savannah, moved his men by way of Florence and Cheraw. Maj. Gen. B. F. Cheatham and Maj. Gen. B. F. Stewart, having come from Augusta, were moving their men toward Fayetteville by way of Newberry, South Carolina. Lt. Gen. Stephen D. Lee and his corps and the cavalry under Hampton were moving northward directly in front of the enemy. Hardee's corps consisted of about 11,000 men, Stewart and Cheatham commanded about 3,200 men, and there were about 6,000 men in the cavalry. Johnson would therefore command about 20,200 men if he could concentrate.[153] Hampton was now the commander of the cavalry corps of the revived Army of Tennessee. His command consisted of Butler's division and Maj. Gen. Joseph Wheeler's corps.[154] It was singularly appropriate that Hampton ended his military career under the command of Joseph E. Johnston, whom he had long admired. Mary Boykin Chesnut, who knew Hampton well, wrote, "Hampton says Joe Johnston is equal, if not superior, to Lee as a commanding office."[155] Wade Hampton IV, now recovered from his wound, was again serving as aide-de-camp to General Johnston.[156]

Johnston faced tremendous odds. As the Union army moved into North Carolina, Hampton's cavalry was screening the move northward of General Hardee's troops. The goal of General Sherman in North Carolina was to move to Goldsboro, be reinforced there by the some twenty thousand men under the command of Gen. John M. Schofield, and be resupplied, both men and material coming inland from Wilmington, North Carolina, that port having fallen into Union hands in early February.[157] After that the strengthened army of General Sherman would move into Virginia, join with the armies commanded by Generals Grant and Meade, and defeat Lee's army, thus ending the war. The Rebel purpose was simply to prevent Sherman accomplishing his goals. General Lee had ordered General Johnston "to concentrate all available forces and drive back Sherman."[158] Johnston, ever the realist, replied to his commanding general, "It is too late to expect me to concentrate troops capable of driving back Sherman. The remnant of the Army of Tennessee is much divided. . . . Is any discretion allowed me? I have no staff."[159] Johnston harbored many resentments, primarily against Davis, for having been relieved of the command of the Army of Tennessee before Atlanta and then witnessing the utter defeat of that army under the command of Gen. John B. Hood at Nashville. Johnston was now picking up the pieces and trying to do anything effective in a situation almost without hope. It is to the credit of Johnston that he tried. In these waning days of the Confederacy, Hampton played a major role in advising his beleaguered commanding general.

Events moved rapidly. By February 23 Hampton was in Chester, South Carolina.[160] Two days later he was in Rock Hill, reporting to Beauregard that General Butler and his cavalry were operating on the eastern side of the enemy.[161] In the following days Hampton moved into North Carolina. On March 3 he skirmished with Kilpatrick's cavalry; the Confederates were repulsed twice.[162] By March 5 Hampton was in Wadesborough.[163] On March 10 General Johnston reported that Sherman was approaching Fayetteville, presumably with the intention of crossing the Cape Fear River.[164]

The ever-aggressive Hampton staged a daring raid on March 10. His scouts found Kilpatrick and his cavalrymen encamped near Fayetteville. Just before daylight Hampton led his men in a surprise attack on the Union camp, literally arousing the Federals from their sleep with terror, riding through, firing weapons, and wielding swords. Kilpatrick, startled from his sleep, escaped on foot in his shirt and drawers. The Rebels captured horses, artillery, and an impressive amount of camp booty, especially impressive for the poorly supplied Southerners. The Yankees fled into a nearby swamp, and while the victorious Southerners enjoyed the plunder of their quick conquest and attempted to harness horses to the captured guns, the Northerners regrouped, swept back into the camp, and regained much that had been lost, including the artillery the Rebels had not been able to remove. Kilpatrick characterized the affair as "the most favorable cavalry charge I have ever witnessed."[165] The Confederates succeeded in capturing 500 Union prisoners and in releasing some 173 Confederate prisoners. General Wheeler was to have come in on the flank, but his troops were themselves bogged down in the swamp.[166] All in all it was an impressive but futile show of Rebel aggressiveness late in the war.

General Hampton stopped in Fayetteville for what he thought would be a leisurely breakfast. His intention was to be the last of the Confederate military in that North Carolina town. He planned to leave town and burn the bridge over the Cape Fear River. His meal was interrupted by cries of alarm that Yankees were approaching. He quickly learned that the intruders were a small group of foragers, operating in advance of the main body. Hampton and his escorts attacked, killed several, and scattered the others. He took several Yankee prisoners, including a scout for Gen. O. O. Howard, Captain Duncan. Afterward Hampton left town and had the bridge burned.[167] When General Howard entered Fayetteville he found several Union men dead in the streets. Captain Duncan later escaped his Rebel captors and reported that one Union soldier was badly wounded "and endeavoring to walk away without arms, when the 'chivilrous' [sic] Lieutenant General Hampton rode after him and hacked him down with his sabre, thus adding to his boasted victims."[168]

Four days later Hampton's men were performing the classic role of screening the withdrawal of an infantry unit. General Hardee's men pulled away from a defensive position at Silver Creek, and the Hampton cavalrymen dismounted and took over those trenches to guard against enemy action while the main body moved to another line. The Rebel intention at this time was to prevent Sherman's reaching Goldsboro, where he would be replenished in men and materiel.[169]

On March 16 General Hardee took a defensive position near Averysboro and fought off the Yankee advance until he found himself being flanked by the more numerous enemy. The Union troops captured 217 men and lost 77 killed and 477 wounded.[170] This was rather costly for both sides, not a minor skirmish.

Then came the last major battle in which General Hampton was a major player. After Averysboro Sherman moved toward Goldsboro for the anticipated union with the troops and supplies from Wilmington. To Sherman's surprise his left wing, commanded by General Slocum, ran into General Johnston's army in an entrenched position. This was the Battle of Bentonville, March 19–20. General Johnston, whose main body of troops were then bivouacked two miles south of Bentonville, had asked Hampton to conduct a reconnaissance of the enemy's position. The cavalry commander recommended a fight before Bentonville. Hampton then put his dismounted men in a defensive line and fought off the advancing Federals until Johnston could get his army in position. Sherman spent all day, March 20, pulling his units together to oppose the Rebels, who were in a V-shaped position around Bentonville. The Confederates stopped the Yankee progress and counterattacked, driving the enemy back until they faced a heavily protected line. That ended the last effective Rebel assault. When Johnston realized he was about to be enveloped, he withdrew toward Smithfield.[171] In the midst of the Battle of Bentonville, the Union Twenty-seventh Corps penetrated the left of the Confederate line. General Hampton's cavalry joined General Hardee's men in an attack on the flank of the advancing Yankees, thereby repelling the Union attackers and saving the Rebels from being routed.[172]

On March 23 Sherman reached Goldsboro and united his army with reinforcements. The Union general then considered his long march virtually accomplished. In his memoirs Sherman wrote of his arrival at Goldsboro, "Thus was concluded one of the longest and most important marches ever made by an organized army in a civilized country."[173] Sherman was confident that he could now join with Grant's army almost at will. The Union army was relatively inactive for some days while General Sherman left for a meeting with General Grant and President Lincoln at City Point, Virginia. It was at that meeting that Sherman gained the impression from Lincoln that the victorious Union should be magnanimous with the defeated Southerners.[174]

The aggressive Hampton was not at rest. On March 24 his men attacked part of the Twenty-fifth Corps at Moccasin Creek. Hampton suggested to Johnston that the Rebels launch an attack at Cox's Bridge.[175] Three days later Hampton was urging General Johnston to aid him by ordering the several brigades of General Wheeler's troops who were operating in South Carolina to join the main body in North Carolina. He also asked Johnston to send orders by telegraph to officers in Georgia and South Carolina to arrest and send to Johnston's army any cavalry absentees they could catch.[176] This request illustrates the serious problem of desertions plaguing the armies of Johnston and Lee in the waning days of the war. Apparently with his commanding general's approval, on April 5 General Hampton sent a telegram to all commissioned officers urging them to arrest deserters from General Butler's command.[177] By the end of March Hampton had in his cavalry corps 4,093 men, down from about 6,000 a month earlier.[178] Reluctant to give up, Hampton asked his commanding general to assist him in securing some torpedoes (mines) from Raleigh that the cavalry commander would use to destroy the railroad bridge at Kinston to disrupt the Union supply line to Wilmington.[179]

Hampton reflected on his losses in a letter to his sister, written on March 30, 1865: "We have all met with great losses and my heart sinks when I think of the suffering the loss of Millwood gives to the girls. . . . If we are spared, I shall try to restore the old house. Did they save many things?"[180] This letter is remarkable for its poignancy and for its insight to Hampton's realizing that the end was near.

In these last days of the Confederacy, the Rebel government expressed its appreciation for the services of the planter-untrained general from South Carolina. On March 9, 1865, Hampton's friend Senator Wigfall introduced in the Confederate Congress a resolution to thank the general for his services to the cause. Congress approved the resolution, and President Davis signed it on March 16.[181]

Then came the end for the army of Joseph E. Johnston. Sherman learned of the surrender of Lee's army on April 9, and he assumed that the war was virtually at an end. Prior to learning the news from Appomattox, Sherman had feinted toward Raleigh with the real intention of interposing his army between the two Rebel armies. The surrender of the Army of Northern Virginia made Sherman decide to seize Raleigh and block any possibility of Johnston's escaping southward. Hampton's cavalry fought Kilpatrick's men as they pushed into Raleigh. Then the peace process began in North Carolina. The messages between the two commanding generals passed through the opposing units that were in closest contact, the Union and Confederate cavalry. On April 16 Hampton sent a message to Kilpatrick that General Johnston would like to arrange a meeting with General Sherman. Hampton suggested that the meeting occur at 10:00 A.M. on April 17 at a point equidistant between the lines.[182] Although the end was near, Hampton was not yet ready to quit. Kilpatrick reported that while negotiations were underway, Hampton's men burned a railroad bridge three miles from Hillsborough.[183] Hampton also accused Kilpatrick's troops of violating the truce in effect while negotiations were under way. The Confederate cavalry commander sent a message to General Kilpatrick to indicate that further loss of life would occur should the Union cavalrymen continue crossing the agreed-upon line between the two armies.[184] In the days in which the peace negotiations dragged on, there were a number of desertions from Hampton's ranks. General Kilpatrick asked his headquarters what he should do with the deserters. His orders were to allow the men to keep their horses but take their arms.[185] The Union forces were apparently not treating the deserters as prisoners of war but releasing them to go to their homes. Sherman was acting as though the war had indeed ended.

The civil authorities of the North Carolina government were more anxious for peace than the Confederate military. On April 19 Gov. Z. B. Vance sent a message to General Johnston to complain that the Confederate soldiers were seizing property belonging to the state of North Carolina, and they were threatening to sack the railcars containing the funds of the state treasury and the state archives. Vance referred to these troops as a mob. General Sherman had offered to provide protection, and Vance, wishing to avail himself of the Federals' protection, asked that the railcars be sent to Raleigh.[186] Johnston replied, asking for details, and the governor responded by listing great quantities of cloth goods (blankets, pants, jackets, and so forth) being seized by the "mob" from the North Carolina quartermaster. Vance wrote that since his state had done more than any other state in clothing the

Confederate army, "I think I can appeal the more strongly to you to protect her against plunder and pillage by an army 'about to be disbanded.'"[187] This is of interest for several reasons: Vance had already given up the struggle, and he placed the welfare of his state over that of the Confederacy, at this time not an illogical attitude.

Sherman offered Johnston extremely generous terms, which, in effect, would have recognized the existing state governments as legitimate. President Andrew Johnson and Secretary of War Edwin Stanton invalidated Sherman's terms and demanded that Johnston's surrender be consonant with the terms offered to General Lee at Appomattox. If Johnston stalled, hostilities must be resumed.[188]

In these last days of the Confederacy, Hampton was the main liaison between the estranged General Johnston and President Davis. While the truce negotiations were taking place, Johnston sent Hampton to Greensborough (now Greensboro) with instructions to go on to Salisbury to meet with President Davis, who after the abandonment of Richmond had been moving southward. Hampton learned that Davis was not in Salisbury, so he sent a message to Charlotte, assuring the president he and many of his officers and men were willing to join the presidential staff in escaping to the west of the Mississippi and continuing the struggle for independence. Hampton indicated that he preferred continuing the conflict to the possibility of being forced back into the Union and then being drafted "alongside of our own negroes" to fight in a war with Europe. Presumably Hampton anticipated that the United States would go to war to remove the European presence from Mexico, where the Emperor Maximilian was ruling with the backing of European powers. Hampton assured Davis, "My men are in hand and ready to follow me anywhere. I cannot agree to the terms proposed." He went on to say that he hoped that Texas would hold out. "If I can serve you or my cavalry by any further fighting you have only to tell me."[189] This message obviously smacks of desperation. At least some of his men had already deserted. His commanding general was negotiating for peace while his army was literally melting away by desertions. Davis replied that he wanted to talk.[190] Hampton went to Charlotte to confer directly with President Davis. Two days later Confederate Secretary of War John C. Breckinridge sent a message to General Johnston asking him to send a cavalry detachment to escort the president and his party to the Southwest.[191] The world of the Old South was collapsing about them; the confusion is not surprising. Wade Hampton, who was an integral part of that society then in its death throes, was a part of that desperate chaos.

While the Confederate president was inclined to be adamant, there came from within the Davis cabinet at least one call for reason. The able secretary of the Confederate navy, S. R. Mallory, had studied the terms offered by

General Sherman, and he gave thoughtful advice to President Davis. Mallory summarized the terms: cessation of hostilities, disbandment of the armies, restoration of the states to their original positions within the Union, the integrity of the state governments as they existed at that time, the security of the Southern people in their rights of person and property under the U.S. Constitution, and a general amnesty. Mallory recognized that these were indeed generous terms. All of this speaks to the enigma that was William T. Sherman, who virtually invented the modern concept of total war, that is, destroying the will of the enemy people to continue the conflict, and who was extremely magnanimous once the conflict ended. Mallory recommended acceptance of the terms and recognition that Southern independence was a hopeless cause. He thought that nine-tenths of the Southern people favored peace. He also spoke of the "vast army of deserters and absentees from our military service." Mallory predicted that if Johnston were to retreat with his army there would be a continual melting away as the army passed the paths to the soldiers' homes. He recognized that guerrilla warfare was a possibility, but such warfare would be destructive to the Southern people themselves. Mallory expressed the interesting belief that guerrilla warfare cannot be successful when both foes were people of a common origin, a common language, and a common culture. Modern studies of guerrilla warfare can scarcely improve on Mallory. He concluded that Davis had a duty to secure for his people the rights of life, liberty, and property.[192] Davis was convinced, and on April 24 he telegraphed to General Johnston his approval of the proffered terms.[193] Later that same day the Confederate president learned that the Federal government had invalidated General Sherman's proposal.

Events moved rapidly; hostilities would be resumed if a satisfactory agreement were not reached. It is to the credit of General Sherman that he was reluctant to cause any more suffering; the utter collapse of the Confederacy was obvious. On April 25 General Johnston telegraphed to Secretary Breckinridge his refusal to provide any more than a small escort for the escaping Davis. Johnston stated his opinion that the president ought to escape as quickly as possible.[194] Breckinridge quickly replied, asking that Gen. Wade Hampton be designated to lead the escort and that he be allowed to take a sufficient number of troopers.[195] Johnston replied, agreeing to the request.[196] On the following day, Davis sent a dispatch to Hampton asking him, "with the approval of General Johnston," to select a number of men and join the presidential party, leaving General Wheeler in command of the cavalry of the Army of Tennessee.[197] Before this could be accomplished the curtain came crashing down on the Confederate army. On April 26 Johnston agreed to new terms offered by Sherman, according to which the Confederate army was to be disbanded.[198]

When Hampton returned from Charlotte, he found that the surrender was accomplished. There followed a quick series of complications. Hampton informed General Johnston that he did not consider himself bound by the terms, since he was away from the command at the time of the actual surrender, and, furthermore, he was then acting under orders from the president and the secretary of war. "I was carrying out their orders when I learned of your surrender." He went on to state that if Breckinridge considered Hampton to be surrendered, he would concede.[199] On April 26 Hampton asked Breckinridge for a ruling. Was he properly embraced by the surrender?[200] The secretary of war replied that in his opinion since Hampton was not present with the army at the time of the surrender he was free "to come out."[201] Word that Hampton was preparing to continue the war reached the ranks of the cavalry. At least part of General Butler's cavalry and Hart's artillery left the main body, presumably to reform under General Hampton. On learning of these developments, General Johnston sent instructions to order the troops returned to the Army of Tennessee of which they were a legal part.[202] Hampton responded with an apology. He reminded General Johnston that the general had ordered Hampton to go and confer with President Davis. During the time Hampton was conferring with the president they concocted a plan whereby Davis was to move to the Southwest with Hampton in command of a military escort. Hampton reported that Davis had ordered him to execute this plan and that he was proceeding with it.

Hampton found himself faced with a true dilemma. On one side he could agree that he had been surrendered and leave the fleeing Davis to his fate, and on the other he could deny that he had been included in the peace terms and perform his agreed-upon duty to Davis. If he chose the first alternative he would feel that he had betrayed an honorable commitment to the Confederate president. "I shall never cease to reproach myself." Hampton recognized that accompanying Davis might mean that he was becoming an outlaw by disobeying a lawful command to surrender to U.S representatives. He concluded by stating his determination to go with Davis because "I believe it to be my duty to do so." He declared that he would ask no troops to join him. If any chose to join him of their own accord, "They will be stragglers like myself."[203]

General Johnston sought to remove any doubt that Hampton and all other Confederate soldiers in the area were subject to the surrender; his headquarters stated that the general's command extended from North Carolina to the Chattahoochee River, which included most of Georgia.[204] Consequently all Confederates in the area were surrendered. A study of the records vindicates Johnston's ruling; his command included the Army of Tennessee and all troops in South Carolina, Georgia, and Florida. Hampton's rather irrational actions can only be interpreted as acts of desperation; he had lost so much that was dear to him. Furthermore, Hampton had not fought this war from a campstool; he had often led his troops from the front. That meant that he had firsthand seen his men, including his son, killed by the detested enemy.

Fortunately, he worked through this time of desperation without doing harm. It is of course significant that such leaders as General Lee, President Lincoln, and Secretary Mallory had feared the horrors of the war being continued by partisan or guerrilla tactics. Just as fortunately, the Union general in immediate opposition favored a distinct policy of mercy.

Events demonstrated the best side of General Sherman. The general deeply resented the statements made by Secretary of War Edwin Stanton, when the president's cabinet rejected the general's first offer of peace terms. The secretary of war accused General Sherman of having been "bribed by Jeff Davis gold." Stanton obviously wanted Sherman to push on for a victory of vengeance. The assassination of Lincoln had fueled the feeling for a more harsh victory. Sherman retorted that there had been no trouble with Johnston's army. One may wonder whether he knew of the agonizing of Wade Hampton. The Union general went on, "The South is broken and ruined and appeals to our pity. To ride the people down with persecution and military exactions would be like slashing away at the crew of a sinking ship. I will fight as long as the enemy shows fight, but when he gives up and asks quarter, I cannot go further." Sherman especially resented the charge that Stanton had aired in a news release that Sherman was a party to allowing Jefferson Davis to escape. The general denied moving the command of General Stoneman to facilitate Davis's escape, but he did refuse to use his army to hunt down the Confederate president.[205] Sherman was indeed a wonderfully complicated man. The Columbia, South Carolina, *Phoenix* of May 5, 1865, published a general order of General Sherman to his troops informing them that Gen. Joseph. E. Johnston had surrendered all Rebel forces east of the Chattahoochee River. The order went on to instruct the Yankee victors to receive "our hitherto enemies . . . in a spirit becoming a generous army." Sherman ordered his subordinates to loan mules, horses, and wagons and to issue provisions "to relieve want and encourage inhabitants to resume their peaceful pursuits and to restore the relations of friendship among our fellow citizens and countrymen."[206] This was in a newspaper published in a city still in ruins from Sherman's march.

Hampton tried to act properly. He learned that part of Butler's cavalry and Hart's battery had left camp. On the night of April 26 he rode to overtake the departing troops, catching them on the morning of April 27. He explained that they were legally surrendered and that they should return to the army to be properly paroled. There followed an emotional parting of the general from his loyal troops. Hampton later said that the men of Hart's battery, upon being convinced to join the surrender, "threw themselves upon their captured guns (for they had no other) and, passionately kissing them, wept like children."[207] Hampton then rode on to Charlotte, accompanied by a small escort. In Charlotte he learned that the presidential party had moved on to Yorkville,

South Carolina. Hampton left his escort in Charlotte, gained a fresh horse, and rode through the night. He swam the Catawba River and reached Yorkville early on the morning of April 28. There he met his wife, who had come there after the loss of Columbia, and he found that he was again one step behind the Confederate president, who had gone on to Abbeville. General Wheeler came at the request of Mrs. Hampton, and they convinced the exhausted Hampton that there was nothing more that he could or should do.[208]

Hampton's war was over. He had proved himself a superb military commander. Douglas Southall Freeman, one of the most distinguished scholars of the Confederate military, wrote of Wade Hampton: "In all the high companionship of knightly men, none had exemplified more of character and of courage and none had fewer mistakes charged against him. Untrained in arms and abhorring war, the South Carolina planter had proved himself the peer of any professional soldier within the bounds and opportunities set for a commander who did not have complete decisions of strategy to make. There is nothing to indicate that he would have failed in a higher command."[209] For all of this glory, his cause had lost, and he had lost much with it.

Now came the task of picking up the pieces. Hampton's adjustment to peace was not easy. On May 10 he wrote to a "Dear Captain" that he did not consider himself surrendered since he was absent from the command at the time the terms were agreed upon. He told this now-unknown captain, "If any opportunity offers later, we can avail ourselves of it. If I determine on any course, you shall hear from me."[210] He struggled with several alternatives before accepting parole[211] and began making the adjustment to peace.

FIVE

The Prostrate State

Hampton returned home to find much of his former life in ashes. As Sherman's army moved into North Carolina in March 1865, one of the Union officers thought back on their activities of the last month and wrote: "We have destroyed all factories, cotton mills, gins, presses and cotton, burnt one city, the capital, and most of the villages on our route as well as most of the barns, and out buildings and dwelling houses, and every house that escaped fire has been pillaged. . . . There was a recklessness by the soldiers in South Carolina that they never exhibited before and a sort of general 'don't care' on the part of the officers."[1] The Northern journalist Sidney Andrews visited Columbia in September 1865, seven months after Sherman's visit, and recorded his findings: "It is now a wilderness of ruins. Its heart is but a mass of blackened chimneys and crumbling walls. Two-thirds of the buildings in the place were burned, including without exception everything in the business portion."[2] The Yankee tourist also commented on the poverty of the defeated South Carolina. "The people of the central part of the State are poor, wretchedly poor: for the war not only swept away their stock and material resources of their plantations, but also all values, all money, stocks, and bonds, and generally left nothing that can be sold for money but cotton, and only a small portion of the landholders have any of that."[3] Professor Marion Lucas concluded from his careful study that a total of 458 buildings, or one-third of Columbia, was destroyed by the fire.[4]

Perhaps the most serious losses were not in material things but in humanity. The state had lost 12,977 killed, or about 23 percent of the arms-bearing population, and some of these would have provided the needed leadership. People of both races faced the possibility of starvation. The Freedmen's Bureau was distributing rations to more than 10,000 people, black and white, by September 1865.[5] On May 12, 1865, the *Columbia Phoenix* reported that in the last six days, 163 families had been furnished five days of rations from the U.S. Army Commissary. Those receiving rations included the old aristocracy: "From early dawn until late afternoon a crowd of chivalry are constantly surrounding the Provost Marshall's and Commissary's offices, anxious to take any oath or obligation that may be offered them in pledge of future good and loyal conduct. Utter destitution seems to prevail beneath nearly every roof and were they not privileged to be pensioners upon the bounty of the government they have outraged it would be hard with them indeed."[6] Simply put, many of the men who should have been leading South Carolina in this most difficult of times were not there, and those who were there faced threats far more basic than the correct philosophical stance of a defeated people. This was the Columbia and South Carolina to which Hampton returned. Mary Boykin Chesnut recorded a telling statement from one Isabella of Columbia: "General Hampton is home again. He looks crushed. How can it be otherwise? His beautiful home is in ruins, and ever present with him must be the memory of the death tragedy which closed forever the eyes of his glorious boy, Preston!"[7]

Prior to the war Hampton had only a marginal interest in politics. While he served respectably in both the South Carolina House of Representatives and Senate, he had not emerged as a leader. His fame as the most prominent Confederate officer from his state propelled him into a role of political leadership soon after the cessation of hostilities. There appeared in the *Columbia Phoenix* of May 9, 1865, a letter from an unnamed paroled soldier who urged his fellow South Carolinians to recognize that the war was over. "Go to work. Select your representatives to the legislature and Congress. Select good men. Choose among the first as the immediate representative from Richland General Wade Hampton, . . . the right man for any place involving responsibility, talent, courage, patriotism, all the virtues you need in office."[8] Hampton's motive for entering politics in the early period sprang from the noblesse oblige of a Southern aristocrat and former military leader. After he himself had played with the idea of first guerrilla warfare and then life as an expatriate in Mexico or Brazil, he decided to make the best of life in his home state, and he urged other veterans to do the same. Sadly, in later years he needed to hold office as a means of livelihood.

As Hampton began to emerge as a political leader, it was not immediately clear what his political stance would be. Would he as a former major owner of slaves be an embittered reactionary, fighting one last-ditch battle after another, trying somehow to regain whatever possible of his lost grandeur? Would he be a bigoted racist, embittered by the new power of the freed slaves? It took some time for Hampton to emerge as the moderate conservative that history would label him. There were some puzzling vacillations before he settled on a middle-of-the-road policy. He had at first to worry about such basics as where he would live. Hampton and his wife initially moved into an overseer's house on the Sand Hills plantation, and they then went to Cashiers Valley,[9] presumably for recuperation from the rigors of their recent life. Before departing Columbia, Hampton's daughter Sally married John Cheves Haskell, a veteran with one arm[10] who would in time become a Hampton political ally.

Meanwhile, the state began its struggles to adapt to its new status. In the days immediately following the collapse of the Confederate government, the occupying Union troops provided the only semblance of the order normally provided by the duly constituted government. This is not to say that there were no attempts by civilians at restoring order. On May 12 Gov. A. G. Magrath issued a proclamation recognizing that hostilities had ended and directing all officers of the state to reopen their offices and resume their duties.[11] Events proved, however, that restoring the old order was not to be that simple. Indeed, the old order was no more. Governor Magrath was arrested on May 25 and taken as a prisoner to Fort Pulaski, near Savannah. A writer in the *Columbia Phoenix* commented, "That such an arrest should take place in the capital of South Carolina and in the case of its executive should be conclusive as to the complete moral and physical prostration of the country."[12] In local communities the already-serving officials made some attempt at carrying on, but there was no civil authority over the state. On May 26 the *Columbia Phoenix* printed the announcement that the United States military had superseded the civil government of the city and the state. Lt. Col. N. Houghton served as the local commandant with headquarters in a building on the South Carolina College campus. Citizens were invited to go to that office to obtain paroles and take oaths of allegiance.

The military authorities assumed responsibility for law and order. Interestingly, the Columbia city council continued to function, albeit beset by problems of lack of funds.[13] On July 3, Lieutenant Colonel Houghton, commandant of the Columbia Post, issued a decree that the mayor and council of Columbia would continue to function, but as a relief committee with responsibility for caring for needs of the poor and supplying the city with fresh water and other necessities. The mayor and council would be subject to the commandant. Taxes assessed by the mayor and council would be paid to the office of the commandant.[14] A group of concerned citizens of Charleston selected a delegation to go to Washington and petition President Andrew Johnson for a provisional civil government. In like manner, a group of citizens convened on June 14 in Columbia and drafted a petition asking President Johnson to take the necessary steps to restore civil government.[15]

President Johnson began the process of reconstruction by appointing Benjamin F. Perry as the provisional governor on June 13, 1865. A longtime friend of the Hamptons, Perry, a well-known Unionist who had supported his state after secession, served at the pleasure of the federal president and with the support of the Federal troops stationed in the state. Hampton made his support of Perry clear from the beginning of the provisional government. The general wrote to the provisional governor, "It was with the greatest satisfaction that I saw your appointment as Governor and I read it as the only gleam of sunshine which has fallen on the state since this black cloud has spread over the horizon." When Perry returned to Columbia after meeting with President Johnson in Washington, he met with a group of leading citizens, including Wade Hampton.[16] He followed federal instructions in calling for the election of a convention to do the necessary restructuring of the state government. It is important that President Johnson had, on May 20, 1865, issued a general amnesty, pardoning the former Confederate Rebels, except for the wealthiest and the highest-ranking civil and military leaders. That exception included Hampton. Individual former Confederates could apply singly for their pardons, which the president granted freely. Extant papers do not reveal precisely when Hampton obtained his pardon, but he obviously received a pardon, else he could not have been politically active. The general applied for amnesty in August 1865.[17] It is assumed that Hampton was pardoned by the general act of Congress in 1872. According to Governor Perry's proclamation the delegates to the convention and the voters who chose the delegates must be loyal citizens who had been subject to the president's amnesty, and they had to be eligible to vote according to the constitution and laws of the state effective December 20, 1860, the date of secession.[18] There was no consideration of suffrage for freed blacks. All of this is significant because from the beginning of this conservative reconstruction many of the leaders were prominent Confederates, and their thinking had not changed much. On July 20 Governor Perry directed the civil officers of the state to resume their functions.

The work to reestablish civil government was made difficult by punitive actions of the federal government and by the recalcitrant attitude of the leading political figures of the state. The Federals strove to collect the state's part of the direct tax levied by an act of Congress in 1861. This was a direct tax on real estate in the entire country, intended to help defray the costs of the war. Subsequent acts indicated that the tax would apply even in the insurrectionary states. Union officials imposed on Charleston and its environs a special tax of $185,000 to close partially the gap between what the state was deemed to owe and what could realistically be collected from "the prostrate state." Union agents descended on the state like vultures to confiscate cotton that had belonged to the Confederate government. Since the agents received a commission of 25 percent of their seizures, their interpretation of what the Rebel government owned was elastic, much to the damage of South Carolina farmers. There was also a tax of from two to three cents per pound of cotton, a tax to run for three years.[19] These collections were a form of reparations. The recalcitrance on the part of the defeated leaders unfolded with their attempts toward resurrecting something of the old way of life.

In the elections for the convention, Hampton was chosen as a delegate from Richland, but he was in North Carolina and did not learn of his election in time to participate.[20] Contrary to the directions of the provisional governor, the voters obviously elected a number of delegates who were excluded from President Johnson's amnesty and who had not yet obtained an individual pardon. On October 17 the *Daily Phoenix* published a notice that President Johnson had signed pardons for the members of the convention, and those pardons had been forwarded to Governor Perry for distribution.[21] Perhaps but not likely, Hampton received his pardon with the other members of the convention; it is uncertain because he did not attend. The convention began its sessions on September 13, 1865. Hampton participated only by a letter published in the *Daily Phoenix* of September 27, 1865. He informed the president of the convention that he had learned of his election to represent Richland District, but the word had reached him quite late. He would attempt to reach Columbia as soon as possible.[22]

While in Cashiers he assumed a leadership role in advising his former military colleagues. A number of Confederate veterans thought that living in the Union would be unbearable, so they considered immigrating to more friendly lands. For a time Mexico, under Emperor Maximilian, seemed inviting. The collapse of that regime, at least in part because of the influence of the U.S. government, made that country less attractive. Some went to Brazil, and some of those remained there, but most of the expatriates in time returned to the more familiar South. The most famous of the expatriates, former Confederate Secretary of State Judah P. Benjamin, went to England and began a new and prosperous career in Her Majesty's courts. He was unique; most came back home. Hampton learned while he was in Cashiers that a group of veterans were organizing themselves to immigrate to Brazil, and they had chosen him as their leader. Hampton acquired some information about the prospects. He learned that Brazil would not grant lands to the immigrants, but the Brazilian government would sell lands at about the same price that the U.S. government sold its public lands. One of the attractions to Brazil was that slavery was still legal there. However, Brazilian authorities warned the would-be immigrants that they must not expect to find cheap labor. Slaves in Brazil were very dear; their owners were reluctant to sell.[23]

Hampton addressed a letter to the editor of the *Columbia Phoenix* in which he said, "I doubt the propriety of the expatriation of so many of our best men. . . . The very fact that our state is passing through so terrible an ordeal as the present should cause her sons to cling the more closely to her." He urged all to work to reestablish order, agriculture, and commerce and to rebuild the cities. "I recommend that all who can do so should take the oath of allegiance to the United States government, so that they may participate in the restoration of civil government in our state." He went on to say that if these efforts failed then he and others might wisely consider finding a home in another country. He promised to gather information about other countries in the unlikely event that efforts to rebuild the state failed. He wholeheartedly endorsed Benjamin F. Perry as provisional governor, calling him "a distinguished citizen of our state . . . , an honest man and true patriot." Hampton anticipated that Perry would call for the election of a convention to reestablish a regular government. He urged his fellow South Carolinians to elect the best possible representatives. Harking back to a complaint he and Perry shared, Hampton urged citizens not to elect politicians who cried out for war but managed to avoid its hardships. Reflecting his classical education, "The Roman Senate voted thanks to one of their generals because in the darkest hours of the republic he did not despair. Let us emulate the example of the Romans and thus entitle ourselves to the gratitude of the country." He concluded, "I invoke my fellow citizens, especially those who shared with me the perils and the glories of the last four years, to stand by our state manfully and truly."[24]

While Hampton took the high road in considering the possibilities of emigrating, it is significant that some of the Northern press did not interpret his advice to Confederate veterans quite so favorably. A correspondent for the *Nation* noted that Hampton had advised his fellows not to emigrate, but to stay and work for a better day. The correspondent thought that Hampton's better day would include restoration of slavery, not by war, but by developing a united South that would achieve power by an alliance with a national party. "Knowing the country well, he is aware that a 'united South' will hold out great inducements to a party in the North to come to its aid."[25] While the idea of restoration of slavery was far-fetched, the idea of a powerful "solid South" was almost prescient.

Despite the spirit of hopeful determination in the letter just cited, Hampton himself, later in the summer of 1865, showed a more skeptical side. He was probably irritated by such requirements by President Johnson as invalidating the Confederate debt, repudiating secession, and recognizing abolition of slavery. Later events made these requirements seem quite mild, but the reemerging leaders of the South were slow to understand the true nature of their position. This lack of recognition of the realities of defeat merited the sobriquet "bourbons," a people who had learned nothing and forgotten nothing.[26] Notwithstanding the long-standing friendship between the Hampton family and Provisional Governor Benjamin F. Perry, the vacillating general urged the people of South Carolina to go slow in cooperating with the federal government in establishing a civil government. On August 20, 1865, Hampton wrote an open letter to the mayor of Columbia, James A. Gibbes, saying that he opposed the tenor of a recent public meeting, which apparently adopted resolutions aimed at restoring the civil government, presumably referring to the meeting of June 14, 1865, cited earlier. The general stated his opinion that South Carolina was either a member of the federal union or it was a conquered territory. If secession had never occurred in a legal sense and the state had never left the Union, as President Lincoln had maintained, then it was improper to request readmission to the Union. If South Carolina was a conquered territory it was then the responsibility of the conquering power to provide an appropriate government. Hampton thought it demeaning that his state was expected to adopt a constitution that would be acceptable to Massachusetts and not necessarily acceptable to the people of South Carolina. He preferred a military government to such humiliation. "The people, though conquered, will not have the additional humiliation and reproach which they would bring on themselves, if they consent to destroy their own constitution which was bequeathed to them by their fathers."[27] This attitude was in sharp contrast to the moderate Hampton yet to emerge.

There are likely two explanations for Hampton's attitude at that time. He was probably still bitter from the outcome of the long struggle with such tragic consequences for himself, and Southerners did not at first trust Andrew Johnson, who was widely quoted by radical Republicans as having said, "Treason must be made infamous and traitors must be impoverished."[28] In late May a reporter recorded the opinion of Gen. Joseph E. Johnston that Andrew Johnson was a radical and a man of strong prejudices.[29] Once Johnson's true policies were learned, Southerners voiced wholehearted support. Julian Selby in the *Columbia Daily Phoenix* of June 26, 1865, praised Johnson for stopping the arbitrary arrests of former Confederate officers and for taking steps to restore civil government.[30] In November 1865 General Johnston evinced his change of opinion by telling an interviewer, "President Johnson is a great man."[31]

The delay in time between events in Columbia and elsewhere and Hampton's responses was caused by the isolation of the Hamptons in Cashiers Valley. Columbia was itself isolated in that there was no railroad service for several months after Sherman's visit, so thorough had been the work of the Yankee soldiers. The Northern reporter Sidney Andrews, who was touring South Carolina in the summer and fall of 1865, reported that Hampton addressed a letter to the people of his state, stating, "It is our duty to support the President of the United States so long as he manifests a disposition to restore our rights as a sovereign state." Andrews did not give the date for this statement, but it probably referred to Hampton's letter of July 27, 1865. Andrews interpreted Hampton's statement as an example of the arrogance of South Carolina.[32] Such eager endorsements of Johnson's policies by Southern leaders added to the already-growing distrust of the president by the Republicans.

While at Cashiers Hampton took time to defend his role in the loss of Columbia and its subsequent burning. He had read General Sherman's official report in which the Union general blamed General Hampton for the burning of Columbia, stating that Hampton had the city's extensive supply of cotton moved into the streets and set afire to prevent its falling into the hands of the

Yankee conquerors. The fires purportedly set by Hampton's orders were spread by the high winds of the night of February 17. Sherman specifically stated, "I charge General Hampton with burning his own city not with malicious intent. . . . Our officers and men worked well to extinguish the flames." Hampton wrote a letter to the editors of the *Day Book* of New York, denying Sherman's charge. Rather, Hampton explained that General Beauregard had ordered the cotton placed in the streets, and Hampton warned the Creole general against firing the cotton, stating that it could easily get out of hand. With Beauregard's approval, Hampton instructed his troops not to burn the cotton. He went on to say that when he and his troops evacuated Columbia, no cotton was burning. Hampton charged the Union troops with actually torching the city, pointing out that his own homes were burned about two miles out of town, which was certainly not the result of flames being blown from the burning cotton.[33] This controversy haunted Hampton for the rest of his life.

In August of that summer Hampton received a letter from Gen. Robert E. Lee, which must have given great satisfaction. Speaking of the last days before the surrender at Appomattox, Lee wrote, "If you had been there with all of your cavalry, the results at Five Forks would have been different." The commander of the Army of Northern Virginia was planning to write a history of his campaigns, and he wanted Hampton to send him a narrative of his part in the campaigns.[34]

Of all the adjustments required of the defeated state, the building of effective relations between the two races was the most difficult. On July 10, 1865, the *Columbia Daily Phoenix* printed an interesting notice from the military commandant. The Federal military authority had become aware that many black persons were declining to make contracts for work, and many of those who had negotiated contracts left their places of employment in violation of the contracts. The commandant stated, "It is hereby ordered that those refusing a fair contract or leaving their places of employment without consent of military authorities or their employers shall be put to hard labor by the military." Freedmen wishing to visit other places had to have passes from their employers.[35] This is of interest because it shows that the attitude of the occupying troops toward the freedmen was not very different from that of the white Southerners, especially that of the former slaveholders. It is also significant that Gen. Benjamin F. Butler, in command of that part of Louisiana under Federal control in 1862–1863, initiated policies not unlike the Black Codes later enacted by the conservative governments established with the support of President Johnson in 1865. Butler's labor regulations for freedmen insisted that the free blacks work under contracts with the planters. The freedmen were to avoid vagrancy. Once under contract the freedmen could leave the plantations only with passes from their employers.[36] Lest one think that Butler's policies were a personal peculiarity, it is noteworthy that the essence of his policies was continued by his successors Gen. Nathaniel Banks and Gen. Stephen A. Hurlbut.[37] The Black Codes adopted by the South Carolina and other Southern legislatures reflected a similar attitude. White South Carolinians came to appreciate this kinship of attitudes with white occupying troops. In sharp contrast, white South Carolinians were deeply hostile to black occupying soldiers, but in September President Johnson had the black troops withdrawn from the interior of the state and assigned to the coastal region.[38] White South Carolinians even came to prefer the presence of white Federal troops to the radical Republican rule.

The workings of the convention of 1865 had great significance for Wade Hampton. The convention met in the First Baptist Church of Columbia on September 13, the same site where the Secession Convention had met in 1860. At first glance the important aspect of the gathering was whom the electors had chosen. Twelve had been members of the Secession Convention, and many had been Confederate officers. There were four generals and six colonels in the membership,[39] and there would have been one more general if Wade Hampton had learned of his election in time to attend. President Johnson set forth modest expectations of this and other conventions, for example, recognize the abolition of slavery, repudiate secession, and invalidate the Confederate debts. The very modesty of President Johnson's directions was itself misleading to the reemerging Southern leadership. The president endeared himself to the defeated South by the generosity of his amnesty and by the freely granted individual pardons. As Johnson drew down upon himself the condemnation of the Republicans, he drew the applause of the Southern whites, and each response fed on the other. Unfortunately for the white South, the radical Republicans were the strongest of the factions, and they grew stronger because of the unrealistic words and deeds of the vanquished South and the increasingly isolated president.

Whether to grant suffrage to freed blacks should have been a key issue for the convention. President Johnson himself did not recommend black suffrage, and his stand on the issue reinforced the opposition of white Southerners even to consider such a measure. Christopher Memminger, the former Confederate secretary of treasury, in looking back on Reconstruction in later years, remarked that the South would have been wiser to have granted suffrage to the freedmen, but, he explained, President Johnson "held up before us the hope of a 'white man's government,' and . . . it was natural that we should yield to our old prejudices."[40] The delegates were also acutely aware that black suffrage was denied by a number of Northern states and restricted by others. Only in the New England states, where there were few blacks, was black suffrage on an equal basis with whites.[41] General Hampton became a progressive in promoting the idea of a qualified suffrage for freedmen. His twofold problem was that the white population thought it was too much to offer, and the Republicans and black population thought that it was not enough.

Next in importance to whom the electorate had chosen was the attitude of those chosen. First, there was a general attitude toward accepting the fact of defeat. Leaders such as Robert E. Lee and Hampton had urged all to accept defeat and make the best of things. Significantly, Hampton was sometimes linked with Lee as the South's natural leaders. A correspondent for the *Nation* wrote, "The Southern people can be reached quickest through the medium of such men as R. E. Lee and Wade Hampton."[42] Next, however, was a feeling that they had to make rather few adjustments to regain admittance to the national congress and full status as members of the federal union. After all, this thinking seemed to be supported by the president. The provisional governor had met with Generals Meade and Quincy Gilmore (the former in command of the Atlantic coast region and the latter in command of South Carolina), and he secured an agreement that the civil courts could resume their traditional roles. Military courts would function only in those cases in which a black person was a party. Governor Perry complained that the presence of black troops was disquieting to black workers, and the generals agreed to withdraw black troops from most of the state, moving them to the low-country.[43]

On September 14 Governor Perry addressed the convention. He told the delegates that to extend suffrage to freedmen would be an act of madness, for if blacks were enfranchised the large landowners would be able to control hundreds of black voters. This attitude became standard stock-in-trade of the upcountry politicians who feared an alliance between the lowcountry gentry and black voters. There was some basis for this assumption; General Hampton thought the old leadership would be able to control black voters if they were treated with courtesy and at least some measure of fairness. Thus the age-old animosity between the upcountry poor whites and the lowcountry gentry was entangled with the race issue, and Wade Hampton was in the midst of it. Perry's stance against black suffrage notwithstanding, the governor urged the convention to treat the freedmen and women with justice and humanity and "attach them to you as strongly in their new condition as they were whilst your slaves."[44]

Perry and the majority of South Carolina whites vastly underestimated the value the black population assigned to being truly free. Perry declared, "this is a white man's government and intended for white men only." He cited the Dred Scott decision, which had ruled that black people were not citizens, as though the Civil War had had no effect on that decision. The governor's recommendations included changes to achieve a greater degree of democracy in allowing the population to elect the governor, lieutenant governor, and presidential electors. He told the convention of his relief that the black troops were being withdrawn from most of the state because of unsavory conduct.[45]

It is significant that in this time of rising hope among the old white leadership freedmen were also expressing their expectations. A group met on St. Helena Island and submitted a petition to the convention, urging that black citizens be granted suffrage with no qualification not also applied to the whites. Their resolution contained this ringing statement: "We will never cease our efforts to obtain a full recognition of our rights as citizens of the United States and this commonwealth."[46]

That eloquent appeal notwithstanding, the convention adopted a constitution with no provision for suffrage for the freedmen, but there were elements of reform. The convention recognized the abolition of slavery. The new constitution included such democratic provisions as equalizing representation for the upcountry and low country in the state senate and providing for popular election of the governor and lieutenant governor and of presidential electors. Upon the recommendation of Governor Perry, the convention established a commission to study and recommend laws for the protection and regulation of freedmen.[47] Perry told the delegates, "The Negro is innocent of all that he has gained and all that you have lost, and he is entitled to your sympathy and kindness, your protection and guidance." The commission having been approved, Perry appointed Armistead Burt and David Wardlaw, both prominent jurists and representative of the ancient regime, as commissioners.[48] These able men had a less than adequate understanding of the political realities of the nation in late 1865. They were likely motivated by sincere desires to regulate the labor of the former slaves in a manner not unfavorable to the planters and to protect freedmen in their new status as freedmen. Governor Perry reported to President Johnson that the legislature was "considering a wise, just, and humane system of laws for the government and protection of freedmen in all their rights of person and property."[49] This attitude was not significantly different from that of some of the Federal officers in command of the occupying troops, but those officers could be excused more easily than the leaders of the defeated cause.

The convention adopted a resolution to petition President Johnson for clemency for Jefferson Davis, Alexander Stephens, former governor Magrath, and former secretary of the Confederate treasury G. A. Trenholm.[50] This action was another indication of the Convention's measure of comfort with President Johnson.

The convention made provisions for a general election of the new government. Ninety-two members of the convention petitioned James L. Orr, a well-known Unionist, to allow his name to be put before the South Carolina voters as a candidate for the office of governor. With some reluctance Orr accepted their nomination.[51] Meanwhile groups of citizens in Charleston and elsewhere met and nominated Wade Hampton for the office of governor. The *Phoenix* on October 11 published an announcement that General Hampton had declined to be a candidate: "Highly appreciating the confidence of his fellow-citizens throughout the state, it is proper to make this announcement to prevent embarrassment to his friends. . . ." This edition of the newspaper also included an announcement that President Johnson had congratulated the provisional governor for the work of the convention.[52]

It is interesting that at the same time in Georgia the former Confederate major general John B. Gordon, who was a military colleague of Hampton's and who would be a political ally in the future, was refusing to be a candidate for the office of governor of that state. Gordon, like Hampton, informed the people of his state that there were other able candidates, and all must support President Johnson in his work to defeat the efforts of Northern radicals to crush the South.[53]

Despite Hampton's urging to the contrary, on October 18, 1865, the people of South Carolina almost elected him governor. The totals were 9,928 for Orr and 9,185 for Hampton. This was of course a remarkable reading of the general's popularity.

The new legislature met on the South Carolina College campus on October 25 and elected John L. Manning and Benjamin F. Perry to the U.S. Senate. Manning was the widower of Hampton's aunt Susan, who had died in 1845, and Perry was the former provisional governor and a longtime friend of the Hamptons. The U.S. Senate, under the control of the Republicans, refused to seat both of them, and the lower house refused to seat the congressional delegation. In December the legislature voted to ratify the Thirteenth Amendment, and Secretary of State Seward proclaimed the amendment properly ratified, including South Carolina in the necessary three-fourths states voting positively.[54] The combination of the rejection of the newly elected representatives and senators and including the state's vote on the Thirteenth Amendment was especially galling to South Carolina conservatives.

In December 1865, the legislature enacted the Black Code to regulate the labor of the freedmen and women and the black race in general. This legislation guaranteed to black citizens the right to own property, to sue and be sued, to testify in court cases in which they were involved, and to enter into marriage contracts. The code protected former slaves from eviction from the plantations where they lived before January 1, 1867. The more negative provisions restricted their access to the trades by requiring special licenses and taxes, provided capital punishment for such crimes as rape of a white woman, homicide, insurrection, stealing of a horse or mule or baled cotton, and housebreaking. The code provided for punishment by whipping, which was obviously reminiscent of slavery. Black persons could not serve in the militia, could not sell produce without special permission, and black workers were referred to as servants and their employers as masters.[55] The effect of the Black Code of South Carolina and the similar codes of the other Southern states was to infuriate the Republicans and others in the North and undermine the efforts of the moderates for an easy reconstruction. It was indeed a costly misreading of the political climate of the nation. The Black Code gave many in the North reason to question what had been gained by the very costly war. Gen. Daniel Sickles, the commander of the Department of South Carolina, swiftly declared the Black Code invalid, ruling that only those laws applicable equally to all citizens were valid.[56] The code is therefore of interest only as a reading of the temper of the white leadership.

General Hampton published a letter to the people of South Carolina in the *Daily Phoenix* of November 15, 1865, in which he expressed his gratitude for the recent unsolicited vote. He indicated that since he was about to leave the state for an indefinite time he wanted the people to know his reasons for not wanting the honor of being elected governor. First, he was aware that the convention had with an impressive unanimity approached James L. Orr to be a candidate, and he felt that the election of one so recently a general in the Confederate service might be embarrassing to President Johnson, who was working admirably for reconciliation. Next, he concluded by saying he had personal reasons, which, though unstated, one may assume were his need to work to recoup the family fortune. Hampton went on to offer some advice to his fellow South Carolinians. He hoped that they would avoid partisanship. He believed that although President Johnson had no constitutional authority to order the state to conduct a convention, he did have the right as a conqueror to offer terms, which the state had obviously chosen to accept. The general urged the state to abide honorably by the accepted terms. He recommended that the state support Johnson "so long as he manifests a disposition to restore all our rights as a sovereign state." He went on to express a magisterial view not meaningfully different from the antebellum states' rights creed. "Here is our country—the land of our nativity, the home of our affection. Here all our hopes should centre; here we have worshiped the God of our fathers; here amid the charred and blackened ruins are the sites we once called our homes and here we buried the ashes of our kindred. All those sacred ties bind us to our state and they are intensified by her suffering and desolation." He concluded with prescience, "Whenever the state needs my services she has only to command and I shall obey."[57]

In the fall of 1865 the general was getting about the business of making a living. In trying to renew his fortunes in Mississippi, he was confronted with an accumulation of unpaid debts. He made no payments during the war. On January 9, 1862, a notary filed a protest that Hampton had made no payments on his obligations to the Bank of Louisiana.[58] A cashier of the Bank of Louisiana had written to General Hampton in February 1865 to remind the general of his indebtedness and to indicate that the U.S. commanding general of the Department of Louisiana had ordered the liquidation of such debts.[59] The general's financial problems were looming over him. On October 10, 1865, the *Daily Phoenix* reported that the Negroes who were once the slaves of Wade Hampton were being employed as day laborers by their former master at the rate of ten dollars per month for men and eight dollars for women, board included. The optimistic Hampton planned to produce eight hundred bales of cotton in the coming season.[60] The general experience of this time would indicate that Hampton was overly optimistic, both with his plans for employing former slaves as wage workers and with his plans for such a productive crop. The freedmen usually refused to work in gangs as too reminiscent of slavery; they preferred to farm their own portion of the land to working as day laborers, a preference that ultimately led to the share-cropping system. Another reason for the failure of the wage system was that the white landowners often lacked the necessary cash to pay wages prior to the harvesting and marketing of the crops.[61] The *Phoenix* article pertained to Hampton's efforts on his South Carolina lands, but his major effort at resuming the role of planter was in Mississippi.

Back in his home state the general made an interesting address to an audience at Richland Fork on November 22, 1865. A group consisting of white and black citizens had invited Hampton to "consult" on the future of Richland District. His comments were indeed revealing. The South's system of labor had been swept away "by a single despotic stroke of the pen." Slavery was indeed dead. "The sooner we recognize and act upon this fact, the better it will be for all parties." He urged his white audience to deal equitably with the freedmen and -women who would be farmworkers. He urged the freedmen to make contracts and work for white men. He assumed that black workers would be able to support themselves and "put something up for a rainy day." He added, "The Yankees don't care for you, and they would be perfectly willing to see you die off, so that room can be made here for their poor people." Most telling of all, "But you must not think, because you are free as the white people, that you are their equal, because you are not. You will have to do a great many things you cannot do before you begin to be as great as they are. You will have to be able to write a book, build a railroad, a steam engine, a steamboat, and thousands of other things you know nothing of." He recommended that the freedmen become friends with whites who would help freed blacks to rise. He warned his black audience that the president would not give them land. They had been given freedom at the cost of from eight hundred dollars to one thousand dollars per head, and "The President thinks as I do, that is enough."[62] As harsh as these opinions sound, they were not wide of the center of the thinking of most of white America of this time; this was the era of social Darwinism, the influence of which increased with the passing of time.

The primary difference was that this was an expression of a man who had been defeated in defense of slavery, and the ruling party in Congress wanted to see more evidence of their victory. Hampton's own thinking went through some interesting changes.

On December 18, 1865, Hampton was on his way to his Mississippi plantations. While on a riverboat sailing up the Mississippi he wrote to his sister to say that his vessel was "full of Yankees but William Blanton and his mother are on board so that we have some decent company." His soon-to-be-employed freedmen had gone ahead, and they were "all well and in good spirits."[63] His wife, Mary, did not initially accompany the general; he would have her come out later.

Hampton's spirit of optimism continued after he arrived at the plantations. He reported to his sister that the blacks seemed happy to see their former master. These hands wanted their South Carolina relatives to join them in Mississippi. The general asked his sister to help him by getting Taylor, a neighbor, to hire up to one hundred blacks to come west. The general would pay their passage. Harking back to his sporting interests, he asked Fisher to get the five dogs in the keeping of a Dr. Ray and keep them until his return to Columbia.[64] A few weeks later Hampton wrote that he hoped to make something that year, "if the Yankees do not interfere with me. They seem disposed to give me some trouble and my place and that of Mr. Davis are the only ones in the state not given up. But I am in possession." His concern about his land being confiscated was unduly pessimistic. The Mr. Davis was probably Joseph Davis, the brother of Jefferson Davis. The Davis Bend plantation reverted after the war to the Confederate president's brother, who later sold the land to Benjamin Montgomery, the leader of a black community.[65] Union-sympathizing neighbors, the Duncans, would have been safe since they were loyalists. They were at home and had called on Hampton.[66]

By March 1866 Mary and their son McDuffie joined the general in New Orleans. The Hamptons saw Mrs. Jefferson Davis, and it was a pleasing reunion of friends.[67] The Hamptons soon took a boat up the Mississippi, a trip that Mary did not take well. When they disembarked, she was ill enough that they stayed one night with the Duncans before proceeding on to Wild Woods. Interestingly, Hampton now found these neighbors very kind;[68] in the midst of the war he had referred to his Union-sympathizing Mississippi neighbor as "a contemptible traitor."[69] The Duncans later enabled Hampton to keep some of his land after bankruptcy.

Things seemed to be going well for the Hamptons in the first spring of peace. In June 1866 a correspondent for the Memphis *Argos* wrote that Lieutenant General Hampton was active as a planter on the shores of Lake Washington in Mississippi. The house that the general had built before the war, Wild Woods, was still there, and it served as the Hampton home. The general was devoting himself "chiefly to the general pursuits of a Southern gentleman—books, planting and the chase." The reporter believed that the former slaves were working well and happily.[70]

The issue of who was responsible for the burning of Columbia continued to pop up from time to time. On March 22 General Sherman published a letter to Benjamin Rawls of Columbia, who was petitioning Congress for payment for damages to his property in the fire of February 17, 1865. Sherman insisted that the U.S. government could not agree to any compensation since that would be an admission of guilt. The Union general argued, "I from what I saw myself have no hesitation in saying that [Hampton] was the cause of the destruction of your property. Your true remedy is against him." Sherman repeated the charge that Hampton had ordered the cotton in the streets set ablaze.[71] Hampton in Mississippi learned of this from reading the published proceedings of Congress, and he fumed. In a letter to General Beauregard, he spoke of "that scoundrel Sherman." He had asked Beauregard for corroboration of the explanation that he (Hampton) realized that the Yankees could not possibly ship the cotton since they were destroying the railroads, and then asked that the cotton not be burned. Beauregard replied to Hampton and confirmed his colleague's memory. The Creole general remembered that the only thing burning when the Confederates left Columbia was the railroad depot, which had caught fire from an explosion. Hampton thanked Beauregard for his support.[72] The feelings between Hampton and Sherman were indeed bitter. The *Richmond Times* reported that Sherman referred to Hampton as an "impudent Rebel" and a "whining cur." The *Times* writer ventured that Sherman would not say that face-to-face.[73]

Dr. R. W. Gibbes published in the *Daily Phoenix* a letter to the Charleston *News*, reporting that he was responsible for gathering a group of citizens in Columbia who were taking on the task of studying the burning of Columbia. They intended to gather affidavits from witnesses and other evidence and then write a synopsis, all so that historians like George Bancroft could have access to the truth. Gibbes stated that he could not himself maintain absolute objectivity since he saw his residence pillaged and destroyed by Union soldiers. He and his daughters and granddaughters had been driven into the streets "to wander through Sherman's pitiless fire-storm and licensed soldiery."[74] On learning of this committee, Hampton wrote to the chairman, Chancellor Carroll, urging him to get affidavits from Gen. M. C. Butler, one of the last to leave Columbia in the evacuation, from Capt. Rawlins Lowndes, who was on Hampton's staff, and from the lady superior of the convent.[75]

Hampton continued to work at making Wild Woods profitable again. In June 1866, he wrote to his sister that Mississippi was pleasant, and they would remain for the summer. The black hands were working well, and Hampton hoped for a good crop. Speaking of the hands, "They give no trouble and behave well." Meanwhile a new home for the Wade Hamptons was under construction in Columbia.[76] The general named this new home located near the ruins of Diamond Hill (in present-day Forest Hills) "Southern Cross."[77]

Despite his earlier intention to remain in Mississippi through the summer of 1866, Hampton returned to Columbia in July. He undoubtedly checked on the progress of his new house, and he also began gathering papers to send to General Lee. Writing to General Lee to report on that process, he commented, "I am not reconstructed yet." He informed his former commanding general that he had declined an offer to serve as a cavalry officer in Europe. "I shall never draw my sword again except for my own country."[78]

In the summer of 1866 Andrew Johnson sought to build a party that could get him reelected in 1868. The Republican Party in 1864 had reshaped itself into the National Union Party in order to attract the support of the war Democrats. Accordingly, that party nominated Johnson, a Southern unionist Democrat, as the vice-presidential candidate. Lincoln having been martyred, Johnson then found himself somewhat alone. Which party would support his election, the Democratic Party he left or the Republican Party he had never really joined? Johnson reasoned that his best chance was to continue as a National Union candidate. By mid-summer the formerly Confederate South saw Johnson as their champion, and conservative leaders were quite willing to fall in line. The question was whether the South, not yet readmitted to the Union, could be of any real help. The Johnson supporters scheduled a convention for Philadelphia, August 14, 1866.

Gov. James L. Orr agreed to conduct a state convention that would select delegates to send to the National Union Convention in Philadelphia.[79] The state convention met in the First Baptist Church of Columbia on August 1, the same building where the Secession Convention had met in December 1860. The delegates elected Orr as president and Wade Hampton and three others as vice presidents. Orr explained to the convention that the purpose of the National Union movement was to "solidify the vote of the North and West against the radicals." The convention resolved that it approved the policies of President Johnson for restoration of the Union. The delegates chose Governor Orr to lead the delegation to Philadelphia. Hampton was not a member of the delegation, presumably by his choice, since he was popular enough to have been chosen as a vice president of the convention.[80] Orr entered the Philadelphia convention arm in arm with Major General Couch of Massachusetts, setting the tone of unity, North and South. When Orr addressed the convention, he said that the South had seceded because it believed it had that right under the Constitution. He went on to say that the war had settled that question, and the South acceded to the results.[81]

When Hampton returned to South Carolina as a vanquished hero, his reputation as a military leader was such that many in the state expected him to assume a role as a political leader. Those expectations gave him opportunities to serve as a spokesman for the state, and it appears that he willingly moved into the position of political leadership, in contrast to his low political profile before the war. In August 1866 he wrote a remarkable letter to President Johnson, a letter that had all the earmarks of a statement written on behalf of the white leadership. The letter was published in the August 25, 1866, edition of the New York *Metropolitan Record*. Hampton sent the letter to John Mullaly, the editor and a Southern sympathizer with whom the general corresponded from time to time. It is puzzling that one can now find little mention of this letter in the South Carolina papers. In this public letter, Hampton sought to inform the president of the true conditions of South Carolina. He first expressed gratitude for Johnson's role in protecting South Carolina and other Southern states from the clutches of the radical Republicans. "We of the South feel, that to you we owe it, that life itself is not utterly crushed out of our unfortunate country—that law and order are surely, though slowly, extending their protection over our people." Hampton believed that the fanatics sought as the price for reunion the complete degradation of the South, a fate that the general thought was worse than that of Poland and Hungary. Hampton did not find the president faultless, since he had extended certain terms to the South as conditions for readmission to the Union, conditions the South had met and had still been denied representation in Congress. The Johnson terms to which Hampton referred were the recognition of the abolition of slavery and the repudiation of the Confederate debt. The general stated that while he had some reservations about the constitutionality of these terms, they were accepted. One must note that they were not accepted with quite the cooperative spirit that Hampton implied. The imagery of Hampton's letter portrayed the defeated South sitting like Rachel, "weeping for her children and would not be comforted because they were not." The general's own losses gave that image special poignancy. When Hampton mentioned Johnson's amnesty, he noted exceptions, which included the writer of the letter, comparing those exceptions to the purpose of the British in executing Admiral Byng, "shooting an admiral to encourage the others." Hampton said that he could not think of one act of reconciliation on the part of Congress.

He stated a particular resentment for the stationing of black troops in the South, "pouring into our whole country a horde of barbarians—your brutal negro troops under their no less brutal and more degraded officers." Hampton complained of the insult in black troops' tearing Confederate buttons from the coats of Confederate veterans and the killing of at least one former Rebel. The general then complained about the "hydra-headed monster, the Freedmen's Bureau," an organization he thought guilty of swindling the black man and plundering the white man. The general noted with bitter appreciation the demands that the Southern states ratify the Thirteenth Amendment. "We are states when our votes are needed to ratify a constitutional amendment, but in all other respects we are only conquered provinces." Hampton made a strong argument for justice for the imprisoned Jefferson Davis, noting with accuracy that Southerners then had greater love for Davis than when he headed the Rebel government. "We feel that he is vicariously bearing our sorrows." Hampton urged the president to give Davis a fair trial. There is tragic irony in Hampton's statement urging the president to allow the South to care for the freedmen without outside interference. "I am sure that the Southern states would protect him and give him all the rights he is capable of enjoying, if he is left to their care." He warned Johnson against trusting Southerners who too readily protested their love for the Union. Better to rely on those who fought loyally for the South, but who recognize the reality of defeat. The general concluded, "It is for you, Sir, to redress these evils under which we groan."[82]

There is no indication of how Johnson received this letter, but he was surely in agreement with much of it. There is interesting irony in the fact that Hampton's enemy General Sherman was on the side of reconciliation. The *Daily Phoenix* quoted the New York *Commercial Advertiser* in noting Sherman's frequent expressions of indignation that the Southern states were still deprived of representation in Congress after so long a lapse of time since the end of the war.[83]

In October 1866 Hampton spoke to a gathering of Confederate veterans at Walhalla, South Carolina, urging them to abide by the terms of peace. Hampton recommended the National Union Party as a way of supporting the work of President Johnson, a man of "strong intellect, . . . firm purpose, and . . . indomitable will." The general admitted that he did not agree with the president on every point, but he especially appreciated Johnson's defense of the South and of the Constitution. Hampton was sharply critical of the North for excluding the Southern states from Congress while insisting that they ratify the Thirteenth Amendment. Yet, Hampton avowed that slavery was well gone, and former slaves should be treated well. "As a slave he was faithful to us, as a freedman let us treat him as a friend."[84]

The Walhalla speech drew a sharp reaction from Union officials and from the Northern press. The *New York Times* editorialized, "Their [Hampton's and the South's] complaints of a breach of faith are utterly without foundation."[85] The commander of Union troops in South Carolina, General Sickles, in a report to the secretary of war, indicated that he had prohibited associations and assemblies of Confederate veterans for the purpose of perpetuating the rebellion. He commented that he had heard of Hampton's speech in Walhalla, and he had heard that the Rebel general had spoken of the operations of troops under the command of Sherman and Sheridan in a manner possibly provocative of hostility to the government of the United States.[86] Sickles promised to investigate the matter, suppress such gatherings, and admonish Hampton, if that proved to be merited. Apparently Sickles's investigation led to nothing disturbing, because nothing more was heard of these concerns.

Sidney Andrews, the Northern correspondent who toured and reported on the postwar South, gave Northern readers a critical reaction to Hampton's statements. Andrews noted that he could find in South Carolina little pretense of love for the Union, finding instead a passionate devotion to the state. He remarked, "There is no occasion to wonder at the admiration of the people for Wade Hampton, for he is the exemplar of their spirit—of their proud and domineering spirit." Andrews characterized the attitude evinced by Hampton as "cool arrogance."[87]

On the national scene the Republicans, in their determination to make secure the gains of the war, having lost patience with the president, took advantage of the North's angst about the attitude of the conservative leaders whom Johnson's policies had allowed to resume control of the former Confederate states. The more radical faction determined to gain control of Congress in the fall elections of 1866. With that majority they could enact legislation of their pleasing over any presidential veto.

The battle between Johnson and the Republicans had been brewing for months before the election of 1866. In the spring of 1866, Congress overrode Johnson's vetoes to extend the life and powers of the Freedmen's Bureau and to pass a civil rights bill. The strengthened Freedmen's Bureau was authorized to assume jurisdiction in cases involving blacks and to punish state officers who denied blacks the civil rights afforded white people. The civil rights bill defined all persons (except Indians) born in the United States as citizens and defined those rights that were not to be denied because of race.[88]

The Republicans indeed strengthened their majority in the elections of 1866, and they loomed large in the 40th Congress; thus came the radical Reconstruction. The lines between the Republicans and their opponents (Democrats and Johnson National Unionists) were clearly drawn. White Southerners interpreted their hopes as being closely tied to Andrew Johnson; as his stock declined so did theirs. The president encouraged the natural defiance of the former Rebels, and with his encouragement, out of the former Confederate states, only Tennessee failed to ratify the Fourteenth Amendment. This refusal to cooperate with the congressional majority fueled the growing hostility toward the conservative South. One result was the passage over presidential vetoes of the Reconstruction Acts of March 2 and 23, 1867, which divided the South into five military districts, each under a brigadier general, whose instructions were to conduct elections of constitutional conventions to draft state governments acceptable to Congress (providing manhood suffrage and ratifying the Fourteenth Amendment). These acts disenfranchised Southerners who had leading roles in the recent rebellion.[89] President

Johnson appointed Gen. Daniel Sickles as commander of the second military district, which included North and South Carolina.[90] White Southerners were acutely aware that the provisions for black suffrage applied only to the former Confederate states. It is against this national background that one must view the emergence of Hampton as a political leader of Reconstruction South Carolina.

One significant indication of Hampton's emergence as a political leader of South Carolina—and of the South—is the amount of national attention he attracted. The *New York Sun* reported on the general's participation in an interracial meeting in Columbia in March 1867. Hampton was one of several speakers, both white and black. The *Sun* found the black attendees to be friendly to Hampton and inclined to vote regardless of race for the best possible representatives to the forthcoming constitutional convention, and the audience resolved that Congress should repeal the laws that disfranchised former Confederate leaders.[91]

Similarly the *Richmond Times* praised General Hampton for his attempts in the meeting of March 1867 to convince blacks that there was no natural conflict between white capital and black labor and that both races would be well served by voting for the best possible candidates, without regard for race.[92] It is significant that Hampton shared the platform with other conservative whites and with several prominent black leaders, including William Beverly Nash, who for a time gave Hampton his support.[93] Obviously Hampton assumed that the natural roles for the races were capital for whites and labor for blacks, and he assumed that the white race would provide the best candidates. Hampton told the audience that he would support suffrage based on literacy and property for both whites and blacks, even if the Supreme Court were to rule the Reconstruction Acts unconstitutional.[94]

Wade Hampton's statement that he supported a qualified franchise for freedmen became an important part of his political persona. While this stance placed him in advance of many of his contemporaries, he was in fact a conservative in the tradition of Edmund Burke, who had maintained that a proper ruling majority should consist of those qualified by tradition, station, education, property, and morality.[95] Also Hampton was conferring from time to time with other Southern leaders. His correspondence with General Beauregard has been noted. He and J. B. Gordon of Georgia conferred on occasion, and the *Daily Phoenix* reported that the general had met Richard Taylor in New Orleans to share thoughts about the Southern situation.[96]

The proof of Hampton's pragmatism was how he in these stressful times developed his basic political stance. He described his strategy in a letter to James Conner, his comrade in arms and future political ally. Hampton wanted every eligible white man to vote in the forthcoming election of delegates to the constitutional convention and when possible attend the convention. He would have white candidates seek the votes of black citizens. "We can control and direct the negroes if we act discreetly, and in my judgment the highest duty of every Southern man is to secure the good will and confidence of the negro. Our future depends on this." Hampton thought it at least possible that the Supreme Court might declare the Reconstruction Acts unconstitutional, but he declared to Conner that even if the Court so ruled he would support suffrage for blacks based on educational and property qualifications. Presumably, he would apply the same qualifications to whites and blacks. The general stated that he was willing for the state to send black representatives to Congress. "They will be better than anyone who can take the oath and I should rather trust them than renegades or Yankees." He concluded, "Disfranchised, unpardonable and unrepentant rebel, I live solely to try to help my state, and, failing in that, to suffer with her."[97]

Lest modern students of history judge Hampton too harshly for his desires to control the black voters, it should be noted that the well-known unionist B. F. Perry held much harsher views. Perry described the black people then assuming political powers as "an inferior race, utterly ignorant and debased."[98] Perry opined, "General Hampton and his friends had just as well try to control a herd of wild buffalo as the Negro vote."[99] The former provisional governor probably understood the realities of the state's politics better than General Hampton. In the following month Hampton assured John Mullaly, his New York correspondent, that he could live with black suffrage. Hampton expressed regret that Governor Orr had severed his ties with the Democratic Party. The general still had hopes that the Democrats could regain influence. His letter to Mullaly was a mixture of hope and despair. "Nothing keeps the people from starvation but the kind charity of friends. God send us deliverance."[100]

Hampton's appeals to black citizens seemed to demonstrate an attitude of acceptance of the inevitability of the Reconstruction policies of the Republican Congress and, even more important, a determination to work within the system. Privately, however, he suffered not unnaturally from despair that the society in which he had thrived was disappearing. In March 1867 Hampton wrote to Mrs. Edward Carrington (Elizabeth Preston) of Virginia, "The war was full of sorrows and griefs to me, but peace has been worse; so much so that I often wish I had fallen when our flag was waving in triumph." Then followed a statement that went far in explaining Hampton's basic philosophy: "But as it has pleased God to keep me here, I accept my position and I shall try to fulfill my duties. My household has been bereaved of one who was very dear to me and it is hard for me not to murmur. But God's will be done."[101] The death was probably either that of the Hampton's infant daughter, Catherine Fisher (whose death occurred just before he wrote this letter), or that of his favorite sister, Fisher Hampton, who had died the previous December.[102]

How were the black citizens, then beginning to realize their dreams of both freedom from slavery and freedom to participate in their own governance, receiving from their former masters these rather halting expressions of cooperation? Their reactions were, not surprisingly, mixed. At a meeting of blacks in December 1866, a missionary preacher advocated resolutions to support universal amnesty to reenfranchise the former Confederates and universal suffrage to enfranchise blacks. At an AME church meeting in January 1867, there was an appeal for funds to send representatives to Washington to present the resolutions pertaining to amnesty and suffrage to federal officials. W. B. Nash, a rising star among black politicians, declared that he was not willing to seek amnesty for such men as General Hampton, "when their hands are stained with the blood of our people."[103] This was the same Nash who at times supported Hampton.

It has been noted that white Southerners often found much to appreciate in the white occupying troops. The *Daily Phoenix* expressed pleasure in learning that Gen. Daniel Sickles had reorganized the military posts in South Carolina and that the commander of the Columbia post, Brevet Brigadier General Green, would remain with his command. "An efficient officer, excellent disciplinarian, a courteous, unobtrusive gentleman, General Green has won the esteem and confidence of this whole community."[104]

Hampton's policies of pragmatism began to draw support from other influential white citizens. In July 1867 former congressman W. W. Boyce wrote an open letter to urge white citizens to follow Hampton's lead. "Show yourselves to be friends of the colored people—recognize what is legal and inevitable in regards to the political rights of the blacks."[105]

The general spent much of his time in 1866 and 1867 in Mississippi, trying to reestablish the family fortune as planters. Unfortunately, things did not go well for Hampton and for other Southern planters. The entire agricultural South suffered from declining prices for cotton, unstable labor conditions, and poor weather. These difficulties came at a time when the planters had virtually no financial cushion to absorb even one or two bad crop years. In April 1867, Hampton wrote to a firm in New Orleans to apply for a loan to assist in getting that year's crop planted and cultivated. He indicated to the would-be creditor that he planned to expand his production of cotton by an additional 250 to 300 acres. He and others compounded the problem of falling prices for cotton by additional production.[106] In June 1867 Hampton wrote to the executor for the estate of Bond I'on, to whom the general owed payments on a mortgage for nineteen thousand dollars, executed in 1850. He wrote, "It has been a source of great regret to me that I have not been able to make provision for the debt due to the estate of Col. Bond I'on, but I have had absolutely no means at my disposal. My crop failed last year, not even repaying the advances I had obtained to cultivate it and you are aware of the result of my efforts to sell my lands." He hoped for a better crop in the forthcoming harvest, and he still hoped to sell some land. He promised a payment as early as possible. The general ended the letter on a plaintive note: "No legal steps can hurry that moment, for it is only a question of ability to pay."[107] The debts that Hampton assumed in the expansive years before the war became an unbearable burden in the difficult postwar years. The general and others tried to raise funds by disposing of some of their lands, but there were few buyers. A year later the general executed a mortgage to Henry W. Conner for nine thousand dollars, using as collateral the entire crops of his Mississippi plantations, plus mules, horses, and utensils.[108] Thus were his Mississippi fortunes doomed.

The military authorities scheduled an election in November 1867 to determine the state's decision about electing another constitutional convention. The Reconstruction Acts virtually ensured a black majority and thereby increased the level of anxiety in the white community. In its August 28, 1867, edition, the *Daily Phoenix* published a letter dated July 31, 1867, signed by over sixty white South Carolinians addressed to General Hampton, seeking his advice about the forthcoming election of a convention. The general replied in a letter dated August 7, 1867. He reiterated an argument made to Columbia Mayor James G. Gibbes two years earlier, stating his belief that South Carolina was either in the Union with rights equal to those of other states or it was a conquered territory. Hampton argued that the state would be wiser to remain passive until the federal authorities made explicit what was expected of the vanquished. Better to be under military rule than to be humiliated. Hampton commented that the treatment of the South had been Punic, perhaps meaning almost a salting of the earth. He believed that the constitution of 1865 was a mistake, and the ratification of the Thirteenth Amendment also a mistake. This argument had remarkable consistency in that Hampton had earlier stated that the federals treated South Carolina as a state when they wanted the amendment ratified, but not as a state to be represented in Congress. He accused the Republicans of perverting the traditional belief in government with the consent of the governed in order to perpetuate the party in power. His definition of "the governed" included literate or propertied citizens, meaning a majority of whites. Making no distinction between presidential and congressional policies, Hampton pointed out that each concession (ratification of the Thirteenth Amendment, revocation of secession, and repudiation of the Confederate debt) had brought fresh demands for more concessions. In fact, South Carolina had not yet repudiated the war debt. He reasoned that the promise of restitution of representation had proved to be a Trojan horse with an ensuing Iliad of woes. He bemoaned the disenfranchisement of the most intelligent citizens and the enfranchisement of ignorance and inexperience. Hampton assumed that the disenfranchisement was perpetual. He was particularly chagrined that those who had served the state in the recent war, those who believed that they were obeying the commands of the state, would be denied the franchise, while those who shirked their duty would be enfranchised. Better, he believed, to have no representation in Congress and wait for a time of more equitable treatment.

Still, he urged forbearance and harmony in dealings with blacks. "Let our people remember that the Negro has, as a general rule, behaved admirably, and that they are in no manner responsible for the present condition of affairs. Treated fairly, the blacks will learn that their best friends are the traditional leaders. I deprecate universal suffrage, not only on general principles, but especially in the case before us, because I deny the right of Congress to prescribe the rules of citizenship in the state." He went on to cite the Dred Scott decision as denying the citizenship of the black race. The states, however, could bestow that citizenship, and Hampton argued that the Southern states would be wise to do so. "We have recognized the freedom of the blacks, . . . let us recognize in the same frank manner, and as fully, their political rights as well." Hampton recommended equal suffrage for all races based on "slight educational and property qualifications for all classes."[109] The citing of the Supreme Court decision of 1857 was rather unrealistic, but he was indeed trying to reach over the span between being himself a slaveholder to being a leader of the not-yet-reconstructed state, and that was quite a stretch. The *New York Herald* editorialized on Hampton's advice to his people, finding much to applaud but noting that he professed devotion to the Constitution he had fought a war to destroy.[110] The *New York Times* was even more favorable to General Hampton, endorsing his belief that the Southern states should enfranchise the blacks. "The South very naturally objects to universal Negro suffrage because they know that the great body of the Negroes are utterly unqualified for it." The *Times* stated the belief that most intelligent Southerners favored black suffrage,[111] proving that even that newspaper could be unrealistic.

William J. Armstrong replied in a letter to the *Daily Phoenix* to Hampton's letter, and injected a remarkable note of realism. He pointed out that Hampton (and by inference the Southern states) made no distinction between the leadership of the president and that of Congress, and that Congress more accurately reflected the thinking of the North. He also indicated that the Emancipation Proclamation had, on January 1, 1863, changed the war from a struggle to preserve the Union to a revolution, which made it impossible to restore the Union as it had been in 1860.[112]

In the way of understanding Hampton's deprecating universal suffrage, students of later times must understand that there were few champions for universal suffrage in the mid–nineteenth century. As an example, the erudite scholar-historian-member of Parliament Thomas Babington Macaulay held the belief that universal suffrage without universal education would be fatal to the good purposes of government and incompatible with civilization.[113]

On September 12, 1867, Gen. E. R. F. Canby replaced General Sickles in command of the second district.[114] White South Carolinians found even less to complain of in Canby than they had in Sickles. In general, the relations between the conquered whites and the occupation troops were remarkably good.

It is noteworthy that the freedmen, and those whites allied with them, proceeded to organize for political action. A convention of Union Republicans met in Charleston on May 9, 1867, and then adjourned to meet again in Columbia on July 24. This party declared for universal suffrage, ad valorem taxes, and sale of unoccupied lands to the poor. Blacks organized units of the Union League throughout the state for the purpose of supporting the Union Republican Party and its platform. Members of the Union League swore to vote for the Republican candidates and causes, branding the Democrats as the party of slavery and secession.[115] F. L. Cardozo, future secretary of state and future state treasurer, one of the most prominent black leaders, served as president of the State Council of the Union League. R. H. Gleaves, another prominent black leader and future lieutenant governor, served as state treasurer.[116]

On October 16 General Canby issued General Order Number 78, directing the citizens of the state to vote on November 19 for or against a constitutional convention.[117] In preparation for the election the conservatives met in a convention on November 7. These men represented the white conservative elements of the state. Wade Hampton was a delegate from Richland District. The convention elected James Chesnut of Camden as presiding officer and B. F. Perry and Hampton as vice presidents. This body, representing the old white leadership facing with desperation the forces before which they sensed themselves powerless, expressed their thinking in a series of resolutions addressed to the populace. The instant emancipation of approximately 4 million slaves was disastrous. While gradual emancipation would have been a wiser course, it was beyond recall. Later observers are almost overcome by the question of where that wise sentiment was in 1860, when Hampton's English friend urged his Southern friends to follow the example of the Czarist Russians, who were emancipating serfs with at least some concern for their possession of land in the status of freedom. The delegates recognized that labor was the major problem of South Carolina in 1867. Somehow the people must deal with that and other realities without stooping to sanction the legality of the Reconstruction Acts. They opined that Congress had sown the seeds of discord by disenfranchising the white population and granting that privilege to uneducated blacks. "The fact is patent to all that the Negro is utterly unfitted to exercise the highest function of the citizen. . . . We should not consent to live under Negro supremacy, nor should we acquiesce in Negro equality." The convention protested these congressional acts "on behalf of the Anglo-Saxon race and blood."[118] Lest one, in the spirit of present thinking, overly condemn this thinking, one should remember that by the late nineteenth century the most articulate minds in America were expressing similar thoughts about the superiority of the Anglo-Saxons over other peoples. Apparently, Hampton was rather quiet in this convention, likely indicating that he realized the essential futility of trying to win over the black vote.

The election resulted in an overwhelming approval of the constitutional convention. The delegates assembled in Charleston on January 4, 1868, to compose the new constitution, the Reconstruction Acts having made the 1865 constitution obsolete, confirming the reality of the revolution then occurring. Seventy-six of the 124 members were black. Two-thirds of these were former slaves. That these citizens not yet three years away from slavery were to participate in forming a new government was indeed revolutionary. The leadership, however, generally lay with the white portion of the convention. Albert G. Mackey, a Unionist of long standing, served as president. Thomas J. Robertson, a wealthy businessman and later senator, was a competent leader. Franklin J. Moses, Jr., son of the able jurist, an outspoken advocate for secession in 1860, and future governor, was among the white leadership. Future governor D. H. Chamberlain was also a member of that impressive leadership. The black leadership included Cardozo, the remarkable Robert Smalls (a former slave who took a Confederate ship over to the Union forces near Charleston and who later held important political positions, including a seat in Congress), A. J. Ransier (later a member of the U.S. Congress), and N. B. Nash (member of the state legislature in 1868–1877). The convention composed one of the state's best constitutions, which Simkins and Woody concluded "had the earmarks of theoretical perfection." The constitution laid the groundwork for universal education, provided for manhood suffrage, removed all vestiges of slavery, and provided for a militia without regard to race. Thereafter the people were to vote for presidential electors. The school system was to be managed by a popularly elected state superintendent and by a school commission in each county. Attendance at school was compulsory for children ages six to sixteen.[119]

Prior to adjournment, the convention transformed itself into something like a Republican convention to nominate candidates for the election scheduled for April 1868, an election to serve as a referendum on the constitution, and for the election of the new government. This convention was functioning much like the white convention of 1865. The nominees were Robert K. Scott for governor, Lemuel Boozer for lieutenant governor, Francis L. Cardozo for secretary of state, Niles G. Parker for treasurer, Franklin J. Moses for adjutant and inspector general, D. H. Chamberlain for attorney general, and Justus K. Jillson for superintendent of education. Scott was from Ohio, and he had served as assistant commissioner for the Freedmen's Bureau. Boozer was an attorney from Lexington. Cardozo was the only black nominee. Parker, from Massachusetts, had commanded a company of black troops. D. H. Chamberlain, probably the most able of the lot, a Yale graduate who had studied law at Harvard, had served as an officer in a black regiment. He came to South Carolina after the war to become a cotton planter on the coast. Typical of the many Yankees who tried this venture, he failed as a planter and turned to politics.[120]

On April 2, 1867, delegates from the various Democratic clubs around the state convened in Columbia. The Democrats elected Amistead Burt of Abbeville as their presiding officer and B. F. Perry and John S. Preston as vice presidents. Hampton was not a delegate, probably because he was in Mississippi at the time. The convention urged the people to vote against the constitution. Despite the beliefs in the inferiority of the black race held by many, if not all, of the delegates, the convention resolved to grant blacks suffrage with proper qualifications when that was constitutionally possible. The Democrats nominated for governor W. D. Porter of Charleston, who was serving as lieutenant governor under Governor Orr, and for lieutenant governor Thomas C. Perrin of Abbeville. Porter declined the nomination and urged voters to concentrate their efforts on defeating the constitution, thereby removing the necessity of a new governor. The convention issued an address to black people, urging them to support the white Democratic leadership and condemning the white Republican leadership as corrupt and unworthy of black support. These were the people being branded as scalawags and carpetbaggers. "Remember that your race has nothing to gain and everything to lose if you invoke that prejudice of race which since the world was made has ever driven the weaker tribe to the wall." The convention issued a special appeal to white voters, which included statements demonstrating the difficulty of appealing successfully for black support while at the same time declaring their inferiority. The appeal to whites urged them to vote against the constitution, and stated opposition to the ratification of the Fourteenth Amendment. "It provides not only for our government by the Negroes, but that our sons and daughters shall be educated with their children on terms of equality, and they shall have the right of taxing our property ad libitum and spending the money as they please, whilst at the same time they contribute comparatively nothing to the treasury." The concern that non-taxpayers will tax the propertied was a recurring theme of Reconstruction. The delegates stated their preference for military government rather than living under the proposed constitution. The convention also adopted an address to Congress to protest the prospect of radical government. "We do not mean to threaten resistance by arms, but the people of our state will never quietly submit to Negro rule. We will keep up the contest by moral agencies, political organization, every peaceful means until we regain control." That statement of determination was of course prophetic. The convention elected the absent Hampton chairman of the State Executive Committee.[121]

The election of April 1868 resulted in an overwhelming victory for the Republicans. The entire Republican slate of candidates for state constitutional offices and for seats in Congress won. In the newly elected state Senate only 6 Democrats won seats, contrasted to 31 Republicans. In the House of Representatives, there were 14 Democrats and 124 Republicans. On May 22, 1868, Congress declared that South Carolina was eligible for representation as soon as its legislature ratified the Fourteenth Amendment. On July 7 the new legislature voted favorably on the amendment. By General Order Number 120, General Canby on June 30, 1868, ordered Governor Orr and Lieutenant Governor Porter to vacate their offices so that the newly elected could assume their roles. Radical Reconstruction was then a fact. Shortly afterward, Canby declared that military rule had ended.[122]

Although Hampton was absent from the state during much of these turbulent times, his name remained before the public. He had been elected to the state executive committee, and in the *Daily Phoenix* of April 16, there appeared a letter signed "Columbia," which decried the absence from power of such traditional leaders as John S. Preston and Wade Hampton. The writer spoke of Hampton as South Carolina's Washington and Preston as its Demosthenes. Columbia hoped that the rule of the federal bayonet would soon pass so that the state's Washington and Demosthenes could return to "their political mansions."[123]

The Democrats continued their efforts. On May 13 a large group of Democrats, including Hampton, met in Gregg Hall in Columbia. This convention elected Hampton as chairman of the committee to seek Democratic candidates for local offices.[124] In June the *Daily Phoenix* reported that a number of Democratic conventions in various districts were nominating Hampton to be a delegate to the upcoming National Democratic Convention.[125] The state Democrats convened on June 9 and elected Hampton as a delegate. At the close of the convention the chairman invited the general to make some closing remarks. Hampton received a standing ovation, which he acknowledged with deep emotion.[126]

In the wake of this revolution, the Democratic State Executive Committee, chaired by Wade Hampton, issued *The Respectful Remonstrance on Behalf of the White People of South Carolina against the Constitution of the Late Convention of That State, Now Submitted to Congress for Ratification*. The remonstrance specifically objected to the powers the constitution would give to black justices of the peace, presuming that they would be ignorant; objected to authorizing the legislature to establish and support a standing army ("The purpose of this section is to enable the legislature to keep up a regular force of five or ten thousand Negro soldiers to suppress and keep in subjection the white race, after the U.S. forces are removed from South Carolina"); objected to enfranchising all black males while disenfranchising whites who had held

Confederate offices ("The superior race is to be made subservient to the inferior race"); objected to the establishing of free schools for black children and white children together and for the care of old black people; objected to prohibiting the paying of the war debt; and objected to the almost exclusive taxing of property owned by whites, many of whom had been disenfranchised. The remonstrance reiterated the determination to pursue relentlessly the goal of regaining control of the government for white people. They also repeated the pledge to support suffrage for both races "under proper qualifications as to property and intelligence."[127]

Hampton's reputation as a spokesman of the postwar South continued to grow. In the spring of 1868, he gave the commencement address at Washington College in Lexington, Virginia, the institution of which Gen. Robert E. Lee was president. Lee's reputation was by then soaring, and to speak at Lee's college was a signal honor. Appropriate for General Lee's guest, Hampton spoke on the topic "Duty," and he spoke of his profound respect and veneration for the former commander of the Army of Northern Virginia. Hampton urged on the graduates the obligations of duty, such as the Romans charging their young men to "see that the republic suffers no harm." General Hampton remarked that the graduates faced an especially difficult time, in which the constitution written by the land's best intellects had been destroyed by arbitrary powers. Also appropriate for Lee's graduates, the speaker recommended that these young men model themselves after their president, "whose inspiration has been patriotism and whose pole star duty."[128]

While it is safe to assume that Hampton had received a parole some time after the surrender, he had not been included in any of the declarations of amnesty, because of his wealth and because of his high rank in the Confederate service. On July 4, 1868, President Johnson issued a general amnesty that significantly extended the reach of executive clemency to include all who had earlier been excluded, except for those under presentment or indictment (for example, Jefferson Davis).[129] This amnesty obviously included Hampton, and it freed him for some political activity. The Fourteenth Amendment, however, still prohibited his holding office, until Congress acted in 1872.

The Democratic Party convened in New York City in July 1868, and Wade Hampton was a delegate from South Carolina. Hampton and his fellow South Carolinians, aware that their too-obvious participation could embarrass the Democratic efforts in Northern states, went to the convention determined to be relatively quiet. The Democrats had been tainted by their sympathy for the South during the recent war, a sympathy that had sometimes reached into treason.

Those intentions notwithstanding, Hampton became embroiled in a controversy of some importance. The ultimate victory of the Republican candidates, U. S. Grant and Schuyler Colfax, was broad enough that General

Hampton's role did no real harm to the party, but it was important in his own political career. He served as a member of the platform committee, the duty of which was to define for the public the philosophy of the party. The platform called for immediate restoration of all states to their rightful places in the Union, for amnesty for all, for a reduction in the standing army, for abolition of the Freedmen's Bureau, and "all political instrumentalities designed to secure negro supremacy"; and the platform stated that only the states could define the qualifications for suffrage, that the Reconstruction Acts were unconstitutional, and that "our soldiers and sailors who carried the flag of our country to victory against a most gallant and determined foe must be gratefully remembered."[130] The precise wording of the platform statement about the Reconstruction Acts became controversial for Hampton. The wording was that the acts were "unconstitutional, revolutionary, and void." Those words were not actually inconsonant with the platform in general; rather, the controversy was about the influence of a former Confederate general in "dictating" such a statement.

The convention nominated Horatio Seymour for president and Francis P. Blair for vice president. Seymour had served as governor of New York, and he was reputed to have been sympathetic to the South. Blair had served as a general in Sherman's army.[131] Hampton's support for Blair, even delivering one of the seconding speeches, was one of the interesting ironies of these times. Soon after the nominations had been made, Hampton addressed a large gathering in the front of Tammany Hall. Speaking from a balcony, he thanked the audience for their kindness to their Southern visitors. He explained that they had come with the intention of remaining quiet, lest they prove to be an embarrassment to the party they wanted to support. Hampton told the crowd that he had at first voted for Andrew Johnson, then for G. H. Pendleton of Ohio, and in later balloting for Winfield Scott Hancock—"one of the most gallant of your soldiers," a Union general whom he had faced on several battlefields, including Burgess Mill, where Preston Hampton had been killed—and finally for Seymour, who ultimately secured a unanimous vote. He pledged the South's support for Seymour and Blair. The general then described conditions in his home state, stating that the legislature of South Carolina, "from whose halls used to go as high intellect as ever came to the halls of Congress," was dominated by blacks who having collectively paid no more than seven hundred dollars in taxes will now levy the taxes. He assured his listeners that he and the other Southerners were men of honor who when "we said 'war' meant war and when we said 'peace' meant peace," but not the peace imposed by the radicals that subjected the defeated South to rule by ignorant blacks. While he was speaking several paper lanterns caught fire, and as they were being extinguished, Hampton remarked that he never liked fire at his rear.[132]

Ruins of Millwood, Hampton's boyhood home.
Courtesy of the South Caroliniana Library, University of South Carolina, Columbia

Hampton Plantation. State of Mississippi historical
marker near site of Wild Woods Plantation.
Courtesy of Nancy Bridges, Glen Allan, Mississippi

Left: Mary Singleton
McDuffie Hampton. Portrait
by John Wesley Jarvis, 1846.
*Courtesy of Historic Columbia
Foundation, Columbia, South
Carolina*

Gen. Wade Hampton.
*Courtesy of the South Carolini-
ana Library, University of South
Carolina, Columbia*

Lt. William Preston Hampton. From Edward L. Wells,
Hampton and His Cavalry in '64 (1899)

Wade Hampton, 1876.
*Courtesy of the South Caro-
liniana Library, University
of South Carolina, Columbia*

Left: "Democratic Citizens in Columbia Carrying Hampton in Triumph." From *Frank Leslie's Illustrated Newspaper*, January 6, 1877.

> *Courtesy of the South Caroliniana Library, University of South Carolina, Columbia*

"Box and Cox." From *Frank Leslie's Illustrated Newspaper*, January 6, 1877.

> *Courtesy of the South Caroliniana Library, University of South Carolina, Columbia*

BOX AND COX.

CHAMBERLAIN—"*Will you come down and fight, so that I can call in the troops to suppress you?*"
HAMPTON—"*No?*"   CHAMBERLAIN—"*Well, then, stay where you are.*"

Martin W. Gary.
Courtesy of the South Car-
oliniana Library, Univer-
sity of South Carolina,
Columbia

Benjamin Ryan
Tillman.
Courtesy of the South
Caroliniana Library,
University of South Caro-
lina, Columbia

Elder statesman Hampton.
Courtesy of the South Caroliniana Library, University of South Carolina, Columbia

Southern Cross, Hampton's Columbia home. Left to right: LeRoy Youmans, Chief Justice Henry McIver, Hampton, Col. Joseph D. Pope, Gen. Samuel McGowan
Courtesy of the South Caroliniana Library, University of South Carolina, Columbia

Hampton, commissioner of Pacific Railroads, in his Washington, D.C., office.
Courtesy of the South Caroliniana Library, University of South Carolina, Columbia

Hampton and Col.
Thomas Taylor.
Courtesy of the South Caro-
liniana Library, University
of South Carolina, Columbia

Hampton in his last years.
Courtesy of the South Caroliniana Library, University of South Carolina, Columbia

Statue of Wade Hampton by Frederick W. Ruckstull. Installed on the State House grounds in 1906.
Courtesy of the South Caroliniana Library, University of South Carolina, Columbia

On July 24 the general went to Charleston to report on the convention and to drum up support for the party. A crowd met him at the railway station and escorted him to the home of Gen. James Conner. That evening he addressed a large gathering of the Democratic faithful, speaking from a platform draped with U.S. flags. In discussing the platform adopted by the convention, the general said that he, as a member of the platform committee, originally asked that they adopt a statement that suffrage belonged to the states as they existed "up to 1865." When delegates from the North complained that such a statement would make their campaigns difficult, Hampton withdrew his request. The committee simply resolved that the definition of suffrage was a responsibility of the states. Hampton was pleased to tell his audience that he succeeded in getting included a statement—"and we declare that the reconstruction acts are unconstitutional, revolutionary, and void"—adding, "This is my plank in the platform."[133] When such Republicans as James G. Blaine accused the Democrats of being subject to dictations from such Rebels as Hampton, the South Carolinian was forced to explain his role a bit more modestly.[134]

Hampton, serving as chairman of the South Carolina Democratic Central Committee, issued a call for the party to convene in Columbia on August 6.[135] When the Democrats met and considered their own platform, they declared "that the political control of South Carolina belongs of right and by inheritance to the white inhabitants thereof." Yet, in the same collection of resolutions was a statement that the Democrats recognized the legitimate results of the war. The convention requested the Central Committee to invite orators from the North to come and canvass the state.[136] Apparently the conventioneers thought that such visitors would assure South Carolinians of the wisdom of supporting the national party and at the same time assure the nation that this state was participating in national affairs as a state with equal rights and responsibilities. Meanwhile Hampton himself did some canvassing. In mid-August he addressed a large audience in front of the old courthouse in Greenville, where he was recognized as the "idol of the up-country as well as of the low and middle country of the state."[137]

The state had indeed reentered the Union, although not on the terms that Wade Hampton would have chosen. On July 15 the legislature had ratified the Fourteenth Amendment, signed by Governor Scott, F. J. Moses, Jr., as Speaker of the House, and D. T. Corbin as president pro tempore of the Senate. In accordance with the Reconstruction Acts, General Canby issued an order remitting to civil offices the authority exercised by the military to that time.[138] At least technically, the Reconstruction process had been completed in South Carolina. In keeping with this progress, the Democratic Central Executive Committee released a letter to the public stating that there should now be no disabilities in suffrage since the restrictions in the Fourteenth Amendment applied to office holding, not to voting.[139] Their purpose was of course to encourage whites to vote for the Democratic ticket.

General Hampton and the other members of the Central Committee wrote to John Quincy Adams, the grandson of the sixth president, Democratic mayor of Boston, and candidate for governor of Massachusetts, to invite him to come to Columbia to address a large audience.[140] Adams accepted the invitation in a lengthy letter setting forth some of his thinking on the problems of Reconstruction. For example, he ventured that the politically unwise Black Codes had brought on the demands for universal manhood suffrage as a means of protecting blacks from any form of renewed slavery. Adams himself preferred a literacy qualification for voting. He further assumed that if the Democratic Party lost the coming election it would in part be because many Northerners feared that a Democratic success would jeopardize the results of the recent war.[141]

On October 12 Adams addressed the Columbia gathering, sharing with them his unvarnished opinions, as only an Adams could do. In an interesting way the Adams message fit the belief structure Hampton, through all his vacillations, had been building. To the extent that the general faltered in implementing his beliefs, which he did, later students should remember that implementing them on the South Carolina ground was much more difficult than the theorizing of an Adams from the ethereal atmosphere of Braintree. It is possible that Adams helped in shaping Hampton's theories. The New England visitor reminded his audience that he was the grandson of "one of the earliest opponents of your peculiar institution" and that he himself had been a loyal supporter of Lincoln. He said that the fate of the South lay in its own hands. Noting that the country was suffering greatly from intemperance, Adams reminded his audience that the South had been guilty of intemperance in seceding because it did not trust slavery in the constitutional process of the U.S. government, and now the Republicans were guilty of intemperance because they did not trust white Southerners. "I take it that no one denies the cause of that action [the war] was the apprehended danger to slavery from the result of the election of 1860." The leaders of the nation the South sought to build saw slavery as its cornerstone. In claiming to be a sovereign nation, the South gave up any claim to statehood in the Union, and in fighting and losing a war, the South could be expected to be subjected to any terms the victor set forth. The North on the other hand insisted that the Southern states had never and could never give up their statehood. Both were then at fault, the South in claiming the rights of statehood that they had fought to be free of and the North in insisting that the South had not seceded and then treating them as though they were conquered territories. Adams stated his own belief: "The war was to subdue insurrection, not to conquer a nation; you were defeated Rebels, not conquered alien enemies, and the union was re-established, not extended over your territory. It was upon this theory that the government of the United States proceeded at first to renew what were called the practical relations of the states to the union, and you gladly accepted this view of the case and did all in your power to resume your vacant places." Adams pointed out that the South had little choice, but he thought that the South had acted in good faith. Congress had in fact assumed the position of the South in the war and acted as though Southerners were indeed alien enemies in a conquered territory. Adams noted that the Republican leadership, and especially Senator Sumner, whose "mind is theoretical and extreme," chose to misinterpret your participation in the Democratic convention, declaring that Southerners (Hampton) had "dictated" the terms of the platform in such a fashion as to deny the results of the war. The vagrancy laws in the Black Codes were paraded before the North to prove that white Southerners were seeking to reestablish slavery in another form. Adams insisted that the minimum the North expected of the South was renunciation of the doctrine of secession, extirpation of slavery, fair treatment of freedmen, and equal rights of all citizens to travel and speak freely in any state. While Adams himself disliked universal suffrage, he thought that the South had brought it on itself and would have to live with it. He urged patience, saying that the educated and propertied class would eventually be in control. He feared that the present system of Reconstruction would encourage demagogues to stir up strife between the races for their own benefit. He pleaded with his audience to avoid racial hatred, and, in words that proved to be prophetic, said that "it is essential that the dangerous element of hostility of race should be kept out of the calculations. If that poison once fastens firmly on your vitals, your political future is desperate."[142] Ultimately Hampton's policies of moderation failed, and the body politic was indeed poisoned by racism to the benefit of generations of demagogues.

General Hampton replied to Adams by asking him to take the word home that the South was united in accepting the results of the war. The issue of slavery had been settled forever. "So far as I am concerned, I assert and claim to have been the first to accept the results of the war. . . . I recognized the freedom of our former slaves, and was the first man in the state to address the colored people and tell them they were free." Hampton told Adams that the recent Democratic convention in South Carolina had declared its willingness to grant blacks the same suffrage they enjoyed in Massachusetts.[143]

Then came another opportunity for Hampton to develop and explain his political philosophy. G. L. Park of Stevens Point, Wisconsin, wrote an open letter to General Hampton, saying that since so much weight was put on every utterance of the general, he wanted to know Hampton's precise beliefs about the recent war and its results. Park pointed out that many Northerners believed that Hampton was still working for the "lost cause." The general replied in a letter dated October 17, indicating his understanding that the main causes of the war were secession and slavery. The former was the primary cause, and the latter was introduced afterward. Hampton asserted that he accepted the war's verdict on both issues. Furthermore he strongly supported equal civil rights for both races, and he specifically supported suffrage based on qualifications of literacy and property. Hampton indicated that he was aware that the radicals were accusing him of having dictated the statement in the Democratic platform that the Reconstruction Acts were "unconstitutional, revolutionary and void," but he insisted that those actual words were introduced by a delegate from Connecticut; Hampton simply assured the Platform Committee that those words would be pleasing to the South. The general reiterated his belief that those acts were unconstitutional. Finally, he said that he wanted the Southern states restored to the Union with "all their rights, dignity, and equality unimpaired."[144]

The same issue of the *Daily Phoenix* carried a letter to the public from the Democratic State Central Executive Committee, signed by Wade Hampton and others, noting with regret the news that there had been several murders that might have been politically motivated. Specifically, the three men named were Rep. James Martin, killed in front of the Abbeville Courthouse; B. F. Randolph, a black carpetbagger from Kentucky and former army chaplain and prominent member of the 1868 Constitutional Convention, who was killed as he got off a train in Hodges; and Sen. Solomon Washington Dill, a white man, presumably Republican. The committee wanted the public to know that such acts by lawless individuals brought discredit to the people of South Carolina. The committee adjured all to remain peaceful in the days approaching the election, disapproving even incendiary language.[145] This was the committee's response to the activities of the Ku Klux Klan, which had become active in South Carolina in 1868 after the radical constitution was approved. There is no real reason to doubt the sincerity of this statement; Hampton normally disapproved of violence, and, moreover, violence might encourage federal intervention with troops. Governor Scott met with Col. L. D. Childs, a friend of Hampton's, and stated that if Hampton did not act to dampen violence, there could easily be a race war, especially since both races were armed. The message from Hampton and the Democratic Executive Committee apparently had a calming effect; the amount of violence lessened.[146]

The efforts of the Democrats notwithstanding, the Republicans won the election of 1868 at both the state and national levels. Hampton, as president of the Central Committee, published a letter congratulating the people for their efforts in the canvass. He urged the faithful to maintain the party structure, assuring them that victory will come later. "From failure gather wisdom; out of defeat get patience and resolution."[147]

On the following day the Central Committee issued another letter deploring the violence related to the election just past. "The Club [Central Executive Committee] abhors acts of intemperance and violence growing out of political excitement." Those acts, although committed "under circumstances of severe provocation and trial," were seen by the Club with abhorrence.[148] As if to bring the campaign to closure, Hampton and several other leading Democrats called on Governor Scott to indicate that they accepted the results of the election, pledging they would confine their opposition "to peaceful and lawful limits." The *New York Times* praised this attitude: "The step taken by the South Carolina democrats is eminently prudent and cannot be too soon imitated by the same class in other states."[149]

Despite pleas that Democrats maintain their political structure and that citizens refrain from violence, and the pledge that Democrats would serve as a loyal opposition, white Democrats generally withdrew from political life after the election of 1868 and concentrated instead on economic matters. Hampton himself dropped off the list of officers of the State Central Committee of the Democratic Party.[150]

For the next several years the general focused his attentions on earning a livelihood for his family. Since the end of the war Hampton had divided his time between Mississippi and his home state, trying desperately to wrest a living from the Mississippi lands. Poor crops, a poor market, and unsatisfactory labor all contrived to sink Hampton deep in debt. In March 1868 he wrote to his friend Armistead Burt, "unfortunate results of two years planting have rendered it impossible to recover from my losses."[151] He strove in Mississippi to try to save those plantations from complete failure. In December 1868 Hampton filed for voluntary bankruptcy in the court of Jackson, Mississippi, listing liabilities in excess of one million dollars and assets nearly all of which had been mortgaged, many dating to the years before the war. One of the most interesting debts was to the estate of the late Stephen Duncan, his neighbor of Northern origins and sympathy, whom the general had disliked as a traitor during the war. His son Stephen Duncan, Jr., proved to be a valuable friend, in that he had inherited mortgages exceeding one hundred thousand dollars on the Walnut Ridge Plantation and then bought some of the other mortgages from the banks to keep them from foreclosing on Hampton. The general struggled for years to make these payments. It took two years for all of the claims against the Hampton estate to be filed with the court. By order of Judge R. A. Hill on July 13, 1870, Hampton was discharged from all debts that existed on December 29, 1868. Nevertheless, he continued the payments to Stephen Duncan, Jr. In 1869 and 1870 he actually bought back some of the Mississippi lands that had been confiscated for taxes. In September 1868, the Diamond Hill estate near Columbia and some of the Hampton's personal property were sold at public auction.

Hampton was the only bidder for his home Southern Cross, which he bought back for one hundred dollars.[152]

Back on his Mississippi plantations, the general tried to make a go of it. A number of his friends lent him assistance. In February 1869 the general wrote to Col. L. D. Childs to thank him for his help. "I am sanguine that I can succeed and at all events it is better to die in harness than to rust out." Hampton reported to his friends that things were going well. "The negroes are working well."[153] That favorable statement about black labor notwithstanding, the general ultimately found it too difficult to get the freedmen to work in gangs as they had in slavery. The freed blacks found that form of work too much like servitude; they wanted to work their own lands. That desire, coupled with the shortage of money for the black laborers and for the white landowners, led to the practice of sharecropping. In 1871 Hampton wrote to Armistead Burt that he could not get the blacks to pick the cotton. "I shall rent all the land I can this year so that the negroes may work their own cotton."[154] One may assume that the rent was paid in cotton. Some of Hampton's neighbors became so discouraged by the difficulties with black labor that they considered importing Chinese coolies, as the Californians had.[155]

Most, but not all, of Hampton's notes wound up in the possession of Stephen Duncan and, after his death, in the possession of Stephen Duncan, Jr. In 1868 the general's debt to Duncan neared one million dollars. In that year Hampton declared bankruptcy, and Duncan forced sales and then purchased the lands himself, which he then leased back to the general with the stipulation that annual payments would allow redemption of the lands. By selling off some of the land and further mortgages, Hampton in the mid-1880s had regained some of his former estates, specifically at least parts of Wild Woods plantation in Greenville County and Walnut Ridge in Issaquena County.[156] The general struggled to keep afloat. Duncan did not hold all of the mortgages. On November 19, 1868, the Chancery Court of Greenville County, Mississippi, ordered sale of a portion of the Hampton lands to satisfy a mortgage possessed by M. B. Portman and Edward J. Barron.[157] It was in all an agonizing process (and bewildering to researchers). In May 1869 the same Chancery Court ordered the sale of the plantation Wild Woods, Hampton's Mississippi residence.[158] Hampton managed to retain possession of Wild Woods by an obligation to make annual payments to Stephen Duncan.[159] Annual operations at times involved other mortgages. In March 1872 Hampton borrowed $3,500 from Richardson and May of New Orleans to purchase supplies and pay for cultivation, for which he mortgaged the crop for that year. This loan bore an interest of 10 percent.[160] On July 11, 1878, Hampton signed an indenture to pay Stephen Duncan, Jr., $20,335.18 over a period of years to regain possession of Walnut Ridge.[161] Hampton retained possession of Wild Woods and conveyed it to his son Wade IV, who bequeathed it to his widow, Kate.[162]

Duncan, Jr., similarly conveyed a portion of the plantation Walnut Ridge back to Wade Hampton, and possession passed on to Wade IV and after his death in 1879 to Kate, who managed these operating farms.[163] Apparently, by 1900, Hampton was no longer in possession of Mississippi lands. His son McDuffie Hampton remained active in Mississippi; he was trading in lands in Issaquena County in 1899.[164]

The general continued to be vitally interested in the affairs of his home state. In April 1869 he wrote to his Charleston friend James Conner that he had hopes of paying off his debts. Although Hampton was not involved in politics at this time, the interest was still there. He commented to Conner, "we cannot be extricated from our deplorable condition by any help from abroad; we must work out our own political salvation." The general was pleased that South Carolinians were organizing an agricultural society and that there was a move to organize a historical society focusing on the South. Hampton and many others wanted to ensure that the Southern side of history was preserved and recorded.[165] In July 1870 Hampton, as president of the Survivors Association, published a brochure apparently distributed to veterans, asking them to send copies of their unit rolls to the Bureau of Records, Survivors Association of the State of South Carolina. Col. Edward McCrady, Jr., was to collect this information.[166] McCrady became a significant historian of South Carolina.

Hampton apparently understood that he would have to look beyond planting to earn the kind of livelihood he wanted. In 1869 he joined with his Confederate friend Gen. John B. Gordon of Georgia and others to form the Carolina Life Insurance Co. They tried to involve General Lee, but he declined. Jefferson Davis became the president of the company.[167] Hampton's former military and later political colleague M. C. Butler served as a general agent for the company.[168] The insurance business took Hampton to Baltimore, where he, as a vice president of the company, managed a branch office. He still went to Mississippi from time to time, trying to salvage those plantations.

Mary McDuffie joined him in Baltimore in 1872,[169] but she had by now become almost an invalid. It is not possible to know her precise illness, but some form of depression was apparent. Dr. D. H. Trezevant of Columbia had diagnosed her illness as a form of hysteria, and that finding had been confirmed by Dr. Noll, who came from New York to examine Mary.[170] It is probable that her health had been hurt by childbirth. The family had grown in these troubled years. The first child by Mary McDuffie Hampton, George McDuffie, was born in 1859. Mary Singleton, known as Daisy, was born in 1861. Alfred was born in 1863. Catherine Fisher died soon after her birth in 1867.[171]

While Hampton was at his business in Baltimore the world learned of the death of Robert E. Lee in Lexington, Virginia, October 1870. The Baltimore Society of Confederate Soldiers and Sailors invited Hampton to give an address in memory of the great General Lee. The canonization of Lee had begun, and General Hampton contributed to the process by speaking of "our great leader," "the illustrious chief," and "the first soldier of our time." True to his classical learning, Hampton compared Lee to Aeneas; "When the Trojan chief flying from his ruined city, under whose 'high walls' he had prayed to die, was urged by the Carthagenian Queen to recount the misfortunes of his country, with a heart broken by the loss of friends, of kindred, and of native land, he exclaimed: 'Infandum, Regina, jubes renovare dolerem; quoque miserrina ipsi vidi.'" Hampton told his audience that both Light Horse Harry Lee and his son had fought for the same principle, the right of self-government. The memorial address included a summary of Lee's career, military and civilian. In reviewing Lee's great failure at Gettysburg, Hampton indicated that the Confederate general was forced to fight at a disadvantage because of the absence of J. E. B. Stuart, who should have kept his commander informed of the enemy's movements. "There can be no doubt that General Lee when he invaded Pennsylvania did not intend to deliver battle unless the advantages of position were in his favor, and these he had every reason to suppose his superior skill could enable him to secure."[172] Hampton's definition of the cause of the war as having been for self-determination was quite in keeping with the general trend in the Southern reinterpretation of the "lost cause" in these years. While self-determination was not a completely inaccurate description of reasons for Lee and Hampton's going to war, it does put aside the issue of slavery that Alexander Stephens during the war defined as the "cornerstone" of the Confederacy.[173] It was more comfortable to define the war as having been fought for a people's right of self-determination, a cause that a later Southerner, Woodrow Wilson, raised to a level approaching holiness. The Lee Memorial Association was organized in October 1870. Gen. John C. Breckenridge served as president and Hampton as one of the several vice presidents.[174]

While Hampton's main reliance for a living was the insurance business in Baltimore, he returned to the Mississippi plantations from time to time. On one of his stays in Mississippi there occurred an interesting and revealing incident. There was a small railroad station on the edge of the Wild Woods plantation where the trains stopped to leave and pick up the mails. On a Friday afternoon the general returned from a hunt to stop at the station and get his mail. His clothing had the smells of horses and dogs. A Northerner got off the train to have a look around and, smelling the hunter who was wearing a tattered old Confederate uniform jacket, remarked, "All Southerners must live in the woods or a barn." Hampton, ignoring the stranger, proceeded to a barrel for a drink of water. The stranger then ventured that the Southerner should be drinking with his horses. The general then gave the Northerner an open-handed slap. Hampton remarked that his father would not abide an insult and neither would he. The stranger got up and boarded the train.[175]

The general was gravely concerned by the need to earn a livelihood. In 1870 he wrote to Joseph E. Johnston to ask for a recommendation to the viceroy of Egypt, who Hampton thought might offer employment as a military officer.[176] Nothing came of this; it was another indication of Hampton's desperate financial situation.

Even while living in Baltimore, Hampton continued to be obsessed by the desire to justify his actions relative to the burning of Columbia. In December 1872 he wrote to Dr. Trezevant that he hoped to be able to testify before the international commission established by the Treaty of Washington—established primarily to consider claims of the U.S. government against Great Britain for the damages done by the Confederate cruiser *Alabama*, built in a British shipyard. Hampton wanted to be a witness in determining whether the U.S. government was responsible for the destruction of British property in Columbia.[177]

Continuing in the redefining of the causes of the war, Hampton delivered an address at Warrenton, Virginia, on June 23, 1873, at the dedication of a monument to the Confederate dead. He told his audience that the Southern cause was just, defeat notwithstanding. "Why should we admit we are in the wrong?" Harking to the cause of self-determination, "If we were wrong in our struggle, then was the Declaration of Independence a terrible mistake, and the revolution to which it led a palpable crime; Washington should be stigmatized a traitor and Benedict Arnold canonized as patriot. If the principles which justified the first revolution were true in 1776 they were no less true in 1861." In a very moving passage, the general asked his hearers, "Can the father forget his boy struck down by his side in the very prime of manly strength and youthful beauty?" He declared that the South should accept its defeat with its legitimate consequences, but they must not "basely hug their chains." He urged the audience to work to lift "the prostrate country from the dust and hold in reverence and honor those who gave their lives."[178]

On October 29, 1873, Hampton addressed the Southern Historical Society in Richmond, Virginia. He again stated that the war had been fought for the Constitution as it had been intended by the founding fathers. He saw his native South as the victim of corruption and vice, a land where "intelligence, experience, patriotism are placed under the rude feet of ignorance, folly, cupidity, and barbarism." He did not blame the freedmen for these evils, saying that they were being misled by unscrupulous outsiders.[179]

Meanwhile, the general's business efforts continued to fall short of the success he so badly needed. In September 1873 Jefferson Davis wrote to Hampton to report that the Carolina Insurance Co. was in serious trouble. The former Confederate men who bought the policies were dying young, and many of those who survived had great difficulty in paying the premiums; and the agents were often not aggressive in pressuring their clients. Then the company merged with the Southern Life Insurance Co., which was close to bankruptcy itself. The company continued to decline, until it was bankrupt in 1876.[180] As the insurance business floundered, Hampton attempted to find other sources of income. In 1872 he invested modestly in the Baltimore Fire Extinguisher Works, which yielded little.[181]

Tragedy continued to haunt the general's personal life. As the health of his wife worsened, Hampton decided to take her from Baltimore to a more restful place in Charlottesville, Virginia. He asked Thomas and Anna Preston to allow the Hamptons to live with them until Mary's condition improved.[182] The Hampton party consisted of the general, his wife, Miss Nelson (apparently a companion for Mary Hampton), Wade IV, and two servants, one of whom would sleep in the room with Mary Hampton.[183] The general devoted his attentions to his wife, withdrawing from public life for most of a year, during which time the general's brother Kit, his son Wade IV, and his son-in-law John Haskell managed the plantations.[184] Mary McDuffie Hampton died on March 1, 1874, in Charlottesville. Hampton brought her body back to Columbia for burial in the Trinity churchyard. The general's sisters assumed the responsibility of raising the younger Hampton children.[185] Hampton was soon back in Columbia;[186] he thenceforth divided his time between his hometown and his holdings in Mississippi.

During much of the radical reconstruction of his native state (1868–1876), General Hampton was for the most part preoccupied with making a living and caring for his family. He divided his time between South Carolina, Mississippi, Maryland, and Virginia, appearing in his home state from time to time, never completely divorcing himself from the affairs of South Carolina, maintaining just enough presence to retain the image as the natural leader of South Carolina's conservatives. It is necessary to review the events of radical reconstruction to understand Hampton's role in bringing the era to an end.

During the administration of Gov. Robert K. Scott, 1868–1870, the radical Republicans became ensconced in power with all the attending good and evil, and it was indeed a time of mixed good and evil. Black South Carolinians enjoyed an exhilarating taste of citizenship, and some of the non-Southerners whom Hampton called foreigners, popularly called carpetbaggers, brought an element of progressivism in instituting a public commitment to such worthy causes as public schools, care for the destitute, and even redistribution of land. The good efforts were, however, besmirched by corruption and ineptitude of staggering proportions, such that the radicals lost the confidence of not only "respectable" white South Carolinians but also of the national Republican Party, without whose support the new regime simply could not survive.[187]

About 60 percent of the South Carolina population was black, and congressional Reconstruction policies gave them their day in the sun. Black members held a majority in the South Carolina House of Representatives and a majority in the joint meetings of the House and Senate in the entire nine years of Reconstruction, 1868–1877. Still, there was never a black governor, never a black senator from this state, and never a black judge in any of the eight circuit courts. There was a black lieutenant governor, adjutant general, treasurer, Speaker of the House, and president pro tempore of the Senate, and blacks filled nine of the twenty congressional seats. Blacks were in the majority in the Senate for the session of 1874–1875. Only one black served on the state Supreme Court.[188]

Governor Scott was not essentially a wicked man, but he was weak, and the legislature ran amok. Scott made efforts to placate the traditional white leadership by recommending that the general assembly memorialize Congress to relieve the whites of South Carolina of their political disabilities, a measure that would surely have pleased the former Confederates.[189] There were a number of efforts at good government. Under Scott's leadership the legislature passed a progressive civil rights bill forbidding discrimination by common carriers and by licensed businesses, and the legislature placed free public schooling on a permanent footing.[190] Also under his leadership, the legislature in 1869 in accordance with the Constitution of 1868 established the Land Commission to buy lands from large estates and sell smaller parcels of land at reasonable prices, primarily to assist freedmen in becoming landowners, not tenants. The new owners were to pay for their farms in installment payments for five years. The Land Commission became mired in corruption, but after being reformed it achieved a measure of success. Approximately two thousand small farmers purchased their lands from the commission.[191]

Racial tensions were heightened when in March 1869 South Carolina ratified the Fifteenth Amendment, which forbade the use of race to deny the right to vote. For a combination of reasons Klan activities increased in 1869, and Governor Scott responded by securing an act reorganizing the state militia as the National Guard of South Carolina. The guard was open to both races, but whites refused to join, and it became all black. By the fall of 1870, almost one hundred thousand blacks had joined the militia. These units were important in black political life.[192] Whites responded with Klan activity and the somewhat more respectable rifle clubs. The state was becoming an armed camp.[193] There is some significance in the fact that the state's most violent period was a time when Hampton was politically inactive and for much of this time out of the state.

The combination of a black majority and pervasive corruption proved to be fatal to the fundamental hopes of Reconstruction, that is, building a society of equality and fairness. Walter Allen, author of a study of the administration of Daniel H. Chamberlain, obviously approved by the subject, wrote of the radical regime prior to that of Chamberlain, "Corruption ran riot; dishonesty flourished in shameless effrontery, incompetency became the rule in public office."[194]

The highest elected officers were not without talent, but most became in some way stained by corruption. N. G. Parker, treasurer, had come to South Carolina as an officer in a black regiment. He served through both of the Scott administrations. Daniel H. Chamberlain, probably the most able of the lot and the one who emerged with the best reputation, served as attorney general, but even he was tainted by questionable financial dealings with Parker and Scott. Francis L. Cardozo, an able black official who served as secretary of state from 1868 to 1872 and then as treasurer in the administrations of Moses and Chamberlain, was also tainted by charges of corruption, but he still emerged with a relatively good reputation, at least in the opinions of later students. Cardozo was a graduate of the University of Glasgow and a Presbyterian minister. He went to Charleston as the principal of the Avery Institute and entered politics as the leader of the South Carolina Union League. There was an attempt to impeach Cardozo in 1875, but no charges were proved. The radical legislature elected Thomas J. Robertson to the U.S. Senate in 1868, and he served until 1877. Frederick A. Sawyer, who was also elected to the Senate in 1868, served until 1873, and was replaced by the notoriously corrupt John J. "Honest John" Patterson.[195]

In 1870 Robert Scott won reelection, but there was enough alarm about corruption to bring about an opposition movement within the Republican Party. The white leaders met in June 1870 in Columbia to decide on their most appropriate action. Recognizing that there was no chance of a Democratic victory at that time, this gathering decided to throw its support to the reform branch of the Republican Party. The dissident Republicans organized as the Union Reform Party and nominated Richard B. Carpenter, a circuit court judge, for governor and the former Confederate general M. C. Butler for lieutenant governor. The reform effort failed, and Scott continued in office for another term.[196] Hampton played no role in this election.

Richard Zuczek, author of *State of Rebellion*, a study generally sympathetic to the era of the black majority, concluded, "the period from 1872 through 1874 [Scott's second term] saw the worst corruption and abuse in any state during Reconstruction." Two examples will serve well enough. A. O. Jones, the clerk of the House of Representatives, reported a charge of $125,000 in one session for sherry, brandy, and whiskey. The cost for the state's printing in 1872 and 1873 was $450,000, compared to $63,000 for the state of Ohio for the same period.[197] Printing was first contracted to the Carolina Printing Co., owned by Governor Scott, Attorney General Chamberlain, Treasurer Parker, and others. Later contracts went to the Republican Printing Co. owned by Joseph Woodruff, clerk of the Senate, and A. O. Jones, clerk of the House of Representatives.[198] One of the more lasting effects of corruption in the Reconstruction administrations was the accumulation of a large public debt, which grew astronomically during the two terms of Robert Scott.[199] Prior to the

Constitutional Convention of 1868 the state debt stood at $8,378,255, but the convention, acting in accordance with the wishes of the Washington government, invalidated war debts of $3 million. A committee of the legislature in 1871–1872 pegged the public debt at $29,158,914.47. When Franklin Moses, Jr., took office in December 1872 he reported, "There is no money in the Treasury with which to meet either the current expenses of the state government or its long and outstanding liabilities."[200]

As noted earlier, the state in the years of Governor Scott descended into the depths of racial violence, for the most part whites on blacks. Also noted earlier, the state militia had become a black organization, and the whites responded with the Ku Klux Klan and the many rifle clubs. Most of the violence occurred in the upcountry counties, where the black population was smaller. In May 1870 Congress passed the Enforcement Act to discourage election fraud. This law forbade bribing voters or punishing voters for their choices. This is of special interest because white Democrats became adept in shaping election results by threatening blacks with eviction from land, denial of employment, and denial of credit in order to ensure that they either voted Democratic or stayed away from the polls. The Enforcement Act made it a felony to conspire or to use disguises to infringe on basic voters' rights. This impressive legislation was not well enforced. For one thing Gen. Henry W. Halleck, commanding the Division of the South, did not really want to involve his troops in interfering with civil matters, and the federal judiciary was not equipped for such an extensive undertaking.[201]

Governor Scott, realizing the inadequacy of the state agencies in coping with widespread violence, appealed for help from the federal government. In 1871 General Sherman sent into South Carolina four companies of the Seventh Cavalry and five companies of the Eighteenth Regiment. In March 1871 Scott met with a number of the conservative white leaders and appealed for their help in restoring peace, and they agreed upon a truce. The white leaders agreed to use their influence for peace, and the governor agreed to disband the black militia in Union, York, and Chester counties, three of the more violent counties. Fortuitously, there was a move among whites in some of these counties for pacification. On April 20, 1871, Congress enacted another Enforcement Act, which became known as the KKK Act, allowing the president to suspend the writ of habeas corpus in finite areas affected by insurrection.[202] In the following October, President Grant suspended the writ in nine upcountry counties of South Carolina, and federal agents arrested 533 men.

The white leadership came to the defense of the arrested whites. During most of this time Hampton was not politically active, but he became involved in the defense of the KKK defendants, writing to the conservative jurist Armistead Burt to suggest that the white leaders hire distinguished defense lawyers from the North.[203] The white leadership raised a defense fund of ten thousand dollars and employed Reverdy Johnson, a well-known conservative who had served as U.S. attorney general, and Henry Stanbery, who had been a member of Andrew Johnson's defense team before the Senate. Within months fifty-four of the defendants had been convicted and sentenced, thirty-eight had been acquitted, and thirty cases dismissed. Within the next three months eighteen more were convicted, and eighteen pled guilty. Most of the remaining cases never came to trial. Since murder was a state, not a federal, crime, the most severe sentences were for five years in prison, and these sentences were for findings of conspiracy to deprive citizens of their rights.[204] All of this activity achieved at least relative peace.

A congressional committee investigated the siege of violence, and Hampton was called to testify. He told the committee that the condition of South Carolina under the radicals was one of taxation without representation and representation without taxation. Hampton denied any knowledge that the Democrats were acquiescing in violence as a means of suppressing black political activity. He did note the presence of black intimidation of blacks inclined to support the Democrats.[205]

Because of the restoration of a greater degree of order and because of the growing national outcry against corruption associated with Reconstruction, the national government was losing interest in the former Confederate states. In 1872 Congress failed to pass a civil rights bill put forward by Sen. Charles Sumner, and Congress enacted the Amnesty Bill, restoring the right to hold office denied to former Confederates by the Fourteenth Amendment. In April 1872 Congress refused to extend the president's suspension of the writ of habeas corpus in South Carolina. In early 1873 federal authorities withdrew some of the troops from South Carolina.[206]

The conservatives of South Carolina objected to the rule of the radicals for many reasons—race, educational level, and the influence of the Northern victors are just a few. There was also a growing concern that the legislature was dominated by people who paid little or no taxes, while the real taxpayers were in the minority and forbidden to hold office until the Act of Amnesty of 1872. As Hampton had noted, it amounted to a new expression of taxation without representation. The white conservatives saw the public debts mount higher and higher and the rate of taxation approach confiscatory levels. Actually, some of the legislators intended the taxes to be confiscatory. Those radicals wanted taxes to be especially high on unused lands to force owners either to cultivate the land or sell it. High taxes would also force large landowners into insolvency and the loss of their lands for unpaid taxes. The forfeited lands would then presumably be sold in smaller parcels to transform South Carolina into a state of small landowners. The tax income would also provide the state the means to offer public services not customary in the years of the old regime, for example, adequate public schools, a modern penitentiary, and care for the destitute. Taxes indeed rose to new heights. Whereas the state paid a total of $600,000 in taxes in a year under Governor Orr, in 1870 the total reached $2.8 million.[207]

Taxation was the radicals' most effective means of forcing at least some redistribution of land. In 1873 the state seized 270,000 acres for failure to pay taxes; in the next year the total reached 500,000.[208] The twelve counties in which the greatest amount of land was forfeited for failure to pay taxes were the twelve counties in which the proportion of black voters to white voters was the highest. The census of 1890 indicated that in South Carolina a total of 13,675 black farmers owned their farms. Of these only 4,000 had gained their lands through government action.[209] The problem was that not enough freedmen had the funds to purchase land at any price.

Both the passionate desire of the freedmen for a redistribution of land[210] and the fundamental failure of the federal government to answer those desires are worthy of further comment, even in a biography of one who was only indirectly involved in this particular aspect of Reconstruction. The black slaves were obviously accustomed to farmwork, and their desire to own land was quite natural. Their revulsion at working in any system evenly remotely resembling gangs led to their reluctance to work as day laborers and ultimately to the share-crop system, which was in effect a system of virtual serfdom. Black South Carolinians escaped from the bonds of that serfdom only with the New Deal and World War II. In retrospect some redistribution of lands would appear to have been a matter of justice and political and economic wisdom. Only the federal government could have effected this revolutionary reform, and the economically conservative Republican Party did not have the stomach to confiscate lands, even from their defeated enemy.[211] It is of more than passing interest that South Carolina accomplished more than any other Southern state in its attempts at land redistribution. Still, the fundamental failure to make adequate provision for land for the freed slaves was tragic, and it doomed South Carolina and the South to decades of struggle that could have been eased by a more thoughtful and daring policy for assisting the former slaves in adjusting to freedom. Recall that Hampton's English friend T. W. Probyn had written a letter in 1860 stating his belief that the American South should make some adjustment in the peculiar institution or risk being run over by the progressive movement of the nineteenth century. Probyn cited the work of Czar Alexander II of Russia in freeing the serfs. The Russian government freed the serfs just weeks before the firing on Fort Sumter, and the Russian government made provision for a distribution of land to the former serfs. The Oxford historian of Imperial Russia, Hugh Seton-Watson, noted the irony that the U.S. government failed to make any provision for lands for former slaves even though the white landowners of the South had been defeated and were at the mercy of their victors, while the landowning nobility of Russia remained powerful after the emancipation of their serfs.[212] In looking back one may conclude that this country lost an opportunity to put former slaves in the position of landowners from which they could have progressed as independent and responsible citizens. South Carolina did more than any other Southern state in redistribution of land, and that was largely a product of this state's having a black majority that had its time in power. General Hampton entered this era as a major landowner, and at the end of his life he was without property, the result of bankruptcies and sales and losses for failure to pay taxes.

In 1871 the Charleston Chamber of Commerce sought to address the white conservatives' complaint that the non-taxpayers were overtaxing the taxpayers and then squandering the funds. The chamber, obviously speaking for business interests, pledged resistance in paying for the bonds then being issued by the legislature. The chamber sent out a call to the taxpayers of the state to elect delegates to convene in Columbia to consider possible responses to this crisis. The first Taxpayers Convention met in Columbia on May 9, 1871. This was the first halting step white conservatives took toward redemption, that is, redeeming the state from radical (black, scalawag, and carpetbagger) control. Hampton was not present; this was his time "in the wilderness." His absence notwithstanding, the white conservative leadership was there: Armistead Burt from Abbeville; Johnson Hagood from Barnwell; John L. Manning and J. S. Richardson from Clarendon; M. C. Butler, Martin Gary, and M. L. Bonham from Edgefield; and William H. Wallace of Union. Daniel H. Chamberlain, the carpetbagger future governor, was also there. This was the cast of characters for the redemption drama in which Wade Hampton would be the protagonist. The convention resolved that the recent issue of bonds known as "the sterling loan" was without legal status and therefore were not binding on the taxpayers of South Carolina. The convention warned would-be buyers of these bonds to beware. The convention also decided to recommend that the legislature enact laws to assure the state's sixty thousand taxpayers representation at least in proper proportion to the ninety thousand nontaxpayers who were at that time in power. The Republican future governor Daniel H. Chamberlain made an interesting argument in favor of the idea of proportional representation: "Do you not believe, for a moment, that when you put into an ignorant assembly, many of whom cannot read nor write, forty-seven gentlemen, whom I might select in this body, that you would not shame them into decency or frighten them from crime."[213] There is little wonder that white conservatives would be attracted to Chamberlain, while many black Republicans came to suspect him of treason to their party. The convention urged the legislature to find ways of economizing, such as reducing the number of government employees. Significantly D. H. Chamberlain introduced a resolution to recommend that the state investigate acts of violence and seek corrective measures. The resolution included in its concern about violence "larcenies and incendiarism by deluded Negroes." Delegates conferred with Governor Scott, and the chief executive admitted that government printing had been "a flagrant fraud upon the public treasury."[214] The Taxpayers Convention accomplished nothing immediately, but the views expressed are interesting.

The election of 1872 revealed fissures even within the Republican Party. Governor Scott lost favor with his party; there was even an attempt at impeaching him in 1872. The Scott era ended after his second term. In that year the Republican Party nominated Speaker of the House of Representatives Franklin J. Moses, Jr., for governor and R. H. Gleaves for lieutenant governor. The white conservatives saw Moses as a traitor; he, the son of the chief justice of the state Supreme Court, had served as a secretary to Gov. F. W. Pickens and had played a role in pulling down the stars and stripes and raising the state flag over the conquered Fort Sumter in April 1861. Gleaves was a black teacher from Barnwell. After the war he became a radical and reaped the contempt of most whites of the state. Unfortunately his record of corruption was such as to merit that contempt. James L. Orr led a portion of reform Republicans in a revolt. The reformers nominated Reuben Tomlinson for governor. Tomlinson was a Quaker from Pennsylvania who had worked with the Freedmen's Bureau. While Hampton was in Baltimore during the election of 1872, he participated by making a speech in which he urged the South to work for redemption.[215] Concerning the national election of 1872, Hampton thought the National Democrats to be wise in backing the nominee of the liberal Republicans, Horace Greeley. He wrote to John Mullaly, expressing his hope that the South Carolina Democrats would support Greeley.[216]

In February 1874 the conservatives met in the second Taxpayers Convention, and they again deplored the corruption and extravagance of the radical government. The convention drafted a memorial to be sent to Congress and the president, and the delegates agreed to organize taxpayers' clubs in the counties to serve as watchdogs for conservative interests. The memorials achieved nothing, but this second convention was another step toward an effective organization of the conservatives.[217] Martin Gary, soon to be Hampton's primary antagonist, in an address to this convention spoke of Hampton as being an "incorruptible patriot," but he blamed the general for having supported qualified black suffrage, "the present cause of our woes."[218]

During the time the second Taxpayers' Convention was in session, the most gifted of the state's black Republicans made a remarkable speech to an audience of black South Carolinians. Robert Brown Elliott was one of the state's representatives in Congress, and on January 6, 1874, he delivered a superb speech in defense of the civil rights bill sponsored by Sen. Charles Sumner. His speech was actually in response to an attack on the bill by the

Georgia congressman Alexander Stephens, the former vice president of the Confederacy. The bill did not pass until the following year, but Elliott was widely acclaimed for his effort. He returned to South Carolina still basking in national attention. The Republicans of Columbia Ward Two asked Elliott to address them on February 16 in the Columbia Courthouse. It is possible that he was testing the waters for a run for the office of governor. His speech proved to be both shocking to his audience and revealing of his understanding of the realities of the political situation in the Palmetto State. The congressman commented that he knew that the second Taxpayers' Convention was then in session. Rather than disparage that gathering of white conservatives, including some Republicans such as D. H. Chamberlain, Elliott said that the other gathering was "no sorehead movement." He told his audience that the state government was a disgrace, and that since blacks were in the majority of voters they had to bear responsibility for that disgrace. The Taxpayers' Convention was seeking to do "the work which it was the duty of the Republican Party to have accomplished." Most damaging of all, he said, "To mention South Carolina is to merit the sneers of the commonwealths of the North." The national Republican Party was ready to disassociate itself from their brothers in this state.[219] The withdrawal of the national Republican Party from a commitment to the future of the Southern black population was of course one of the fundamental causes of the failure of Reconstruction.

In summer 1874 South Carolina reached a new and more threatening status as an armed camp. In response to the white rifle companies, Governor Moses began a reorganization of the state militia, already almost entirely made up of black citizens. In February 1874 the legislature permitted the chartering of paramilitary units, and blacks joined in great numbers. Some of these informal units were armed.[220] The presence of so many armed black neighbors added to the level of panic among the whites. Nowhere was the danger more obvious than in Edgefield County, where the whites gathered in a public meeting to discuss the best response to a series of burned houses, gin houses, and barns, all assumed to have been the work of black arsonists. The meeting resolved that anyone, white or black, caught in an act of firing a structure would be summarily lynched. Former governor M. L. Bonham was reported to have told the gathering that "it not infrequently happens that such a course was necessary for the righting of social wrongs, but it was desirable to make the announcement to the world." Martin Gary urged his fellow citizens not to wait on the slow process of the law.[221] Statements by such leaders as Bonham and Gary should qualify the usual assumption that lynching was always the doing of the white "trash" part of society. It might well be that Bonham and Gary did not handle the rope, but they gave their blessings to the process.

By 1874 an increasing number of the Republican leaders realized that reform in some measure was a necessity, else their rule would end in disgrace.

There was a mounting protest from within the state (witness the two taxpayer conventions), and many knew that the reputation for corruption in the South Carolina Republican administration had become known nationwide. In that year James S. Pike, an ardent abolitionist, associate editor of Greeley's *New York Tribune*, noted Republican, and former minister to the Netherlands, published a short book about Reconstruction South Carolina titled *The Prostrate State: South Carolina under Negro Government.* The book, based on his visit to the state in 1873, was an unrelenting attack on the black-dominated regime. Pike's opinions reached a wide audience with considerable credibility. Members of Congress read from Pike's book to demonstrate the depths to which Reconstruction had sunk. Pike's observations were biting and memorable. "The present government of South Carolina is not only corrupt and oppressive; it is insulting. . . . It is barbarism overwhelming civilization by physical force." The author blamed the U.S. government for maintaining blacks in an unnatural position of power. Pike was blatantly racist. "Sambo takes naturally to stealing, for he is used to it. It was his notorious weakness in slavery, and in his unregenerate state he is far less culpable than the whites." There was enough truth in Pike's judgments to make them damaging. A reviewer in *Literary World* noted that Pike as an abolitionist could "hardly be accused of color prejudice."[222] Pike had met and talked with Wade Hampton at an agricultural convention in Washington. The general had informed Pike of oppressive taxation by the radical government and of corruption among the white radicals who unscrupulously used black voters.[223] Without question *The Prostrate State* played an important role in the ultimate failure of Washington to support the Reconstruction regime.

The year 1874 was a pivotal one. The Republican Party nominated Daniel Chamberlain for governor and R. H. Gleaves for lieutenant governor. It is of more than passing interest that the editor of the Charleston *News and Courier*, Francis Warrington Dawson, a member of the Republican convention of 1874, opposed the nomination of Chamberlain. Later this influential newspaperman supported Chamberlain and then switched to Hampton. He then became a leader in the state Democratic Party. There was by this time a growing feeling, even among the ruling party, that some significant measure of reform was necessary. Once again there was a reformist bolt from the regular Republican Party. The Independent Republicans nominated Judge John T. Green, who had also bolted the regular party in 1872, for governor and Martin R. Delany, a well-educated black who had served as an U.S. Army officer during the war and had been an employee of the Freedmen's Bureau afterward, for lieutenant governor. James Chesnut of Kershaw, chairman of the Democratic Executive Committee, called for a convention of conservatives, those favoring an honest government. This gathering was essentially a continuation of the taxpayers conventions. The conservatives convened in

October 1874 and endorsed the candidacies of Green and Delaney. Chamberlain and Gleaves won by a vote of 80,402 to 68,818.[224] In the midst of the excitement about the election of 1874, four prominent white conservatives, former governor A. G. Magrath, Francis W. Dawson, James Conner, and George Trenholm, went to see President U. S. Grant to plead for his intervention in the "prostrate state." They specifically asked the president to endorse a reform candidate, Joseph B. Kershaw of Camden, described by Dawson as a "symbol of aristocratic integrity."[225] Grant refused to become involved, probably in part because of reports of white violence. The president's support actually went to D. H. Chamberlain, who was in fact tainted by his own involvement in scandals of the earlier Republican administrations. However, Chamberlain emerged in the campaign and after his inauguration as a genuine advocate of reform.[226] He was the best educated—Yale and Harvard —and the most talented of the white Republican leaders.

By the end of the administration of Governor Moses, there was mounting evidence of the depths of corruption to which the radical government had sunk. There were hearings pertaining to the charges that Sen. "Honest John" Patterson had acquired his office by bribery. Several members of the legislature testified that Patterson had promised them bribes for their votes. He was never convicted, but the public believed him to be guilty.[227] In Moses's last report to the legislature he indicated that the state debt stood at $15,851,627.35, and he commented, "The public funded debt of South Carolina stands as the opprobrium of the state, and the dishonoring symbol of its wholly violated faith to its creditors."[228]

Republicans suspected their own leaders. During the gubernatorial campaign Robert Brown Elliott resigned from Congress and ran for the state House of Representatives to represent Aiken County, a seat he easily won. When the House met to organize, they elected Elliott as Speaker. There was a widely circulated rumor that Chamberlain and Elliott had agreed that in return for Elliott's support the governor would seek and win reelection in 1876 with Elliott as lieutenant governor. After the reelection Chamberlain would get himself elected to the U.S. Senate, resign as governor, and make Elliott the first black governor. It was an interesting possibility, but the two were fated to become earnest enemies, rather than cohorts in a secret deal.[229]

The new governor created tensions in his party by making five commitments: to achieving an end to corruption, to laying a foundation for equality of civil and political rights for both races (few advocated social equality), to reducing taxes, to safeguarding the public treasury, and to supporting honest men in office. There was a significant opposition to the governor from his own party within the legislature. Possibilities of collusion with the governor notwithstanding, House Speaker Robert B. Elliott and black leader W. J. Whipper became outspoken opponents of Chamberlain. Whipper, a lawyer from Michigan, played important roles in both the constitutional conventions of 1868 and 1895 by being an advocate for the cause of women's rights.[230] All of the reasons for the split between Chamberlain and Elliott are not clear, but one incident in the fissure occurred in December 1874 when the Speaker supported Whipper for the First Circuit bench against the governor's choice of Col. J. P. Reed, a white conservative who had only recently joined the Republican Party. Reed won the election largely because of the political work of Governor Chamberlain.[231] Elliott and other radicals were bothered by Chamberlain's backing a white conservative over a prominent black Republican, albeit one of a tarnished reputation. They in time became convinced, probably correctly, that Chamberlain preferred the company of white conservatives to that of the black voters who had elected him. From the beginning of Chamberlain's term he demonstrated considerable independence from his Republican legislative colleagues. The governor vetoed nineteen bills, and in part because of his support from white conservatives, the legislature did not succeed in overriding any of them.[232]

Governor Chamberlain launched his reforms in his inaugural speech by expressing the opinion that the tax evaluations of the past administrations had been "unjust and oppressive."[233] He estimated that in the last year of the Moses administration a total of $376,832.74 had been appropriated for contingency expenses. He recommended that thereafter those items that were indeed necessary be covered by distinct appropriations. The contingency fund should not exceed $10,000 to $12,000. After expressing his concerns about the past administrations' mismanagement of the public debt, the governor told the inaugural audience, "It now becomes our paramount duty to labor to restore our ruined state credit by the only means apparently left to us—a prompt, unhesitating, and conscientious discharge of every obligation under the law which authorizes the consolidation of the public debt. In this way we may hope, little by little, to win back some part of the public credit, the loss of which is among the saddest calamities which have befallen this state."[234] Such statements obviously turned away the support of the ensconced radical leadership, and at the same time awakened support from the white conservative community.

Governor Chamberlain's reforms were quite remarkable. There were an impressive number of prosecutions of radical politicians for various crimes. For example, the former treasurer Niles G. Parker was found guilty of malfeasance in office, and the chairman of the House Ways and Means Committee was indicted for bribery. The new governor was also effective in reducing the expenses of government. Chamberlain enhanced his reputation for responsibility by pushing the state to improve its educational system, pointing out that less than half of the children eligible for elementary and secondary education were actually enrolled and that the average school year was only five months. He pleaded for public support, specifically recommending a high school for each county.[235]

Governor Chamberlain recognized the danger to the state in the presence of the two opposing armed camps: the black militia, and the paramilitary units and white rifle clubs. This armed hostility made South Carolina a virtual tinderbox. The problem was especially acute in Edgefield County. In early January 1875, Gen. M. C. Butler and several others went as representatives of a public meeting in Edgefield to see Governor Chamberlain, specifically to protest the fact that Ned Tennant, the black commander of the Edgefield militia, had rearmed his men, contrary to the governor's earlier instructions; the men were drilling regularly, much to the consternation of the white community. The governor sent Judge Thomas J. Mackey to investigate the situation in Edgefield. Acting on the judge's advice, in January 1875 the governor ordered the Edgefield militia to disarm and the Edgefield rifle clubs to disband.[236] On the night of January 13 M. C. Butler's home burned. After a brief search, Butler and his comrades found a black man who confessed to having burned the house on the orders of Tennant. The sheriff issued a warrant for the arrest of Tennant, but the militia leader refused to be arrested. The sheriff then allowed Butler to form a posse. The result was a gunfight in which two black citizens were killed. Tennant and others fled.[237]

Chamberlain's efforts for reform reaped impressive support from the conservative white community. On March 12, 1875, the editor of the Charleston *News and Courier*, Francis W. Dawson, wrote, "No honest man, Republican or Conservative, can hesitate to give full credit on this point to the Republican governor, who, without counting the consequences and looking only to the public good, has stood like a wall of adamant between the public robbers and the honest and law-abiding people of this state." One proof of white conservatives' support for Chamberlain came in March 1875 when the Republican majority in the legislature sought to impeach State Treasurer Francis L. Cardozo. The governor defended the treasurer and with the support of the conservative legislators saved him.[238] It is significant that the *News and Courier*, speaking for white conservatives, supported the black politician Cardozo,[239] who was apparently a man of talent and integrity. The support that the scalawag Chamberlain and the black Republican Cardozo drew from the whites is indicative of a possible working compromise between white conservatives and reform Republicans of both races. On March 11 the Charleston newspaper editorialized, "We believe that through him [Chamberlain] and by the line of conduct which he pursues can the conservative citizens, as well as the Republicans, attain most quickly and easily that reform of abuses and the reduction of taxes which are vastly more important than any political victory."[240] There was in the spring of 1875 a real possibility of a cooperative relationship between the radical Republican government led by a Northern white pledged to reform and the traditional white conservative leadership. The legislature, dominated by blacks, was not supportive of the governor, but such black leaders as Cardozo were on Chamberlain's side, as were the probable majority of the black voters of the state. The flaw was in the violence boiling over in Edgefield and then elsewhere. Ultimately such violence forced Chamberlain to cast his lot with the blacks and thereby lose the support of the majority of whites. But that split did not come until the summer of 1876.

In May 1875 Governor Chamberlain received an invitation to address the literary societies of Erskine College, an invitation indicative of growing acceptance by the whites of South Carolina. Chamberlain wrote to the societies to decline, expressing genuine regret, saying that he had previously accepted an invitation to speak at the commencement of the law department at Yale, his alma mater. The governor told the Erskine students that had he received the two invitations at the same time, he would have come to Erskine.[241]

Chamberlain continued to represent the interests of fiscal responsibility. In the spring of 1875 the two houses of the legislature passed a bill known as the Bonanza Bill, intended to legalize the vast indebtedness incurred by the previous radical administrations. The governor vetoed this measure, indicating to the general assembly his wish that the state work toward paying off part of the debt and reducing part of the debt according to the validity of the obligations. In a letter to the Speaker of the House, Chamberlain noted that part of the state's debt consisted of "certificates for legislative expenses . . . made to cover for vast frauds."[242]

The governor's efforts reaped for him an astonishing array of support from the state and national press, and this was at a time when the nation in general was losing patience with the whole idea of radical Reconstruction. A writer for the *Kingstree Star* commented, "That he is a Republican we care not; what we want is an honest government, no matter by whom. This we believe Governor Chamberlain will give the people of South Carolina, so far as he is responsible for it, if he is properly sustained."[243] The *News and Courier* itself indicated, "Two years of such noble work as this will cause him to be hailed as the savior of South Carolina." The *Nation* wrote of Chamberlain, "we can assure him of the sympathy of honest people all over the union, as one who is really defending civilization itself against barbarism in its worst form." The Republican *Boston Advertiser* noted that in the Chamberlain administration there were no more calls for Washington to intervene to sustain the Republican administration, "such as were frequent under the corrupt regime of Moses. While the people of South Carolina were plundered and harassed by an administration of scoundrels, they were as unreconciled and troublesome as the white people of Louisiana are now. When their just rights were respected, they forthwith respected the rights of others."[244] On September 3 the *News and Courier* printed quotations from newspapers in Marlboro, Abbeville, and Greenville to show the breadth of support for Chamberlain.[245] Such support for this carpet-bagger was remarkable, but the events of the next year revealed a fragility not suspected by these admirers in 1875.

In the summer of 1875 the State Sinking Fund Commission brought suit to recover funds alleged to have been improperly taken by the former state treasurer N. G. Parker. Governor Chamberlain and the current treasurer Cardozo testified against Parker, and the court found for the plaintiffs, ordering Parker to refund $75,000 to the state. The press covered the trial in detail, and again the conservatives were pleased with the governor. Treasurer Parker escaped from jail, was caught, and placed in jail again. He then secured his release by a writ of habeas corpus, issued by Judge T. J. Mackey, who released Parker on a bail of $2,000. The former treasurer then promptly left the state.[246] The Parker case reflected favorably on Chamberlain and added further discredit to the radicals.

In the midst of this "era of good feelings" in South Carolina, the white conservatives of Mississippi were engaged in a campaign of violence and intimidation to regain control of that state. The South Carolina press covered the Mississippi campaign with interest, usually portraying the Mississippi campaign as relatively free of violence. On September 9, 1875, the *News and Courier* noted, "The white people of Mississippi are making a determined effort to relieve themselves of the corrupt government under which the material interests of the state have continued to retrograde since the close of the struggle, and to establish an honest government." It is also significant that Gen. John B. Gordon of Georgia was active in the Mississippi campaign.[247] No Southern politician crossed more state lines in the effort to overthrow the radical regimes than Gordon. He was akin to Hampton in advocating a moderate approach. On September 21 the *News and Courier* printed a letter from Gov. Adelbert Ames of Mississippi, a native of Maine and son-in-law of Benjamin Butler, to the U.S. attorney general, asking for federal aid in suppressing white violence.[248] The Mississippi campaign would have great meaning for South Carolina; there were many similarities between the conditions and attitudes of the two states. For example, the white Mississippians had a great distaste and fear of the armed black militia. In October 1875 the white leaders of Mississippi reached a compromise with the scalawag Governor Ames, whereby the governor agreed to disarm the black militia and the white leadership pledged their efforts for a fair election free of violence.[249] Lest one believe that all of the South Carolina press reported favorably on the Mississippi election, it should be noted that the Republican paper of Columbia the *Union Herald* was often critical of the tactics of the Mississippi Democrats. A year later the *Union Herald* quoted James Redpath of the *New York Times*, who had informed a committee of the U.S. Senate investigating the Mississippi election that the black people of Mississippi, in counties where they outnumbered whites, were overawed by a system of organized terror. If less violent means failed to deter blacks from political activities the whites turned to murder.[250]

The era of good feelings in the Palmetto State was interrupted from time to time by acts of violence, which were indeed harbingers of even greater troubles to come. The radical boss of Newberry County, Joe Crews, was mortally wounded in an ambush in early September. Crews was a member of the House of Representatives, serving on the Ways and Means Committee; therefore, he was politically important.[251] This was unquestionably a political assassination; Crews was detested by the conservatives of that county.[252] Speaking for the conservatives, the *News and Courier* editorialized that the murder of Crews was wrong but that the state was better off without him. "By threats of causing their houses and barns to be burned down, by parading a list of citizens whom he intended to accuse of Ku Kluxism Joe Crews held Laurens subject to his will."[253]

For a time, in this era of good feelings for South Carolina, Governor Chamberlain was able to maintain reasonable support from the black community, largely because he was Republican, and they had been propagandized to vote Republican. He also had a surprising degree of support from the white conservative leadership, surprising because he was Republican, and the white community was averse to voting Republican. To maintain this balance between the two racial camps was a difficult feat. It was of course fragile because of basic racism and conflicting interests—for example, the conservative demand for lowering taxes and the black community's wish for public services that could be financed only by taxing the property owners. Underlying all of this was the basic truth that the Republican regime had been discredited by corruption. Fragility notwithstanding, Chamberlain's administration was a genuine success, at least for a time. One proof of the administration's success was that Chamberlain had been able to collect taxes with remarkable efficiency. In November 1875 the governor reported that the state in the last year had collected a total of $1,155,201.68, failing to collect only $12,519. This means that the public failed to pay 0.8 percent in taxes, a significant measure of public confidence, especially from a public thoroughly aroused by the several Taxpayers' Conventions as to the evils of unfair taxes. The governor had also succeeded in reducing government expenditures. He had, for example, reduced the contingency appropriation by 65 percent, and he reduced the expenses for public printing from an average annual cost of $181,209.95 to $50,000.[254]

In September 1875 the *News and Courier* reviewed the record of the South Carolina Democratic Party since the war and recommended cooperation with Chamberlain. In 1868 the Democrats tried what became known as a straight-out policy, a policy of putting forth a full slate of Democrats for all offices, encompassing no compromise with the Republicans. In the following elections, there were varying attempts at supporting reform Republicans, and not one of those efforts was successful. The writer noted that the South Carolina Democrats were wise to give their attention to local concerns. "The National Democracy are our natural and chosen allies, but it is South Carolina first, and National Democracy next." The *News and Courier* noted that the New York Democrats had recently nominated a Republican for the office of secretary of state. The writer encouraged South Carolina Democrats to "persevere in their policy of cooperation."[255] Events bore out the paper's prediction of success when conservatives joined with independent Republicans in the fall municipal elections in Charleston to oust the radical C. C. Bowen from the mayor's office and elect in his place the former Confederate general George Irving Cunningham. This was an effective coalition of white conservatives, blacks, and independent Republicans.[256] The *Boston Advertiser* wrote of Chamberlain, "He has made the protection of the white people as much his care as the protection of the negroes and zealously fostered the idea that . . . just and honest government is right for all."[257]

In November 1875 Chamberlain made his second annual report to the legislature. His program was to lower taxes, to exercise greater care in disbursing public funds, and to achieve an equitable adjustment of the public debt. The *News and Courier* praised the governor, noting that he "is resolute to carry on the good work of retrenchment and reform which began with his administration and his words will be hailed with satisfaction by every lover of honest and equal government."[258]

In December 1875 former governor Benjamin F. Perry wrote to the *News and Courier* to support the paper's policy of encouraging cooperation with the Republican Party. Perry thought that a straight-out policy would be folly. He wanted all interested in honest government to unite to "purge the legislature and public offices of roguery, corruption, and incompetency." Perry had opposed Chamberlain in the last election but later recognized that he had been mistaken, indicating his belief that Chamberlain's administration had been "honest, wise, patriotic." Perry wanted Democrats to be open to cooperating with black voters, noting that a straight-out policy was likely to alienate blacks from whites.[259]

Governor Chamberlain endured one more crisis in 1875. On December 16, 1875, while the governor was out of town, the legislature elected former governor F. J. Moses as judge of the circuit court in Sumter and W. J. Whipper as judge of the Charleston circuit court. Both of these men had tried unsuccessfully for judicial office in earlier sessions; Chamberlain had opposed them. The governor thought that he had the assurances of the Speaker of the House R. B. Elliot that the elections would be delayed until his return to Columbia. The governor had in a Republican caucus months earlier denounced Whipper as "incapable and corrupt."[260] Chamberlain described Moses as "covered deep with charges, which are believed by all who are familiar with the facts, of corruption, bribery, and utter prostitution of all his official powers to the worst possible purposes." Francis J. Moses, son of the chief justice of the South Carolina Supreme Court, was in fact notoriously corrupt. Chamberlain charged that Moses had spent his last hour in the governor's office signing a total of fifty-seven pardons.[261] The governor considered the election of these two reprobates as perhaps the worst calamity to fall on any Southern state in this difficult time. Chamberlain perceptively feared that this election would encourage the Democratic Party to reorganize and redouble its efforts for a straight-out victory over "this terrible crevasse of misgovernment and public debauchery." Lest anyone doubt that this election added fuel to the fires of racism, the *News and Courier* described the election of Whipper and Moses as a "carnival of robbery and ruin which the leaders of the negro ring are seeking to inaugurate." Later this influential newspaper editorialized that the election of Whipper and Moses was "a part of a deliberately formed plan to Africanize the low-country of South Carolina."[262] Chamberlain countered by refusing to sign the commissions for the two elected judges, using a subterfuge. Both of the judges whom the two were to replace had been elected to complete vacated terms. The constitution provided for terms of four years, and the governor reasoned that the two judgeships were not properly vacant until after the next general election, which meant that the next elected legislature should properly conduct the elections for these two seats.[263] Chamberlain's reaction against these elections did much to endear him to white conservatives. In the midst of the Whipper-Moses fracas the Charleston New England Society invited the governor to come address them. Chamberlain had to decline the invitation, and he wrote to the society this warning for the white race: "The civilization of the Puritan, and of the cavalier, of the Roundhead and the Huguenot is in peril."[264] With that kind of statement there is little wonder that Chamberlain appealed successfully to white conservatives.

It is worth noting that not all opposition to the judicial elections came from whites. Robert Smalls and other black members of Congress from South Carolina denounced the action of the legislature. Smalls described the event as a "calamitous blunder which puts in jeopardy Republican ascendancy in that state." Smalls said that the previous conservative judges should have been left in office. He described Whipper as "no lawyer and unfit for office" and Moses as "known to every man in South Carolina to be a scoundrel."[265] Chamberlain and Congressman Smalls were correct in fearing that the legislature had endangered the future of the Republican regime. The events of the next year bore out their prophetic fears, and this was when Wade Hampton entered the limelight of politics.

On December 27, 1875, there was a public meeting in the Hibernian Hall in Charleston, called to protest the election of Whipper and Moses. Gen. James Conner, a conservative aristocratic supporter of cooperation with Chamberlain, addressed the gathering. "No people has ever endured so much so patiently and so long. We have never organized for resistance. We have sought relief through conciliation and compromise; I do not condemn it. I say it was well; for had it not been tried, there are those who would have claimed that it was the true remedy and the sole panacea for all our ills. We have tried it, and have demonstrated by failure its utter inefficiency." This from a moderate who supported the Republican Chamberlain! He still urged white conservatives to support Chamberlain, but there was now a militancy, which when turned toward Chamberlain, would doom that reformer carpetbagger to defeat. Conner went on, "Every man, young and old, from the mountains to the seashore, must be organized, ready and willing to meet every issue as it may arise, and to hold the next election as the paramount duty of the hour, that to which every interest must be subordinate and every difference of opinion sacrificed." Col. B. C. Pressly also addressed the assembly and said that South Carolina did not support lynching, but lynch law is better than no law. Pressly then demonstrated an amazing combination of beliefs by saying that if the legislature dared to impeach Chamberlain, the members should fear for their lives.[266] The combination of support for lynching with support for the carpetbagger governor was indeed amazing. At this time the militant fervor was directed against the Republican legislature, not against the Republican governor.

Walter Allen, who wrote about Chamberlain's administration, provided an excellent insight to the political significance of the legislature's election of Moses and Whipper. Allen quoted H. V. Redfield, correspondent of the *Cincinnati Commercial*: "For a long time the whites have wanted a sufficient excuse to rise up and overthrow the African government under which they live; and now they have it."[267] This judgment might have been too cynical, but there was much truth in it. The election of Moses and Whipper also added to the disillusionment of national Republicans in the cause of Reconstruction of the South. On January 12, 1876, the *Columbia Register* quoted *Harper's Weekly* in urging members of Congress to look at South Carolina, where the "colored legislature" had elected two notoriously corrupt men to the bench.[268] There was still a considerable number of white conservatives who were willing to support Chamberlain, but they had doubts that he would receive the Republican nomination. The State Executive Committee of the Democratic Party met on January 6, 1876, to begin developing their plans for the elections of that year.[269]

The last years of the radical regime were Hampton's time in the wilderness; he was busy trying to make a living, trying to salvage his estates as they slid into bankruptcy, and working with the troubled insurance businesses. During much of this time Hampton was actually out of the state, in Baltimore, Charlottesville, and Mississippi, and only occasionally in South Carolina. In a letter of February 1874 to John Mullaly, Hampton said that he had known little of public affairs for two and a half years; his time had been consumed by out-of-state business and his wife's declining health.[270]

In November 1874 the general was at Delmonico's in New York City, attending a meeting of the New York Young Men's Democratic Club. The papers noted that the Confederate general shook hands with Major General Averill, "who had led many a charge of the union horse in the shadows and passes of the Blue Ridge." Hampton addressed the club and noted with gratitude the recent Democratic victories in the North, having won a majority in the national House of Representatives in 1874. Hampton predicted that the Democratic Party would lead the nation to a "future in which shall be no North, no South, no East, no West."[271] New York governor Samuel J. Tilden, the future Democratic candidate for the presidency, was at the same meeting.

The following April the general was back in Mississippi. He wrote to Mrs. Thomas L. Preston, with whom he and his family had lived in the months of Mary McDuffie Hampton's decline to death, that he was trying to make a go of things in Mississippi. He hoped to save one plantation by selling the other two, but it was not easy to find a buyer in those hard times. "If this can be done, I can, by living here, make a support for my family, but I do not fancy the idea of becoming an overseer. Nothing can be made, however, unless I remain on the place."[272] Hampton's reluctance to function as an overseer and his failure to remain on the land were undoubtedly factors contributing to his ultimate failure as a postwar planter.

On July 2, 1875, John S. Preston, who had married Hampton's Aunt Caroline, delivered a stridently unreconstructed speech at the University of Virginia. Preston told his audience that the people of New England were "rotten root and branch." He said that for a Southerner to visit the North was "to crawl on our bellies to Negro and New England temples" and "pray them not to give back our happy homes, not to give back our slaughtered children, but to let us be one of them." The papers, including the *News and Courier*, were critical of Preston, saying that his uncompromising attitude could only hurt the South, which was at that time moving toward what could be a satisfactory compromise with the reforming Republicans. The *News and Courier* compared Preston's extremism to that of Wendell Phillips of New England.[273] General Hampton wrote to his aunt Caroline that Preston's indiscretion "was in the time and place of delivering the speech and not in the speech itself."[274] It is difficult to make much of this response, since Hampton was not likely to be critical of his relative-in-law, especially to his aunt.

Hampton himself managed to stay before the public in what were essentially nonpolitical appearances. In February 1875 he spoke to a reunion of the Washington Light Infantry, largely about his grandfather's role in the Battle of Eutaw Springs.[275] On July 22, 1875, the general addressed a reunion of the Hampton Legion.[276] In July 1875, the *News and Courier* announced that General Hampton, that "gallant soldier and gentleman," would address the Washington Artillery on Washington's birthday in 1876.[277]

SIX

The Election of 1876

Just as Governor Chamberlain had feared, the South Carolina Democratic Party revived in 1876, but that is not to say that the party was totally inactive in the preceding year. In many ways the two taxpayers' conventions presaged the revival of the Democratic Party; the taxpayers' unions faded into the Democratic clubs at the various levels of the state. Thomas Y. Simmons of Charleston, representing the National Democratic Executive Committee, summoned the state Central Committee to meet on January 6, 1876. When that committee met, M. C. Butler was the chairman. The other members were F. W. Dawson, editor of the *News and Courier*, emerging then as a leading Democrat, Johnson Hagood of Barnwell, William Wallace of Union, William D. Simpson of Laurens, M. P. O'Connor of Charleston, John S. Richardson of Sumter, S. P. Hamilton of Chester, Henry McIver of Chesterfield, William Sellers of Marion, Martin Gary of Edgefield, and Wade Hampton of Richland. Neither Hampton nor Gary, who was to be the chief Hampton antagonist, was present for the initial meeting. The committee issued an address to the state, announcing its intention to revive the party and asking interested individuals to organize Democratic clubs at the local level. The goal of the revived party would be to obtain "honest and economical government." The committee expressed its confidence in the sitting Republican governor, appreciating his efforts at "reform and retrenchment." Still, the committee envisioned party organization in every precinct.[1]

The appeal from the Democratic Committee for grassroots organizations had a quick effect. The *Columbia Register* of February 13, 1876, reported organizational meetings in Anderson, Greenville, Marion, and Walhalla.[2] The issue of February 26 reported organizational meetings in Kershaw, Spartanburg, and Barnwell counties.[3] In response to the leadership's urging that Democratic organizations begin at the precinct and township level, the *Columbia Register* of March 3 reported meetings at Walnut Grove and Cedar Springs in Spartanburg County and Moon township in Newberry County. A resolution adopted by the Moon Democratic Club caught the fervor of the moment: "the line of demarkation . . . [is] so strictly and thoroughly drawn between us and the corrupt party now disgracing this state that no true and honest voter can doubt or hesitate as to which side it is his duty to take his stand."[4]

The Whipper-Moses incident had created a fissure in the conservative support of Chamberlain, but the support held together in the first part of 1876. In the spring of 1876 there was good reason to believe that if the Republicans nominated Chamberlain for a second term he would receive the votes of the majority of the conservative whites; and that union of white leadership with the reformist Republicans, white and black, could have had hopeful significance for race relations in South Carolina. Francis W. Dawson, the Englishman-Charlestonian, who was the influential editor of the *News and Courier*, supported the compromise between the conservatives and Chamberlain. His editorials argued that the compromise, often called fusion, could succeed in the election of the reformist governor only if the black voters cooperated. Ironically, Dawson, like many of his colleagues, assumed that the corruption in the Republican regime was the result of the black majority in the legislature, and the newspaper made that clear.

One of the reporters for the *News and Courier* was R. Means Davis, a good mind, later a writer of South Carolina history and professor at the University of South Carolina. A year after the election of 1876 Davis observed the actions of the convention of the Episcopal Diocese of Charleston in refusing to admit black delegates. Davis wrote in his notebook: "Thus, in Charleston, the stronghold of fusion political policy, a firebrand was thrust in this religious-social question. Here was another disturbing element. If the whites could not admit blacks to church conventions, how could Democrats allow blacks in political office? The Republican politicians were shrewd enough to ask these questions."[5]

Dawson became the leading proponent of fusion politics. He was at the same time a leading Democrat, serving as the secretary of the state Democratic Executive Committee. He urged his fellow Democrats to nominate and work to elect a straight-out ticket, save for the office of governor.[6] Dawson's newspaper in the months after the Whipper-Moses fiasco received some pressure to support a straight-out policy, but Dawson withstood it until other events occurred in the summer of 1876.

It is significant that the movement for a straight-out policy had racist overtones from its beginning. For example, on January 6, 1876, the *News and Courier* published a letter signed "Payson," in which the writer expressed exasperation with the attempts by whites to conciliate the black voting majority. Payson thought that the efforts at conciliation had achieved only "disgraceful corruption," another indication of the assumption that the prevalent dishonesty in government was a result of black participation. One wonders how Payson explained the rampant corruption of the all-white Grant administration. Many, perhaps most, South Carolinians believed that Republicans were without morals, and black Republicans were even more immoral. Payson concluded: "And now, Mr. Editor, I have come to what I regard as the plan for our redemption—and that is a straight-out, thoroughly organized Democratic opposition."[7] Payson was prescient, even in using the word "redemption," for that is the term South Carolinians had used to indicate the seizure of the reins of power from black and white Republicans. All of this notwithstanding, Dawson stuck by his support of fusion until well into the summer of 1876.

On January 10, 1876, the *News and Courier* published a story that gave the Democratic Party a war cry for its forthcoming campaign. The Republican judge Thomas J. Mackey spoke to an audience in Chester and quoted Sen. John J. Patterson as having replied to someone who mentioned the efforts by Governor Chamberlain for reform: "Are you going to let Chamberlain frighten you off with his cry of reform and economy? Why, gentlemen, there are five years of good stealing in South Carolina yet."[8] Conservative support for Chamberlain was not restricted to Charleston. There were pockets of support and opposition scattered about the state. Within a week there were public meetings in Laurens and Georgetown, which passed resolutions endorsing Chamberlain.[9]

Edgefield County was the center of the opposition to fusion politics and of support of a straight-out Democratic effort. Martin Gary of Edgefield was the leading spokesman for the straight-out policy. Gary was a Harvard graduate, a former brigadier general in the Confederate army, having served for a time in the Hampton Legion,[10] and he was an ardent racist.

Gary modeled his political efforts in 1876 after the Mississippi plan of intimidation and violence. It is interesting that the *News and Courier* and to a lesser extent the *Columbia Register*, the most influential papers advocating fusion of white conservatives with reformist Republicans, also advocated that South Carolina Democrats follow the lead of the Mississippi plan. The difference was in how Gary and the newspapers interpreted the workings of that plan. Gary was attracted to the side that threatened violence and the use of it on occasion; the very influential *News and Courier* and the less influential *Columbia Register* chose to view the Democratic campaign in Mississippi as a moderate effort. For example, a correspondent of the Columbia paper wrote from Mississippi during the campaign to predict that a significant number of black Mississippians would vote for the Democratic ticket, inspired by the promise of honest government.[11] After the Democratic victory in Mississippi the *Columbia Register* enthused: "The overthrow of Ames and the Radical monstrosity in Mississippi is proof positive that no Southern state need long remain under Ethiopian rule, if the people of that commonwealth address themselves properly to the task of redemption." To indicate its belief in a moderate policy, the paper went on, "It is urged that a revolution at the ballot box cannot be consummated in South Carolina, except by prevailing upon the negroes, by hook or by crook, to vote the conservative or Democratic ticket." In what came close to a cry for Wade Hampton, the writer continued, "we believe that the people of South Carolina only require a quickening touch, a master hand at the helm, a clarion voice calling upon them to rally, so that in the future, as in the days gone by, upon the broad shield of honor shall be inscribed this golden legend:

> The greater glory of a free-born people
> Is to transmit that freedom to their children."[12]

A letter in the Martin Gary papers, written by S. M. Ferguson of Mississippi to T. G. Parker of Charleston, set forth the case for the Mississippi plan. Ferguson had specifically observed the campaign in Washington County, where Hampton had planting interests. Ferguson reported that there was no bloodshed in that county. White Democrats had let it be known that if any white Democrat were harmed then every white Republican in the county would be murdered. Democrats made it a point to attend all Republican rallies. These Democrats "denounced the radical rascality to their faces." Black Mississippians saw their white leaders either cower or withdraw.[13] This was indeed the political plan that Gary and his cohorts promoted.

The *Columbia Register* closed out the year 1875 by endorsing the Democratic effort in Mississippi. The paper quoted Mr. Redfield of the *Cincinnati Commercial*, who, according to the *Columbia Register*, judged the Mississippi campaign to have been well and fairly done. The Columbia paper summarized the Mississippi plan as urging Democrats to organize, vote at full strength, enlighten the black voters, and secure a following among honest Republicans. To remove all doubts as to the role of black voters in the radical regime, the Columbia writer opined: "The blacks are notoriously incompetent to govern wisely or well; they elected a miserable set to office."[14] This was of course a rather bland interpretation of the campaign in Mississippi.

It is significant that six months later the Republican newspaper the *Union Herald*, relying on James Redpath of the *New York Times*, concluded that the Mississippi campaign was based on intimidation and actual violence, including murder. Redpath believed that the well-known L. Q. C. Lamar, "who wept over Sumner's coffin lid," owed his election to the U.S. Senate to many violations of civil rights.[15] The Reconstruction historian Eric Foner concluded from his studies that the Mississippi campaign of 1875 was a "violent crusade to destroy the Republican organization and prevent blacks from voting."[16] These differences in interpretation of the Mississippi campaign help in understanding how members of the South Carolina Democratic Party could vary so drastically in emulating the Mississippians.

Martin Gary was until his death in 1881 the primary antagonist to Hampton and the ideas represented by Hampton. After Gary the next great opponent to Hampton was Benjamin Tillman, also from Edgefield and a protégé of Gary. Martin Gary and the thinking he represented are worthy of some detailed treatment in this study of Hampton. The ties between Gary and Tillman were significant and longstanding. In 1857 Martin Gary, as a member of the Edgefield jury that had found George Tillman, older brother of Benjamin, guilty of manslaughter in the death of Henry Christenson (the jury sentenced Tillman to serve two years in prison and to pay a fine of two thousand dollars), signed a petition to Governor R. F. W. Allston, asking that the sentence be reduced and the prisoner released. Tillman had for a time fled the state.[17] George Tillman was released, and he achieved success in politics, serving for a time in Congress. That one could serve time in prison for manslaughter and still be an officeholder is an indication of the degree to which the South Carolina public tolerated violence among "respectable" people. This tolerance of white violence makes the oft-repeated white charge that black people were prone to violence more difficult to understand. The Tillman regime was in fact marked by more violence than earlier periods.

Gary was one of the severest critics of the morality of the Republican regime. Yet he was himself not without stain. One of the scandals in which "Honest John" Patterson was involved was a scheme in which he and his associates managed to purchase at a bargain rate the state's shares in the Blue Ridge Rail Road. Mart Gary was associated with Patterson in this scheme.[18] It is doubtful that Gary or Patterson profited by this arrangement, but their attempt was less than honorable. Gary and M. C. Butler were also accused of having accepted a promise of payment to try to influence the Taxpayers Convention of 1871 to declare state bonds valid. Those promising payment planned to purchase the bonds at a reduced amount and then profit by an increase in their value after the convention endorsed the issue.[19] The most important aspect of Gary's opposition to Hampton was racism. Gary's attitude toward the black race was one of raw contempt and violence. He will later make much of Hampton's dining with blacks at the home of the president of Claflin University.[20] Unfortunately Gary's views became those of the majority of the white population. The sad choice was between the paternalism of Hampton and the hatred of Gary, and too many South Carolina white people ultimately chose the latter.

It is noteworthy that those in South Carolina who opposed the policy of fusion had some support from without the state. On January 16, 1876, the *Columbia Register* quoted the *New York Sun* in chiding South Carolina Democrats for being slow to organize for an independent effort. The writer for the *Sun* thought that Governor Chamberlain had humbugged the Democrats with his talk of reform. The *Columbia Register* at this time disagreed with the *Sun* and continued to urge cooperation with the reformist governor.[21]

Governor Chamberlain understood quite well that he needed the support of the national Republican Party to win reelection and keep the Republican Party in power in South Carolina. Sen. Oliver P. Morton of Indiana accused Chamberlain, because of his opposition to the seating of Moses and Whipper, of treason to his party by "truckling to" the conservatives. Chamberlain replied, "If South Carolina is to be given up to the opposition it will be because you, and others whom you can influence, fail to help me and my friends to 'unload'—to use the current phrase—the infamy of these judicial elections."[22]

Chamberlain's gaining support from white conservatives by his reforms and by his rejection of Whipper and Moses indeed caused a serious fracture in the South Carolina Republican Party. The black Republican Whipper was by no means muted. He called the governor "a black hearted traitor."[23] Whipper represented a significant portion of the black leadership who saw Chamberlain as selling out to white conservatives. The Republicans met in convention in April 1876 to choose delegates to the national Republican convention. Chamberlain won election as a delegate but only with great effort. After a stirring speech he defeated "Honest John" Patterson as a delegate-at-large.[24] The effort the governor had to make to be elected as a delegate was a measure of the fissure in his party. At one point Judge T. J. Mackey charged, "We are met here today, face to face and eye to eye, [with] the banded robbers that have plundered the state." The black politician S. A. Swails asked, "What do you mean?" Mackey replied, "You are one of them; you are their head and front." In the heat of these charges R. B. Elliott drew his pistol. Although no one was struck or shot, such bitterness weakened the party for the forthcoming campaign.[25]

Through the spring of 1876 the Democrats in the state continued to divide over the issue of fusion. The upcountry counties tended to support a straight-out policy, and Charleston led the move for fusion—supporting Chamberlain for governor and an otherwise full slate of Democratic candidates. For example, the *Edgefield Advertiser* editorialized for a straight-out plan and indicated that the sentiment for that policy was gaining support in Anderson and Union counties. The *News and Courier* argued strongly and regularly for fusion.[26] The Democrats of Greenville County met in convention in February and resolved: "That we favor no further efforts to compromise with the Republican Party, as all attempts at coalition only tend to demoralize and disintegrate the Democratic Party." It is also significant that the Greenville Democrats invited all citizens regardless of race to join the party,[27] apparently following a model resolution circulated to county organizations by the state executive committee, which included this statement: "We invite our coloured friends to unite with us in our efforts to secure the peace, harmony, and prosperity of our country by joining our organization and subscribing their names to the roll."[28]

Whereas the most obvious spokesman for the straight-out plan in the upcountry was Martin Gary of Edgefield, the most prominent supporters of fusion were Francis Dawson and James Conner of Charleston.[29] Conner wanted the Democrats to court the black vote, assuming that white leaders could, by befriending blacks, control their political decisions. Conner was even willing to support the election of black congressmen, as long as the white leadership could control the state government.[30] In this Conner and Wade Hampton were in agreement. The general had written to Conner on April 9, 1867, that he would willingly let black Republicans have seats in Congress if the conservatives could regain control of the state government.[31]

Events will indicate that Martin Gary suffered from no such paternal softness in his attitude toward black South Carolinians. Gary had addressed the Taxpayers Convention of 1874 on the issue of race, arguing that the white fusion with the Union Reform Party in the election of 1872 had failed to induce a significant number of blacks to vote with whites for reform. Gary did not believe that the state's blacks were arrayed against whites as Democrats but against whites as a race; therefore, he saw the issue before the state as one of race. "It was certain that God had destined the Caucasian race to rule the other." Whites therefore must unite as a race.[32] Gary specifically blamed Wade Hampton for his early advocacy of a qualified suffrage for blacks, believing that to have given black South Carolinians an entering wedge for universal black suffrage.[33]

The state Democratic Executive Committee issued a statement calling for the first of two state conventions to meet on May 4 to select delegates for the national convention. The next convention would select candidates for state offices. The committee reported that blacks were joining the party in the upcountry counties.[34]

One of the reasons the election of 1876 has received much attention from historians is the role of violence in the campaign. In recent decades historians have usually focused on intimidation and violence by white conservatives or Democrats. It is important in studying that violence by whites to understand that those whites thought, rightly or wrongly, that they were themselves under threat of violence from their black neighbors. Alfred B. Williams, a young journalist who followed the Hampton campaign, reported that within one week there were three incendiary cases in Abbeville County alone. There the house of J. C. Pressly and the barns and gins of William Agnew and J. B. Moore were burned, presumably by incendiaries. White conservatives were convinced state law enforcement officers had little interest in solving such crimes.[35] The combination of that perceived threat of violence with the obvious corruption in government and the burden of heavy taxation made whites feel their civilization faced possible destruction. The result was an attitude among whites quite like that of a people at war. The editor of the *News and*

Courier, obviously thinking of the centennial of the American Revolution, wrote on July 4, 1876, "Just as surely as the white colonists were relieved by their own efforts from British tyranny, so shall the white citizens of South Carolina be relieved, in one way or another, from the reign and rascality of the so-called Republicans."[36] A people at war often consider any act of violence against the enemy as necessary for the just cause. White conservatives conducted their campaign with a frenzy like that of a people threatened with extinction. The Democrats of 1876 probably "fought" that campaign with a greater fervor than they had fought the Yankees in 1861–1865. In March 1876 the *Columbia Register* reported that a cotton gin had been burned in Lexington County, apparently an act of incendiaries. The writer commented, "Is it any wonder that retaliation is meted out to the incendiaries, murderers, and thieves, when these diabolical deeds are of such frequent occurrence?"[37] In part because whites owned most of the newspapers, the acts of black violence received more publicity than similar acts by whites. White Democrats generally believed that the corrupt government was incapable of protecting its citizens, thereby justifying vigilantism. The editor of the *Columbia Register* wrote, "The burning of gin houses, robbery of stores, a general destitution and idleness, and the murder of citizens for money, are the legitimate effects of a government whose power is lodged in corrupt and imbecile hands. The general assembly is the most demoralizing institution in this state. It sets an example of systematic spoliation."[38] It is significant that rifle clubs and Democratic organizations were often synonymous and that rifle clubs had military organizations, complete with commanding officers, noncommissioned officers, and wagons containing supplies for three days.[39]

Since Edgefield County was the germinal center for the most radical of Democratic tactics, it is worthwhile to follow in some detail the resolutions of that county party. In a March meeting of the Edgefield Democrats, George Tillman, brother of Benjamin, offered a resolution that "we are sternly opposed to any fusion, coalition or compromise with even professedly honest Republicans. We cordially invite all voters, whether white or black, and without regard to previous party affiliation to cooperate with us in elevating capable and good Democrats to office." That resolution passed. A more severe resolution offered by Martin Gary failed to pass. The *News and Courier* commented, "How can the Democrats have the face to ask the Republicans to vote for 'professedly' honest Democrats, while those very Democrats flatly refuse to vote for 'professedly' honest Republicans?"[40]

In 1870 and 1871, Congress passed three "enforcement acts," intended to protect the voting rights of black people. The U.S. Supreme Court in *United States v. Reese* (1876) declared portions of the enforcement acts unconstitutional because the Fifteenth Amendment did not extend any positive guarantee of the franchise.[41] This and later decisions did much to vitiate the role of

Washington in controlling the franchise in the states. The *New York Times*, in considering this decision of the Supreme Court, ventured, "This important decision marks the beginning of a new era in the political relations of the Negro in our Southern states."[42] While this opinion was ultimately true, in the near future the federal government yet had a role to play.

Still it was true that even in the spring of 1876 the national Republican Party was losing interest in the efforts of Reconstruction. In April Governor Chamberlain wrote a letter to President Grant to explain the issue of the election of Moses and Whipper to the South Carolina bench. "The election of these two men sends a thrill of horror through the state." Chamberlain wanted state and national Republicans to join him in denouncing this act of the Republican legislature.[43] It took more than the election of Whipper and Moses to get Grant involved in the South Carolina race.

Rifle clubs played an important part in the Democratic campaign. The Democratic Convention of Richland County met in the quarters of the Richland Rifle Club. Not at all incidentally, that convention elected one black man, Robert Adams, as a delegate to the state convention.[44] In the same month the officers of the U.S. Eighteenth Infantry stationed in Columbia entertained the Richland Rifle Club, complete with the post band.[45] This was simply another indication of the normally good relations between the occupying Yankee troops and Southern whites. There was some irony in this entertainment in that within a short time those troops would be called upon to restrain rifle clubs, without much success, perhaps in part because of a basic racial sympathy.

Even Governor Chamberlain had had good relations with some rifle clubs. In December 1876 Robert H. Hemphill testified to the congressional investigating committee designated to investigate the possibility of fraud in the campaign of 1876 that he organized the first rifle club in the upcountry in May 1876, in Abbeville, and he did so with the consent of Governor Chamberlain. The club made Chamberlain an honorary member.[46]

The Democratic Party convened for the first convention of 1876 on May 4 in the House chamber of the capitol. Wade Hampton was not a delegate, but most of the men who would play leading roles in the campaign were there: M. L. Bonham, M. C. Butler, Edward McCrady, Jr., James Conner, Martin W. Gary, George Tillman, Benjamin F. Perry, and A. C. Haskell, to name a few of the most prominent.[47] The most important purpose of this convention was to elect delegates to the national convention. It was also possible for this convention to nominate the slate for the fall election, but the majority wanted to wait until later. The fusionists wanted to wait until the Republican convention had made their choices. The *Columbia Register* editorialized that the Democrats needed a gubernatorial nominee who could give the party a greater stimulus than the current abstract discussion, and the party should wait until after the Republican convention so that they could more effectively take advantage of the divisions in the opposing party.[48] Delegate Martin Gary introduced a resolution that the convention present a slate of candidates for all offices, a straight-out plan. This resolution failed to pass. The convention decided to authorize the executive committee to call for a convention at a time it thought most advantageous.[49] In his advocacy for a straight-out plan, Gary charged, "The great commercial city of Charleston is surrounded by a horde of black barbarians." Gary was seldom hesitant to reveal his racism. In a similar vein, M. C. Butler told the convention, "The only way to redeem the state is to nominate a true, liberal, moderate native, with a like ticket, and carry the war to Africa." Butler argued that the South Carolina Democrats must follow the example of their brothers in Mississippi. The convention responded with resounding applause.[50]

After the Democratic convention, as before, the *News and Courier* continued as the leading voice for a fusion campaign, recommending that the Democrats wait until the Republican convention had made its choice, and, assuming that that party nominated Chamberlain, the Democrats should nominate a full slate save for the office of governor, then should try to elect Chamberlain and a Democratic legislature. The editor made a point that had considerable meaning in the dispute following the election: the Board of State Canvassers was composed entirely of Republicans, and that body had the power to decide on protests and disputed counts. The writer made a statement that his Democratic colleagues hotly contested in the following November, "The action of that Board is final and without its certificates the members of the legislature have no prima facie right to their seats." All of this meant that the Democrats stood little chance of winning without a fusion with Governor Chamberlain.[51]

Many of the leading Democrats were convinced that they must win a significant number of black votes if they were to have a chance in the coming election. The census of 1875 indicated a black majority in the voting age of 110,744 blacks to 74,199 whites, a daunting majority of about 35,000.[52] In the edition of May 14, 1876, the *Columbia Register* quoted a letter written by a black citizen published in the *Barnwell Sentinel:* "There must be a change and if that change is not made, we are a lost race of people. We want, we must have a change for the better." The *Columbia Register* recommended seeking the black vote, using the phrase "carrying the war to Africa."[53] When this newspaper used that phrase it meant wooing the black vote; when the more ardent racists used it the meaning was more militant. That Columbia paper originally supported a policy of fusion. After the May convention the *Columbia Register* shifted to a position of warning Democrats of the dangers of compromise with the Republicans.[54]

The editor of the *News and Courier* voiced a warning that was of immense importance in the campaign of 1876. "The experience of the past year ought to satisfy the most sanguine Democrats in the South that the National Democracy will not go out of its way to benefit the South and the necessities of their position compel them to show no favor whatsoever."[55] Indeed, Southern Democrats, like Hampton, realized that the national party would be cautious in demonstrating much support for Southerners who had served prominently in the Confederacy. Hampton would be charged with having ignored the national party, even of favoring the Republican candidate Rutherford B. Hayes.

Historians have been intensely interested in the prevalence of violence in the campaign of 1876. One of the first important incidents occurred when rice-field laborers, all of whom were black, began a strike in the area along the Combahee River. The rice planters had reduced the pay for a day's work from fifty cents to forty cents, and a number of the more aggressive workers decided to threaten the crops by a walkout. The violence lay in their efforts to prevent their less aggressive coworkers from working.[56] The strike dragged on for some time, and it took on political importance. Some of the planters and other Democratic voices urged the governor to intervene.[57] Many of those same Democrats later decried Governor Chamberlain's proclivity to intervene in local affairs. When Chamberlain became involved in the strike, he offered amnesty to offenders if they agreed to a truce. The *News and Courier*, which was still defending fusion, criticized the governor's too-quick offer of amnesty.[58] Ultimately the Combahee strike was settled by essentially local efforts. The governor asked Rep. Robert Smalls, the influential black leader known as the "King of Beaufort," to go with the county sheriff to quell the disturbances. Smalls reported to the governor that there was no need for the militia. He and the sheriff successfully negotiated an end to the strike. Smalls negotiated safe passage for a rifle club that had tried to intervene and had come under siege by the militant strikers. Several ringleaders were arrested, and the local planters made concessions. The Beaufort trial justice dismissed the charges.[59]

On May 26 the *News and Courier* reported that Mr. and Mrs. Harmon, of near Abbeville, had been murdered by several blacks. A mob apprehended several suspects. At least one confessed, and all suspects were summarily killed by the mob. The several deaths are important, and the white defense of the mob is also revealing of the temper of the time. The Charleston paper indicated that circumstances in South Carolina justified the resort to lynch law. "The Negroes overwhelmingly outnumber the whites in the state. They are passionate and heedless and have a narrow sense of moral responsibility." The editor insisted that such crimes required swift retribution, and that justice was not available in South Carolina at that time.[60] The *Columbia Register* also gave a justification: "Lynch law was a necessity in newly settled regions before civil government with its protection and security had been extended to them." White people had despaired of depending on the courts for justice.[61] The

Edgefield Advertiser editorialized: "The time has come in Edgefield for the people to save themselves."[62] Governor Chamberlain reacted sharply to the lynchings, stating in a proclamation, "This state is not a new or improperly organized community in which concerted violence must sometimes supplement or supersede the law."[63] Such arguments, cogent and just though they were, because they tended to place him in defense of South Carolina blacks against the whites, probably contributed to the ultimate failure of the fusionist movement. Almost as Gary had said, it was a question of race.

By the end of May the *Columbia Register* was in full support of a straight-out policy for the Democratic Party. The editor reminded Democrats that Chamberlain declared himself to be a loyal Republican. The Columbia paper argued that this election should be one of parties, not of candidates.[64]

During these events Wade Hampton was on his plantations in Mississippi, rather detached from the politics of his home state. The *Columbia Register* reported that the native South Carolinian classical scholar William Pinkney Starke, who had been teaching at Urbana University in Ohio, was with Hampton in Mississippi. The Columbia paper expressed the hope that Starke would return and enrich his home state with his talents. The writer apparently assumed that Hampton would remain on his plantations.[65] Nevertheless, the general was back in South Carolina to deliver an address at the Confederate Home in Charleston on June 29.[66]

The *Columbia Register* in June predicted an overwhelming move to a straight-out policy, supporting this assumption with statements from the *Camden Journal*, the *Abbeville Medium*, the *Keowee Courier*, the *Charleston Journal of Commerce*, and the *Abbeville Press and Banner*, all pushing for a full Democratic slate.[67] With the exception of the Charleston paper, these were all upcountry papers. The fire-eater R. B. Rhett, Jr., had just begun the *Journal of Commerce* in Charleston. In late June there came another indication of upcountry–lowcountry excitement about fusion when the *Greenville News* editorialized that if the Democratic state convention chose to support Governor Chamberlain, "we would see the whole thing d----d before we would have anything to do with the ticket."[68] On July 4 the *Columbia Register* stated its position rather succinctly: "Governor Chamberlain is an honest man, but he represents a notoriously corrupt constituency and, in supporting him, the corrupt constituency is supported."[69]

In late June the South Carolina delegation left for the national Democratic Convention in St. Louis. Wade Hampton was not in that number. The delegation included M. C. Butler, M. L. Bonham, Benjamin F. Perry, M. P. O'Conner, and J. C. Sheppard.[70] The convention nominated New York governor Samuel Tilden for the presidency and T. A. Hendricks of Indiana for the vice presidency. The next duty was to return home and select the South Carolina candidates.

Back in South Carolina, M. C. Butler let it be known that he intended to nominate Gen. Wade Hampton for governor. The *News and Courier* responded to this news by restating its support of fusion, but noted that if the Democratic Party were to decide on a straight-out plan and nominate Hampton, it would support the party and the candidate. "There is no office in her [South Carolina's] gift of which he is not worthy."[71]

On July 4, 1876, there occurred in the little town of Hamburg, just on the South Carolina side of the Savannah River opposite Augusta, an incident that brought down all hope for a compromise between white conservatives and Governor Chamberlain, thereby wrecking a chance that whites could have joined with some Republicans, white and black, in support of honest and economical government. Hamburg was a small town that had brief importance as the terminus of the railroad from Charleston. Once a bridge was built over the Savannah River to Augusta, Hamburg's significance waned. By 1876 the village was known as an essentially black community, complete with black officeholders. On July 4 Doc Adams was drilling his black militia unit in the streets of Hamburg when two white men from Edgefield County, Henry Getzen and Thomas Butler (no relation to M. C. Butler), tried to pass through the street in their carriage. The white men demanded that the militia make way for their passing through. Harsh words were exchanged, which both parties considered insulting. After some arguing, a rainstorm forced the troops to move, and the white men continued on their way.

Then came the violence. On July 6 the two men from Edgefield returned and filed a complaint with the black magistrate, Prince Rivers. The magistrate attempted to conduct a hearing on the charge of misconduct against the officers of the militia unit. Doc Adams proved to be uncooperative, and the magistrate fined him for contempt and then delayed the hearing until July 8. When the two plaintiffs returned they were accompanied by M. C. Butler as their counsel and by an undetermined number of whites from Edgefield. A number of whites also came over from Augusta, and the gathering took on the aspects of a mob. M. C. Butler demanded the militia unit give up its arms. Threatened by the presence of the large gathering of whites and by the demand that they disarm, the militia retreated into a brick building, where they soon found themselves under siege by a mob of about two hundred men. Firing began; the first shots came from whites. A white man named McKie Meriwether was shot and died. Whites then fired with abandon, some even pulling a cannon over from Augusta. When the cannon was fired several times into the side of the building, some of the militia sought to escape by running from the building. Several were wounded and one was killed as they ran. The remaining militia, about thirty, surrendered. After these men were captured, members of the white mob summarily shot and killed about seven of the prisoners. This was the Hamburg riot or massacre, an event that assumed great political significance. The initial white response was one of shock and disapproval. After Governor Chamberlain's response, which tended to blame white South Carolinians in general, white spokesmen shifted to a mixture of disapproval and justification.[72]

Benjamin R. Tillman, younger brother of George Tillman and future nemesis of Wade Hampton, was one of the participants in the Hamburg riot. Tillman went to Hamburg on July 8 as a member of the Sweetwater Sabre Club. He later wrote of that event: "It was our purpose to attend the trial to see that the young men had protection and, if an opportunity offered, to provoke a row, and if one did not offer, we were to make one." He was a member of the group that fired on the fleeing blacks. Tillman was later proud of his role in the affair.[73]

Area newspapers stated their positions. The *Augusta Constitutionalist* editorialized, "That excesses were committed and disgraceful outrages occurred none will deny. The perpetrators should be brought to justice."[74] The Republican *Union Herald* informed its readers that there were "seven prisoners who were shot down like rabbits long after they surrendered." The *Union Herald* was correct in declaring that the cause of the violence was the demand that the militia yield its weapons. It is interesting that even this Republican paper, one of the owners of which was Governor Chamberlain, stated "the presence of armed bands of Negroes is a menace to any community."[75] The editor of the *Columbia Register* wrote, "We are far from justifying or apologizing for the killing of the men after they had surrendered and were powerless. We think that we can assure our readers that General Butler has nothing to do with such a deed as that." The editor was confident that Butler was "cool and circumspect, as he always is and not moved by any revengeful or passionate feeling." The *News and Courier* stated: "We find little, if any, excuse for the cowardly killing of the seven negro prisoners." Moving toward what would become a justification, the editor continued, "The presence of armed bodies of negroes is a threat to any community, but we do not understand that the danger was such as to justify the whites in demanding the surrender of the arms or in laying siege to the house in which the negroes took refuge and killing the negroes who sought to escape."[76]

The first accounts had M. C. Butler present through the entire fight, thereby placing him in at least quasi command and therefore quasi-responsible. Later reports, which Butler himself supported, had Hampton's political colleague leaving the scene before the prisoners were killed.[77] Butler told the press that he did not even know how many were killed. Butler insisted that he left just as the men were surrendering.[78] A writer for the *Union Herald* made a trenchant comment on Butler's claim to have been absent. "It was ever thus. He was far away from the frightful scene. That was what the 'best citizens' said when the Klan had been indiscreet to get caught in 1870–1871.

The privates went to Albany Penitentiary, while a leader remained at home to 'deplore' the 'rashness' of an 'infuriated crowd.'"[79]

Governor Chamberlain sent Attorney General Stone to investigate. Stone concluded that the order to surrender arms was without legal justification, and that M. C. Butler was in charge throughout the affair.[80] Francis Dawson, editor of the *News and Courier*, understood the political potential of the Hamburg riot, and he wrote in the July 13 edition: "to the unthinking masses, in such a county as Edgefield, the Mississippi plan is the Hamburg plan." Dawson feared the people of the North would interpret a straight-out Democratic ticket as a plan to win by intimidation,[81] which is precisely the charge made by Chamberlain and many others. Actually there is no direct evidence that the Hamburg riot was part of a planned strategy. However, the violence at Hamburg was a reflection of an attitude propelling the likes of Martin Gary and M. C. Butler and many in the white population. Ben Tillman later claimed that the Hamburg riot was part of a "policy of terrorizing the negroes at the first opportunity by letting them provoke trouble and then having the whites demonstrate their superiority by killing as many as was justifiable."[82] This statement, however, came years later when Tillman sought to gain credit for his racism and for his role in the campaign of 1876.

On July 20 the *News and Courier* expressed the hope that Governor Chamberlain would not use the incident at Hamburg as an excuse to involve federal troops "to prop up the waning fortunes of South Carolina Republicans."[83] On July 18 the *Columbia Register* reported that the governor had indeed requested federal intervention.[84] Chamberlain did not at this time request federal troops. He wrote to President Grant to inform him of his interpretation of recent events and to seek assurance that the general government would intervene if it proved necessary. Some of the governor's comments were quite perceptive. "Why do not the colored race return this violence with violence? Why do they suffer themselves to be terrorized, when their numbers greatly exceed those of their enemies in the localities where many of these outrages occur?" Chamberlain's explanation was that they, the black race, had been acclimated to white dominance by years of slavery. The governor noted that whites were the more intelligent, they owned four-fifths of the property, and they thus had the superior position of power. Perhaps of most interest in the year 1876, Chamberlain said that these acts of violence tended to frighten black voters away from the polls. He perceptively feared that the Hamburg riot foreshadowed "a campaign of blood and violence, such a campaign as is popularly known as the 'Mississippi plan.'" Federal intervention might become necessary to preserve good order.[85]

President Grant replied to the governor, promising to give all aid legally possible. There is little question of Grant's sympathy. He described the Mississippi campaign as having been one of "fraud and violence such as would scarcely be accredited to savages, much less a civilized and Christian people."[86] The president was, however, under intense pressure to avoid further use of troops in the South. Ohio Republicans warned Grant that if he sent troops into Mississippi their party would likely lose the next election in Ohio. Grant did not order troops into Mississippi, partly to save Ohio for his party.[87]

The coroner's report included M. C. Butler and Ben Tillman as participants in the Hamburg riot. The emergence of Tillman is of importance in the Hampton saga.[88] Tillman later with considerable pride confirmed his participation. The state brought charges of murder against seven of the whites and charges of being accessories before the fact against a large number of others, including M. C. Butler and Ben Tillman.[89] The Aiken bar offered their services in defense, but neither ever came to trial.

In the midst of these events there were calls for two significant conventions. The executive committee of the state Democratic Party issued a call for the next convention to meet on August 15, 1876.[90] Speaker of the South Carolina House, Robert B. Elliott, called for a meeting of black representatives to consider their situation since the Hamburg riot, "in view of the gross and unprovoked outrages that are daily committed upon our colored brethren throughout the state."[91] The responses to these calls for conventions are interesting. The *News and Courier* expressed regret that the Democrats would meet before the Republicans made their choice. The early meeting meant that the convention would almost surely decide on a straight-out policy.[92] The *Columbia Register* thought that the calling of an "indignation" meeting of black representatives was a mistake. The representatives will "exchange horrible stories, utter a great many denunciations, distort and pervert facts and perhaps succeed in provoking feeling against themselves instead of conciliating it."[93]

The black convention met and published their plea for national sympathy in pamphlet form, citing the oppression under which the black race lived in South Carolina and asking Governor Chamberlain to use all appropriate powers to bring the culprits, including M. C. Butler, to justice.[94] They believed the Hamburg massacre was part of a deliberate plan to intimidate the black population before the fall election.[95] Predictably the *Columbia Register* found the report of the black convention false. "The predominance of injury and wrong is mostly on the side against the whites."[96]

Upon learning more about Hamburg, Chamberlain became outspoken in his indignation and thereby removed himself from any real possibility of political support from white conservatives. A letter the governor had written to South Carolina senator Robertson was published and brought a sharp reaction. Chamberlain said the "victims at Hamburg were murdered in cold blood after they had surrendered and were utterly powerless." Insightfully, the governor wrote, "It is said, as usual, that the niggers were impudent." Chamberlain had no doubt that the whites were the aggressors.[97] The governor addressed a black audience and condemned the conduct of the whites at Hamburg. The *Columbia Register* complained that the governor was overlooking the "dozens of stealthy and bloody murders, hundreds of house burnings, robberies without number, and crimes without name," charging that these crimes were ignored because they were committed by the same people who kept the governor in office.[98]

Wade Hampton was not totally uninvolved in the politics leading to the Democratic Convention. Hampton wrote to Martin Gary that he intended to attend the convention, and he believed that it would decide on a straight-out ticket. General Hampton's division with Gary was essentially the disagreement between the moderate Hampton and the extremist Gary. In the letter of July 25, 1876, Hampton cautioned Gary, "We must be gentle with our Charleston friends, appealing to them to go with us. The *News and Courier* must either be made to sustain our policy or to quit the party [Democratic] which it is defeating and disgracing."[99] Hampton obviously favored a straight-out policy, and the *News and Courier* held out for fusion until the convention made its decision. In early August the Charleston paper rejoiced that Democratic clubs in Charleston, Orangeburg, and Sumter were supporting fusion.[100] Even the *Columbia Register*, which supported a straight-out policy, was cautious about the chances of Hampton being elected. A Marlboro planter wrote to the newspaper, "the name of General Hampton is electric, and will thrill through the nerves of every white man in South Carolina." The editor replied, "There is not a nobler being on earth than he." Yet the editor predicted that he would be defeated by the Republican majority.[101] Francis Dawson of the *News and Courier* also expressed admiration for Hampton, but he doubted that a former Confederate general could be elected in the face of a large black majority.[102] The *News and Courier* thought that the nomination of a former Confederate would be supplying capital to the radical Republicans of the North, and the party should nominate a civilian.[103] But General Hampton, like Dickens's Barkus, was "willing." On August 10 the general wrote to the *Columbia Register* to say that he favored a straight-out policy and that if the delegates thought he was the best candidate to bring the various elements into harmony, he would be willing to accept the nomination. The editor replied that he hoped that Hampton would not be the choice because he did not believe the general could be elected.[104]

It is of interest that the white community was at this time not unified in interpreting the Hamburg riot. The Democrats of Aiken County met on August 5 to elect their delegates to the state convention. That gathering of Democrats in the same county where the Hamburg riot had occurred resolved "that the killing of unarmed negroes following the collision between whites and blacks at Hamburg, in this county, on the 8th of July is, if true as alleged, a most atrocious crime and should be punished to the full extent of the law."[105] There was, however, a growing sense that the Hamburg riot had made the chance of a fusion between Democrats and Chamberlain quite unlikely. Gen. J. B. Kershaw wrote to the *Columbia Register* to indicate that he would not accept the Democratic nomination. He ventured that the "unhappy affair at Hamburg" left no alternative for the Democrats but straight-out policy.[106] After the Tillman regime was established, white South Carolinians tended toward unity in interpreting the Hamburg riot as a victory for the righteous cause of civilized society. Ben Tillman and M. C. Butler both claimed credit for leading whites at Hamburg.[107]

The Republicans staged a rally in Edgefield on August 13, and that gathering proved to be a harbinger of things to come. Governor Chamberlain, Congressman Smalls, Judge T. J. Mackey, and others were to address the faithful. About 1,500 black and white Republicans gathered in front of a stand at the academy just out of town. When the Republican dignitaries took the stand, some six hundred mounted whites rode up and demanded a division of time. The governor assented, and he spoke first, addressing the needs for reform. General Butler spoke next, bitterly denouncing the governor for charging him with being a leader of the Klan and for having been responsible for the killings at Hamburg. Butler told the audience that if Chamberlain and Smalls could not provide proof, they were liars. He denied any complicity in the murders at Hamburg. Judge Mackey then spoke to endorse Chamberlain. Martin Gary then gave what the press described as a "very hot speech," accusing the governor of corruption. Judge Mackey tried to answer those charges, but because of interruptions from Democrats in the audience he gave up. At this point, the speakers' stand collapsed, leaving only Butler upright, all to the merriment of the Democrats. The Chamberlain party then left, heckled by much of the crowd. A number of whites followed the governor's party to the rail station. One shouted, "There's our Congressman Smalls; let's kiss him." Others shouted, "Let's ask the Governor for a lock of his hair."[108]

The Democrats followed this pattern in many of the hustings of 1876. This was a part of the Mississippi plan adopted and followed by the more aggressive white conservatives, apparently never fully approved by Wade Hampton. Some of the mounted men wore red shirts, either adopted from the movement led by Giuseppe Garibaldi in his campaign for Italian nationalism or a takeoff from the political expression "waving the bloody shirt," meaning the Republican tactic of working up enthusiasm for that party by recalling the Republican leadership and sacrifices in the bloody Civil War. The red shirt became the popular uniform of the Democrats in this spirited contest. A. B. Williams, a participant in the campaign, wrote that the first regularly uniformed red shirts appeared in the rally at Newberry on September 18.[109]

The Hamburg riot was of political significance for many years. In early August the coroner's jury in Aiken County charged M. C. Butler and a number of others with murder, and they were to be arrested.[110] The political pressure was such that the defendants were released on bail of one thousand dollars and never brought to trial. In 1876 Butler heatedly denied having been responsible for the Hamburg killings. In the election campaign of 1894, when Butler was pitted against Ben Tillman in a race for the U.S. Senate, both he and his opponent vied for credit for the murder of blacks at Hamburg.[111] Racial attitudes had changed. In 1876 there was a chance that some blacks would indeed vote for the Democrats, and there was some national sympathy for the plight of black Southerners. By the 1890s the majority of white Democrats, partly because of the leadership of Ben Tillman, had given up on wooing black voters and were committed to a hard policy of proscription of all black political activity. Furthermore there was little national interest in the condition of the black race. This was the era of "manifest Anglo-Saxonism."

Meanwhile Democrats, especially M. C. Butler and Martin Gary, applied unrelenting pressure on General Hampton to accept the nomination for the office of governor. It is obvious that Butler and Gary thought they stood a much better chance in defeating the Republicans if their frontrunner was a man of the reputation of Wade Hampton. The plan was to nominate a man of unquestioned character who could represent the state in its best light while the campaign itself could use all of the tactics of intimidation that had been effective in the Mississippi campaign of the previous year. As the state celebrated the centennial of the Battle of Fort Moultrie in Charleston on June 28, General Hampton was the grand marshal of the parade, a role that reminded Butler and Gary of the prominence of the general. Hampton returned from Charleston to Columbia by train, and he rode in the same car with two fusionists, Johnson Hagood and J. B. Kershaw, and with the most outspoken advocates for the straight-out plan, Butler and Gary. Butler and Gary took this opportunity to pressure Hampton to agree to the nomination. They surely based their pleas on patriotic duty to the state. The general, still struggling to recoup the family fortune, was reluctant. He was certainly no longer a man of wealth, and such a race would necessarily be a sacrifice. Apparently, Hampton gave at least tentative assent, impelled by his sense of patriotic duty.[112]

The Democratic Executive Committee of Edgefield County adopted a plan of campaign modeled after the Mississippi experience. It became known in South Carolina as the Mississippi plan, the Edgefield plan, or the shotgun plan. The main tenets were that every Democrat should be a member of a Democratic club and:

> Each club should have a roster of every voter, white and black, in the township or region the club represented.
> Every club member should be armed [the clubs often became synonymous with the rifle clubs]. The clubs should have a military organization and supplies for three days' action.

The clubs should demand that at least one of the three election managers be a Democrat.

The clubs should have a representative present when the votes are counted and demand a duplicate of the results.

The clubs should send a committee to Columbia with the duplicates to ensure an accurate count by the State Board of Canvassers.

Every club should provide transportation for voters to the polls.

The clubs should be alert to prevent underage blacks from voting and to prevent multiple voting.

Every Democrat should control the vote of one black, either by intimidation, by purchase, or by keeping him from voting.

Democrats should attend every Republican meeting to demand a division of time to challenge their statements, call them liars, cheats, or thieves.

Democrats should realize that argument serves no purpose with blacks; they can only be influenced by fear and cupidity ("treat them so as to show them you are the superior race and that their natural position is that of subordinates to the white man").

Clubs should let it be known that they will hold radical leaders responsible for any bloodshed, any house burnings, and voting irregularities.

Members of the county executive committees will visit the area clubs.

There should be five mass meetings in the counties, concentrating on July and August.

The counties should choose good candidates, preferring native whites to carpetbaggers.

There will be no financial assessments until the cotton harvest.

All transactions should be secret.

The clubs should enroll boys from age sixteen and up.

The watch word would be "Fight the devil with fire."

Organize black Democratic clubs or pretend to have organized such clubs.

The uniform is the red shirt.[113]

Gary told his followers, "Never threaten a man indiscriminately if he deserves to be threatened, . . . for a threatened radical or one driven off by threats from the scene of his operations is very troublesome, sometimes dangerous, always vindictive. The necessities of [the situation may] . . . require that he should die."[114] Neither Hampton nor the state executive committee ever adopted this plan; yet it was important enough in the campaign of 1876 that those bloody tactics tainted them.

As the time for the next Democratic convention drew near, the various county Democratic organizations met and decided to support either a straight-out policy, which meant nominating a full slate at that meeting, or the fusion policy, which meant waiting on the Republican convention to see whether they nominated Chamberlain for a second term. The party in Abbeville County voted to watch and wait, Chester decided on the same policy, Beaufort voted for the straight-out policy, York wanted to watch and wait, Fairfield voted to watch and wait, and both Anderson and Richland voted to support the straight-out policy. The Richland party elected Wade Hampton as a delegate.[115]

The number of counties voting for the possibility of fusion notwithstanding, Chamberlain was during this time taking a position relative to the violence in Hamburg that made it less likely he would receive the support of conservative whites. On August 9 the *Union Herald* published the letter Governor Chamberlain had written to President Grant on July 22, in which he told the president he assumed that the whites demanded the militia yield their weapons because the militia was black and Republican. Chamberlain interpreted the Hamburg riot as part of a deliberate plan to terrorize blacks so that they would withdraw from political activity. He informed the president that the black population tended to be impotent in the face of aggressive whites because blacks had become accustomed to subservience. The governor speculated that in every community in the South there were a number of white men accustomed to violence and lawlessness, "over whom their betters have little influence." Chamberlain asked the president whether the general government was willing if necessary to send aid to suppress an insurrection.[116] On July 26 President Grant replied to the governor's letter, agreeing with Chamberlain in condemning the atrocities. Grant promised "to give every aid for which I can find law or constitutional power."[117] White conservatives could scarcely forgive these appeals for federal force to be used against South Carolina whites. In late August, Secretary of War J. D. Cameron, on the advice of President Grant, asked General Sherman, the commanding general of the U.S. Army, to be prepared to send troops to assist in preserving order in South Carolina. The *News and Courier* reported this to South Carolinians, and the paper indicated that two companies of the Eighteenth Infantry Regiment were being transferred from Atlanta to Edgefield County.[118] All of this helped to steel white conservatives to make a desperate campaign to defeat the radical regime.

Sen. John B. Gordon of Georgia became a gadfly for Democrats seeking redemption. He appeared in the South Carolina campaign from time to time until the state's redemption was completed. Gordon gave a speech in Alabama in the summer of 1876 in which he sought to set a tone of moderation for the Democrats. Speaking to an audience of Alabama blacks, he said, "You have had Democrats rule here in Alabama, and they have robbed you of none of your rights. Here the interests of the white man and the colored man are identical; a good government for one is a good government for the other."[119]

During much of the summer of 1876 General Hampton was at his lodge at Cashiers in North Carolina; from there he made his decision. He had attended the celebration of the centennial of the Battle of Fort Moultrie in late June and had been pressured on his return trip to accept the gubernatorial nomination. M. C. Butler continued the pressure by correspondence. Hampton's war comrade deliberately withheld details of the Mississippi plan he and his Edgefield clan had decided to pursue. Butler knew that Hampton would never agree to such a strategy.[120] The general's formal answer came in a letter to the *Columbia Register*, published on August 9. Hampton informed the people of South Carolina that he was opposed to any compromise with the Republican Party, but he would acquiesce in the policy decisions of the Democratic convention, whatever they might be. He indicated that a number of friends had urged him to accept the nomination for governor, but he was reluctant. Still, "I recognize, however, the paramount claim which the state has, in this supreme hour of her mortal suffering, when she is struggling not only for existence, but for all that makes life worth possessing, upon every son who loves her." He was willing to accept the nomination, sacrificial though that would be, if the convention chose him. The general hoped for unanimity. His purpose would be to redeem the "prostrate state."[121] The editor of the *News and Courier* commented on Hampton's letter: "We hope that General Hampton will not be nominated, because we do not believe it possible to elect him." The editor promised, however, to support the general if he became the nominee.[122]

The Democrats convened in Columbia on August 15. It soon became clear that the straight-outs would have their way. Wade Hampton was a delegate; so were M. C. Butler, Mart Gary, and James Conner. The editor of the *News and Courier*, Francis Dawson, was not there.[123] The next day General Butler nominated Wade Hampton to be the Democratic candidate for governor. Hampton replied with reluctance but a willingness to accept the will of the party. The general noted that because of his military record his nomination might hurt the national Democratic campaign. "These are grave topics, gentlemen, and I implore you to look over the whole field and not let any kindness for me lead you astray." He left the convention so that the discussion would be free of any hesitancy to discuss his strengths and weaknesses. The party made an overwhelming decision for the general. He accepted and then set the tone for the campaign: "Let us bear and forbear, work and pray, and devote ourselves to the cause with the fire and impetuosity of the Southern nature."[124] He promised his best efforts for decency, honesty, economy, and integrity. The convention proceeded to select a full slate, a straight-out ticket: R. M. Sims of York for secretary of state, Hugh S. Thompson of Richland for superintendent of education, W. D. Simpson of Laurens for lieutenant governor, Johnson Hagood of Barnwell for comptroller general, E. W. Moise of Sumter for adjutant and inspector general, and James Conner of Charleston for attorney general.[125] The *News and Courier* described the gubernatorial candidate as a moderate in all things.[126]

Recent Democratic victories in the Deep South gave the South Carolina party genuine hope, despite the significant black majority. The *Columbia Register* quoted a Columbus, Georgia, newspaper in considering the recent Democratic win in Alabama: "It will cause exertions to be redoubled by all Democrats. South Carolina may even be won."[127] The Republican *Union Herald* published a letter from "a colored man" that gave the Democrats good advice. The writer was disturbed that no white man was speaking up for the black people of South Carolina. He was disappointed that a man as "high toned and magnanimous" as General Hampton argued for no compromise, no fusion. This correspondent thought that if the Democrats appealed for black votes, there would be no need for intimidation or bribery in the coming election.[128] Thoughts such as the one expressed by this black correspondent influenced Democratic policy makers, but so did the thoughts of those promoting the shotgun policy. It is significant that on a motion by Martin Gary, Gen. Samuel Ferguson of Mississippi was given the privilege of the floor at the South Carolina convention. Ferguson also spoke to a celebration after the convention, advising South Carolinians from experiences in Mississippi.[129]

The platform of the South Carolina Democratic Party accepted in good faith the Thirteenth, Fourteenth, and Fifteenth Amendments. The party endorsed the national platform and the candidacies of Samuel Tilden of New York for president and Thomas A. Hendricks of Indiana for vice president. The platform indicated the Democratic belief that no real reform could come from the Republican Party, which had been responsible for fraudulent elections, mismanagement of the state's finances, exorbitant taxes, and poor management of charitable and penal institutions.[130]

Ironically, while the Democratic convention was in session, the *Columbia Register* published reports from the committee of the U.S. Senate designated to investigate the Mississippi election of the previous year. The majority report found that the Mississippi election was "carried by systematized outrages and intimidation." The minority report, written by Sen. Thomas Francis Bayard of Delaware, blamed preexisting conditions in Mississippi for any violence that might have occurred during the campaign. Bayard noted, "Every murderer and ravisher convicted in the state was pardoned for money."[131] That was of course much like the South Carolina rationalization for white violence.

After the nominations by the Democratic convention, the red-shirt campaign began in earnest. Edward Wells, who served with Hampton in the war and who knew and admired the general, in his *Hampton and Reconstruction*, certainly not a work of detached objectivity, stated the case for the campaign succinctly and even poignantly: "As to fraud, it is true that the prostitution of the principle of free suffrage had been so complete, the ignorance and corruption of the Negro voters had been so flagrant and shameless for a decade past, and the cheating in counting votes so patent—the entire thing such a farce and tragedy combined—that it could not but bring into contempt the very name of voting. It cannot be wondered at that, under such circumstances, many, indignant and disgusted, should, under the temptation of the issues involved, be carried away by the sophistry that the end justifies the means, and imitate, as far as able, the practices of the adversaries."[132]

The campaign of 1876 proceeded, and it was surely the most spirited engagement of the voting public in South Carolina history to that time. Ironically the next such demonstration of frenzied popular excitement would be the Tillman campaign of 1890, which lowered the curtain on the Hampton era. There was a political rally in Columbia on August 16, complete with a torch light parade in which mounted rifle clubs played a major role, including the Hampton Sabre Club. The parade ended the at the state house grounds, where Hampton and a number of other Democratic stalwarts addressed the crowd. Among the speakers were Colonel Ferguson of Mississippi, M. C. Butler, and Martin Gary. There were several transparencies, one with a picture of General Hampton and beneath the picture, "We Take Ours Straight"; another read "The State's True, Tried, and Trusted Son."[133]

Those conservatives pushing the Mississippi strategy wanted Democrats attending every Republican meeting to challenge radical spokesmen, to intimidate the Republicans, especially black Republicans. Conservatives wanted to make the Republican candidates look corrupt, weak, and even hopeless in the face of the onslaught by determined white Democrats. The usual scheme was to learn where the Republicans were to hold a rally, then get the word out for rifle clubs, Democratic clubs, and even whites not members of any organization to appear at the right time at the opponents' rally. When the Republican meeting was about to begin, a large number of mounted whites would appear, many wearing red shirts and perhaps armed. The horsemen would ride next to the speakers' platform, encircle it, making a threatening cordon between the speakers and their sympathetic audience. The white leaders would demand a division of time, ostensibly giving each side an equal opportunity to discuss the issues of the canvass. In actuality, the whites often shouted down the Republican spokesmen, challenging their statements, insulting them, even threatening violence, but never actually committing a physical offense, denying the opposition the excuse to request the protection of federal troops.

A Republican meeting in Barnwell can serve as an example of the red-shirt strategy. The Republican leadership decided to conduct a rally of the faithful in what had been a Republican stronghold. In the election of 1874, radicals carried Barnwell County by a margin of 1,500 votes. This therefore should have been a friendly gathering. Governor Chamberlain was to be the chief speaker. As the rally was about to begin, a large number of mounted men rode up and took positions around the platform. The governor spoke for about an hour, during which he was interrupted several times by impertinent questions from the Democrats. The whites demanded a division of time and the governor yielded. The first conservative speaker was W. Gilmore Sims, who called the governor "a carrion crow, a buzzard who came down to prey upon our people and steal from them their substance." Then came a loud rebel yell. The Republican judge R. B. Carpenter then strove to speak above shouted questions and taunts. The next conservative speaker was George Tillman, candidate for Congress from the Fifth District. The prominent black Robert Smalls then occupied that congressional seat. Tillman sought to incite his followers and frighten his opponents by pointing to the governor and Judge Carpenter and saying, "Why don't you hang 'em? Hang 'em now! Begin at once and if you men of Barnwell are too cowardly to do it, send a telegram to Edgefield and I will guarantee enough of trusty men to come here and do it for you." Incredibly the meeting broke up quietly, but understandably many in the audience were sufficiently intimidated to question whether they wanted to support the Chamberlain ticket openly.[134]

On August 25 the Democrats held a huge rally in Charleston. There was again a torchlight parade and brilliant transparencies; one read, "Hampton Will Wade In," and another quoted the general: "We recognize the change in the Constitution, and we propose to obey the laws like good citizens."[135] Rifle clubs played a major role in the Democratic campaign. Governor Chamberlain came to understand that the clubs were indistinguishable from clubs of the Democratic Party and were responsible for much of the intimidation of black and white Republicans. Chamberlain eventually banned these organizations, but they had not always been in disfavor with the radical governor. As late as June 28, 1876, Governor Chamberlain and General Hampton were guests of honor at a Palmetto Day celebration hosted by the Palmetto Rifle Club. At the end of the celebration, the club gave the governor three cheers.[136]

Conservative whites did not interrupt every Republican meeting. The Republican *Union Herald* reported a peaceful meeting of the faithful in Winnsboro at which there were present a total of 1,500 people, of which approximately 300 were Democrats. The conservatives apparently conducted themselves with unwonted courtesy. The newspaper indicated in what was probably a biased reading, "After the meeting, the Governor was entertained and called upon by a number of the best conservative citizens of the town, who expressed their confidence in his desire to work for the good of the whole people."[137]

As much as Martin Gary was determined to prevent black votes, General Hampton was determined to convince a number of blacks to leave the party of Lincoln and vote for the Democratic ticket. Some have suspected that this was a conscious plan, something of a "bad cop–good cop routine": Gary and his followers would practice threats and violence to keep away black voters while Hampton presented the case for equal treatment for blacks under a Democratic regime, which would have the added benefit of being free of corruption. To have participated in such a devious scheme was completely out of character with Wade Hampton. Nothing in his long career would give credence to such a possibility. He was anything but disingenuous. Furthermore, there is some evidence to belie this charge. A significant enmity developed between Hampton and Gary, and an important part of that enmity was the difference between their attitudes toward the black race. Samuel J. Martin, a recent biographer of M. C. Butler, found that Butler deliberately withheld from Hampton the harsher side of the Edgefield plan (another name for the Mississippi or shotgun policy). Martin concluded that Hampton and Butler were "forever estranged" because of Butler's deceit in keeping his senior uninformed about the dark side of the campaign of 1876. This biographer concludes that the relationship between the two was thereafter one of a "chilly peace" in which they occasionally worked together effectively and were occasionally friendly in part because they sometimes had a common enemy.[138]

In every speech during the campaign Wade Hampton promised the black people of South Carolina equal treatment in the forthcoming Democratic government. He often reminded his audiences that he had been an early advocate of black suffrage. "I shall be the governor of the whole people." He promised improved public schools, and he pledged support of the Thirteenth, Fourteenth, and Fifteenth Amendments to the constitution. Hampton often said, "If there is a white man in this assembly [who] because he is a Democrat or because he is a white man believes that when I am elected governor, if I should be, that I will stand between him and the law or grant him privileges or immunities that shall not be granted to the colored man, he is mistaken, and I tell him so now that if that is his reason for voting for me, not to vote at all."[139] Hampton's promising equal treatment meant political equality, not social equality, and even in the consideration of political equality Hampton assumed that he and others of "the better classes of whites" could shape the political activities of black people. Hampton had stated, not in a speech, "As the Negro becomes more intelligent he naturally allies himself with the more conservative of the whites."[140] It behooves modern students of this era to remember the relative attitudes of South Carolinians of this time. While Wade Hampton's attitude was assuredly one of paternalism, the comparison should not be between Hampton and the liberal of the late twentieth and early twenty-first centuries, but with others of his time. W. W. Ball, an earlier student of the Hampton era, wrote, "The other type of South Carolinian was a dull brute who killed negroes without provocation, who hated all negroes and shot one on the roadside to slake his bloodthirst."[141] In his acceptance speech to the Democratic convention Hampton had said, "I shall be governor of the whole people, knowing no party, making no vindictive discrimination, holding the scales of justice with firm and impartial hand, seeing, as far as in me lies, that laws are enforced in justice tempered by mercy, protecting all classes alike, and devoting every effort to the restoration of prosperity and the re-establishment of honest government."[142] This then was the contrast between the paternalistic General Hampton and the more racist whites.

General Hampton obviously did not attend all Democratic rallies; there were many without him, and those without the general tended to be more threatening, the Barnwell rally, for example. In late August there was a Republican rally in Newberry at which Chamberlain spoke. Hampton not being there, J. N. Lipscomb gave the Democratic response to the governor. The *Union Herald* described Lipscomb's speech as a harangue in which "all decency was abandoned."[143] Yet the Democrats were not abusive at every encounter with their opposition. The *Union Herald* reported on a rally in Camden at which Col. William Shannon and Gen. John D. Kennedy gave the Democratic response to Governor Chamberlain. The Republican paper noted the Democrats "uttered no single word of abuse of any individual."[144] Kennedy and Shannon were of Hampton's class. In 1880 E. B. C. Cash killed Shannon in a duel.

Hampton made a constant appeal to black citizens, and there was at least some response. The actual total cannot be determined and has been the subject of much debate. Even in Walhalla, where the black population was a small minority, Hampton promised equal treatment for all citizens.[145] The Republicans planned a rally for August 26 in Manning. When the Democrats learned of the Manning meeting, they canceled plans for a rally of their party so that they could attend the opposition gathering. At the Manning rally Democrats demanded and achieved a division of time. One of the conservative spokesmen was a black man named Matt Brooks.[146] The Democrats often made a point of having a number of blacks in the parade of mounted red shirts. There were even a number of black red shirt clubs. In Barnwell County Sandy Sanders, a black man of undisputed courage, organized a black red shirt club of about 100 members. By the end of the campaign there were a total of eighteen black Democratic clubs with a membership totaling 668. Black bands performed for a number of the Hampton rallies.[147]

The possibility of black citizens voting Democratic was of considerable importance in the campaign. It is not possible to determine precisely how many black South Carolinians voted for Wade Hampton. Chamberlain thought that only about three thousand blacks voted for the Democratic candidate. Hampton thought that the number could have been as high as seventeen thousand. Edmund L. Drago, the author of a recent study of this subject, estimates the number to have been about five thousand, which was indeed enough to have given Hampton the margin of victory.[148] Still, a number of authors discount the significance of the black vote. W. W. Ball wrote, "With rare exceptions the bolder and more aspiring black men stood by their party, and many of the negro Democrats were of the lazy, good-natured . . . most expectant of tips from white people." Ball told a story from his family of someone offering to pay black voters to spend election day at home. Only one accepted the offer.[149] Blacks who considered voting for the Democratic Party were subjected to threats from their own race. Black women were especially determined to keep their men faithful to the party of Lincoln, often threatening to have nothing to do with the men "unmanly" enough to consider voting with conservative whites. Some Democratic blacks were attacked and beaten.[150] On August 25 the editor of the *Columbia Register* urged Democrats to protect black Democrats from threats from their own race.[151] Blacks wanting to support the Republican Party were subjected to threats of violence from Martin Gary's followers and, perhaps most effectively, threatened with economic discrimination by the more wealthy whites. The Aiken County Democrats met in early August and resolved to do no business with Republicans, even to fire all employees who intended to vote for radicals.[152] Other Democrats followed this plan, and that was probably the most effective form of intimidation. On October 2 the *News and Courier* urged its readers, "If you want a porter, employ a Democrat; if you want a driver, employ a Democrat."[153] Hampton disclaimed any responsibility for this tactic.[154]

General Hampton was reputed to have been a kindly, paternalistic slave owner, the kind of master people of the aristocratic class usually aspired to be. Rev. Francis Davie, a former Hampton slave, wrote this letter to the general:

Dear Marse Wade:
Seeing you are nominated for governor by the white people and hearing you have promised the black man all the rights he now has, and knowing you were always a good and kind man to me when your slave and knowing you are a good and kind man who will do what he promises. I write to say that I will vote for you and will get all the black men I can to do the same. I have bought a piece of land in York county and am trying to make a support for my family which I can do if we have good laws and taxes.
My wife, Flora, is living and we have but one child whom we wish to educate. Please write to me, care of Dr. T. C. Robertson, Rock Hill, S.C.
Your friend and former slave,
Rev. Francis Davie[155]

This was of course precisely the image Hampton wanted to project to his black audiences. There is reason to believe that it had a limited effect in the charged atmosphere of 1876, but even a small effect could have been important in the outcome of the election. The general read the Davie letter in a number of his speeches.

In late August, Governor Chamberlain announced he was appointing the commissioners of election for each county, and he intended to appoint two Republicans and one Democrat to each commission. Since the Republicans had a clear majority, this was a fair decision. The governor assured the public, "I intend to appoint only fair minded and just men." He asked for suggestions.[156]

There came in this time an important indication that states with radical governments badly needed to achieve stability. The trustees of the Peabody Fund met at White Sulphur Springs and decided not to offer any grants to South Carolina or to Florida "until there is a change in their state governments."[157] The Peabody Fund became an important effort to lift the defeated South to its feet. The refusal to consider these two states was another indication that the North had tired of the efforts of radical Reconstruction.

The possibility that some blacks would support the Hampton ticket was an inflammatory issue with both races. The Hampton and Tilden Colored Clubs met on September 6 in Archer's Hall in Charleston. The black hatred for any of their race drawn to the Democrats brought on a fracas. The Live Oak and Hunkadory (black Republican) clubs faced the Democrats as two mobs. There was some firing of weapons from both sides, resulting in one white man being mortally wounded.[158] The Republican *Union Herald* denounced threats from the black Republicans. "We denounce the conduct of the rioters who attempted to ill treat men because of their political action."[159] The white leaders disagreed about whether there should even be attempts to attract black voters.

While most black citizens saw the Republican Party as their champions, worthy of loyal support, a number of blacks were disillusioned with the Republicans because of their record of corruption. In a remarkable demonstration of objectivity the Republican *Union Herald* on September 12 commented that the radical-controlled states of Florida and South Carolina were the "two worst-ruled states in the union."[160]

The *News and Courier*, under the editorship of Francis Dawson, jettisoned objectivity after the Democratic convention and threw its full weight behind the campaign of Hampton and company. On July 13 Dawson had ventured that a straight-out strategy could win only by the use of "fraud or force."[161] On July 20 the editor announced his change of heart. "We have supported Governor Chamberlain's reform measures, and we have frankly expressed our opinions of the Hamburg riot, but must protest against any move which wears the appearance of taking advantage of a local disturbance to prop up the waning fortunes of South Carolina Republicanism."[162] Dawson even defended the whites in the Hamburg riot. By December 1876 the editor described the Republican governor as a "chameleon, taking the hue of what he feeds on."

Both Chamberlain and Dawson had entered the year 1876 as moderates, and both had been drawn to opposite extremes, one of the real tragedies of this drama.[163]

With the passage of time both parties worked themselves into a frenzy, but because of the intimidation by white conservatives, white enthusiasm was more effective. After a Democratic rally in Belton, a correspondent wrote, "Politics are all the go now-a-days in our county. The Democrats have entered the campaign with vim and determination."[164] This is not to conclude that black Republicans had no determination. At a radical meeting at Macedonia Church, black horsemen initially surrounded the site and would not allow mounted whites to enter. After some negotiations, whites were allowed to divide time with their opponents.[165]

On September 2 General Hampton formally launched his campaign with a rally in Anderson. Every store was closed to allow maximum participation in the parade, which concluded at the Collegiate Institute. Hampton told the Anderson audience that he had assured his black workers in Mississippi they would retain all of their rights under the Democratic regime. W. D. Simpson, the Democratic candidate for lieutenant governor, followed Hampton (there was no division of time with Republicans), and he made similar promises to black citizens. Then came rallies in Walhalla and Pickens, complete with torchlight parades.[166] At the rally in Greenville there was a transparency showing the goddess of liberty with sword in hand and with shackles falling to the ground. The body of Chamberlain lay on the ground. The printed message was "The Prostrate State."[167]

A writer for the *Columbia Register* reported on September 9 that radical leadership was encouraging secret meetings of their faithful and avoidance of joint discussion.[168] In truth, Republicans were somewhat intimidated by their opponents. Chamberlain made fewer appearances thereafter; conservative enthusiasm was having effect. Chamberlain was scheduled to speak in Marion on September 8, but he declined.[169] Hampton ridiculed his opponent for not appearing on the same platform to discuss the issues.[170]

The Democratic campaign became a smooth operation. The ubiquitous senator John B. Gordon of Georgia appeared with Hampton at the Spartanburg rally. In Greenville former governor Benjamin F. Perry, who had earlier declared South Carolina to be a white man's government, introduced Hampton who promised that if elected he would know "no race, no party, no color."[171]

The Republican convention began on September 12 in the hall of the House of Representatives. Chamberlain secured the nomination for a second term, but not without opposition. Robert B. Elliott nominated T. C. Dunn to oppose Chamberlain, and in his speech the black Speaker of the House of Representatives read a letter in which Chamberlain said that he was running for office to keep South Carolina from being run down by "Negroism." Elliott also charged that the governor had overstepped the bounds of the law in denying commissions to Moses and Whipper. When Chamberlain secured the nomination, he pleaded with the convention to complete the ticket with men who were sympathetic with his plan of reform. "If I am not surrounded by such men, it will be a difficult question for me to determine whether it will be worthwhile for me to undertake to carry the canvass." The governor's plea notwithstanding, the Republicans completed their ticket by nominating R. H. Gleaves for another term as lieutenant governor, F. L. Cardozo as treasurer, R. B. Elliott as attorney general, James Kennedy as adjutant and inspector general, and T. C. Dunn as comptroller general.[172] Walter Allen, the author of a study of the Chamberlain administration, commented, "Probably nothing did more to perfect the consolidation of the Democratic Party and destroy all hope of support for Governor Chamberlain from that quarter than the nomination of R. B. Elliott for Attorney General, and the re-nomination of Comptroller General Dunn. Both of these men had been pronounced as bitter enemies of reform." Years later Chamberlain wrote to the famous abolitionist William Lloyd Garrison that he, Chamberlain, had made a grave mistake in not refusing to run on the same ticket as R. B. Elliott. "His presence on the ticket gave offense to honest men of both races."[173] The animosity between Elliott and the reformist Chamberlain can be misleading. Elliott, too, had claims to political integrity. In the 1872 race with the notorious "Honest John" Patterson for election to the U.S. Senate, Elliott refused to be bribed and lost the election.[174]

As to the Chamberlain letter in which he referred to the dangers of "Negroism," there is not much doubt that, his support of black suffrage notwithstanding, the governor shared many of the racial prejudices of the rest of white America of his time. His prejudices, like those of mainline America, hardened as the years passed. In 1901 in an article for the *Atlantic Monthly* he stated his belief that a victory by his party in 1876 would have foisted on the state a government not "fit to be endured."[175] Still, in the heat of the campaign of 1876, the Republican governor spoke out bravely for the cause of the black citizens. To a Beaufort audience he said, "If I had to choose between an ignorant ballot and an educated ballot controlled by prejudice, I would say give me the free ballot and I can make it an intelligent ballot. The only way to work out of the difficulties which now surround us is to accept freedom for every man in all its length and breadth and trust that freedom will build up and lead the people into intelligence, frugality, and all the civic virtues."[176]

The platform of the South Carolina Republican Party pledged support for the ticket of Rutherford B. Hayes and William A. Wheeler and expressed appreciation for the administration of U. S. Grant, "so honestly and economically conducted." The party condemned the conservative strategy of disrupting Republican meetings. In keeping with the tradition of progressivism in the radical regime, the platform endorsed the reform of biennial sessions of the legislature and line-item veto for the governor.[177]

The relationship between the candidates Wade Hampton and Samuel J. Tilden proved to be one of the more controversial aspects of the campaign of 1876. Hampton understood at the time of the state convention that his nomination might be something of an embarrassment to the national party. Some elements of the national party had flirted with treason during the war, and having a prominent Confederate general seeking the gubernatorial chair in South Carolina might aid the Republicans in waving the "bloody shirt." After his nomination Hampton wrote to Tilden to assure him that they could work together for the good of the national and state parties. Tilden never answered the letter, and the national party refused to give any financial support to its South Carolina partisans.[178] The Palmetto State, which had led in secession, was indeed a pariah state in the nation's view. There is no question that Hampton saw his primary responsibility was to win in this state. He even said, "It is not Tilden we are working so much for as relief from the rule of the robbers here at home."[179] On September 19 Hampton wrote to Manton Marble, a close associate of Tilden, "Of course we are anxious to aid in the general election, but you can understand our solicitude to find out how we can best do this. The Committee [the South Carolina Democratic Executive Committee] say they can get no suggestions from the National Committee and even no reply to communications. This has discouraged them and they are at a loss what to do. . . . The vote of the state can be secured for Tilden, and I think that we can have a quiet election if we can raise funds to preserve the peace."[180]

When Martin Gary became an avowed enemy of Wade Hampton, the Edgefield Democrat leveled a number of charges against the general. One of those charges was that Hampton had betrayed the Democratic Party by actually joining in a plot with representatives of the national Republican Party to support the election of the Hayes-Wheeler slate of electors from South Carolina. Gary was angry about Hampton's oft-repeated statement, "So help me God! I am no party man." Gary recalled that the straight-out Democrats had nominated Hampton, and the nominee was guilty of appealing to Republicans, especially black Republicans.[181] Although it is not likely that Hampton was in a conspiracy to support Hayes and Wheeler, it is true that he scarcely mentioned the national ticket in his speeches, and when one considers the lack of interest from the national Democratic Party there is little wonder that Hampton responded with less than enthusiasm. This also made it easier for Hampton to refrain from contesting the victory of the state's Republican electors. In a number of his speeches he made it clear that blacks could vote for the South Carolina Democrats and for the Hayes-Wheeler electors if they felt so moved.[182]

There was indeed some affinity between Hampton and Rutherford B. Hayes. Hampton's general philosophical beliefs were essentially those of a Whig, although he had never been a member of that party. Wade Hampton II was an active Whig, but thanks to the dominance of John C. Calhoun, the Whig Party was not a real choice for the third Hampton. When Hayes and others like him in the Republican Party wanted to appeal to white conservatives in the South they thought their most likely prospects were leaders such as Hampton who had Whiggish roots. The Republican efforts to attract conservative whites did not succeed in that generation, but Southern conservative Democrats developed a longstanding tradition of voting with Republicans on many issues.

The Democratic rally in Abbeville on September 15 became important in the internal struggles in the party, in part because of the appeal for Republican support. Gen. Robert Toombs of Georgia was the guest speaker. He was followed by a show of support from the other party. Circuit Court Judge J. Thompson Cook, a Republican, spoke to endorse General Hampton. Cook had been elected to replace James L. Orr, when Orr vacated the office to become minister to St. Petersburg. Circuit Court Judge Thomas J. Mackey, another Republican, also came over to Hampton's side. The support of the judiciary became an important part of the Democratic victory. Judge Cook was especially critical of the Republicans for having R. B. Elliott on the ticket.[183]

The Ellenton riot occurred on the day after the Republicans nominated Chamberlain for his second term. The riot continued for several days, and resulted in the deaths of between thirty and forty black men, including Simon P. Coker, a member of the state legislature. Two white men were killed and a number wounded. It began when two black men invaded the home of Mrs. Alonzo Harlee, whose husband was working in the fields. Mrs. Harlee chased the men away with a gun. The Harlees then sounded the alarm, and white men gathered, armed and mounted. Johnson Hagood, a prominent Hampton ally, received authority from the sheriff to organize a posse comitatus. The white posse confronted an armed group of black men, and they engaged in a firefight. The black men vented their anger by destroying railroad property and several houses and gin buildings, and the whites hunted down the black men, who hid in the woods. A company of U.S. infantry finally restored peace.

The recurrence of violence—the riot in Charleston instigated by blacks on September 6 and the Ellenton riot begun on September 19—moved federal authorities to take action. Gen. Thomas H. Ruger, in command of the Department of the South, moved his headquarters to Columbia. He then moved several infantry units from Columbia to outlying districts.[184]

A. C. Haskell, chairman of the State Democratic Executive Committee, wrote a public letter to Governor Chamberlain, charging him with seeking federal troops to aid the Republican cause. He further asked the governor to deny the rumor published in New York newspapers that the governor of South Carolina was going to purchase twenty thousand stands of weapons to arm the black people of his state.[185] Hampton joined in this attack by stating in his speeches that if the governor could not maintain order he should resign so the Democrats could achieve stability.[186] Chamberlain replied in a public letter, denying that he had sought the intervention of federal troops and charging the Democrats with responsibility for the Hamburg riot. He stated that he was not sure who had instigated the Ellenton riot, but he noted that most of the dead were black.[187]

The next day the governor issued a proclamation ordering rifle clubs as armed combinations operating illegally in the state to disband and cease to exist. Chamberlain gave the clubs three days to obey his order; that failing, he would proceed to raise the necessary force to restore order. The proclamation implied that the governor would suspend the writ of habeas corpus, should that be required to achieve peace. The state Democratic Executive Committee replied immediately, stating that the state was in a period of "profound peace." The committee charged that blacks incited the Ellenton riot.

General Hampton entered this argument by writing a public letter to Chief Justice F. J. Moses, asking him whether in his opinion there was such unrest in the state to justify the governor's proclamation. The chief justice replied that his observations were limited to Sumter and Richland counties, but he had seen no evidence of violence in that part of the state. A. C. Haskell wrote similar letters to Associate Justice A. J. Willard and to Circuit Court Judges T. J. Mackey and Thompson H. Cook, and all replied that they had observed no violence. Judge Mackey went beyond saying that he had observed no violence. "I solemnly protest against the proclamation of Governor Chamberlain as absolutely false." The *News and Courier* noted that the white men charged with crimes at Hamburg and Ellenton were ready to stand trial.[188] T. J. Mackey, who had earlier supported Chamberlain, became a staunch Hampton ally.

In the face of violence obvious to later scholars, it is not easy to understand these statements from respectable citizens. While blacks were responsible for some of the violence, there is no doubt that their race suffered the most. Only a partial explanation can be offered. The campaign operated on two separate levels, one led by Hampton avoiding violence but tolerating implicit intimidation by the mounted red shirts and the other led by Mart Gary avowedly encouraging threats and actual violence. The fact that the South Carolina press was in the main controlled by Democrats made it possible to present the violence as black inspired and of little consequence. Even the Republican *Union Herald* presented the opinions of whites, for example, assuming that the arming of blacks was more dangerous to the peace than the presence of white rifle clubs. How does one understand Wade Hampton as a man of integrity tolerating such violence against blacks? He later testified that he had spoken at fifty-seven rallies, and "I never saw an organized armed body of men at any of those meetings."[189] The majority report of the U.S. Senate committee that was charged to investigate the election of 1876 concluded that "General Hampton took no part in the campaign [terror]. . . . General Hampton was not permitted to hear any one urge violence, nor did he ever see any armed man, nor did he personally know of any physical violence or unlawful intimidation."[190] The growing enmity between the general and Gary indicated that Hampton was not comfortable with the shotgun policy. He apparently thought that winning the campaign was important enough to keep disagreements within the Democratic Party below the surface. Perhaps most important is the fact that the people of South Carolina had worked themselves into a warlike frenzy, and wars often make the end justify the means. Add to this that much of the North had tired of the whole mess of Reconstruction. Both the *New York Sun* and the *New York World* reported that Chamberlain had given up on reform.[191]

A. C. Haskell, chairman of the State Democratic Executive Committee, wrote to R. B. Elliott, chairman of the Republican Executive Committee, to challenge the opposing party to conduct joint meetings for debate of the issues. Elliott initially offered to meet with the Democrats in five places in the upcountry and five in the lowcountry. When the Democrats refused to make any changes in their schedule, these negotiations fell apart.[192]

On October 16 the *News and Courier* reported accurately that Governor Chamberlain had requested federal troops.[193] The prospective involvement of federal troops became an explosive issue. President Grant issued a proclamation recognizing that there were combinations in South Carolina threatening the peace, and he ordered rifle clubs to disband. Secretary of War J. D. Cameron instructed Gen. W. T. Sherman to order all available troops to report to General Ruger in South Carolina.[194] The Democratic Executive Committee responded in a published letter: "We know that our homes are in peril and that our women and children are exposed to the horrors of ruthless butchers and barbarity. But, nevertheless, we advise and command, so far as our authority goes, that every such rifle club . . . be disbanded, and that the members thereof be held in future only by ties of humanity which bind all men together."[195] Rifle clubs continued underground, often mockingly changing their names. One club in Columbia became the "Hampton and Tilden Musical Club with Twelve Pound Flutes." Others became "Tilden's Mounted Baseball Clubs."[196] The *News and Courier* commented that the purpose of the federal troops was not so much to ensure that blacks voted according to their convictions as to ensure they voted Republican.[197]

The rifle clubs were a formidable force. In a letter to the *New York Times*, dated October 25, 1876, Governor Chamberlain estimated that there were in

South Carolina 213 rifle clubs with an average membership of sixty, totaling between sixteen thousand and eighteen thousand. Chamberlain thought that the clubs had killed fifteen Republicans, whipped several hundreds, and threatened thousands.[198] *Harper's Weekly* ventured, "There is no more doubt that it is the purpose of Wade Hampton and his associates to suppress and destroy the colored vote than there was of their intention formerly to carry slavery into the territories. The rifle club and Ku Klux are simply suckers from the root of slavery."[199] These comments would seem to indicate that Chamberlain had the backing of the North, but ultimately that was not true.

During this time federal troops were dispersed to a number of locations in the state. In mid-October General Ruger assigned Company G of the Eighteenth Infantry Regiment, commanded by Lt. R. F. Bates, to Newberry. There were then fourteen separate posts in the state.[200] It is not possible to measure the effect of the presence of federal troops, but it is safe to assume that black Republicans were encouraged by the evidence of support from Washington. On the other hand, the spectacle of large numbers of mounted red shirts was intended to overawe blacks by the appearance of such white power. James Conner, who campaigned closely with Hampton, thought that the federal troops counterbalanced the effect of the red shirts and significantly reduced the number of blacks who voted for Hampton.[201]

The Democratic campaign continued with increasing momentum. A number of prominent black citizens announced support for Hampton. Martin Delany, the reform candidate for lieutenant governor in 1874, and Stephney Riley, a well-known stable owner in Charleston, "crossed Jordan" to the conservative side, and the Democrats made the most of it.[202] Part of the strategy was to emphasize, even exaggerate, the number of blacks who came out for Hampton.

A number of the state's most prominent citizens published a letter to "The People of the United States," stating the case for the conservative cause. "For ten long years the white people of South Carolina have endured a condition of things which any Northern state would have been tempted to throw off in two years at the point of a bayonet. At last there is a determined effort. It is not true that South Carolina is in insurrection, nor is the state disloyal to the United States, nor do the white people intend hostility to the colored people of the state. The rifle clubs are not outlaws. The president has been deceived." The letter stated that black people incited the acts of violence, especially near Charleston. The letter recalled that Governor Chamberlain had not long ago feared that "the civilization of the Puritan and the cavalier, of the Roundhead and Huguenot is in peril." The writers insisted that the peril was even greater in 1876. The authors of this letter included Bishop W. M. Wightman of the Methodist Church, Bishop W. B. W. Howe of the Episcopal Diocese of South Carolina, the Catholic bishop

P. M. Lynch; several Lutheran, Baptist, Presbyterian, and Reformed Episcopal clergy; and several bank presidents.[203] It was in all an impressive array of leaders who subscribed to the leadership of Hampton.

Hampton urged his followers to treat the federal soldiers as friends and make them ambassadors for the state. General Hampton told his followers that these troops "were no longer our enemies, but are the best friends we have in the North." His appeal was effective in part because the federal soldiers were often in sympathy with white South Carolinians. Some of the "best" homes entertained federal officers. Several Charleston leaders actually asked General Ruger to protect the whites of their city from black violence.[204]

All of this notwithstanding, the presence of more federal troops brought about an improved situation for the Republican cause. Authorities arrested about two hundred white suspects accused of participating in the Ellenton riots. Hampton telegraphed to his allies Johnson Hagood in Barnwell and George W. Croft in Aiken to "urge our people to submit peaceably to martial law. I will see and consult with them." The courts released the arrested men on bail; few were ever tried.[205] On October 19 the *Union Herald* reported that four companies of infantry were coming from Fortress Monroe to South Carolina.[206] A day later that Republican paper reported that other companies were coming from such places as Atlanta, Maine, Massachusetts, and Pennsylvania.[207] The spirits of the radicals, blacks and whites, received a boost from the federal troops, although the individual troopers were often quite sympathetic with South Carolina whites. Democratic leaders interpreted the reinforcement of the troops already in the state as a victory for the radicals. James Conner wrote to his wife, "Our chance to carry the Negro was not by argument of reason but by letting him see that we were stronger, to impress him with a sense of our power and determination—hence the demonstrations we made."[208] This statement from Conner, a close associate of General Hampton, sets forth insight into the degree of intimidation to which Wade Hampton probably agreed—the display of white power by the overawing presence of the mounted red shirts, but falling short of actual violence or direct threats. Conner thought that the presence of additional federal troops vitiated the effect of the red shirts.[209]

In the face of complaints from Republicans about conservatives' interrupting their meetings and mass intimidation of blacks, the spokesmen for white conservatives presented a united front of denial, whether from Hampton and the party leaders or from representatives of the judiciary and clergy. A. C. Haskell replied to a complaint from Governor Chamberlain: "not an instance can be proved when a Republican in this campaign has been intimidated by a Democrat."[210] Even former governor R. K. Scott issued a statement that he found the state to be remarkably peaceful.[211] There is little doubt that conservatives were winning the propaganda battle. The Republican paper the *Union*

Herald noted in the issue of November 22 that three out of four of the great dailies of the North were willing to see Chamberlain defeated by Hampton.[212]

On October 17 a clash between the two races occurred at Cainhoy, near Charleston. A number of white conservatives took a boat from Charleston to Cainhoy, where they were to have a joint meeting with black radicals. Both sides had agreed to come unarmed. When the whites discovered that the blacks had hidden a supply of arms near the site of the meeting, the two sides engaged in a fight that inspired the whites to retreat to Charleston.[213] The large black majority in the Charleston area allowed blacks there to be more aggressive, and whites were forced to be more defensive.

Republican leader E. W. M. Mackey, who later served as the Speaker of the Republican House of Representatives when the state had two opposing lower houses, spoke to a largely black audience and made some interesting charges against Hampton. He said that some of the Hampton lands had come from the shady Yazoo land scandal, an essentially correct charge. Mackey then said that the Democratic candidate was not even a legal resident of the state; he was instead a resident and landowner in Mississippi. In fact Hampton functioned as though he had dual citizenship in the two states. Mackey charged that the general was not financially responsible, having declared bankruptcy and being still very much in debt. Furthermore Hampton had been a director of the Citizens Savings Bank, which had failed, causing serious losses to many people.[214] There was some degree of validity in all of these charges. Republicans had usually been reluctant to level personal attacks against the icon Hampton.

The Democratic campaign concluded with giant rallies in Charleston on October 30 and in Columbia on November 4. In Charleston Hampton addressed a large crowd at White Point Gardens and a black audience at the Academy of Music. The only disturbance came when several blacks threw bricks at black Democrats in the parade. In Columbia the parade went from the corner of Sumter and Gervais streets to the fairgrounds, where Hampton spoke. The Hampton and Tilden Music Club participated in the Columbia parade.[215] From August 16 through November 4, General Hampton addressed fifty-seven audiences, and he had spoken in every county but Lexington.[216]

The people voted on November 7, and there was relative quiet in the state. There was evidence of intimidation of blacks by whites and blacks by other blacks, but all in all there was relative peace. B. H. Hughes, black, testified to the house committee that several hundred black citizens in Allendale could not vote because of threats from a crowd of white roughs.[217] Coleman Beatty, black Democrat, testified of black intimidation of black Democrats.[218] Captain E. R. Kellogg of the Eighteenth Infantry testified that Martin Gary failed to properly restrain his followers, and the result was that a number of blacks were too frightened to vote.[219] Wiley J. Williams and Abraham Lauhan, managers of ballot box 1 in Edgefield, submitted a signed affidavit that the Democratic manager illegally took the ballot box into the county courthouse, where white men crowded the entrance to make it difficult for blacks to vote, while some whites voted four and five times. Only about thirty-five blacks voted, and they were escorted in and out by a U.S. marshal.[220] Alfred B. Williams in his *Hampton and His Red Shirts*—a rather biased treatment—admitted with humor that there was white fraud, quoting Judge Mackey: "The wise and patriotic women in Edgefield, foreseeing troublesome times ahead, had developed amazing and unprecedented zeal and industry in producing male offspring in the years 1854 and 1855."[221] That was Williams's sardonic explanation for the Georgians who crossed the state line to cast votes in Edgefield. There was unquestionably fraud by both Democrats and Republicans. Nevertheless voting day was rather peaceful.

The real complications came with the counting of the returns. The commissioners of election (two Republicans and one Democrat) in each county tallied the county votes and forwarded the results to the Board of State Canvassers in Columbia, the body charged with tallying the state's totals. The Board of State Canvassers consisted of Secretary of State H. E. Hayne, Treasurer F. L. Cardozo, Comptroller General T. C. Dunn, Attorney General William Stone, and Adjutant and Inspector General H. W. Purvis. Hayne, Cardozo, and Dunn were themselves candidates for election. This board was to report their counts to the secretary of state. The Democratic leadership, led by Gen. James Conner, appealed to the Board of State Canvassers to refrain from ruling on protests, arguing that the board should function only as a ministerial body, not in any way judicial. R. B. Elliott represented the Republican leadership in insisting that the Board of Canvassers should indeed rule on contested results. The board held that they could decide contests in the elections of members of the general assembly; the general assembly itself would decide the elections of governor and lieutenant governor, the board acting only in a ministerial role in reporting returns for those offices. When the board refused the conservatives' plea, the Democrats appealed to the State Supreme Court, a body consisting of three Republicans, two of whom were sympathetic to conservatives.[222] Chief Justice F. J. Moses, the father of the former governor, was friendly to Hampton. Associate Justice A. J. Willard was a white Republican whom Hampton had befriended in the Cashiers, North Carolina, community. The third associate was J. J. Wright, a black Republican, more loyal to his party.[223] The initial count gave Hampton a lead of 92,261 to 91,127 for Chamberlain. The results changed when the Board of Canvassers decided to reject the votes from Laurens and Edgefield counties because of suspected fraud. The total vote in Edgefield exceeded the number of registered voters. That decision would of course throw the election to the Republican candidates.

The results were amazingly close. Hampton won in most of the upcountry counties; his largest majorities were in Edgefield, Greenville, and Spartan-burg counties. He also won in Abbeville, Aiken, Anderson, Barnwell, Chesterfield, Horry, Lancaster, Laurens, Lexington, Marion, Marlboro, Oconee, Pickens, Union, and York counties. He lost in Beaufort, Charleston, Chester, Clarendon, Colleton, Darlington, Fairfield, Georgetown, Kershaw, Newberry, Orangeburg, Richland, Sumter, and Williamsburg counties. It is interesting that Hampton lost his home county. By the uncontested national count, Tilden won 184 electoral votes; he needed 185 to be elected. Three states were subject to contests: Florida, Louisiana, and South Carolina. One vote from the three states would elect Tilden; Hayes needed all three states.[224]

The Democratic leadership petitioned to have the election in Charleston County declared null because of widespread intimidation of black Democrats. This was in part to counter the Republican charge of fraud in Edgefield and Laurens counties.[225] One last incident of violence occurred in Charleston on November 9 as crowds gathered on Broad Street to read the bulletins on the election returns. Someone in the black crowd opened fire, and whites returned fire. The result was the death of one black person, with eight wounded, and the death of one white person, with twelve wounded. U.S. troops arrived to disperse the crowds and end the violence.[226]

On November 10 a crowd of Democrats gathered in Columbia in front of the office of the State Democratic Executive Committee. At 2:00 P.M. someone draped from an office window a picture of Wade Hampton with "Our Governor" printed below. The crowd responded with great enthusiasm. A band played, and Hampton came out to address the crowd, thanking them for their loyal support.[227]

The Supreme Court ordered the Board of Canvassers to count the returns and report the results to the court. Associate Justice J. J. Wright dissented from the majority in the order that the count be reported to the court,[228] which later played some part in ending his judicial career. The Board of Canvassers defied the court by meeting, rejecting the returns from Laurens and Edgefield counties, and then issuing certificates of election to the Republican candidates from the two contested counties, to all Republican candidates on the state ticket, and to the Republican electors for president and vice president.[229] That action would have assured the Republicans a majority in both houses of the legislature. The Board of Canvassers then adjourned sine die.

The Supreme Court held the members of the Board of Canvassers in contempt and ordered their arrest. Federal attorney D. A. Corbin then filed with federal judge Hugh L. Bond a petition for a writ of habeas corpus. The judge, holding that the State Supreme Court had exceeded its jurisdiction since the election of electors was a federal matter, ordered the prisoners released.[230]

At the request of Governor Chamberlain, on November 28 General Ruger stationed a company of troopers in the state capitol, thereby bringing about another burning issue. On that day the Republicans certified by the Board of Canvassers assembled in the House chamber. The Democratic claimants came as a body, including the Democratic claimants from Edgefield and Laurens counties. The federal sentinel at the entrance of the House chamber refused to admit those from the contested counties, even though they had certificates of election issued by the Supreme Court. The sentinel acted on instructions from John B. Dennis of Chamberlain's staff. The rebuffed Democrats then left as a group. Wade Hampton and A. C. Haskell tried to enter the House chamber as spectators, but they too were refused. The Republican House proceeded to organize and elected E. W. M. Mackey as Speaker. The Democratic newspapers branded the Mackey House the "bayonet" house. The Mackey House initially consisted of fifty-nine members; all but three were black. The legal quorum should have been sixty-three—the House membership was 124—but the Republicans reasoned that the exclusion of the members from Edgefield and Laurens lowered the quorum.

An immense crowd of angry whites gathered before the capitol. There was real danger of a mob attack on the State House; the company of troopers could have been overwhelmed. A federal officer asked Hampton to try to maintain peace. The general stood on the front steps and addressed the crowd, urging all to disperse peacefully. He pleaded, "One act of violence may precipitate bloodshed and desolation. I implore you, then, to preserve the peace." The crowd, many of whom were armed, went away quietly. It was indeed a great act of leadership. Several weeks later a participant in that huge crowd wrote to Hampton, "I was in front of the state house on the 28th when you came out and asked us to leave, I was the first to leave, tears came to my eyes. In 5 minutes there were not 10 men left who would not obey General Hampton." The legislative bodies proceeded to organize. The Democratic claimants to the House assembled in Carolina Hall and elected William H. Wallace of Union as Speaker, thereby creating South Carolina's legislative schism. The Wallace House initially consisted of sixty-four members, but within a short time five members (four black and one white Republican) coming over from the Mackey House augmented it. The Mackey House declared the Republican contenders from Edgefield and Laurens counties officially elected. The Senate meanwhile met as one body with a Republican majority, excluded the Democrats from the two contested counties, and elected the radical S. A. Swails as president pro tempore.[231] The senators from Laurens and Edgefield counties were not administered the oath of office. The senator-elect from Edgefield was Martin Gary.

Hampton and other Democratic leaders complained of the partisan use of federal troops, specifically in excluding certain Democrats on instructions from Governor Chamberlain. President Grant, sensing how unpopular the political use of troops could be, sent instructions: "I want to avoid anything like an unlawful use of the military."[232] General Ruger then determined on a more neutral stance, and on November 30 the members of Wallace House were allowed to walk into the House chamber and occupy their seats, much to the consternation of the Mackey House when they later returned to the chamber. Both speakers occupied the podium, and members of both houses co-occupied the chamber, camping there with blankets and meals brought in for the next four days. It was of course a scene of tension and occasional humor.

On November 30 Hampton telegraphed to President Grant that the Democratic members were in the House chamber. He informed the president that General Ruger was determined to remove the eight members elected from Edgefield and Laurens counties, although they had been certified elected by the State Supreme Court. Hampton insisted that the House, not the military, was itself the judge of whom it would admit. "We seek only a constitutional legislature peaceably assembled for the good of the state." In what some interpreted to be an offer to bargain, Hampton assured Grant, "The Legislature will not interfere with the presidential electoral vote."[233]

On December 3 Hampton received an anonymous letter warning that Governor Chamberlain had brought about one hundred black Hunkidories from Charleston, who on order from the governor would by force evict the contested Democrats from Laurens and Edgefield counties and thereby incite violence, which would give General Ruger the excuse to bring in his troops. Hampton telegraphed to Secretary of State Hamilton Fish a copy of the letter signed "A Hayes Republican of the Stripe of Evarts and Bryant." The general pleaded, "I implore you gentlemen to take measures to prevent bloodshed."[234] Grant made no reply, likely considering the message to be impertinent. Still, the president knew that the use of troops in a civil affair was becoming unpopular in the North. The Democratic leadership decided to summon about three thousand red shirts to Columbia for a show of strength but to avoid a direct act of violence by having the Wallace members vacate the chamber on December 4. The Democrats reassembled in the Southern Life Insurance Building.[235]

On December 5, 1876, the Mackey House met with the Republican-dominated Senate and declared Chamberlain and R. H. Gleaves elected as governor and lieutenant governor. Chamberlain took the oath of office the next day.[236] The Republican governor recognized in his inaugural address that his side was losing the propaganda war in the North. "I am appalled when I see the North, that portion of our country which is secure in its freedom and civil order, and the great political party which has controlled the republic for sixteen years, divided in its sympathy and judgment upon such questions. . . . There are Republicans who permit the errors which have attended the first efforts of this race in self-government to chill their sympathies to such an extent that they stand idly by, and practically say that the peace of political servitude is better than the abuses and disquiet which newly acquired freedom has brought."[237] Chamberlain understood quite well that the corruption of the black-dominated government had left a heritage of vulnerability.

Meanwhile, the tide was indeed turning to the favor of the Democrats. The State Supreme Court on December 6 ordered the secretary of state to deliver the returns for governor and lieutenant governor to Speaker Wallace, in effect ruling that the legal House of Representatives was the body over which Wallace presided.[238] Several taxpayers petitioned Judge R. B. Carpenter to issue an injunction prohibiting the banks that were depositories for the state's funds from paying out state funds on requests signed by F. L. Cardozo, acting as state treasurer. The judge issued a temporary injunction.[239] This tactic proved to be shrewd and effective, in that the Chamberlain administration was virtually starved out of effectiveness by the injunction and by the refusal of the white population to pay taxes to Republican officers.

On December 14 the Democratic House and eleven Democratic senators voted that Hampton was elected, and the new governor took the oath of office administered by the Republican judge T. J. Mackey and delivered his inaugural address, speaking from a stand built in front of Carolina Hall. Hampton's opening statement set a significant tone: "After years of misrule, corruption, and anarchy brought upon us by venal and unprincipled political adventurers, the honest people of the state without regard to party or race with one voice demanded reform and with one purpose devoted themselves earnestly and solemnly to the attainment of this end." He reminded his audience that the conservative party had pledged all citizens of South Carolina of both races and parties would be treated as equals in the eye of the law. "We owe much of our late success to these colored voters who were brave enough to rise above the prejudice of race and honest enough to throw off the shackles of party in their determination to save the state." He again reminded his listeners that he had been an early advocate of qualified suffrage for freed slaves.[240] Hampton expressed profound gratitude for the victory, saying that the people had "with a lofty patriotism never surpassed, with a patience never equaled, with a courage never excelled, and with a sublime sense of duty, which finds scarce a parallel in the history of the world, . . . subordinated every personal feeling to the public weal and consecrated themselves to the sacred work of redeeming the prostrate state."[241] This statement captured the zeal and devotion of the campaign rather well, a campaign that had been interpreted as virtual war.

Public finances immediately became both a burden for the Hampton administration and a weapon to be used in unseating the opposing administration. The newly sworn governor sent notices to the Carolina Bank and the Central National Bank that they should dispense public funds only when the requests bore his signature. On the same day Dr. J. F. Ensor, the superintendent of the lunatic asylum, informed Hampton that his institution would soon be forced to close for lack of funds. Ensor was already using his personal credit for operational funds.[242] The Democratic Executive Committee urged all taxpayers to refuse to pay taxes to the Chamberlain government.

Some of Chamberlain's appointees began deserting the Republican ship. The *News and Courier* reported that Chamberlain had sent a pardon to Superintendent Parmele of the state penitentiary, which Parmele refused to honor.[243] Hampton was not hesitant to seize power. He published a letter to the people of the state indicating that he intended to name all county officers within his powers, and he asked for recommendations. Hampton assured the public that no one would be removed from office simply because he was a Republican.[244] He also sent a letter to Chamberlain: "I hereby call upon you my predecessor in the office to deliver up the great seal of the state together with the possession of the state house and records." Chamberlain replied, "I do not recognize that you have any right to make the foregoing demand."[245] Hampton's office was in the rooms previously occupied by the Democratic Executive Committee, located on Richardson Street.[246]

Office seekers soon besieged the newly installed governor. Interestingly, the applicants often cited their military records, their mistreatment by Republicans, and their needs. Hampton received a recommendation that he appoint Benjamin F. Mays as county treasurer of Edgefield County, citing Mays's service in Hampton's command and the fact that the radicals had burned the Mays mill.[247] Thompson Earle sought appointment as superintendent of the state penitentiary, stating that he could make the penitentiary "a source of revenue for the state."[248] The possibility of using convict labor for revenue appealed to Hampton, but he retained the Republican-appointed Parmele as superintendent. Letters requesting patronage typically cited military records, wounds, devotion to the Democratic Party, destitution, and competence.[249] One applicant wrote that he had served in the Twelfth South Carolina Volunteers, that he had lost his right leg in the war, and "I have a wife and five little ones looking to me for sustenance."[250]

The Democratic legislature also began to function. On December 29 the Wallace House met with Democratic senators and elected M. C. Butler to succeed Thomas Robertson as U.S. senator. Interestingly, Martin Gary received five votes and Robert Smalls received three votes.[251]

On December 20 the *News and Courier* gave a significant insight into the intensity of the Democratic campaign by publishing a report on incendiarism for the year 1876, indicating a total of 104 in the state through December 17. White people, especially in rural areas, greatly feared burnings by blacks. The report indicated that the number of cases increased during the political campaign; from an average of 4 to 8 per month to 18 in October, 22 in November, and 25 in December to the day of the report.[252]

The Democratic legislators joined Hampton in the effort to unseat their rivals. The Ways and Means Committee of the Wallace House voted to urge the citizens of the state to refuse to pay taxes to the Chamberlain administration and instead to pay voluntarily a portion of their taxes for the year to the Hampton government.[253] This appeal ultimately worked well enough to vitiate the Republican claims to be an effective government. On December 21 a public meeting was held in Charleston in the Hibernian Hall, representing the "bulk of property and wealth of the city." The participants resolved to support the Hampton government with their taxes.[254] Hampton asked the people to pay one-tenth of the taxes paid in the last year, assuring them that those payments would be counted properly in the taxes due for the year 1877. The Republican *Union Herald* stated that if Hampton could secure support by a voluntary tax, "we should be ready to acknowledge that the 'starve 'em out' policy might possibly succeed."[255] It did indeed succeed.

The fundamental conflict between the thinking of Wade Hampton and that of Martin Gary became more obvious in the critical time of dual governments. Gary considered the avoidance of violence advocated by Hampton to be a basic betrayal of the state's honor. Hampton, on the other hand, was determined to deny the opposition the excuse to call for a massive military intervention and to avoid losing the propaganda war in the Northern press. His determined stance for peace notwithstanding, the general was unwaveringly bent on serving as governor. He assured one crowd of anxious supporters, "The people have elected me Governor, and, by the Eternal God, I will be Governor or we shall have a military governor."[256]

On December 23 Hampton wrote identical letters to the two presidential claimants, Hayes and Tilden. The results of the presidential election had not yet been determined. He enclosed a copy of his inaugural address, delivered as "the duly elected governor of South Carolina." He assured them that "profound peace prevails throughout the state" and that the people were determined to let the courts decide all questions pertaining to the election. Because of the sympathy of the State Supreme Court, that was a safe way to secure a Democratic victory. The general's real objection was to the use of the military to prop up the opposing administration. He insisted to the two presidential claimants, "[The people] condemn any solution of existing political problems that involves the exhibition of armed force." Hampton proposed to "unite the people of all the State in an earnest effort to preserve the peace, to sustain the laws, and to obey the Constitution." He concluded by saying that an important part of the state's problem "must ultimately depend on yourself or upon your distinguished competitor for the Presidency."[257]

The Republican judge T. J. Mackey delivered Hampton's letter to Governor Hayes. While Judge Mackey was in Cincinnati, a reporter from the *Cincinnati Enquirer* interviewed him. Mackey told the reporter that the contest in South Carolina was a "struggle between the white civilization of the nineteenth century and the barbarism of Africa, augmented by the villainy of the carpetbaggers."[258] The *Union Herald* noted that using Mackey to deliver the message to the Republican candidate made some of the more ardent Democrats uneasy.[259] Martin Gary later used Mackey's role as an intermediary as a part of his charge of a conspiracy between Hampton and Hayes.

The *News and Courier* reported on December 29 that the committee of the U.S. House of Representatives that had investigated the election in South Carolina, having conducted hearings in Columbia for a period of three weeks, decided by a majority vote that the election had resulted in victories for the Hayes electors and for Hampton and the Democratic ticket. The majority also ruled that the Ellenton riot was not of political significance. The committee's main purpose was to rule on the election of presidential electors; everything else was incidental.[260]

Governor Hampton issued a New Year's message in which he called upon all faithful and law-abiding citizens to pay one-tenth of the taxes they had paid in the previous year "to maintain the government of their choice." The conservative governor noted that the "charitable and penal institutions of the state are now suffering for want of proper supplies, and it is to meet their needs which appeal to us so strongly that funds are now required."

Newspapers also reported that Hampton had received a letter from William Preston in Cincinnati, indicating that he had heard that T. J. Mackey had sought to represent Hampton in dealing with Hayes, offering Hampton's support for Hayes in opposition to the Northern Democrats in return for Hayes's support for the Democrats in South Carolina. Hampton replied that no one was authorized to make bargains for him or the party.[261] Such rumors became part of the growing enmity between Wade Hampton on one hand and Gary and later Ben Tillman on the other. On January 10, 1877, the *Augusta Chronicle and Sentinel* printed a story about Judge Mackey's "embassy" for Governor Hampton, indicating that a number of Northern Democratic newspapers were condemning the use of a Republican in such a role as "likely to injure the Democratic Party and to weaken the possibility of inaugurating Tilden." The *New York World* reported that Senator Robertson of South Carolina had been heard to say that the South Carolina Democrats preferred Tilden, but they would assent to the election of Hayes provided they could get a Democratic government in their state.[262]

There were a series of public meetings around the state, each meeting resulting in resolutions to support the Hampton administration with voluntary taxes. Interestingly Martin Gary presented the resolution that the people of Edgefield join in support of the Hampton government.[263] Governor Hampton received a petition from a number of rice planters, promising to pay the voluntary tax of 10 percent of the previous year's tax. This petition was signed by an impressive collection of the lowcountry aristocracy: Daniel Heyward, Joseph Manigault, John Rutledge, Woodward Barnwell, Allen S. Izard, and L. A. Cheves.[264]

A reporter for the *News and Courier* informed his readers of the activities of the opposing administrations. He had recently observed federal troops in quiet possession of the capitol, taking their meals in Governor Chamberlain's anteroom. The reporter visited Governor Hampton's office and found him busy naming people to fill various offices, including agents to collect the voluntary taxes. The writer noted, "He who can collect taxes is Governor of South Carolina." Governor Chamberlain told the reporter that he had no funds for such agencies as the lunatic asylum and the penitentiary. The court injunction against payments from the depository banks was still in force.[265]

There was mounting evidence that the conservatives were winning. The *News and Courier* reported on January 10 that several hundred citizens of Charleston County had paid their voluntary taxes.[266] There were more meetings of citizens pledging their support of Hampton in Abbeville, Columbia, Newberry, Oconee, and Walterboro.[267] The Hampton government was indeed functioning. The Democratic leader was appointing county auditors, treasurers, and trial justices (justices of the peace).[268] Hampton also removed some people from office. A letter from the Democratic governor's secretary, dated January 9, 1877, indicated the removal of a number of trial justices from office.[269] The governor even undertook to obstruct the collection of taxes by Chamberlain's agents by instructing the county solicitors to seek court injunctions prohibiting the collection of taxes by those representing the Republican administration, basing this action on the ruling of the State Supreme Court that the Mackey House was not legal and that that body had no right to enact taxation.[270]

The dual governments in the state capital were repeated in a number of the counties where there were competing claimants for offices. Hampton blurred party lines by seeking to strengthen his appeal to dissatisfied Republicans by appointing some of their party to offices. The Orangeburg Democratic Executive Committee recommended that Governor Hampton appoint James Van Tassell, Republican, as county auditor. Van Tassell had recognized Hampton as governor and had thereby offended the Republicans of that county.[271] There was indeed some bipartisan support for Hampton. The governor received a petition signed by Democrats and black Republicans of Sumter County, recommending the appointment of P. B. Gaillard, Republican, as a trial justice.[272] James H. Rion of Winnsboro recommended that the governor appoint Willard Richardson, Republican, as school commissioner of Fairfield County. Richardson had voted for Hampton.[273]

The Republicans sought ways to fight back. The black Republican leader W. B. Nash addressed a Republican meeting in Columbia, urging his audience to respond to the economic boycott by Democrats by their own boycott; they should refuse to buy from merchants who were not Republican.[274] In this contest there could be little doubt which side would triumph.

Governor Hampton received a number of pleas for relief from the loss of lands for failure to pay the high taxes enacted by the radical regime. Mrs. D. E. Conner of Reevesville wrote, "We have been run nearly to death for the last 10 years by the radicals." Her lands had been sold for taxes by the sheriff. "I know no other help but you."[275] The Democrats tried to respond to this and other cries for help.

On January 12 the *News and Courier* printed a letter from "A Tilden Democrat," accusing Hampton of having betrayed the Democratic Party by a bargain with Rutherford B. Hayes. The writer admitted that Tilden had opposed the nomination of Hampton and had given the latter no assistance in the campaign, but he asserted, "It is not too much to say that the state was lost to Tilden and the national Democracy through the policy pursued by General Hampton."[276] The Tilden Democrat also accused Hampton of having betrayed the straight-out Democrats who had nominated him by failing to appoint any straight-out members to the party executive committee and of having followed a campaign policy of "milk and cider" instead of the bold and aggressive plan recommended by the straight-outs. By "milk and cider" the writer meant a policy to conciliate the blacks.[277] Party chairman A. C. Haskell answered the letter from "A Tilden Democrat" by publishing the letter written to Tilden at the time of the Democratic convention, the letter Tilden never answered, and the letter to Manton Marble, a Tilden associate, expressing consternation at the lack of support from the national party but denying any agreement to dump the national ticket in South Carolina.[278] Haskell said that after the Republican convention Judges Cooke and Mackey, both of whom were Republicans supporting Hampton, came to the Democratic Executive Committee to say that they would support Hampton and to urge the state Democrats to abandon the national Democratic ticket. The committee welcomed the support of the judges but declined to dump the national ticket.[279] The Democratic leaders obviously thought that the black people who voted for Hampton voted for Hayes, and that gave the Republican electors their victory. The best support for that supposition was that the two Republican judges, Cooke and Mackey, had actively encouraged black voters to vote for Hampton and Hayes. Many South Carolina Democrats who were supporters of Hampton manifestly had faith in Hayes. Gen. J. B. Kershaw in a speech delivered in Lancaster told his audience, "Even though the dearest wish of hearts be defeated by the failure of Mr. Tilden to be elected president I still have full faith that with Hayes as president of the United States justice will be done throughout the whole land."[280] There is little doubt that Martin Gary either wrote or inspired the letter from "A Tilden Democrat."

While the Democrats generally had the support of the South Carolina judiciary, it was not uniform. On January 30 Governor Hampton pardoned Amzi Roseborough, a black man. The sheriff of Chester County refused to recognize Hampton's decree as legal. Counsel for the prisoner brought suit to enforce the pardon, and the presiding judge, T. J. Mackey, ordered Roseborough released, ruling that Hampton was the legitimate governor. In another and similar case Judge R. B. Carpenter ruled that Hampton had not been properly declared elected since the House of Representatives had acted without meeting with the full Senate.[281]

As the year 1877 bore on, there were increasing indications that the support of Republicans for the Chamberlain administration was wearing thin. The Republican senator T. J. Robertson, who had already announced that he would not seek reelection, delivered a speech in the U.S. Senate in which he commented that in the recent election in South Carolina, black intimidation of blacks was more significant than white intimidation of blacks. He also ventured that the transfer of power to the Democrats would be beneficial to all in his state.[282] The *Columbia Daily Register* on February 28 reported that 115 black citizens of Anderson County and 983 black citizens of Barnwell county had paid the voluntary tax to the Hampton government.[283]

A reporter for the *New York Tribune* interviewed President Grant and quoted him: "In South Carolina the contest has assumed such a phase that the whole army of the United States would be inadequate to enforce the authority of Governor Chamberlain. The people of the state have resolved not to resort to violence but adopted a mode of procedure much more formidable and effective than any armed demonstration. They have refused to pay taxes to Governor Chamberlain and it would be useless for him to expect to maintain his authority for any length of time."[284] Thus the president, who had tended to back Chamberlain, was beginning to give way. Republican nominee Hayes was even less inclined to support the Chamberlain effort.

Hampton sought to present his case to Congress by sending a pamphlet of sixty pages, arguing for the validity of the Democratic government and stating that Chamberlain was utterly unable to govern. Meanwhile, the state suffered. Commerce languished, trade had virtually ceased, capital was turned away, and industry was paralyzed. The lawfully elected were barred from the capitol by troops.[285]

In February 1877, President Grant issued a proclamation forbidding the "so-called rifle clubs" from participating in a parade on Washington's birthday in Charleston. The Charleston Democrats chose to interpret the president's order as prohibiting a parade to honor the first president. Governor Hampton issued a proclamation on February 20 calling on all organizations to postpone celebrations of Washington's birthday. "If the arbitrary commands of a chief executive, who has not sought to emulate the virtues of Washington, deprives the citizens of the privileges of joining publicly in paying reverence to that day so sacred to every American patriot, we can at least show by our obedience to constituted authority, however arbitrarily exercised, that we are not unworthy to be countrymen of Washington."[286] Hampton found himself in sympathy with Hayes, but he never exhibited much sympathy for his old military opponent.

Meanwhile in Washington the electoral commission established by Congress to determine the outcome of the disputed presidential election was completing its work, and the result was by then obviously to be a Republican victory. The *News and Courier* on February 27 printed an appeal from Governor Hampton urging the people of South Carolina to accept the commission's decision peacefully: "better to suffer defeat than to incur the imputation of acting in bad faith."[287] At long last the election of 1876 reached its denouement with the commission's declaring for Hayes and Wheeler. Much has been written about possible agreements between Southern Democrats and the lieutenants of Rutherford B. Hayes, much of it pointing to an informal agreement that the Southerners would acquiesce in the election of Hayes in return for pledges that the Republican president would support federal funds for a Southern transcontinental railroad (the Texas and Pacific Railroad), fund internal improvements in the South, and withdraw federal troops from Louisiana and South Carolina, thereby allowing the Democrats to take over those two states.[288] Hampton did not engage in the direct negotiations. He had little interest in any part of the agreements other than the withdrawal of federal troops. L. Q. C. Lamar of Mississippi, who was in many ways cut out of a cloth similar to that of Hampton, played a much more active role. Lamar was intensely interested in funds for internal improvements in the South, especially railroads and rivers.[289] Nevertheless, Hampton benefited from the agreements, and he did indeed sympathize with Hayes.

After Hayes took the oath of office on March 4 the struggle in South Carolina moved swiftly to a conclusion. On the day after the inauguration, Stanley Matthews, one of Hayes's lieutenants, wrote to Governor Chamberlain urging him to give up, stating that the maintenance of the South Carolina Republicans in office by troops was an embarrassment to the new administration. Secretary of State designate W. M. Evarts endorsed the letter. There is no doubt that Hayes approved of this appeal. Chamberlain replied, refusing to surrender: "There are better ways to conciliate and pacify the South."[290] The Republican governor pleaded, "to permit Hampton to reap the fruits of a campaign of murder and fraud, so long as there remains power to prevent it, is to sanction such measures."[291] The election having been determined, Southern leaders pressed for quick action. Sen. J. B. Gordon was promptly in

Washington exerting pressure on the White House.[292] Hampton was represented by a whole delegation in Washington, including A. C. Haskell, Gen. John B. Kershaw, Judge T. J. Mackey, and even former governor R. K. Scott, who was now supporting Hampton. Senator-elect M. C. Butler was already there. The South Carolina Republican House and Senate had elected former district attorney D. T. Corbin to replace Robertson in the U.S. Senate. Hence, there was a standoff between Butler and Corbin.[293]

Negotiations intensified in the time after Hayes took office. Republican judge T. J. Mackey was one of Hampton's primary intermediaries with Hayes. The judge sent Hampton a telegram on March 10 assuring him, "All of the President's friends are with us."[294] Hampton had sent Butler a telegram on March 7 assuring him that there would be no violence when the troops left.[295] Lamar wrote a sharp letter to the new president, reminding him of Southern support and expressing impatience. On the next day Hayes invited Hampton and Chamberlain to come to Washington to confer.[296] Judge Mackey telegraphed Hampton, "Come and end our long agony peacefully. Gordon agrees with me."[297] Hampton replied to the president on March 26, accepting the invitation to "place before you my views of the impediments to the peaceful and orderly organization of a single and undisputed state government and the best methods of removing them." He made it clear that the troops occupying the capitol were the impedimenta. Hampton told the president that they should resolve their problems "not by resort to force but by legal and constitutional agencies." He asserted that no "proscription shall be exercised here on account of political opinions." Both races will receive equal protection of the laws.[298]

In the midst of these events, South Carolina Chief Justice F. J. Moses died on March 6.[299] The election of a successor to Moses involved Hampton in an important controversy with the Gary faction. Governor Hampton had had friendly relations with the late chief justice. On January 15 the governor had written to Justice Moses to inform him that the Democratic administration would continue his salary. "I suppose that I am only authorized to recognize claims accruing since the 14th of December last. . . . I hope that your health is re-established and that this fine weather will restore your strength."[300]

Hayes had invited both Chamberlain and Hampton. The Republican was in Washington on March 27. Hampton left for Washington on the next day, assuring his faithful that he did not intend to ask the president to recognize him as governor. He was already governor; he would ask for the removal of the troops. The trip to the nation's capital was a triumphant procession, with huge receptions, bands playing, and speeches at many stops. His major stops were Florence, Wilmington, Rocky Mount, and Richmond. In Washington he stayed at the Willard Hotel.[301] Hampton sent a note from the hotel to the White House. "I beg you to believe that my anxiety to bring about the permanent pacification of the state—a pacification in which the rights of all shall be safe and the interests of all shall be protected—is as sincere as I feel assured your own for the accomplishment of the same ends." He promised the president that the rights of black people would be "absolutely secure."[302] The general met with the president at the White House on March 29, and the meeting was obviously successful for the South Carolinian.[303] Hampton remained in the capital city for several more days. The pro-South journalist from New York Fernando Wood entertained the South Carolina coterie, including Hampton, James Conner, M. C. Butler, and Francis Dawson, and the rumor was that the president would withdraw the troops.[304] Hampton's Washington trip received national attention. On March 30 the *New York Tribune* noted, "Wade Hampton's presence in Washington excites more attention than of any other public men who have arrived here since President Hayes came. A considerable crowd of people remained around Williard's [*sic*] until 3:00 this morning, waiting to see him."[305] On March 31, while still at the Willard, the general wrote a note to the president, repeating the assurances of their meeting. If the troops were withdrawn from the State House, there would be no violence. He specifically promised to secure the right to vote and public education for the black citizens of his state. Hampton reminded Hayes that the removal of the military would be well received by the whole country.[306]

One part of the negotiations between Rutherford B. Hayes and Southern Democrats was Hayes's desire to get the Democratic-dominated House of Representatives to elect the Republican James A. Garfield as speaker, using an alliance of Republicans and conservative Southern Democrats. While Hampton was in Washington he met Stanley Matthews, a Hayes colleague, who asked Hampton to support the Garfield effort. Apparently, the governor promised to do what he could.[307]

Victory was complete. On April 3 Governor Hampton, still in Washington, telegraphed to Lieutenant Governor Simpson: "Everything is satisfactorily and honorably settled. I expect our people to preserve absolute peace and quiet. My word is pledged for them." The newspapers reported that the president's cabinet met on April 2 and agreed to ask Secretary of War George M. McCrary to prepare orders to have the troops withdrawn from the capitol in Columbia. An interesting indication of capitulation occurred when Sen. "Honest John" Patterson met with Hampton in Washington and pledged his cooperation in what had by then become inevitable.[308] A committee came together in Columbia to plan a proper welcome home for the governor. He was to leave Washington on April 4.[309]

The return to South Carolina was a triumphal journey. A group of sixty South Carolinians met Hampton in Charlotte, and the governor addressed them: "We are bound to carry out in good faith the pledges we made them, that every citizen, regardless of color, shall be equal in the light of the law." A band led the governor from his hotel to the station. Thousands saw him off to Columbia. The train was decorated with wreaths and ribbons. There were additional speeches in Rock Hill and Chester, where the train passed under a triumphal arch. Another arch awaited them in Winnsboro. In Columbia a battery firing a salute greeted the governor. The band of the U.S. Army Eighteenth Infantry led the parade in honor of the former Confederate general. Hampton spoke from a stand in front of Carolina Hall, urging all to forget their party affiliations and renew their faith as South Carolinians. He again pledged equal justice for all.[310] The *New York Tribune* editorialized, "Governor Hampton returns to Columbia one of the most important men in the United States. The future of the whole South may be said to depend in a great measure on him. He can confirm the federal administration in its new policy of non-interference or he can provoke a reaction in public opinion."[311] The governor consistently recommended peace.

Things fell apart for the Republican governor. On April 10 Chamberlain received a letter from Attorney General R. B. Elliott, Superintendent of Education John R. Tolbert, Adjutant and Inspector General James Kennedy, Comptroller General T. C. Dunn, Treasurer F. L. Cardozo, and Secretary of State H. E. Hayne advising him that they had conferred and agreed to recommend that he yield his claims to the office of governor. On the same day troops occupying the capitol received orders to vacate the building. Thereupon Chamberlain issued an address to the Republicans of South Carolina: "I now announce to you and to the people of the state that I shall no longer actively assert my right to the office of Governor of South Carolina." He told followers rather plaintively: "The government of the United States abandons you, deliberately withdraws from you its support, with the full knowledge that the lawful government of the state will be speedily overthrown." And with profound understanding he added, "It is said that the North is weary of the long Southern problems."[312] He concluded, "I devoutly pray that events may indicate the wisdom of this action, and that peace, justice, freedom, and prosperity may hereafter be the portion of every citizen of South Carolina."[313] Chamberlain vacated his office in the capitol a few minutes after 11:00 A.M. on April 11. At noon Mr. Babbitt, secretary to Chamberlain, handed over the keys and records of the office to Wade Hampton Manning, the secretary for the new governor.[314] It all happened peacefully; there was no celebration; it was as Hampton had desired. The *Columbia Register* quoted Sen. "Honest John" Patterson as having said that the surrender of Chamberlain's office to Hampton was "the death knell of Radicalism in South Carolina."[315] And so the era of radical Reconstruction ended. Governor Hampton's next duty was to consolidate the powers attendant to his office.

Chamberlain's farewell address was poignant and tinged with bitterness. Later in his life his attitudes toward Hampton and the black race shifted with those of the nation, and he actually regretted his attempts at extending the era of black rule. He expressed great appreciation for the role played by Wade Hampton, saying that Hampton deserved to be ranked with John C. Calhoun as the two greatest leaders produced by the Palmetto State. He asserted, "Totally unlike Calhoun, Hampton's strength of leadership lay, not in intellectual or oratorical superiority, but in high and forceful character, perfect courage and devotion to what he conceived to be the welfare of South Carolina. Not even Calhoun's leadership was at any time more absolute, unquestioned, and enthusiastic than Hampton's in 1876; and it was justly so from the Democratic point of view, for he was unselfish, resolute, level-headed, and determined. He was for the hour a true natural leader; and he led with . . . prudence and aggressiveness."[316] And this was praise from his erstwhile enemy.

SEVEN

In Office

Governor Hampton moved swiftly to consolidate the authority of his office. His colleagues in office were a mixed group. He faced a Republican majority in the Senate, where there were eighteen Republicans and fifteen Democrats. In the House Republicans still held fifty-five seats, and the conservatives held sixty-nine. The judiciary was essentially Republican, but of a kind generally acceptable to Hampton and his followers. The chief justice had died recently; the two remaining were Republican. Hampton would support the election of Associate Justice A. J. Willard as the next chief justice. Six of the eight circuit court judges were Republicans, and two congressmen were Republican. Sen. "Honest John" Patterson had two more years in office.[1] Wade Hampton Manning, the governor's secretary, wrote letters to the Republican leftovers in the cabinet-level offices, Henry E. Hayne, secretary of state, R. B. Elliott, attorney general, John R. Tolbert, superintendent of education, James Kennedy, adjutant and inspector general, and F. L. Cardozo, state treasurer, asking them to hand over their keys and records to their Democratic successors. Manning acknowledged that the courts would have to make the final judgment as to who rightfully held these offices, but the business of government must proceed meanwhile.[2] The Republican officeholders answered Manning's letter collectively, refusing to yield their offices, arguing that they had been legally elected on November 7, 1876, and they had been certified by the State Board of Canvassers. The governor replied that he was considering having the offices locked and sealed until the Supreme Court ruled on who had been properly elected.[3]

On April 18 Governor Hampton attended a celebration in Charleston. The train was decorated as it had been on the trip from Charlotte to Columbia. Under the headlight was a picture of the governor. In Charleston St. Patrick's Band saluted the governor by playing "Dixie," and the Washington Artillery led the parade. The celebration lasted two days. Hampton spoke to crowds at the Academy of Music and at City Hall. He told the Charlestonians that when he was in Washington several Republicans asked him for advice on how to restrict the black vote. He replied, "We don't want the vote of the colored man taken away or restricted, for besides the friendship we bear their race, their right to vote gives us more votes in Congress, and when peace comes we are satisfied that the best men in both races and parties will vote together for the common weal." He also reiterated his promise for better education for black citizens.[4] These statements are important indications of Hampton's sincerity in assuring justice for black citizens. If he had been cynical in making promises to black voters before the election, there would have been some change in the tone of his speeches after he was in office. On the contrary, he was consistent in his promises to deliver on the pledges.

One of the most important indicators of Hampton's sincerity vis-à-vis his campaign promises was his record in patronage. There was the usual clamoring for office, especially for a party long out of office. In his study *South Carolina Negroes, 1877–1900*, historian George Brown Tindall found that the Democratic governor appointed a total of eighty-six blacks to office, all minor offices. In some cases Hampton appointed his Republican opponents to office. He appointed the former lieutenant governor, R. H. Gleaves, and the Republican Martin Delany, who had supported the general in 1876, to the office of trial justice. In August 1877 former governor R. K. Scott told a newspaperman, "Hampton is honestly carrying out the promises he made during the campaign. He has already appointed more colored men to office than were appointed during the first two years that I was governor."[5] A compilation from the "Letters of Appointment" in the Governor's Papers in the South Carolina Archives of black men appointed indicates these numbers: two clerks of court, one coroner, sixteen county commissioners, twenty-six election commissioners, seven jury commissioners, twenty-eight trial justices, ten notaries, one pilot commissioner, five probate judges, one sheriff, one steamboat commissioner, three county treasurers, and seven others to offices not named.[6] The total exceeds Tindall's count; he likely did not count some of the more minor offices. In referring to the appointment of black citizens to office, the *News and Courier* noted rather tellingly, "Of course the endeavor is made to avoid putting colored persons in positions where they would or could be peculiarly offensive."[7] This editorial comment is probably an accurate insight to the attitudes of the time. In the light of that attitude the Hampton record is rather good.

The new governor issued a proclamation convening the general assembly in a special session on April 24.[8] There would be several pressing issues for the legislature; two of the foremost were the election of a new chief justice and the state budget. Hampton let it be known that he wanted the Northerner and Republican associate justice A. J. Willard elevated to the office of chief justice. This was apparently to reward an able Republican officeholder for his support of the Democrats' claims to the election of 1876, and the naming of a Republican to this high office would be an indication of Hampton's intentions to honor his oft-repeated pledge to be above party. Other Democrats put forward their candidates.

The election of a new chief justice was the first real confrontation between Hampton as governor and Martin Gary. State senator Gary vociferously promoted Gen. Samuel McGowan to be chief justice. The senator objected strenuously to the election of a Republican, interpreting it to be a flaunting of Hampton's debt to the straight-out Democrats who had won the last election for him. Gary believed that General Hampton had been out of the state until just prior to the 1876 Democratic convention, and the general was therefore naïve of the "antecedent history of the state." Gary argued that the straight-out Democrats secured the nomination of Hampton, and the aggressive tactics of the straight-outs, modeled on the Mississippi plan, won the election for Hampton, who then shunned the straight-outs. Gary deeply resented Hampton's oft-repeated statement in the campaign: "So help me, God, I am no party man." The Edgefield senator passionately believed that the Democratic Party could not afford candidates who appeared to be independent.[9]

In the midst of these debates about the wise treatment of the state's black citizens, on one side the moderation of Hampton and on the other side the extreme attitude exemplified by Mart Gary, there was a rather cynical, yet prescient interpretation by a young South Carolinian, Belton O'Neall Townsend. He wrote in the *Atlantic Monthly* that black citizenship depended on the federal bayonet and that when white Southerners had the opportunity they would disfranchise their black neighbors, albeit by legal means. Lest later generations assume that this maverick was an early-day liberal in matters of race, Townsend thought that the blacks of the South were no better fit for citizenship than "a crowd of Irish roughs picked up promiscuously in the street of a northern city."[10] Still, there is no evidence to indicate cynicism in Hampton's pledges to black people.

On the day before the convening of the special session of the legislature, the editor of the *News and Courier* noted that the members of the Mackey House had been guilty of criminal action in declaring vacant the seats claimed by the members of the Wallace House. That was a decision of the Republican House on December 9, declaring the members of the Democratic-controlled House to be in contempt of the legal House. Subsequently, the State Supreme Court declared the Wallace House to be the legal House of Representatives. The editor predicted that the House convening on April 24 would seek vengeance, saying of the Mackey House, "out of their mouth are they judged."[11]

Governor Hampton sent his first message to the legislature on April 26. He urged his colleagues to forget the partisan animosities of the campaign and to rise above party considerations. Hampton expressed a special concern that the legislature determine the state's legitimate debt, and in order to do that he recommended the establishment of a commission consisting of one member from each house, the comptroller general, the treasurer, and three citizens well versed in finances. The governor reported that the voluntary tax and fees had netted a total of $135,859.48. The Hampton administration had disbursed $76,661.09, primarily for charitable and penal institutions. The administration had not dipped into the funds raised by earlier governments because the courts had enjoined against use of those moneys. Hampton told the legislature that he hoped the penitentiary could be made profitable, obviously implying the leasing of prisoners. He expressed confidence in the service of the Republican-appointed superintendent of the penitentiary, Parmele. Concerning the state university, the governor told the legislature that he knew little of the current affairs, but "I am forced to the conclusion that the benefits it bestows under the present system are not commensurate with the expenses it entails. To bring it up to a prior standard, it must undergo a complete reorganization." He recommended that the legislature study the university before proceeding. He urged his colleagues to establish a system of public schools that would place the means of education within reach of all classes in the state. He described the present school system as a "mockery, under which the children have been imperfectly taught. The teachers have been swindled out of their pay, and the money of the people has been squandered." The governor had with him a teacher's pay certificate signed by the three trustees with three *x*'s. He argued for a school system for rich and poor and for black as well as white.[12]

The rather grim comment about the state university reflected the general white attitude toward the racially integrated institution under the Republican administration. Upon recommendation of the governor the legislature elected a new board of trustees. In June Governor Hampton signed three diplomas for baccalaureate degrees, and the university closed, to reopen later after another reorganization.[13]

The Democratic governor tried to continue and improve on the Republican efforts in education. Hampton's plea for an adequate school system for both races was an attempt to fulfill his promise to the black people of South Carolina. "We are bound alike by every consideration of true statesmanship and of good faith to keep up in the state such a system of free schools as will place within reach of every child, the poorest as well as the richest, black as well as white, the means of acquiring an honest and honorable education."[14]

The leasing of prisoners was one of the scandals of this era. The new governor told the general assembly that he wanted the penitentiary to be made profitable by the use of prison labor. It is pertinent to note that the Republican administration of 1872 had provided for leasing convict labor. An amendment to that law in 1874 prohibited the leasing of prisoners to private companies or private individuals. In 1875–1876 Governor Chamberlain attempted to revive the possibility of leasing convicts to private entities, but he failed. Later legislatures relaxed the restrictions. The governor summarized his policies to the legislature: "restore credit, develop resources, heal wounds, secure equal and exact justice, maintain supremacy of the law, diffuse the blessings of education, strive to bind all classes of both races in the bonds of peace, fraternity and piety."[15]

Rep. James L. Orr, son of Governor Orr, chaired a joint committee consisting of the House Judiciary Committee and the House Committee on Privileges and Elections in considering how to accept or reject the members of the Mackey House who were seeking seats in the then-recognized House of Representatives. Fifty-five members of the Mackey House came. The joint committee decided to recommend that some claimants from the Mackey House be accepted and some rejected, according to the merits of their claims. Some were allowed to recant, confess their mistakes, and be seated as legal representatives. Those about to be forgiven came and stood before the Speaker's stand "like a parcel of disgraced school boys about to be lectured." Two of the Mackey House were denied the opportunity to recant. Two resigned. One refused to take the oath. In one case the vacated seat went to the Democrat who had the next highest number of votes in the recent election. In the other case the House directed new elections.[16]

House committees gave special consideration to the Charleston elections, and, on recommendations from those committees, the House decided because of fraud to reject the entire delegation elected from that county on November 7 and to order new elections.[17] The Charleston Democrats then decided to conduct another convention to nominate their slate. James Conner informed the county convention that Governor Hampton wanted the Charleston Democrats to give black people of that county fair representation. Consequently the slate of seventeen candidates included three black men.

The Democrats followed a similar policy in their selections for offices in Orangeburg, Sumter, and Barnwell counties.[18] For example, the chairman of the Orangeburg Democratic Executive Committee recommended that "an opening be left for the appointment of a colored trial justice provided a fit and competent person for the position can be found."[19]

The balance of power was shifting. The proceedings in the lower house reduced the number of Republicans in the House to thirty-seven. The Senate under Lt. Gov. William D. Simpson admitted the four Democrats from counties where the elections had been contested, and that reduced the number of Republican senators to fifteen.[20]

The *News and Courier* noted that there was a significant opposition to the election of Republican Willard to the office of chief justice, as Governor Hampton was insisting. Some Democrats said they would rather cut off their arms than vote for a carpetbagger. The editor, increasingly the voice of conservative Democrats, insisted that the need for party unity and the need to express confidence in the new governor required all Democrats to vote for Willard.[21] Governor Hampton indeed insisted on the election of Willard, and

Gary opposed him in a bitter speech, charging that the governor was promoting a corrupt carpetbagger.[22] Gary was likely encouraged in his opposition to Hampton by reading in the *News and Courier* that a correspondent for that newspaper reported that President Hayes approved of the actions of Governor Hampton and predicted that the Democratic Party in South Carolina would soon break into several factions. Hayes also predicted that the Republicans in South Carolina would nominate Hampton in 1878.[23] Following the lead of the governor, the legislative Democrats met in caucus and voted to nominate Willard, and the legislature subsequently elected him chief justice. This was a bitter defeat for Gary and an important victory for Hampton. The *News and Courier* gave this election an interesting interpretation: "Liberality in union is announced and affirmed as the governing idea of the Democratic Party in South Carolina. In other words the principles and policy advocated by Governor Hampton during the canvass and after the election have carried the day. The Democratic Party opposes thieves but not all of Northern birth."[24] Later events proved that Democrats followed such a policy as electing this New York Republican only because of the influence of Wade Hampton. Gary was in fact nearer to the heart of the average South Carolinian. Senator Gary said of the election of Willard, "This choice is a dictation of Governor Hampton."[25]

The election of Willard drew national attention. The *News and Courier* quoted the *New York Evening Post*, which interpreted the election of Willard as an indication that Hampton "is giving a practical shape to the promises which he made to President Hayes and that he is succeeding in his efforts to establish an era of good feelings."[26] Hampton indeed saw his advocacy of Willard as something the Hayes administration would applaud. On May 13 the governor wrote to Secretary of State William Evarts that his support of Willard and his support of the policies of President Hayes were evoking some opposition, but "Our fight here has not been against Northern men but against a band of plunderers."[27] Hampton later indicated to the secretary of state that every Democrat in the legislature, save one, had voted for Willard.[28] That was impressive party discipline, but the opposition of that one, Martin Gary, was ominous.

Governor Hampton's policies and practices were gaining the approval of not only the Northern press but also of some of the black leadership of South Carolina. W. B. Nash, a prominent leader of the state's black Republicans (he was the vice president of the constitutional convention of 1868), said that upon considering the speeches and actions of Hampton he was willing to throw down his hatchet and urge others to do the same. He wanted the black community to "meet our white citizens in a Christian-like spirit."[29]

The governor was careful to cultivate the approval of the Hayes administration. On April 22, 1877, Hampton wrote to President Hayes to recommend the appointment of Col. F. W. McMaster as a federal revenue collector. Hampton pointed out to Hayes with obvious pride that the state of South Carolina was peaceful after the removal of the federal troops. This was as Hampton had promised in the negotiations leading to Hayes's decision to withdraw the troops from the capitol.[30]

It should be stated that for all the concern about the removal of troops from the protection of Republican administrations in Louisiana and South Carolina there were in fact few federal soldiers in the South. There was in 1876–1877 no mass occupation of a conquered territory. At the end of the year 1876 there were only 3,230 troops in the South, excluding Texas, where the threat of Indian wars presented a special situation, having no relation to the concerns of the former Confederate states.[31] In the years 1876–1878 the greatest military concern was focused on the western Indians.

The special session of the general assembly began consideration of a major issue facing the state, the fact that U.S. District Attorney D. T. Corbin had arrested several hundred whites for crimes allegedly committed in the campaign of 1876, many of them charged with participation in the Ellenton riots. Corbin won indictments from juries consisting largely of blacks and carpetbaggers, since the "ironbound" oath that a prospective juror had not voluntarily participated in the recent rebellion excluded many white Democrats. There were also three South Carolinians still in prison because of convictions in the Ku Klux Klan (KKK) trials. This session of the legislature established a joint committee to investigate the misdeeds of the radical rule of the last eight years. The likelihood that many former Republican officeholders would be charged with crimes presented the possibility of a compromise, which could be face-saving for both Democrats and Republicans. This issue was not finally settled until after the Hampton administration, but the process began under his leadership. D. T. Corbin was also contending with M. C. Butler for the seat representing South Carolina in the U.S. Senate, adding another layer of complexity.

The general assembly and governor moved toward a compromise. The two houses of the legislature passed a joint resolution, dated May 10 and 11, 1877, asking the governor to communicate with the president of the United States to request executive clemency "as circumstances will warrant and upon the assurance that the state of South Carolina will not prosecute those of the other party for similar offenses." The resolution asked the attorney general to nol-pros all cases already commenced.[32] Hampton wrote to the president as the general assembly had asked, and the president replied in a letter in which he reported that the U.S. attorney general had instructed the South Carolina district attorney to prepare for trial only three indictments arising from the Ellenton riots. The other defendants were being told not to bother to prepare for trial. The president commented that it was possible only one case will be tried. The president wrote, "I agree with you that a general amnesty should extend to all political offenses except those which are of the gravest character."[33] These negotiations stretched over several years before being successfully concluded. Corbin did nol-pros his cases. Three Republicans were convicted—Francis L. Cardozo, Robert Smalls, and L. Cass Carpenter—and all were pardoned.[34] In late June 1877 Governor Hampton wrote to President Hayes to recommend a pardon for two South Carolinians who were serving time in the Albany Penitentiary for convictions in the KKK trials. Both had served more than half of their sentences, and both were in poor health. Hampton considered their offenses to be political in nature, and he concluded, "I hope that such events as led to their convictions will be impossible in the future."[35] The following September the governor again wrote to the president to urge a pardon of the two named in the June letter, plus one more convicted of a similar crime. Hampton distanced himself from the KKK crimes: "I have no sympathy with the offenses with which they were charged, but I desire that peace should be firmly established between the races and nothing could tend more to this than a general amnesty." The governor ended his plea with "If you could pardon them at my request it would strengthen my influence in preserving peace."[36] The following year the governor informed the families of those who had fled the state to avoid prosecution for KKK–related crimes that they could safely return to the state; there would be no federal prosecutions.[37]

One of the Hampton policies that became a point of contention was his determination that the state honor its legitimate debts, even at the cost of paying off some debts of questionable validity created by his radical predecessors. This did not mean that Hampton wanted the state to honor all debts without question, but the governor was unalterably opposed to mass repudiation. Mart Gary and his followers were more inclined to repudiation, and they saw Hampton's concerns for funding debts as a way of enriching what Gary called "the bond ring."[38] That kind of populist rhetoric became stock-in-trade in the attacks from the Tillman forces. The governor told a reporter that sustaining the state's debt was of "vital importance."[39]

Gary, in developing opposition to Hampton, carved out a position that could be described as approximately populist. In the Senate he opposed the appropriations bill that included a statewide tax of seven mills, Gary arguing that five mills was enough. He specifically opposed taxation for the purpose of paying any part of the debt recognized by the consolidation act passed by the Republican legislature in 1873, stating that a tax for such a purpose was recognition of the validity of that debt. The Democratic Executive Committee had agreed to recognize as valid the debt that resulted from the process leading to the consolidation act. Gary argued that the Democratic leadership had overreached its authority at that point.[40] The appropriations act finally determined that four mills would be for current expenses, and three mills would be for debt service.[41] The counties could levy no more than an additional tax of three mills for local expenses.[42] The editors of both the *News and Courier* and the *Columbia Register* opposed Gary as an ambitious and disappointed office seeker who threatened the unity of the Democratic Party. Gary replied that those editors were subsidized by the bond ring.[43]

Meanwhile Democratic efforts to rid high offices of Republicans continued. The House of Representatives impeached Associate Justice J. J. Wright for inappropriate behavior and recommended he resign to avoid disgrace.[44] Subsequently, Wright resigned, effective December 1, 1877. The next black justice assumed office in 1985.[45] Governor Hampton found no fault with Wright.[46] The Democrats in the House continued to increase their majority. Soon there were only thirty-seven Republicans left in the House. In the Senate, with the admission of Democrats from four contested counties, there were fifteen Democrats and eighteen Republicans. Two of the Republicans eventually resigned and were replaced by Democrats.[47]

Governor Hampton also contributed to ridding the state of some Republican officeholders, although he made no attempt to "clean house." In discharging Republicans he normally consulted the county delegations. One discharged trial justice from Spartanburg replied with sarcastic humor, "I have this day received a communication from your private secretary, informing me that you have removed me from the office of trial justice. You will please accept my kindest regards for this distinguished favor, and be assured that should a like opportunity be ever afforded, you will find me neither slow nor reluctant to return the compliment."[48]

In early June 1877, the governor approved a joint resolution to establish a commission to investigate state indebtedness.[49] This issue was immensely important to Hampton, who considered the fair treatment of the state's debts a matter of honor. The commission was to report to the next session of the legislature. The governor also approved the joint resolution establishing a commission to investigate the frauds of the radical regime.[50] The special session passed two acts that would have special importance for the black citizens: one allowed the leasing of convict labor to help bear the costs of the penitentiary and the other to prohibit the sale of seed cotton between sunset and sunrise, the latter to inhibit what was considered a crime peculiar to the black race, the theft and sale of cotton.[51] The governor approved both. In February 1878 Hampton approved a bill authorizing the leasing of convicts for the construction of the Greenwood and Augusta Railroad,[52] which proved to be especially brutal to leased convicts. The legislature continued its purging of the government of Republican officeholders. In mid-June the Democrat-controlled general assembly declared the judgeship of the Fifth District to be vacant, unseating R. B. Carpenter. The assembly then elected Gen. J. B. Kershaw to the bench.[53]

After the legislature adjourned Governor Hampton spent a considerable amount of time traveling out of the state. He was quite interested in playing a role in healing the wounds of the war and gaining a renewed respect for the South. In this interest Hampton was perceived as a leading representative of the reemerging South, not unlike the role being played at that time by L. Q. C. Lamar of Mississippi. He received an impressive number of invitations to speak to Northern audiences, including one to participate in the ceremonies honoring the Shield Guards in Auburn, New York. On his way to Auburn he stopped in New York City, where he met with several financiers to discuss loans to South Carolina authorized by the general assembly to pay interest on the state debt.[54] He met and conversed with New York governor Lucius Robinson. Hampton's message to the governor was what he essentially told all his Northern audiences: the conservative or Democratic victory of 1876 was more than a political win; it was a victory for "civilization, for home rule, for good government, for life itself." In discussing Reconstruction, the South Carolinian made a distinction between honest Northerners who had come South and carpetbaggers, whom Hampton described as thieves. He recounted that his legislature had elected a Republican, Willard, chief justice. Hampton assured Governor Robinson of his determination to deal justly with black citizens. "We intend to try and elevate them, and try to show them the responsibilities as well as the blessings of liberty."[55] In Auburn Hampton assured his audience that white people of the South were bound by every legal and moral obligation to protect the rights of black citizens. He was honest in revealing his conviction that the government of the Southern states was best in the hands of the more intelligent and property owners.[56] It is not likely that many in his audience objected to that sentiment.

The topic of finances was of particular interest during Hampton's visit to New York City. Reporters from the *New York Herald* asked the South Carolina governor whether he alone stood between those who would repudiate the debt and their objective. Hampton assured reporters that only a few favored repudiation.[57] The governor succeeded in arranging for a loan to his state, but he learned while in the city that the tax revenues in his state were good enough that there was no need to borrow at that time.[58]

Governor Hampton placed great importance on his pledge to ensure that quality public education would be available to both races. On June 20 State Superintendent of Education Hugh S. Thompson reported that about two hundred thousand dollars would be available for the support of public schools. This referred only to funds to be disbursed from the state government; the poll tax designated for schools was collected and allocated by the counties. Superintendent Thompson urged county boards of education to begin schools and operate them as long as funds lasted. He also recommended that the boards of education include representatives from both parties and both races.[59]

The radical regime had laid the foundation for the state educational system, but their efforts had been halting and often undermined by corruption. The legislature took until 1870 to enact the basic legal framework for public schools. The code enacted compulsory education for a minimum of two years. The schools were to operate under the direction of commissions of education elected in each county. Each county was divided into school districts presided over by three elected trustees. The county commissions controlled the funds and approved teachers. Under the radicals the total appropriations for schools reached a high of three hundred thousand dollars from property taxes and one hundred thousand dollars from the poll tax. However, at least a fourth of this was wasted by corruption. Also, many of the commissioners and trustees were notoriously inept. A significant number of commissioners and teachers were illiterate. Hampton commented on the illiterate commissioners in his initial report to the legislature. In an attempt to improve the number of able teachers, the state in 1873 established a normal school on the state university campus. Conservatives closed the normal school in summer 1877, probably because the state university was being closed.[60] The Hampton regime by the summer of 1877 enacted a special tax of two mills for the support of public schools.

For a time conservatives made an admirable effort to fulfill Hampton's pledge of better schools for children of both races. In the school year 1876–1877, the general turmoil of the state resulted in a decline in school enrollment. Better support from the state led to a significant improvement in enrollment of both races by 1880. The best indication of the seriousness with which the Hampton regime considered their pledge to provide a better school system for both races is in the financial commitments of the conservative legislature under the influence of Hampton. In the year 1879–1880, state appropriations for white schools reached $168,516 ($2.75 per pupil), and the appropriation for black schools reached $182,879 ($2.51 per pupil). With Hampton's departure to Washington and his declining influence in South Carolina politics there came a widening gap between the expenditures for white and black children in the 1880s. When Tillman came to power the gap widened further. In 1894–1895 the state gave white children three times the support it gave black children. Rule by the "wool hats" resulted in an ever-widening gap. In 1927 support for white children was eight times that for black children.[61] While Hampton and his followers insisted on a segregated school system, they did intend to provide equal support. The general assembly gave an interesting insight to this policy when it enacted a law to provide for one university or college for white citizens (presumably the reorganized state university in Columbia) and one for black youth: "which said universities or colleges shall be kept separate and apart, but shall forever enjoy precisely the same privileges and advantages with respect to their standards of learning and

the amount of revenue to be appropriated by the state for their maintenance."[62] It is significant for the future that Martin Gary opposed Hampton
on these measures. Gary was essentially opposed to the expenditure of tax
money paid in large part by whites for the education of blacks. He opposed
any tax support for the university.[63]

The Hampton policies of fair treatment stood a chance of success because
of his immense popularity, although Gary undoubtedly came closer to representing the sentiments of most South Carolinians. Gary and Tillman succeeded in part by appealing to the baser instincts of the populace. Still,
Hampton was not without support in his moderation. In May 1877 the Democratic Club of Abbeville County passed a resolution endorsing the policies of
Governor Hampton. The club pledged its support for the Hampton pledges of
justice "to all citizens without regard to race, color, or previous condition."[64]

While relative peace prevailed between the two races in the spring and
summer of 1877, all was not completely well. There were spasms of violence in
Timmonsville. The town intendant asked the governor for help, specifically
requesting that the governor send a black detective.[65] And there were
complaints of unfair treatment. Rev. H. H. Hunter wrote to complain that
Hampton had promised equal treatment, but so far he had appointed only
Democratic election commissioners. Hunter pointed out that the Democratic
Party was still a minority party.[66] A black citizen of Colleton County, Carlos
Tracy, wrote to complain that he and his fellow black Republicans had felt
endangered since the Democratic victory.[67] Just as important for the future
were complaints from within the Democratic Party. M. M. Thompson of
Charleston, an applicant for appointment as solicitor, wrote to express his dis-
pleasure that the Hampton regime was ignoring the straight-outs in favor of
the fusionists. Thompson said that fusionists were getting the major share of
patronage, while the straight-outs were largely responsible for the victory in
the campaign of 1876. "The straight-outs stepped aside in your election and
let the Fusionists lead in order to secure their adhesion, but they do not intend
to do so again."[68]

The governor received an interesting bit of encouragement from an erstwhile Republican supporter of D. H. Chamberlain. Alfred Williams, intendant of Beaufort, wrote that while he had voted for the Republican candidate
in 1876, he had come to believe in the leadership of Hampton. His faith in
Hampton had increased with learning that Martin Gary was the leading
opponent of the governor. Williams stated that the opposition of Gary would
attract more moderates to the Hampton banner. "This opposition in your
own party can do you no harm; it only adds strength from some of your
former opponents."[69]

The special election in Charleston occurred on June 26 with the Democratic slate winning a complete victory. This slate included three black

Democrats, and that was to the credit of Hampton, who had encouraged the white Democrats to include representation by a number of black Democrats.[70] This was at least in part an honoring of the Democratic pledge to be fair to both races.

The governor took time off for a family reunion and rest. He spent some time in July in Salem, Virginia, where his daughter, his brother Chris, and his three sisters joined him. The people of Salem serenaded their famous visitor. There was some indication of his being ill and this being a time for convalescence.[71] The governor then went on to the fashionable resort of White Sulphur Springs. The governor of West Virginia welcomed Hampton, expressing relief that the Palmetto State had won release from its "Egyptian bondage."[72]

On August 23, 1877, the *Daily Register* published a report of an interview by a correspondent for the *Sunday Journal* of former governor Robert K. Scott. The former radical governor disavowed much of his earlier experience, saying, "I have never had confidence in a government by a population just disenthralled from slavery." Scott thought the best educated should govern. He endorsed the Hampton regime: "the government of Hampton will inspire confidence, as it will be honestly and faithfully administered. Hampton is honestly carrying out the promises he made during his campaign. He has already appointed more colored men to office than were appointed during the entire two first years that I was governor." Scott was reflecting the changing attitude of much of the North to the whole issue of Reconstruction. The Republican Party was washing its hands of the issue.[73] Scott predicted that black people would soon lose interest in politics. "Labor is their field of usefulness."[74]

Hampton enjoyed friendly relations with President Hayes. The mayor of Louisville, Kentucky, wrote to invite Governor Hampton to attend the Louisville Industrial Exposition in September as a guest of that city. President Hayes had agreed to give the principal address to the exposition.[75] The South Carolina governor from time to time recommended candidates to Hayes for federal appointments. In October 1877 Hampton recommended that the president appoint Lucius C. Northrop, a Republican who had supported the Democratic candidate in the election of 1876, as federal attorney for South Carolina. Northrop had even served as an emissary from the South Carolina Democrats to candidate Hayes. Despite opposition from some radical Republicans, Northrop secured the appointment. On October 3, 1877, Northrop resigned as judge of the Seventh Circuit to become the U.S. district attorney.[76] He later served as a federal judge in Colorado. It is not surprising that Hampton's influence with the Republican president was galling to the Republican leaders in South Carolina.[77] E. W. M. Mackey, the former speaker of the radical House of Representatives, said, "It is understood in South Carolina that no man can get a place from this administration [the Hayes administration] unless he gets the endorsement of the Democrats."[78]

Hampton addressed the Winnebego County Fair in Illinois, and then headed South with a stop in St. Louis, where he attended the Industrial Exposition. President Hayes introduced the South Carolina governor to the exposition audience with impressive praise. Hampton responded by lauding the president, specifically thanking him for the "act of kindness and reconciliation and justice that he performed for South Carolina." Governor Hampton and his servant Billy Rose joined the presidential train en route to Nashville, Tennessee. This friendship with the Republican president gave Mart Gary and his followers ammunition for their charges that Hampton was disloyal to Democrats. Reporter Redfield of the *Cincinnati Commercial* wrote of Hayes and Hampton: "These men have a great liking for each other." President Hayes was pleased by how Southerners received his visit. He, like Hampton, was urging union and reconciliation.[79] The governor stayed with the presidential train until it reached Chattanooga. He then went alone to Atlanta, where he addressed the Georgia legislature. Sen. John B. Gordon introduced Hampton, and the South Carolinian responded by thanking the senator for his assistance in the campaign of 1876.[80]

As a result of the work of the legislative committee charged with investigating the scandals of the radical regime, Attorney General James Conner asked the grand jury in Columbia for a bundle of indictments of leading Republicans, including former governors R. K. Scott and F. J. Moses, former lieutenant governor R. H. Gleaves, former treasurer N. G. Parker, former secretary of state and treasurer F. L. Cardozo and H. H. Kimpton, former financial agent for the state.[81] Later the grand jury returned a true bill on Senator Patterson, and the governor initiated a requisition for his return to South Carolina for trial. The specific charge was that he had bribed the legislature to win election to the Senate.[82] The judge in the District of Columbia refused to order Patterson's extradition. The court in Columbia found F. L. Cardozo guilty, and the judge sentenced him to two years in jail and a fine of one thousand dollars. The same court found Robert Smalls guilty and sentenced him to serve three years with hard labor. Both benefited by pardons, but these findings helped seal the doom of the Republican Party in South Carolina. It is noteworthy that Conner did not seek an indictment of Chamberlain. While little came of these efforts, they drew accusations that the Democrats were using a "star chamber" process to rid the state of Republicans.[83] There was a measure of truth in the Republican accusations. Hampton had apparently assured Hayes that there would be no political prosecutions. The Democrats responded that these were criminal, not political, charges. Governor Hampton told a reporter in Chicago that the investigation was bipartisan, and the grand jury was in the majority Republican.[84] Both statements were true. The grand jury decided on true bills against Scott, Gleaves, and Kimpton. Meanwhile, Senator-elect M. C. Butler argued that the best policy was to abandon these proceedings to avoid hurting the image of the Democratic Party in South Carolina and the nation. Nevertheless, Hampton instituted proceedings for extradition of Parker and Kimpton.[85] Neither was ever extradited or tried.

Despite the immense popularity of Hampton there is evidence that his administration was often inefficient. This may in part have been a result of the great efforts to cut administrative expenses. Letters to the governor were sometimes unanswered. On occasion people resigned from office and received no acknowledgment; others applied for positions and received no response.[86] Hampton's financial difficulties continued during his gubernatorial term. His annual salary was only $3,500, hardly enough to relieve him of obligations extending back into the 1850s. J. N. Ballard sold the general some material in Mississippi in 1871, and he had not received compensation. He wrote in 1877 that he had employed an attorney to collect in Mississippi, and the attorney found that the general's lands in Mississippi had been sold for other debts.[87]

The House of Representatives in Washington handed the South Carolina Democrats a tardy defeat when the House refused to recognize the certificates of election from Governor Hampton and Secretary of State R. M. Sims indicating that Democrats O'Connor and Richardson had been elected and instead awarded seats to two black Republicans, Richard H. Cain and Joseph H. Rainey.[88] It would take another election for Democrats to reclaim these seats.

In November 1877 the governor attended the fair in Darlington. In his speech to attendees he again emphasized the two concerns foremost in his mind: an honorable treatment of the state's debt and good relations between the races. He told the audience he was aware that many thought taxes were too high, but "You must remember that we have the honor of the state in our hands, and her just debts must be paid. We mean to put the credit of the state where it was before the war." He then reiterated his belief that all citizens, regardless of race, are due equal protection of the laws. He concluded this part of his speech with a remarkable statement: "I want the colored people to become land owners, for then they will become conservative. I want to see the people of both races living in peace together."[89]

The legislature convened on November 27, and the governor's annual message again indicated Hampton's profound concern with the state's honorable treatment of its debt. He was obviously aware of the forces led by Gary favoring repudiation of much of the debt. The governor warned, "Repudiation would bring inevitable disaster and would entail disgrace." He urged the general assembly to be careful of the interests of creditors who depended on the honor of the state. He recommended a special tax of one-half mill to be designated for the redeeming of the state's bonds. He also reminded the legislature of the party's pledges to provide public schools for all citizens. He recommended ratification of a constitutional amendment providing a special tax, which, joined with the poll tax, would support the schools. The governor also recommended legislative action to reestablish the state university for whites and a similar institution for blacks.[90] It is significant that Senator Gary and five members of the Edgefield delegation signed a letter to the public opposing the amendment for support of public schools, arguing that the state could not afford such a measure.[91] The general assembly followed Hampton's lead and ratified an amendment providing for a tax of two mills for schools.[92]

Democrats scored a victory in Washington when the U.S. Senate recognized M. C. Butler as the senator succeeding T. J. Robertson, handing a defeat to D. T. Corbin, the Republican elected by the Mackey House and state senate in December 1876.[93] Corbin had been serving as the assistant district attorney prosecuting the Ellenton cases. There occurred a series of changes in the state's leadership. W. H. Wallace relinquished his position as Speaker of the House to become a circuit court judge. John C. Haskell, former chairman of the State Democratic Executive Committee, won election to the State Supreme Court. Johnson Hagood became the chairman of the Democratic Executive Committee. L. C. Northrop, Hampton's Republican friend, became district attorney. And James Conner resigned as attorney general, to be replaced by Leroy F. Youmans. The South Carolina House elected John C. Sheppard of Edgefield as its next Speaker. The *New York Times* interpreted Sheppard's election as a defeat for Hampton. The new speaker was from Edgefield and somewhat under the influence of Gary. Hence the Northern paper might have been correct.[94]

The governor had by now achieved a significant status as a recognized spokesman for the South. The invitations came frequently and from a variety of places. Hampton received invitations to speak in Iowa, Virginia, and a special one to speak in the Boston Lyceum at a rate of five hundred dollars per night.[95] He was invited to lecture in Pittsburgh for one hundred dollars per lecture.[96] Benjamin Moorhouse invited the governor to lecture in the largest lecture hall in Trenton, New Jersey, where the South Carolinian would be introduced by governor-elect George McClellan, Hampton's enemy of years ago.[97] Extant records do not indicate which of these invitations were accepted.

Hampton's policy for considering pardons further endeared him to the people of South Carolina. The radical governors had granted pardons freely and scandalously. The Democratic governor informed the state senate that his policy was to refer applications for pardons to the judge before whom the case had been tried, and seek his opinion concerning whether a pardon was justified.[98] In the course of his administration, the governor granted a significant number of pardons and commutations of sentences. He was often generous to black citizens who appealed for clemency based on the prejudice of juries. A group of citizens of Newberry County petitioned for a pardon for

Thomas Keith, who had been imprisoned for bigamy. The petitioners argued that he was convicted in part because he was a black member of the legislature and superintendent of the Alms House. They argued that if Keith had been in private life his misdeed would not have been noticed. Hampton granted Keith a pardon despite a negative letter from the presiding judge T. J. Mackey.[99] The governor granted a pardon to a black youth named Wade Hampton Fraser, convicted of forging a note for $3.50. Fraser had served eight months on his sentence of twelve months.[100] Robert Aldrich of Barnwell wrote to recommend a pardon for Loudon Brown, a black man convicted of a killing that in the common law of the state was usually considered justifiable. Aldrich warned the governor of the need to avoid the appearance that there is one law for whites and another for blacks. Brown received a pardon.[101] A number of black citizens of Georgetown County petitioned the governor to commute the sentence of Friday Castle from death to life imprisonment, noting that five white men recently convicted of the same crime and sentenced to be hanged had their sentences commuted to life. The governor agreed and commuted Castle's sentence to life in prison.[102]

The *Chicago Times* published several stories indicating that there was a rift between Senator Butler and Governor Hampton, reporting that Butler had made a deal with Senator Patterson whereby the latter would support Butler's claim for a seat in the contest with Republican D. T. Corbin in return for Butler's efforts to squelch the charges against Patterson. The editor of the *Daily Register* denied these charges, but the *Times* was likely correct. Butler had come to Columbia soon after his victory in gaining the contested seat, and in a speech of celebration he blamed Hampton's friend President Hayes for having supported the claims of Corbin. Mart Gary spoke at that celebration, praising his friend Butler.[103]

Gary took another shot at Hampton in January 1878, when he charged the chief justice with having been bribed. Gary asked the Joint Investigating Committee to consider the charge against Willard. The chairman of that committee, Sen. John R. Cochran, refused Gary's request, saying that his committee was restricted to considering frauds having to do with public funds.[104]

The Democratic leadership's next step in purging Republican officeholders was an attack on the bench. Six of the eight circuit court judges were Republicans. Attorney General Conner initiated a suit before the Supreme Court that Judge A. J. Shaw had not been properly elected since the constitution required that judges be elected by ballot of the two houses, whereas Shaw had been elected viva voce. Two of the three justices agreed that Shaw had in fact not been legally elected and should yield his seat and so should the other five justices who had also been elected viva voce. The general assembly then conducted proper elections and filled all but two of these positions with Democrats. Two Republicans were returned to the bench: Shaw and T. J.

Mackey.[105] One of the newly elected Democratic judges was Robert Aldrich of Barnwell, who had resigned from the bench in indignation at the power of the military rule of General Canby.[106]

In January 1878 Gary spoke in the Senate to oppose any measure that would provide support for the black college equal to support for the white university. His reasoning was that most taxes were paid by whites, and those funds should not be dispensed equally for both races. The legislation Gary opposed provided for equality of support. The bill passed over Gary's opposition.[107] Governor Hampton had such influence with the legislature that he seldom used the veto. In February 1878 he vetoed a bill that would have allowed any trial justice to assign county prisoners to work gangs or chain gangs. The governor believed that such a law would have smacked of ex post facto qualities, since the prisoners might not have been sentenced to hard labor. In considering the mood of the time for using convict labor to lessen the public expenses, this was a demonstration of impressive ethics. The House of Representatives sustained the veto by a vote of 102 to 10.[108]

In February 1878 the Bond Commission, which had been established to examine the state's indebtedness and make recommendations as to legal obligations for funding, issued a report recognizing the validity of all consolidation bonds, coupons, and certificates of stock that had been properly issued. The commission found that $3,999,147 of the vouchers for consolidation bonds had not been properly issued. The commission also questioned the legality of the bonds issued by the Sinking Fund Commission and the Land Commission. The editor of the *News and Courier* objected to invalidating any part of the state debt, and that opinion probably followed closely the opinion of Governor Hampton.[109] On February 11 the *News and Courier* assured the public that the Hampton administration favored validating all bonds issued under the Consolidation Act of 1873. The governor opposed any compromise resulting in even a partial repudiation of the state's debt.[110] The governor obviously wanted to honor the State Democratic Executive Committee's pledge to abide by the Consolidation Act of 1873.[111] Hampton saw this as a matter of honor, while Gary insisted that the committee had exceeded its authority.

The Charleston leaders invited the governor to participate in the celebration of Washington's birthday in 1878, doubtlessly with special pleasure since one year earlier President Grant had limited that celebration. The honored guest in 1878 was W. H. F. Lee, the son of Robert E. Lee and Hampton's former comrade in arms. Hampton went and delivered a speech of significance. He urged his audience to remain faithful to the pledges of the campaign of 1876. "You have seen that by doing justice to all, recognizing the rights of all citizens of South Carolina, you can carry the state."[112]

The Hampton-Gary dispute still simmered. A reporter for the *News and Courier* noted that Senator Gary in private conversation criticized the governor as a dictator. Gary thought that Hampton violated the trust of his office when he undertook to lobby the legislature for his favorite issues.[113] Actually, Gary's main argument with Hampton at this time was the charge that the governor had violated the trust of the straight-outs. Gary noted, "The main point with Hampton is his neutral position, and his saying 'So help me God, I am no party man.'"[114]

Gary and his followers were suspicious that Hampton would ultimately support a fusion with part of the Republican Party. M. C. Butler shared at least some of this distrust of Hampton. The newly installed U.S. senator wrote to Gary, "If any steps should be taken by anybody to change or subvert the policy by which we carried the state at the last election, he ought and eventually will be eternally damned by the people of the state. I cannot think that Hampton or any other sane man would advise a fusion with the Radical Party, now that we have control of the state."[115]

Gary's strategy was to support the reelection of Hampton as governor, thereby clearing the way for the general assembly to elect Gary himself to the U.S. Senate to replace John J. Patterson. The Edgefield senator hoped in the second Hampton administration to use his influence to surround the reelected governor with men more agreeable to the straight-out philosophy. "The present state officers have not got spirit enough to oppose Hampton when they know that he is wrong." Gary specifically blamed Lt. Gov. W. D. Simpson, former attorney general James Conner, and Comptroller General Johnson Hagood, all of whom eventually became governors. Gary told his followers that Hampton came to South Carolina from his Mississippi plantations just before the election campaign of 1876, and he did not know the realities of politics in the Palmetto State. It was, however, obviously not to Gary's political advantage to oppose the popular Hampton too openly. He even made speeches in which he endorsed the reelection of the governor.[116] Hampton was nevertheless quite aware of Gary's deep-seated opposition.[117]

The influential editor of the *News and Courier* endorsed the renomination of Hampton as governor. F. W. Dawson assumed that the extremists would not want Hampton in office for another term.[118] This was the opening shot of the campaign of 1878. The governor received an invitation to make the first speech of the canvass in Anderson, where he had launched the 1876 campaign.[119]

The issue of the state's debt boiled up again in early 1878. To review the situation: the Republican legislature had in 1873 passed the Consolidation Act, which recognized a total state indebtedness of $15,851,625, of which the act repudiated $5,965,000, leaving a debt of $9,886,625. The act provided for funding the remaining debt with 6 percent bonds at fifty cents on the dollar. The State Democratic Executive Committee had announced in the campaign of 1876 that the Democratic Party considered the Consolidation Act to be the final treatment of the debt; that is, the Democrats would abide by the Consolidation Act were they victorious. Hampton suggested to the special session of the legislature in 1877 that they establish a commission to study the debt and make appropriate recommendations. After that commission was established, the question of repudiation loomed as a major issue. Hampton increasingly viewed even partial repudiation as a breach of honor. Martin Gary led the opposition to funding the debt as a surrender to the rascality of the radicals. Governor Hampton surely regretted his recommendation that the issue be studied. It would have been wiser to assume that the legislature would implement the commitment made by the Democratic Executive Committee. Gary made it a major issue, engaging in a form of class warfare, charging that those who favored funding the debt were under the influence of a "bond ring." The commission, having studied the debt, recommended partial repudiation, specifically recommending repudiation of $3,608,717 of the consolidation debt. The legislature responded with a compromise whereby a court of claims or bond court, consisting of three circuit court judges, would examine the outstanding bonds and determine which were valid.[120] All of this represented something of a defeat for Governor Hampton, since the Democratic Party split over this issue. Ironically, the Republican minority supported the governor on the handling of the state debt. Fear of perpetuating the division within the party made Hampton loath to push too hard to get the entire debt funded.[121]

Francis Dawson of the *News and Courier* was, next to the governor, the most prominent opponent of any repudiation of the state's debt. Dawson thought that the compromise was a serious flaw in the efforts to reestablish the state's credit. New York philanthropist Peter Cooper considered establishing an educational institution at Limestone Springs, but after some correspondence he withdrew. Dawson interpreted Cooper's change of mind as having been caused by his disgust with the general assembly's lack of responsibility vis-à-vis the state debt. The editor charged the general assembly with having "played ducks and drakes with the public credit."[122]

In March 1878 the general assembly and governor redeemed an important and popular campaign pledge by giving some relief to landowners who had lost property for failure to pay taxes. The act allowed lands forfeited for taxes and that remained in the state's hands to be redeemed by the original owners' paying taxes for the fiscal year 1876–1877.[123] The legislature also considered another seemingly innocuous measure, but one that became a class issue. This was the so-called fence law, which required owners of livestock to build fences to protect neighbors' property from being devoured. The issue was offensive to poorer people, who were accustomed to allowing their cows and pigs to range freely. The legislature was sufficiently aware of the sensitive nature of fence laws to allow the counties to vote on fences as a local option.[124] The

Hampton people became associated with the issue of fence laws, and it became one more charge against them as selfish men of property.

Hampton was responsible for a mildly progressive measure in the establishment of a railroad commission. These officers were charged to examine the railroads for safety and general adequacy of accommodations for the public. The commission had the authority to modify rates for freight and passenger service. Disputes arising from these orders were to be settled in state courts.[125] Governor Hampton appointed three men to the railroad commission: Edward Magrath, H. L. Pinckney, and Joseph Winthrop.[126] This is noteworthy because it was before the progressive movement, and regulation of railroads became an issue for progressives.

The general assembly passed several acts designed to limit the power and influence of the black population. The legislature carved a new county, named Hampton, out of the black-dominated Beaufort County, thereby assuring more white representation in the general assembly. The new county received three representatives and one senator, until the next census. Another law forbade the sale of seed cotton after the hours of darkness, to inhibit the widely believed theft and sale by black people.[127]

The attacks on Hampton in 1878 were strong enough to cause some concern among his faithful. The Democratic Club in Aiken passed a resolution endorsing the governor's leadership. The preamble stated, "Whereas there have been attacks on the policy of our beloved Governor, which in our judgment were uncalled for and without reasonable grounds."[128]

In the final days of the legislative session the majority passed a resolution authorizing the governor to discontinue prosecutions springing from the committee that had investigated the scandals of the radical regime. The purpose was to push along the proposed compromise whereby the state would not prosecute the Republicans for their crimes and the federal authorities would not prosecute the Democrats for their excesses in the campaign of 1876 and earlier. Once again, Gary led the opposition. He argued that it was wrong to select a few and to stay those cases because of political reasons. The resolution passed despite Gary's opposition.[129]

The recurring conflict between illicit distillers and revenue agents in the mountains of the state involved Governor Hampton in yet more negotiations with the federal government. The conflict in Pickens County had reflections of Shay's Rebellion and a hero like Robin Hood. Several agents of the U.S. Revenue Service arrested three locals charged with bootlegging. A party of armed mountain men, ostensibly led by Lewis Redmond, confronted Sheriff Jacob Mauldin at the county jail and demanded the release of his prisoners. The men made their escape, and the sheriff chose not to pursue.[130] Circuit Court Judge T. J. Mackey issued a bench warrant for the arrest of Redmond, ordering Sheriff Mauldin to organize a posse to seek and arrest Redmond and his followers. Judge Mackey was far more concerned that these men had violated the state laws in the jailbreak than he was about their violation of federal revenue laws.[131] Subsequently the posse arrested two of the escapees, but they failed to find the elusive Redmond, who by defying the authorities had by now become something of a folk hero.[132] Judge Mackey ventured the opinion that the men arrested by the revenue officers were in fact not guilty. They were presently released for lack of evidence. The judge thought that the revenue officers had mistreated the men. Redmond earned popular acclaim by invading the house where the revenue officers were living and stealing their overcoats. The judge secured a true bill against Redmond and again ordered a posse for his arrest.[133] Redmond's popular support grew apace. The common belief was that he helped the poor while opposing the unpopular revenue agents. In July Sheriff Mauldin gained popular support for himself by declaring under oath that Redmond was not a part of the jailbreak.[134]

Governor Hampton announced that he was seeking an agreement of clemency from the federal government, and he asked illicit distillers to come forward and bind themselves to cease their illegal activities. For his part the governor would use his influence to stay prosecutions. A number of distillers did indeed turn themselves in.[135] In August 187 men pled guilty in the U.S. court in Greenville with the understanding that there would be no prosecutions. They promised good behavior thereafter. Repeated charges that the revenue officers were themselves lawless were having an effect. A grand jury indicted five revenue officers for assault and battery. They were not prosecuted, but the indictment was an interesting measure of public opinion. Hampton complained that the men chosen as revenue officers were a singularly disreputable lot. Some newspapers accused E. M. Brayton, collector of U.S. Internal Revenue, with having charged Governor Hampton for providing the jail-breaking gang with special protection. Brayton denied having made the charge.[136] The commissioner of internal revenue offered a reward of $1,500 for the capture of Redmond. The public was not responsive. The commissioner acknowledged that Governor Hampton had complained about the character of the revenue agents. He said that he would welcome nominations of new officers from the governor.[137] Ultimately, Hampton managed to achieve a general amnesty for distillers; they were required to pledge themselves to abide by the law thenceforth. The amnesty even included Redmond, and Hampton gained more support in the northern corner of the state.[138]

Governor Hampton and the Democrats fired the first shots of the campaign of 1878 in March. The governor accepted an invitation to speak in Anderson on March 26.[139] The trip to and from Anderson turned into a triumphal procession. There were enthusiastic gatherings all along the way: Prosperity, Silver Street, Newberry, Ninety-Six, Greenwood, Hodges, and Belton. He reminded the Newberry audience that he was determined to be governor of all South Carolinians, white and black. Perhaps wistfully, he said, "you have shown them [black citizens] that you do not want to deprive them of any right, any privileges."[140] A few days later he told a crowd in Abbeville, "would it not be the grandest triumph if the colored men throughout the state, recognizing that their rights are safe, come forward and say we are willing to trust our destinies, lives, and fortunes in your hands." He warned his fellow Democrats, "You cannot win permanent success except by doing justice to all men."[141] That statement might well have been the most accurate insight to Hampton's thinking: a paternalistic attitude of sincerely caring for the rights of black brethren, albeit under the watchful care of white aristocratic leadership. Although such paternalism does not stand up well in the light of later times, it was infinitely to be preferred over the more blatant racism of extremists such as Martin Gary and Ben Tillman. Editor Dawson of the *News and Courier* commented, "There is a small faction in nearly every community who prefer to carry elections by the high hand."[142] Dawson was also a bit wistful in estimating only a small faction.

The conflict between Wade Hampton and the moderates on one side and Martin Gary and the extremists on the other continued simmering. In April Gary charged Hampton for having done more that anyone else to make Rutherford B. Hayes president, a charge Hampton promptly denied.[143] In the same month a number of county Democratic clubs adopted resolutions urging the nomination of Hampton for a second term. The resolution from Barnwell included the statement: "We have no use for the hot heads."[144]

Both the Hampton moderates and the Gary extremists had some fear of majority rule. The Hamptonites in some way feared the votes of poor whites more than the votes of black citizens. The more aristocratic element believed they could control the black votes; they increasingly feared the votes of poor whites, especially as Gary and his followers appealed for class-conscious support. The editor of the *News and Courier* in the months approaching the campaign of 1878 wrote, "In this state a large majority of the populace are ignorant, full of prejudice and wholly unfit to take part in the conduct of government." The particular issue when Dawson wrote was whether the counties should conduct primary elections, as the State Executive Committee had recommended.[145] When the editor wrote those words he was probably referring for the most part to black citizens, but as time passed the Hampton followers began to include poor whites in their consciousness of an ignorant populace.

Despite a vocal opposition, Hampton still had impressive support throughout the state. E. P. Clark, correspondent for the *Springfield Republican*, reviewed the record of the governor after one year in office. Clark interviewed a number of citizens, white and black, and found a growing faith in the stability of state government. Benjamin A. Boseman, the black postmaster of Charleston, told the reporter, "We have no complaint whatever to make. He

[Hampton] has kept all his pledges." Ironically, Clark classified the opponents of Hampton as bourbons, "looking to the past." He considered Hampton to be a progressive. The reporter was perceptive in questioning whether any man other than Hampton could implement his policies. He found that the majority supported the man, not his policies.[146] That finding helps to explain what happened when Hampton went to Washington. Even black Congressman Robert Smalls, who had been sharply critical of the campaign of 1876, praised the "just and liberal course of the governor."[147]

There was progress in achieving the compromise proposed by the South Carolina General Assembly, whereby this state would not prosecute Republicans for their abuses of office and the Republican administration would not prosecute white Democrats for their excesses. In May 1878, President Hayes pardoned three South Carolinians held in the Albany Prison for activities as Klansmen.[148] The negotiations extended past Hampton's time as governor; Francis Dawson of the *News and Courier* acted as the principal mediator. Hampton was in agreement with the compromise, as were many leading Republicans and leading Democrats. Neither side could easily afford the bloodletting that continued prosecutions would have entailed. Some of the Republicans wrote to President Hayes to urge him to seek an agreement. On the Democratic side the general assembly itself had taken the initiative. Fortunately for the defendants, U.S. Chief Justice Morrison Waite, who presided over the Ellenton trials, defined for the jury very narrow definitions upon which a finding of guilty could be based. The Ellenton cases resulted in a mistrial, and those cases were ultimately dropped. The Democrats promised to nol-pros the cases against the Republicans, except for cases against Robert Smalls and F. W. Cardozo then in process before the Supreme Court. Both later received pardons.[149]

The proposed amnesty agreement was of vital importance to many in the state. Dr. J. R. Bratton was one of the many citizens who had fled the state to avoid prosecutions for KKK–related activities. His brother, John S. Bratton, wrote to Governor Hampton to plead for the amnesty so the doctor could return home.[150] The governor replied he had the assurance of President Hayes that "your brother and all others connected with the Ku-Klux troubles can return to the state with perfect safety."[151]

On May 19, 1878, the general assembly passed a joint resolution ratifying the constitutional amendment to require each county to impose a tax of two mills on all taxable property, plus a poll tax of one dollar, both designated for support of public schools. The provision for the poll tax included an interesting statement: "No person shall ever be deprived of the right of suffrage for the non-payment of such tax."[152] That assurance would obviously be changed.

In June 1878 the governor went to Baltimore and to the Eastern Shore to participate in a lawsuit pertaining to the defunct Carolina Life Insurance Co.

He was not actually called as a witness, and he visited friends. There is no evidence of inappropriate conduct by Hampton in the demise of the company, but South Carolinians alone lost about a quarter of a million dollars in a depressed time. The *News and Courier* later commented that these people invested their precious premiums and "without any warning the company blew up and went to pieces." The editorial asked, "Where did the money go? . . . The prominent ex-Confederates who managed the affairs of the Company and whose names caused the Southern people to have faith in it owe it to themselves and their own reputations, it seems to us, to give the people who trusted them with their money a frank and complete history of the rise and fall of the Southern Life Insurance Company [the Carolina and Southern companies had merged, to the detriment of both]." About all that can be said about Hampton is that the company provided him with a livelihood for several years. Sen. John B. Gordon of Georgia became involved in a dispute with a political opponent who charged him with mishandling the affairs of the company.[153] The controversy did not seriously hurt Gordon. There is some doubt about the business acumen of these former Confederates, but it is true that many companies failed in this difficult time.

The Democratic Party of Edgefield County in early June defined much of the focus of the dispute within the party by resolving that the issue between white and black South Carolinians was a matter of one race against the other, not a matter of political differences. "White supremacy is essential to our continued existence as a people." Edgefield County Democrats excluded blacks from their ranks. A writer for the Spartanburg *Spartan* wrote that the mass admission of blacks to the Democratic Party would allow lowcountry whites to control huge numbers of votes and thereby control the state.[154] This in part defined the upcountry versus low county split over the race issue. Hampton with his more generous view of black suffrage was associated with the lowcountry gentry.

Governor Hampton accepted an invitation to attend an exhibition at Claflin University, scheduled for June 10-12, 1878. This event became a political issue, revealing the depth of Gary's racism. The *News and Courier* described Dr. E. Cooke, the president of Claflin, as "a warm friend of Governor Hampton."[155] That relationship provided the governor's racist opponents with ammunition, which they used to try to discredit him. After the governor had attended the exhibition, the *News and Courier* reported that Hampton was determined to show the world that he and his administration were determined to educate black youth. Hence, Claflin had become the governor's "special care." Hampton, accompanied by State Superintendent of Education Hugh Thompson, joined President Cooke for a meal.[156] Apparently, they sat with black guests for the meal, and that became an issue in the mind of Martin Gary. The Orangeburg *Times* noted, "The colored people in Orangeburg, as well as elsewhere in our state, have been favorably impressed with the liberal and consistent course Governor Hampton has pursued."[157] Hampton sitting at a meal with the black friends popped up from time to time as an issue.

The town of Blackville staged a grand celebration July 4, 1878, and that occasion led to one of Governor Hampton's most significant speeches. An excursion train brought from Charleston the Washington Artillery and veterans of Hart's Battery. Both units participated in a parade. The thirty-eight guns fired a salute in honor of distinguished guests, which included the governor. Gen. James Conner delivered the primary address, and Hampton spoke briefly, but tellingly, in that his remarks revealed clearly that the major division between Hampton and Gary was the issue of race. The Edgefield Democrats had moved to exclude black citizens from their party, and they had declared the issue between the races was not political but a question of race. The governor warned his Blackville audience against the "machinations of demagogues." Apparently Hampton feared that the sentiments of Edgefield could spread to other counties; else he would not have spoken so aggressively in Barnwell County. "Those who raise the cry that this is a white man's government know that they are thrusting a lighted match into a barrel of powder." The governor declared that if the party went back on its pledges and sought to consider black people no longer citizens, he would then decline public office. He reminded the audience that he and the Democratic leaders had promised black South Carolinians that their best interests lay with the Democratic Party. How could some Democrats now say to black people, "We have no use for you. You shall not vote even in the primary elections?" Hampton viewed this as a dishonorable action. He also warned against the use of fraud in the forthcoming election. "I tell you . . . if you countenance fraud, before very many years pass over your heads you will not be worth saving, and you will not be worthy of the state you reside in." Hampton charged, "The lust for office is the root of the political evil." Presumably, he saw that evil as emanating from Edgefield. Hampton was obviously quite aware of Gary's insatiable ambition for high office. Comptroller General Hagood also addressed the Blackville audience, warning against the dangers of "ku kluxizm."[158] The editor of the Democratic *Daily Register* commented on this situation, "We thought our friends in Edgefield have made a mistake in restricting primary elections to whites when it is clear that hundreds of Negroes voted with them in 1876, and are entitled to participate in the momentum this year."[159]

Gary was quite aware of the Hampton salvos fired at Blackville. He hoped that Sen. M. C. Butler would answer Hampton's Blackville speech. There is no doubt about Gary's ambition for high office. He wrote to a colleague, "I am receiving flattering assurances from a good many people of my chances for the senatorship."[160] It was increasingly likely that Gary wanted Hampton reelected as governor in order to remove the governor as a competitor for the Senate.[161]

Sen. M. C. Butler managed to straddle the fence by maintaining some relationship with Hampton and at the same time placating his Edgefield neighbors. He at this time leaned more to Gary than he did to Hampton. He spoke in his home county and told his listeners, "Well, theoretically, it is not a white man's government . . . , but practically, as a matter of fact, it is a white man's government."[162] In what was likely a slam at the governor, "It has got to be the fashion for some politicians to turn pale in the face and to go off and hide their head if you use the word 'white' in any communication."[163]

While it is clear in retrospect that Gary represented the majority and the future of the state, Hampton was influential enough that he did not stand alone. The Anderson Democrats adopted a resolution endorsing the reelection of Wade Hampton. The resolution recognized "the perfect equality of all its citizens before the law, and the right and privilege of each and all to participate in the benefits and blessings of good government."[164]

The chairman of the State Democratic Executive Committee, John D. Kennedy, sought on the eve of the Democratic convention to clarify the party's stance on the issue of whether black citizens could participate in the party's choices. In an important speech, Kennedy said, "We have been placed in peculiar relations with the colored people, and it would be madness to turn our backs on them. With honest whites and honest blacks closely united in defense of honesty and home rule, we can bid eternal defiance to carpetbaggers, scalawags and any other rascally element that may seek our destruction."[165]

The South Carolina Democrats met in convention on August 1, 1878. Gen. John D. Kennedy, a Hampton man, served as chairman of the convention. The main purposes were to establish a platform and to nominate the slate of candidates for the November election. The convention adopted a platform essentially like that of 1876. The main points were that the Democrats accepted in good faith the three Reconstruction amendments to the federal Constitution, the party called for the cooperation of both races, and they promised equal protection of the rights of all people. It is of some interest that George Tillman, the brother of Ben Tillman, Hampton's future nemesis, moved that the convention urge the next legislature to begin procedures for a new constitutional convention. Tillman derogated the current constitution as the work of "fraud, knavery, aliens, and bayonets."[166] The Tillmans would have their way, but it took almost twenty years. The convention nominated Hampton by a unanimous vote for a second term. He accepted the nomination and promised to work to get a favorable legislature elected.[167]

The Republican convention met within several days. There was a move to endorse the governorship of Wade Hampton, but E. W. M. Mackey successfully led the opposition, and the resolution failed. Nevertheless, the convention decided that it was inexpedient to nominate a statewide slate of candidates. Their focus would be on the election of county Republican legislators.[168] The Republican platform denounced those black people who had voted Democratic and accused the Democrats of having committed fraud in the election of 1876.[169]

One of Hampton's early efforts in the campaign of 1878 occurred in Edgefield. The governor spoke at a Democratic rally at the same site where Chamberlain had been humiliated in 1876. Speaking in the home county of his major opponent, Martin Gary, was somewhat awkward. Hampton told his audience he had heard that he had been charged with traducing the people of Edgefield. He went on to say, "If you the people of Edgefield never have any man to traduce you until I do, you will have an honored and brilliant career." He then thanked the people of that county for their support in the past and assured them, "When I differ from you, it is as one honest man differs from another, and as a friend differs from a friend."[170] Gary spoke to the same rally, telling the audience that he disagreed with the governor on these points: the constitutional amendment requiring a tax of two mills for the public schools, the funding of the state debt, the bill to reestablish the state university, and the usury bill. Gary commented, "We can honestly differ and still be friends."[171] Protestations of disagreements among friends notwithstanding, the Hampton-Gary schism was obvious in the early stages of the campaign. When Gary addressed a rally in Spartanburg, he charged that the election of Rutherford B. Hayes was a "grand usurpation."[172] Since the Edgefield senator openly disapproved of the friendship between Hampton and Hayes, that the governor was his target was obvious.

One of the scandals of this era was developing during the excitement of the campaign of 1878. The governor and general assembly had agreed that the leasing of prisoners was a proper means of saving the state some expenses. Hampton with many others actually hoped that this was a means of making the penitentiary self-supporting. A number of leased convicts were employed in the construction of the Greenwood and Augusta Railroad. On hearing that there might be abuses involved in the work on that project, the governor asked the superintendent of the prison to investigate. Superintendent Parmele reported that those leased prisoners were "well provided for in every particular."[173] Later investigations revealed terrible treatment of prisoners working on that railroad.

During the campaign of 1878 the governor received significant support from the black population. C. Thomas, a black citizen, wrote to the governor to thank him for pardoning several black prisoners. Thomas added, "Allow me, also, General and Governor and Governor General, to compliment you for having performed all your pledges toward the unfortunate African race."[174] Indeed, the governor's record of pardoning black prisoners was remarkable. By the end of August 1878 Hampton had pardoned a total of eighty-one prisoners, of whom sixty-two were black.[175]

In late August, Hampton temporarily withdrew from the race to recuperate from exhaustion. He wrote a letter to the public to indicate that his physician had recommended rest. He left the campaign to rest at his retreat in Cashiers, North Carolina.[176] While Hampton was resting in the valley, the Democrats conducted a rally in Greenville. The leaders invited Martin Gary to speak and join in reviewing the parade. One of the leaders of the parade was Rep. J. W. Gray, who was the commander of the Fourteenth Brigade of the state militia. Gray was pleased to announce, "This is the first instance where colored troops have ever marched in line with the white citizen soldiers of South Carolina. This event is a moral result of the 'Hampton democracy.'"[177]

This threat to the solid ranks of white South Carolinians was too much for Gary to take silently. Gary wrote a letter to the public in which he said, "I suppose that we will next hear of dining or dancing with the colored brothers as the natural result of Hampton democracy." The editor of the News and Courier commented that Gary's remarks would likely shake the Democratic allegiance of the black citizens of Greenville and that Gary was attacking Hampton as a means of positioning himself to be elected to the U.S. Senate.[178] Gary realized that Hampton's attitude toward the black race made the general vulnerable in the eyes of many South Carolinians. Ellis G. Graydon of Abbeville wrote to Gary to encourage his ambition for higher office. Graydon thought that Hampton, once thought of as a "god," was declining in popularity. "They [the people] no longer regard him [Hampton] as infallible but regard him as the exponent of extreme conservatism and niggerism." To remove any doubt that Hampton was most vulnerable because of his fraternizing with the other race, Graydon wrote, "I have been blowing the nigger dining on Hampton and it meets with universal condemnation."[179]

Hampton left his retreat in the valley to make a political speech in Greenville on September 19. Although still weak from his illness, the governor delivered a vigorous speech in which he attacked his opponents head on. He urged Democrats to be loyal to the platform of 1876. He wanted nothing to do with a shotgun policy. Specifically, Hampton recommended that whites recognize the political equality of the races, that the party protect the rights of black citizens, that whites be kind to their black neighbors, that the state provide adequate facilities for the education of both races, that whites encourage black citizens to join the Democratic Party, and those in power demonstrate justice and magnanimity.[180] "In the name of our civilization and of all that has been honorable in South Carolina, in the name of our state and of our God, I protest against any resort to violence . . . or any adoption of the 'shot gun policy.' We cannot do evil that good may come of it."[181]

After the Greenville speech, Governor Hampton informed the executive committee that he did not want to share the platform again with Martin Gary. John D. Kennedy, chairman of the State Executive Committee, informed Gary that his role in the campaign would thenceforth be restricted.[182] Hampton wrote to James Conner that he considered Gary's allusion to the results of Hampton democracy "a piece of impertinence."[183] Gary's backers never forgave Hampton for curtailing the political activities of their hero. C. Baring Farmer of Walterboro wrote to Gary to express his anguish that Hampton was robbing Gary of his "just laurels" for winning the campaign of 1876.[184]

It is of interest that one of Gary's sympathizers was the son-in-law of John C. Calhoun, Thomas G. Clemson, who wrote to Gary to express indignation at the treatment of Gary by the press. "I have lived in monarchies where the press was under censor, but I have never seen a press suborned as that of South Carolina." Clemson, whose attitude toward the black race was like that of Gary, wrote that he had served as an expert witness in a case involving fertilizer, and the jury consisted of some respectable farmers and "one or two gorillas" (presumably black jurors).[185]

Gary believed himself boxed in by Wade Hampton and his followers. The governor restricted his speaking for the Democratic Party, and Francis Dawson, editor of the state's most influential newspaper, the *News and Courier*, often refused to publish material submitted by the ambitious man from Edgefield.[186] Gary's bitterness toward Hampton became a legacy for Ben Tillman and his followers.

The governor went from Greenville to Pickens on a railroad crank car, propelled by two black men, cranking vigorously. He promised the Pickens audience that he was seeking a complete amnesty for the local hero Redmond. He also said that approximately one thousand men had fled the state to avoid prosecution for KKK–related offenses. Those fugitives were then returning, thanks to the governor's efforts.[187] Hampton participated in a gala political event in Charleston on October 2, complete with a parade and a salute of seventeen guns. The governor made an impassioned appeal to black voters to align themselves with their conservative white neighbors. He described the white race as superior, "bearing the flag of civilization and Christianity." He urged the black brethren to vote and, when capable, run for office.[188]

Although the Democrats won overwhelmingly in 1878, the election was not without fraud, and the Republicans were still strong in some of their low-country strongholds. The State Executive Committee virtually admitted in a letter to the public (released in late October) that there was some degree of lawlessness in the campaign. The letter argued that the campaign had been relatively peaceful, but "It is no more in the power of the Democratic Party to prevent occasional and accidental offenses than it is in the power of organized human society to abolish crime."[189] One of the most publicized cases of lawlessness in the campaign involved the prominent black leader Swails, who wrote to the governor to complain that he had been "arrested" by a group of white ruffians, dressed in red shirts, after he left a Republican meeting in Sumter. The whites told Swails that he and his family should leave the state for their safety. Hampton replied rather disinterestedly, suggesting that Swails initiate proceedings through the judicial system. The governor promised to begin an investigation of the possibility of negligence by the local trial justice.[190] This incident received national attention.[191]

The Republicans were not alone in being frustrated. Democrat William S. Drayton of Beaufort resigned as trial justice, largely because of the frustration of being in a county where the Republicans were a commanding majority. Drayton informed the governor, "the Democratic Party is badly demoralized in this section."[192]

The Democrats won a sweeping, but flawed, victory on November 6, 1878.[193] In the next general assembly there were only five Republican senators and three Republican representatives. Hampton had no opposition, but the vote was still an endorsement of the governor. Black Democratic representatives were nominated and elected from Charleston, Colleton, Orangeburg, and Sumter counties.[194] The lack of a formidable Republican opposition and Hampton's pleas for honesty notwithstanding, the election of 1878 was seriously marred by Democratic intimidation and fraud. Republicans filed charges of assaulting an election supervisor, multiple voting, and hindering a federal marshal, to name a few offenses.[195] Hampton later admitted to the U.S. Senate that there was fraud in the election, offering the justification "that cruel wrongs have been inflicted on our people."[196]

The robust outdoorsman Hampton, who had survived three wounds in Civil War engagements, suffered an ironic twist of fate on November 7, the day after the election. He and some friends were to engage in a deer hunt in the Wateree Swamp. Hampton rode his horse to the residence of Mr. Speigner, where before entering the swamp he exchanged his horse for a saddled mule and then rode to meet the group. While the governor was still alone, a pack of dogs chased a deer nearby, and he then left the road to follow the dogs. When the mule became entangled in brush, Hampton threw the bridle over a limb and began to dismount, at which time the mule started. Having no bridle for control, Hampton leapt from the animal and hit the ground awkwardly, breaking his right leg in two places above the ankle, a bone actually protruding from one place. The hunter dragged himself and leaned against a tree. He then sought help by blowing his hunting horn and by firing his gun into the air. The injury occurred at approximately 4:00 P.M.; help arrived at about 6:00 P.M., when a black man in the hunting party followed the shots to where Hampton lay. The hunters obtained a spring wagon and placed a mattress in the bed. A road had to be cut to reach and then take the governor out. The wounded hunter arrived at his home at about midnight, where Dr. B. W. Taylor dressed the wounds. Several doctors came from Augusta and Charleston to assist. They initially agreed that Hampton should recover without amputation.[197]

The people of South Carolina followed the health of the wounded governor with great interest. He was of course confined to his bed, but for some days he seemed to be progressing well. On November 13 Hampton devolved the duties of his office to Lieutenant Governor Simpson. The acting governor sent a message to the general assembly on November 27, in which he made rather daring recommendations for an interim executive. Simpson recommended the enactment of a statewide fence law, requiring owners of livestock to enclose their animals in fences, thereby protecting their neighbors' crops.[198] As noted earlier, that measure later became a point of friction between the more wealthy planters and their poorer neighbors, a division between the Hamptonites and their populist opponents.

In the midst of the excitement of the election and the governor's very serious injury, there was much public discussion of electing Hampton to the U.S. Senate to replace Senator Patterson. There was some interest in electing Gen. James Conner of Charleston, but Conner in a letter to the public declined to be a candidate, and he suggested Hampton.[199] The usual comment was that Hampton had led in redeeming the state, and he could now best serve in Washington. Martin Gary was ambitious to succeed Senator Patterson, and he therefore had urged the reelection of Hampton as governor to keep the way open for his own election to the Senate. Henry Farley, editor of the *Daily and Tri-Weekly Phoenix* of Columbia, wrote to Gary to report a rumor that Hampton had doubts about the constitutionality of his being reelected governor and then being elected to the Senate and resigning from the former to take the latter. Farley's paper was publishing articles urging the retention of Hampton as governor. Farley told Gary that pressure was being applied on Hampton "to make him run [for the Senate] to spite you."[200] Francis Dawson of the *News and Courier* recommended the election of Hampton to the Senate. "It is time when the wisest and truest American should be sent to the Senate."[201]

For days on end the governor's health wavered between improving and deteriorating. The wounds were not healing as well as the physicians had hoped, and they began considering amputation.[202] On December 4 a group of state officials, including the lieutenant governor, the chief justice of the supreme court, the president and clerk of the senate, and members of a joint committee of the legislature, went to the Hampton home in the suburbs of Columbia to inaugurate Wade Hampton for his second term. Wade Hampton IV welcomed the visitors, and the invalid lay propped up in his bed as Chief Justice Willard administered the oath of office. Hampton dictated a message for his visitors to take to the general assembly, thanking them for their consideration.[203]

In the midst of the intense public interest in the governor's health and in the approaching election of a senator to replace Sen. John Patterson, Mart Gary fired off another barrage, hoping to arouse enough interest in himself to win election to the Senate. Gary moved in the state senate to repeal the legislation adopted to determine the state debt and devise measures for funding. He charged that these were measures to please the "bloated bond holders." The *News and Courier* noted that the Edgefield senator had "opened the vials of his wrath" on the governor and others.[204]

On December 10 the doctors told Hampton that amputation was necessary; he took the news calmly. Dr. Taylor amputated the governor's right leg about six inches above the ankle, using a procedure known as Lister's antiseptic process. The operation was successful, and the governor began the long process of recovery.[205] On that same momentous day the two houses of the general assembly elected Hampton to the U.S. Senate, the Senate unanimously and the House with only two votes to the contrary; those votes were for the Republican E. W. M. Mackey. Hampton had sent a message to the general assembly indicating that he was not a candidate for the Senate, but he would yield to the wishes of that body. Even Sen. Mart Gary voted for Hampton, undoubtedly realizing the hopelessness of his own wishes.[206]

Hampton did not resign the office of governor until February 24, 1879, stating in his letter to the general assembly that he delayed resigning in order to complete some unfinished business.[207] It is likely that part of his reasoning for delaying the resignation was that he needed the income—he was so impecunious that an interim between his leaving the salary for serving as governor and going on the payroll of the Senate would have been financially embarrassing. Simpson continued to act as governor during some of the intervening time.

The injury of November 7 and the ensuing amputation proved to be a pivotal event in the life of Wade Hampton. He was sixty years old, not a young man, especially by the standards of the nineteenth century. He had been wounded on three occasions in the recent war, and at Gettysburg his wounds were multiple. At times the wounds received at Gettysburg caused him intense pain. Although he was considered to be a vigorously healthy man, he was showing signs of weariness and declining health prior to November 8. In the summer of 1878 he gave up the grueling political campaign to go to Cashiers for convalescence. After the accident and amputation, from which he recovered slowly, he was never again in vitally good health. A writer for the *News and Courier* reported that Hampton's "nervous system is shattered."[208] He planned to attend the celebration of Washington's birthday in Charleston but canceled for reasons of health.

In his last months as governor, he did escape to Green Pond for fishing. A reporter found him there, a black servant paddling him about the pond. The senator-elect gave a reluctant interview, in which he expressed approval of President Hayes's vetoing a measure that would have restricted Chinese immigration. Hampton thought that the measure would have been less than honorable in violating the existing treaty with China. He supported the Democratic efforts in Congress to abolish the test oath preventing former Confederates from serving on juries and the efforts to prohibit the use of federal troops in elections.[209] Because of his precarious health, Hampton did not attend the extra session of Congress then in process. He told the people of South Carolina that he was in constant communication with Senator Butler and could go to Washington if it became necessary.[210]

Hampton's influence was waning. After he went to Washington, he ceased to be as involved in the day-to-day politics of his home state. He and his closest associates were able from time to time to influence elections in the general assembly, but, as the decade of the 1880s slid by, the influence of Hampton declined and ended with a disastrous defeat in 1890. As long as Hampton was present and in power there was in the Bourbon regime at least lip service for political equality between the races. That lip service was preferable to the alternative represented by Mart Gary and his associates. Hampton and his followers had for a time been able to fend off the raw racism of the Garyites, but it was a losing struggle. Gary died in 1881 with a consequent loss of momentum among his followers, but others soon took Gary's place and in time continued vying for control of the state. Gary in fact represented the popular sentiment of the state better than Hampton. E. B. Cash (the father of E. B. C. Cash, who participated in the last famous duel in the state, killing W. M. Shannon) wrote to Gary that the next generation would be with the Edgefield senator. "Your politics of today will be the politics of South Carolina in five years from this date. Your dash and boldness saved the state in 1876, none can deny it, but now there are many who are afraid to follow your advice."[211] Sadly, Cash was essentially correct.

There is in the Gary Papers in the South Caroliniana Library a manuscript document in Gary's handwriting, apparently intended for publication but never published in its completeness, which sets forth the author's attitude on race as opposed to those of Hampton. This document amplifies Cash's prediction that Gary's politics were those of the future in South Carolina. Gary insisted that Governor Hampton and Maj. Hugh Thompson, superintendent of education, had indeed dined with blacks in the home of President Cooke of Claflin University. This rumor had been afloat in the last Democratic convention, and Gary thought it politically wise not to make a public charge of this "grievous" misdeed. Gary's racist successors would not be so circumspect. Gary recalled that Wade Hampton had been the first white man in the

South to advocate suffrage for the freed Negro, that Hampton had sat on a rostrum with radical leaders, that Hampton had in the last legislature used his influence to defeat a bill outlawing intermarriage, and that the governor had led the move to unite South Carolina College and Claflin in one state university. This was the bill of particulars. In summation: "It will be seen that his dining with these two Negroes at Claflin University is a logical result of his political record in regard to the Negro. . . . The Negro can only be reached through his love of money, his vanity, and his fears."[212]

Again the contrast with Gary does not make Wade Hampton a late-twentieth-century liberal in matters of race. Hampton assumed that he and the other leading whites could control the black votes. As he had said, "As the Negro becomes more intelligent he naturally allies himself with the more conservative of the whites . . . his interests are identical with those of the white race." And Hampton thought that the freedmen had been enfranchised too soon and in the wrong manner, meaning that he preferred a franchise based on some test of literacy and/or property.[213] Still, the policies of Hampton, albeit limited, held infinitely more hope for ultimate racial equality than the policies of Gary, but the policies of the latter became the standard for the next several generations.

F. W. Dawson, the editor of the *News and Courier*, understood the contrast between the policies of Gary and those of Hampton. Concerning Gary's policy of complete proscription of the black population, Dawson wrote, "No state can be ruled by repression and long retain a republican form of government." On the other hand, the *Greenville News*, in support of Gary charged that Hampton was leading South Carolina "into the dark pit of African rule."[214]

In Hampton's lame-duck period there were several events worth noticing. In January the legislature again faltered in its obligations pertaining to the state's debt. Instead of levying a tax sufficient to pay the interest on all of the debt, meaning that part of the debt already found to be valid, and to fund a reserve to pay the interest on the disputed debt should any part of it be found to be valid, the legislature ordered that the funds held in reserve be used to pay the interest on the valid debt.[215] Any repudiation was a defeat for Hampton, who wanted the entire debt funded at a low interest rate, but such penuriousness aided the conservative regime in attaining a reduction of the tax rate from a high of twelve mills in 1876–1877 to a rate of four and three-fourths mills in 1878–1879.[216]

There was also the scandal of irregularities in the campaign of 1878. Sen. James G. Blaine succeeded in getting a committee appointed to investigate that election. The committee was led by Sen. Henry M. Teller and was known as the Teller Committee. Hampton predicted that the committee would find as much corruption by Republicans as by Democrats. He admitted that there had been irregularities by Democrats but that they were the result of the "crimes of the radical regime." The respectable *News and Courier* offered the same justification for the irregularities. Editor Dawson wrote, "Our civilization was at stake. . . . It was necessary to complete the revolution and a revolution without irregularities is as rare as a fire without heat."[217] The committee found that the Democrats had cheated by intimidation and by the use of tissue ballots, used for stuffing the boxes.[218] The committee also noted the absence of prosecutions in the state courts.[219]

In the month before Hampton took the oath of office as a United States senator, the *North American Review* published a remarkable article that reads like a modern panel discussion. James G. Blaine served as the moderator, asking each member of the panel—consisting of Wade Hampton, L. Q. C. Lamar, James A. Garfield, Alexander H. Stephens, Wendell Phillips, Montgomery Blair, and Thomas Hendricks—questions about the status of suffrage for the black race. Lamar indicated that no Southerner of influence believed that the disenfranchisement of the Negro race was politically possible. Hampton stated his opposition to disenfranchisement and his preference for a franchise based on educational qualifications. He thought that suffrage had been bestowed precipitously, and he repeated his belief that "As the negro becomes more intelligent he naturally allies himself with the more conservative of the whites, for his observation and experience both show him that his interests are identical with those of the white race." Stephens's statement was a masterpiece of evasion.[220] The senator-elect left Columbia for Washington on April 15, declaring that he was in better health.[221]

EIGHT

The Senate and Beyond

Hampton's two terms in the U.S. Senate and his service as commissioner of the Pacific Railroads were sadly anticlimactic. He did not prove to be the distinguished senator for South Carolina his supporters had predicted. His health was never again robust. He had always recovered from wounds with amazing alacrity, but such was not the case with the wound suffered on that hunting trip in November 1878. He was also struck by the tragic death of Wade Hampton IV in 1879. For one who suffered so many losses of loved ones this was too much. He was frequently absent from the Senate. This is not to say that he was a nonentity. Senator Hampton was a respected colleague who performed yeoman service for his committees, who gave impressive eulogies for deceased colleagues, equally effective for those from the other party and from the North. But there is no single piece of important legislation bearing the name Hampton. He was on occasion capable of rising above the prejudices of his home state to support such progressive measures as federal aid for education. Still, reading the *Congressional Record* gives the impression that Hampton was a rather passive member. M. C. Butler, his fellow South Carolinian in the Senate, also not a distinguished senator, was more active in the life of the Senate. Hampton's appointment as commissioner of the Pacific Railroads was obviously a sinecure for a loyal Democrat who needed a means of support. Ironically, the attacks made by Ben Tillman on President Cleveland made Wade Hampton a more satisfactory recipient of presidential favor, even though Hampton's years after the governorship were not his best.

Hampton began his service in the Senate in mid-April. The South Carolina congressional delegation met the new senator at the Washington depot April 16; they escorted him to his new quarters on Capitol Hill.[1] On the same day Sen. M. C. Butler introduced the newcomer to the Senate, and Hampton took the oath of office.[2] The president of the Senate appointed Hampton to the Committee on Military Affairs, the Committee on Mines and Mining, and the Committee on Transportation Routes to the Seaboard, a rather undistinguished list, but probably not unusual for a freshman.[3] Hampton gave his greatest effort to the work of the Committee on Military Affairs, which was of course quite logical because he understood military affairs from his own experience and interests. Although the senatorial career of Hampton was not especially significant, it should be noted that he was not hidebound in his partisanship; he was often willing to cross party lines to vote and express his support for what he thought to be the right cause. Also, he strove to appeal to the new postwar nationalism, quite remarkably for one who had given and lost so much for the Confederate cause. His appeals for an end to sectionalism were like those of L. Q. C. Lamar, although he was not as widely recognized as the senator from Mississippi.

A presidential veto gave the senator an early opportunity to demonstrate his independence. President Hayes faced a difficult choice in that the Democrats in Congress managed to amend the army appropriations bill with a rider that forbade the use of federal troops in elections. While the president was obviously reluctant to use troops, he did not want that possibility removed with no regard for extreme circumstances; he therefore vetoed the bill. While the junior senator from South Carolina opposed the use of federal troops—that had been the pivotal issue in the spring of 1877—he did not approve of the legislative method of impairing the support of the national army to achieve a collateral goal. Hampton used his influence to get the army appropriations bill passed without hindrance.[4] The *New York Times* described Hampton as speaking for an hour, standing with his stump resting on his desk, stating that he did not approve of the use of troops in elections, but he disapproved of achieving such goals by unrelated amendments. He found the opportunity for praising Hayes for withdrawing the troops from his state in April 1877.[5]

Despite Hampton's efforts to rise above the sectionalism of a former Confederate, on occasion he found himself defending his section and his own role as a Southern leader. On May 15, 1879, Hampton rose to object to a statement by Sen. William Windom of Minnesota, who had charged Hampton with having inserted in the Democratic platform of 1868 the statement that the Reconstruction amendments were "unconstitutional, revolutionary, and void." When Senator Hampton denied the authorship of those words, Senator Windom read from a South Carolina newspaper an article in which Hampton claimed credit for that statement. Hampton replied that if he did use the words quoted in the newspaper, he meant only that he approved of the statement and "in that sense [it was] my plank."[6]

His defense of things Southern even included the Klan. In a debate over the possible repeal of the test oath for service on federal juries Sen. George Franklin Edmunds of Vermont reminded the Senate that the people of South Carolina had raised money for the defense of Klansmen. Hampton, who had participated in that effort, took the floor and recalled that the senator from Vermont had long ago charged him with being connected to the

Klan. Senator Hampton emphatically denied any relation to the Klan, and he admitted that the Klan had done wrong. "The contribution that was made by the people of South Carolina to defend those men was simply a contribution that was made on the assumption that the law always holds that parties are innocent until proved guilty." Hampton went on, "If there was one man in America who had no knowledge of, no connection with, no sympathy with anything like the ku klux organization, it was myself. I did not know that there was any such organization in South Carolina until those trials occurred."[7] The last statement approaches incredibility, and it is consistent with his attitude toward the fraud in the election of 1876.

On occasion Hampton was driven to defend not only his region but also his own role as a Southern representative. In the debate concerning the possible use of federal troops in elections, one senator remarked that the presence of twenty-two senators who had served in the Confederate army was itself proof of fraudulent elections. Hampton agreed, "She [the South] is reproached, nay, denounced, for sending such men to represent her. She can scarcely be reproached with justice for trusting and honoring in peace the men who risked their fortunes and their lives for her in war." Hampton regretted that there were no more Union veterans on the floor, for surely they would treat the former Confederates with more respect.[8]

During the 1879 recess of Congress Hampton returned and participated in the political life of South Carolina. He and M. C. Butler toured together and spoke to gatherings. They even attended a performance of Gilbert and Sullivan's *H.M.S. Pinafore*. Hampton expressed to his audiences his support of Sen. Thomas Bayard of Delaware for the Democratic nomination in the 1880 convention. Hampton's support of Bayard would last until the convention. His support was based on the belief that Bayard, a future secretary of state and ambassador to the Court of St. James, would be the most sympathetic to the South.

The term "solid South" was by now well in use, often as a term of derision, and the senator referred to the term in his pleas for justice to the black race. "If the people of the South would show that they do not desire to encroach upon the rights of anyone; if they would show that they were acting in strict good faith . . . then they would break down the bloody shirt cry of 'solid South.'" For the forthcoming elections he urged his fellow Carolinians to "Let every man feel that his rights were protected. Let the white man show that he was the colored man's friend." Such behavior would win the elections for the Democratic Party.[9]

There was a widening gap between the senator and his South Carolina constituency. Hampton was aligning himself with a prominent advocate of hard money, Senator Bayard, who believed that money must have a value itself or it must be easily exchanged for value.[10] This attitude was another indication of Hampton's philosophical leanings to the old Whig Party. Hampton agreed with Bayard in wishing to end the legal tender quality of greenbacks.[11] His fiscal conservatism in the face of the depressed conditions of the South was an important reason for his diminishing popular support. The populist movement was demanding an inflated currency to relieve the debtor class. A reporter for the *New York Times* made an interesting and perceptive observation on the waning influence of Senator Hampton. He noted that when the senator urged an audience in Abbeville to treat blacks fairly, many left the grounds, gesticulating and swearing wildly. The reporter also commented that Congressman D. Wyatt Aiken, a disciple of Gary in matters of race, tried to distance himself from Hampton, even assuring his followers that he had not invited Hampton to make such a speech.[12]

In the midst of these political rumblings in South Carolina, the senator was struck by another tragedy. Wade Hampton IV became ill of malaria in Mississippi, and he died on December 22, 1879.[13] The senator was en route to Mississippi to visit his son when he learned that the young Hampton had died. This was the son who was wounded while tending to his mortally wounded brother at the Battle of Burgess Mill in October 1864. There is no doubt that this was a serious blow to the veteran of so many sorrows. He wrote to his sister, "Life seems closed to me, and I have nothing but duty to live for. It is very hard, but I try to say, 'God's will be done.'"[14]

The *New York Times* found the split between Martin Gary and Senator Hampton to be interesting. Significantly for the political element that would advocate an agricultural college, Gary supported a more scientific and practical education, while the aristocratic Hampton reportedly had little sympathy for such needs of the poorer classes.[15]

The Edgefield politician was ambitious to be elected governor in 1880, and he was quite aware that Hampton was backing the candidacy of Johnson Hagood. T. R. Gaines of Orangeburg intended to nominate Gary for governor in the 1880 Democratic convention;[16] Gary therefore became more open in his attacks on the senator. He accused Hampton of selling out the national Democratic Party in the campaign of 1876, specifically charging that Hampton had during the campaign stop in Abbeville recommended withdrawing the Tilden electors from the state Democratic slate. In effect the candidate was supposed to have said to the two Republican judges, Cook and Mackey, who had come over to support Hampton, "If you'll elect me governor, I don't care whom you elect president." Hampton supposedly met with a number of Democratic leaders in Abbeville and argued for deserting the national party, but Samuel McGowan of Abbeville defeated his proposals. These charges were made public by a letter to the newspapers, signed "A Tilden Democrat." Hampton was sure that Gary was either the "Tilden Democrat" or he had inspired someone else to write it. The senator denied the charge, saying correctly that he had sought the aid of the national party in vain, but he never suggested a desertion. He characterized Gary's views as "narrow, unlawful, and dangerous."[17] Gary's charge were proved wrong when McGowen, who was at the Abbeville meeting, denied that Hampton had supported deserting the Tilden ticket.[18]

Gary continued his pursuit of the Democratic nomination for governor by attacking Hampton in newspaper interviews. He told one reporter, "Everyone in South Carolina knows that he [Hampton] has long hated me as the devil does holy water." Gary repeated the charge that Hampton had been guilty of treachery to the national party in 1876, by attempting to ditch the presidential electors and by urging voters to vote for the Hayes ticket nationally and the Democratic ticket locally. According to Gary, Hampton had been a party to "the great presidential fraud whereby the Democratic Party lost Tilden who should have been declared the President of the United States." Gary's drumbeat attacks were having some effect. One reporter declared, "The Gary stock is rising while the stock for Hampton is decidedly on the wane."[19]

Hampton's friend and political ally A. C. Haskell sought to spike the Gary guns by releasing to the press the letter Hampton had written to Manton Marble, the 1876 chairman of the National Democratic Committee, in which the general expressed his concern that Tilden considered him to be an embarrassment to the national ticket. Hampton assured Marble, "With aid from abroad the state can be carried for Tilden. There is no doubt of its being carried for our own state ticket, for our opponents would gladly let us elect ourselves if we withdrew from the presidential contest. Of course we are most anxious to aid in the general election, . . . but we need your advice. . . . If our alliance is a load, we can unload. What are your views?" Haskell also released Marble's reply encouraging Hampton's efforts for both the state and national tickets.[20] The Democratic leader Samuel McGowan wrote a letter to the *Abbeville Journal* in which he exonerated Hampton of the charge of betraying Tilden, assuring everyone of Hampton's desire that both state and national Democratic tickets succeed in 1876.[21]

As early as December 1879 there was much discussion of the forthcoming state elections. Hampton told a correspondent of the *News and Courier* that he preferred to avoid endorsing anyone for the gubernatorial nomination. The senator noted that the South Carolina Democrats could win in 1880 by either of two methods: appeal to black voters or "suppress the majority by fraud." Hampton insisted that both wisdom and duty indicated choosing the first method. He recalled with a less than perfect memory that about forty thousand black men had voted for him in 1876. He had no interest in an alliance with the Republican Party.[22]

The Hampton-Gary feud continued into the year 1880. A. C. Haskell, obviously acting on behalf of Senator Hampton, wrote to the *Abbeville*

Medium to deny that the senator had ever supported ditching the Tilden ticket. Haskell attacked Gary by asserting, "I frankly admit that I do not think General Gary is fit for the high places to which he has aspired." Haskell then accused Gary of having accepted pay to try to influence the Taxpayers Convention of 1871 to endorse the entire bonded indebtedness of the state and to get the convention to recommend that the state relinquish its mortgage on the Blue Ridge Railroad. Haskell also noted that Gary had unleashed his most recent attack on Hampton while the senator was away in Mississippi when his son died. Gary denied all.[23]

With the year 1880 came the usual interest in who would be the next governor. While Hampton did not engage in direct campaigning for any candidate, two things became apparent: the senator did not want the nomination to go to Martin Gary, and his preference was for Johnson Hagood, already established as a Hampton man and generally recognized as a moderate.[24]

Back in the Senate, Hampton continued with his rather pedestrian duties. Civil War buffs of later generations are indebted to Senator Hampton's interest in maintaining a memory of the great conflict. In March 1880 he represented the Committee on Military Affairs in presenting a bill to complete the survey of the battlefield at Gettysburg to identify the positions and movements of all units on both sides. The bill was ultimately enacted.[25] The South Carolina senator also demonstrated remarkable neutrality in presenting a number of bills to provide pensions for Union veterans and one bill to permit the loan of army tents for a reunion of Union veterans in Central City, Nebraska.[26] His interest in military history extended back to the Revolution when he reported for his committee a bill to fund a statue of Gen. Daniel Morgan to celebrate the Battle of Cowpens. The bill passed.[27]

Senator Hampton's proclivity to neutrality and fairness, as he understood it, led him to oppose the Democratic Party in its attempt to eject the carpetbagger Sen. William Pitt Kellogg of Louisiana. The Committee on Privileges and Elections recommended denying a seat to Kellogg, who had originally presented his credentials in January 1877 and had subsequently won his seat from the Republican-dominated Senate. Now with a Democratic majority came an attempt to unseat the Louisiana senator. Hampton argued that the Nicholls government, which had elected Kellogg, was the legally recognized government of Louisiana, and, thereby, the election of Kellogg was valid. Hampton's speech was remarkable: "I recognize painfully in my case how difficult it is to throw off the shackles forged by partisanship, to oppose mandates of party, or to rise superior to that spirit of sectionalism which has so often exercised its malign influence on matters which have come before us."[28]

Accompanying the senator's ability to maintain neutrality in matters pertaining to the recent war and the politics of the Senate was an attitude toward conditions in South Carolina that strained the credulity of informed observers, both then and since. In a debate with Sen. George F. Hoar of Massachusetts, Hampton asserted that seventeen thousand black citizens had voted Democratic in 1876. He told the Massachusetts senator that he had told black audiences that if they were in Massachusetts they could not vote without being able to read and write. That was of course the qualification Hampton had originally recommended. And on the following day Hampton told his colleagues that he wished his state had a qualification like that of Massachusetts. The South Carolina senator assured the Senate that there was no oppression of blacks in his state. "They have the equal protection of the laws." The Senate heard evidence that the South Carolina Democrats printed thousands of tissue ballots for the purpose of stuffing the boxes. Indeed, W. L. Gagggett, a Democratic employee of the *News and Courier*, testified that tissue ballots were used in most precincts in South Carolina.[29]

The South Carolina election of 1880 was the last confrontation between Hampton and Gary, but the issues of contention continued when Ben Tillman several years later assumed the Gary mantle. Again, the primary issue was which approach should the Democrats take toward the black citizens. The *New York Times* quoted Hampton as having said that his party could win either by fraud or by courting black voters. The senator preferred the latter approach.[30] The *News and Courier* recommended that the state recognize the basic right of voting but restrict it by an educational requirement, essentially what Hampton had favored, and by a strict requirement of registration.[31]

Mart Gary sought the gubernatorial position; again the difference between Gary and Hampton was that the former was an unabashed racist and the latter was a moderate. And Gary's prejudices were not restricted to the black race. In 1879 he had written from Hot Springs, Virginia, where he had gone for the health-giving waters, "There has been an excess of Jews here who I hate to look at."[32] When Gary addressed the Democratic convention of 1880, he pictured himself as defending the Anglo-Saxon race. He saw the convention divided between the straight-outs and the fusionists. He expressed contempt for the "aristocratic oligarchy that has ruled the state for one hundred years." Gary accused his opponents of supporting miscegenation and social equality between the races. Gary claimed credit for the Democratic victory of 1876, scoffing at Hampton's claim of having won seventeen thousand black votes.[33] Gary in arguing against funding the state's debt inherited from the Republicans accused the "bond ring" of supporting full funding for their own selfish reasons. Gary charged the unnamed members of the "bond ring" of having engaged in bribery and corruption.[34]

Ben Tillman later used almost the same words in his campaigns. In considering the extent to which the Tillman campaigns of the late 1880s was a continuation of Gary's efforts, it is worthwhile to reiterate the major attacks Gary leveled against Hampton. He attacked Hampton for favoring the election of the Republican A. J. Willard to the Supreme Court, for advocating full funding of the state's debts, for opposing the unseating of several black legislators after the election of 1876, for opposing a law to prohibit usury, for preferring a black senator from Fairfield over a white man, for advocating equal treatment of the white and black colleges (South Carolina College and Claflin), for opposing a law prohibiting interracial marriage, for supporting the constitutional requirement of a tax of two mills for public education, and for having consorted with President Hayes.[35] And a Gary supporter would have added to this list that Wade Hampton had dared to dine with several blacks in Orangeburg.[36]

Hampton did not engage in direct political activity in the process of the gubernatorial election, but he let his choice be known through his lieutenants, such as A. C. Haskell. The senator and his friends wanted Johnson Hagood, a faithful Hamptonite, to be the next governor. The major opponent was of course Martin Gary. The Democratic convention met in Columbia in June 1880. Gary wanted the convention to delay the nominations until another meeting in August, hoping to use the intervening time to build up support for himself. The old guard wanted the selections to be made in the June convention. James Conner, another Hamptonite, moved that the selections be made promptly, and his resolution passed. The convention proceeded to nominate a slate quite acceptable to Hampton: Hagood for governor, John D. Kennedy for lieutenant governor, R. M. Sims for secretary of state, Arthur M. Manigault for adjutant and inspector general, Leroy F. Youmans for attorney general, Hugh S. Thompson for superintendent of education, and J. P. Richardson for treasurer.[37] A remarkable number of these later served as governor, an interesting indication of the extent to which the Hamptonites controlled the state in these postreconstruction years, a fact leading to one of Tillman's chief complaints. The News and Courier editorialized that the Gary canvass was a series of blunders: "His friends so arranged the struggle that the support of General Gary was equivalent to direct and unmistakable opposition and hostility to Wade Hampton."[38] Hampton's son-in-law John C. Haskell responded to Gary's oft-repeated charge that Hampton had sought to betray Tilden in the 1876 campaign in order to boost his own chance of winning by accusing the Edgefield senator of being "an ass masquerading in a lion's skin."[39]

Some of Gary's charges had effect. A writer for the New York Times observed that the Gary campaign had succeeded in arousing some resentment in the upstate against the arrogance of Hampton and his followers, focusing on such issues as high taxes and fence laws.[40]

Meanwhile the senator's service in office proceeded much as it had. He served on the committees on the military, mining and mines, and on a select committee to examine several branches of the civil service. The Senate continued to make use of his military experiences by appointing him to a select committee to consider heavy ordnance and projectiles for the Navy and coast defenses.[41] He presented several memorials from the Charleston Chamber of Commerce, seeking appropriations for the improvement of Charleston harbor.[42]

The Republican convention nominated James Garfield for president, and the Democrats nominated Gen. Winfield Scott Hancock, who had served as an effective leader in the Army of the Potomac. Hancock was the commanding Union officer in the attack at Burgess Mill in which Preston Hampton was killed. Hampton attended the Democratic convention, where he supported the candidacy of Sen. Thomas F. Bayard of Delaware, but when the nominating process was completed he readily pledged his support of Hancock.[43] True to his pledge, the senator, sharing the platform with Zeb Vance of North Carolina, spoke to a gathering in Staunton, Virginia, urging support for the Hancock ticket and warning his audience that a Republican victory could mean no more free elections. The *New York Times* quoted Hampton as saying that Hancock was fighting for the same ideals that Lee and Jackson had sought. Hampton later said that he had been misquoted.[44] The *News and Courier* reported that he had actually asked whether those men who had followed Lee and Jackson could fail to support the Democratic Party.[45]

In September the senator addressed a Democratic audience in Union Square of New York City. The editor of the *New York World* introduced Hampton as having been "one of the bravest soldiers of the Confederate Army" and now "one of the most loyal and honorable senators of the American union." Hampton spoke to the question of whether the South was in fact "solid," arguing that the negativism of the Republican Party had made it solid to the extent that it was solid. Interestingly he recalled that Southern Whigs had been intelligent and patriotic, implying that the Whig philosophical tradition continued.[46] By implication he was placing himself in the camp of the Whig tradition.

Senator Hampton worked hard in the 1880 campaign. In early October the senator participated in a rally in Marion, South Carolina, where he made a special effort to address a large number of blacks in attendance, assuring them of his commitment to protect their rights as well as those of the whites. He made a special point of denying any connection with the Klan.[47] That denial was in part an answer to a charge made by Secretary of the Treasury John Sherman, who when he addressed the National Republican Committee at a Fifth Avenue hotel asked his fellow Republicans whether they would surrender to the Democratic Party, Wade Hampton, and the KKK. Hampton wrote the secretary an indignant letter denying any connection with the Klan and demanding a retraction. Sherman replied that he did not mean to imply a direct connection, but he stated with a degree of accuracy that Hampton had won office in part because of the Klan.[48] Hampton spoke at a number of rallies in his home state, on occasion riding in with men clad in red shirts, an obvious attempt at stirring up the spirit of 1876.[49]

The longer Hampton stayed in Washington, the less was his interest and influence in South Carolina. While the followers of Hampton remained the dominant leaders of the state through the 1880s, their policies became increasingly restrictive toward the black population. In 1882 the general assembly enacted the "eight box" law, requiring voters to identify the correct box for their ballots, there being a separate box for each race. This law was the brainchild of the aristocratic Charlestonian Edward McCrady, Jr., whose intentions were to restrict the voting power of illiterate blacks and whites. In a sense the restriction this law placed on the poorer whites was as important as the limitation of black voting. White conservatives of South Carolina had good reason to fear the ignorant masses, who would find their leader in Ben Tillman. William Porcher Miles, president of South Carolina College, which became a favorite target of the Tillman movement, told a lowcountry audience that "unqualified suffrage is an evil when exercised by the entire adult population of any race or color."[50]

As the decade progressed there were a number of issues dividing the aristocracy and their adherents from the elements represented by Martin Gary and Ben Tillman. The former represented the remnants of the old planter gentry or conservatives and the emerging commercial interests, especially in the lowcountry. The latter claimed to represent small farmers, especially in the upstate. The issues included fence laws, usury laws, the disproportionate representation of the lowcountry in the general assembly, taxes to support public education, and the increasing demands for a separate college of agriculture. The divisions on these issues were not always clear, but this is a reasonably good list of differences. The issue of race overrode all other issues. The conservative elements grudgingly admitted the right of blacks to vote, but favored qualifications of literacy and property. The Gary-Tillman elements wanted to eliminate blacks from all political participation. Unfortunately, the national mood was swinging from support of universal suffrage to acquiescence in disfranchisement of blacks. An interesting indication of the swing in the national mood is that at the end of the 1880s a writer for the *New York Times* commented, "political evils arising from negro suffrage could be cured if any Southern state could be brought to impose a qualification for voters which should apply equally to both races."[51] The possibility that poor and illiterate whites might be disfranchised became an important factor in the ultimate victory of the forces led by Ben Tillman.

James A. Garfield won the election of 1880. Hampton told an interviewer that he would withhold his opinion of the new president until his Southern policy became obvious.[52] On April 9, 1881, after a brief illness Martin Gary died at the age of forty-seven, leaving his dissident element without an obvious leader. The *News and Courier* commented that Gary's policies since 1876 had been "pernicious."[53] The hiatus between Gary and Tillman gave the Hampton conservatives a few years of relative peace.

In the 1880s the Hampton forces accomplished much that they had promised. The state's expenditures were reduced significantly. The *News and Courier* reported that by the time Johnson Hagood was inaugurated as governor in 1880 the state's budget had been reduced to one-fourth of the budget under the radicals.[54] Despite the stringent economy, the appropriations for public schools had increased from $189,352.50 in 1876–1877 to $351,415.50 in 1879–1880.[55] Of this total the expenditure for black schools exceeded that for white schools by $14,383. The explanation for this progress lies in the fact that the redeemers had amended the constitution to establish a special and permanent tax for schools, a measure Mart Gary had opposed because of its support for black education. Superintendent of Education Hugh Thompson was pleased to have delivered on Hampton's promise to place public education within reach of every child, regardless of race. In the early years of conservative rule, the expenditure per black child actually exceeded the per capita expenditure for white children. Appropriations for education increased every year in the 1880s.[56] Perhaps the best indicator of the progress of education for the black population is the fact that in 1865, 95 percent of the black population was illiterate; in 1880 the figure was 78.6 percent; in 1890 it was 64 percent; and in 1900 it was 52.8 percent.[57] Obviously, much of the credit for this progress must be assigned to the eagerness of the newly freed race.

The conservative record on race was less impressive, but better than the record of their successors. The state legislature had enacted in the session of 1869–1870 a civil rights law prohibiting discrimination by common carriers. The conservatives allowed this law to stand, in part because of the conciliatory attitude of Hampton and in part because of the federal civil rights law. The U.S. Supreme Court ruled in 1882 that the federal law was unconstitutional. The South Carolina law remained until John Gary Evans introduced a bill to repeal the state's civil rights law. The Evans bill passed in 1889. There was in these years little social integration and not much integration on the trains because black passengers tended to use second-class cars.[58] In listing items of forward and regressive movement, it should not be forgotten that the conservative legislature enacted in 1882 the "eight box law," requiring some degree of literacy on the part of voters who must determine which box was appropriate for each ballot, and this law was in part aimed at the black population, and to a lesser degree illiterate whites. The Republican vote declined from 91,780 in 1876 to 13,740 in 1888.[59] The 1880s were not halcyon years for South Carolina blacks, and in fact the rift between the races widened, but there were possibilities for progress and reasons for hope for a better future—these possibilities were virtually extinguished in the decade of the 1890s.

It is obvious to later generations that Southern leaders became sensitive to the fact that they had fought a war in large part to preserve slavery, a cause virtually no one wanted to defend in the late nineteenth century, and they consequently set about redefining the causes to emphasize such factors as states' rights, a conservative interpretation of the Constitution and the Jeffersonian ideal of rural life. Senator Hampton was a part of that redefinition. Sen. John J. Ingalls of Kansas charged in a debate that the North had fought to free slaves and the South had fought to perpetuate human slavery. Hampton replied that the North adopted the cause of abolition during the war, not at the beginning. The real cause, Hampton argued, was the integrity of the Union.[60]

In a speech to the Senate on April 21, 1881, Senator Hampton admitted that white people of his state had committed frauds to win the election of 1876. He tried to justify the fraudulent practices by saying in essence that South Carolina was in a state of war. "But I plead justification the cruel wrongs inflicted on our people. Life and the state itself were at stake." He asked his colleagues to imagine Massachusetts overrun by Chinese and whites facing the possibility of being ruled by the Chinese majority.[61] On September 19, 1881, President James A. Garfield died of wounds received on July 2 at the hands of Charles J. Guiteau. Senator Hampton told the press that the assassination was a national calamity, but he viewed the newly installed president Chester A. Arthur as a conservative under whose leadership things should run smoothly.[62]

The year 1882 was an eventful time for the rule of the Hampton conservatives back in South Carolina. Governor Johnson Hagood announced his support of a fence law, requiring owners of livestock to keep them fenced to prevent their damaging neighbors' field crops.[63] As has been noted, fence laws were a class issue. Ultimately, the Tillmanites opposed fence laws as another measure of aristocratic oppression of the poor. Ironically, Tillman, neither a small nor a poor farmer, himself lobbied in support of fence laws in 1881.[64] He was able later to obfuscate that part of his past. In 1882 the legislature enacted fence laws on a local option basis, that is, each county was to decide whether to require that stock be fenced in.[65] Edward McCrady's eight box law also passed in 1882, and this, too, became a class issue, in that the conservative elements represented by McCrady (and Hampton) were willing to exclude illiterate whites along with illiterate blacks. McCrady was fearful that the state was facing an ignorant mass of voters. The most recent census indicated that the state had eighty-five thousand black voters, of whom seventy thousand were illiterate, and seventy thousand white voters, of whom twelve thousand were illiterate.[66] In February 1882 the general assembly enacted a law requiring voters to register, including measures making difficulties for voters who moved frequently from one precinct to another,[67] another measure adverse to blacks and poor whites.

Hampton's service in the Senate continued much as it had. One of the biggest issues of the decade was the level of tariffs. The senator did not play a major role in the tariff debates, but he favored a downward revision, retaining tariffs for revenue, and modest protection.[68] He, like L. Q. C. Lamar, continued to speak for sectional reconciliation. In January 1882 Senator Hampton gave a creditable eulogy for his recent senatorial colleague and former military enemy Ambrose Burnside.[69] Despite his occasional speeches in defense of the South, Hampton, by his conciliatory attitude, earned the respect of colleagues of both parties.

In the spring of 1882 South Carolina Democrats were uncertain who should be the next gubernatorial candidate—and some considered recalling Hampton to the governor's office. Hampton answered these rumors by a public letter in which he disclaimed any interest in serving again as governor, commenting that capable men were available. He went on to express regret at the passage of the fence and registration laws.[70] He later explained his objections to the fence law by saying that it should have been enacted to apply to the entire state at once. He told the interviewer that he expected to withdraw from public office before too long. That statement might have fueled another rumor that he would succeed William Porcher Miles as president of South Carolina College. Hampton said he knew nothing about this possibility, but he would not accept such an offer.[71]

The confusion among South Carolina Democrats, which had stimulated an interest in Hampton as governor, led the party to make a turn slightly away from the Hampton tradition. The *Greenville News* expressed impatience with the monopoly of office by the Hampton clique and suggested George Tillman, elder brother to Ben and sometimes member of Congress. Tillman declined. The Democratic convention, moving somewhat from the Hampton clique, nominated Hugh Thompson for governor and John Calhoun Sheppard for lieutenant governor. Thompson was from a well-known family, and he had served with distinction as superintendent of education, but he was not a Confederate veteran. Thompson was acceptable to the Hampton camp as a compromise candidate. Sheppard was an upcountry choice described by the *New York Times* as a "cheap edition of Mart Gary." The most interesting indication of dissidence in 1882 was the appearance of the Greenback Party, supporting the issuing of greenbacks as legal tender. This party nominated J. Hendrix McLane for governor and secured the support of the state Republican Party. Hampton, fearing a split in the votes of white South Carolinians, said, "Anyone not with us, with the Democratic Party, is a traitor to the state." McLane secured 20.9 percent of the votes, most of which came from black citizens.[72]

Although the senator was not active in the process of choosing the nominee, he did take part in the hustings, appearing in Charleston, Cheraw, Lexington, and Chesterfield. In addition to supporting the Democratic ticket, he addressed a Confederate reunion. He told the veterans that only God could judge whether the Confederate cause was right, but "They fought for what they believed to be right, and no braver, truer, more heroic men ever tread this earth than the soldiers of the Army of Northern Virginia." He urged the veterans to vote for the Democratic slate, arguing that while there were many honorable men in the national Republican Party, the South Carolina Republicans represented "ignorance, superstition, and vice." He denied that there were political rings in the state.[73] Thompson and Sheppard won the election.[74]

It has been noted that M. C. Butler was a more active senator than Wade Hampton. Indicative of the difference is the fact that at the same time Butler was pushing for legislation for the improvement of the Charleston harbor, Hampton was appointed to a conference committee to reconcile differences in regulations for the soldiers' home in Washington.[75] The senator remained before the public. In June 1883 he spoke at the unveiling of a Confederate monument in Camden, South Carolina. He urged his audience to be patriotic to the Union. His speech approached the Lincolnesque: "The cause for which they fought has failed and it is the duty of every patriot in this broad land of ours to endeavor to obliterate the passions engendered by the late unhappy war and to make this country—now consecrated to freedom for all time to come—the happy abode of prosperous and contented freemen." The war had established the integrity of the Union.[76] It was singularly appropriate that Hampton as a spokesman for reconciliation served as the chief marshal at the ceremonies in Lexington, Virginia, in the unveiling of the Valentine recumbent statue of Robert E. Lee.[77]

From time to time Hampton demonstrated remarkable independence. In June 1883 he presented to the Senate a petition from the dean of the law school of Allen University (an institution for black men) and from a number of citizens of Bluffton, praying for national aid for public schools.[78] This interest led Hampton to support the Blair bill for federal aid to the states based on the number of illiterates in each state. Under this arrangement South Carolina would have received a disproportionate share of the funds. Hampton persisted in supporting this measure long after it became unpopular in his state, unpopular because of fear of federal interference in the state's racial status, just as later politicians opposed federal dollars rather than risk threats to racial segregation. In Hampton's time and later, the stated reason for opposing federal aid to education was that such a measure was unconstitutional. Indicative of similar independent thought, when the Supreme Court in 1883 ruled that the federal civil rights law was unconstitutional, Hampton commented to an interviewer that the court's ruling should make no difference in South Carolina, where social relations were set by custom and the state is obligated to provide equal protection of the laws for all citizens.[79] It should be noted that the South Carolina civil rights law, which had been enacted in 1869 and reenacted by the Democratic-controlled general assembly in 1882, was as comprehensive in its provisions as the federal law. The editor of the *News and Courier* saw no reason for changing the South Carolina law in the light of the Supreme Court ruling.[80]

In March 1884 the Senate debated the education bill presented by Sen. Henry W. Blair of New Hampshire. Hampton delivered a speech in support, arguing that such a measure would aid in the progress of the former slaves who lived in the poorest states. This measure would distribute funds according to the rates of illiteracy in each state. Senator Butler opposed the bill, fearing federal interference. Hampton's support of the Blair bill immediately aroused opposition back home. The *Winnsboro News and Herald* commented, "The magic of Hampton's name can no longer sanctify the enormous outrage . . . which the education bill is intended to perpetuate." The *Abbeville Press and Banner* joined in the attack. Hampton replied to the *Press and Banner* that he did not believe the Blair bill would do any harm.[81] Hampton was not a consistent progressive. It should be noted that in June 1884 he voted to prohibit women's suffrage in the territories.[82] He did, however, join the progressives in supporting the Interstate Commerce Commission in 1885.[83]

Some of the glow about the Hampton name had indeed diminished. The opposition to the election of Hampton as a delegate to the Democratic National Convention of 1884 surprised the *News and Courier*. He was nevertheless elected, and he attended as a supporter of Sen. Thomas Bayard of Delaware.[84] Bayard's chances for the presidential nomination were seriously damaged by his having made a speech critical of Lincoln's policies early in the recent war. The Democrats nominated Grover Cleveland.

The election of 1884 was relatively peaceful. The South Carolina Democrats renominated the incumbent administration without dissent. The Republicans did not bother to name a slate for statewide offices.[85] Senator Hampton participated in some of the campaign rallies. He addressed an audience in Anderson, urging the election of Grover Cleveland for president, assuring black voters that the national Democrats would protect their rights.[86] He told a Lancaster audience that he had been mistaken in not supporting Cleveland from the beginning.[87] As the campaign progressed, the senator suffered from poor health, sometimes complaining of severe pain, presumably from the amputated leg. Nevertheless, he addressed crowds in Abbeville, Aiken, Charleston, Hampton Courthouse, Beaufort, and Eastover. On occasion he was greeted by bands of red-shirted riders, reminiscent of the campaign of 1876.[88] On November 14 Hampton joined the Columbia crowd in celebrating the election of Grover Cleveland, assuring black citizens present at the gathering on the state house grounds that they would find that the Democratic Party was their best friend.[89] The general assembly on December 9 reelected Hampton to another term as senator. The editor of the *News and Courier* approved of continuing Hampton in office, describing him as "not meteoric or magnetic, nor is he particularly fond of routine work, but he is a loyal gentleman, who bore good fortune meekly, suffered evil with constancy and through evil or good maintains truth always."[90]

In March 1885 the Department of the Interior, under the leadership of L. Q. C. Lamar of Mississippi, named Gen. Joseph E. Johnston to the position of commissioner of the Pacific Railroads. His duty was to supervise these railroads in their relationship to the national government, which had generously endowed their construction.[91] This is the position Hampton occupied in the 1890s. In June President John M. McBryde appointed Senator Hampton honorary chairman of the Board of Visitors of South Carolina College. Hampton declared that his alma mater was in good condition.[92]

Despite occasional protests, the Hampton clique had been able to maintain reasonable peace through the first half of the 1880s. The year 1885 brought the first significant attacks on the Hampton political edifice. Both the *Greenville News* and the Columbia *Daily Register* complained about the monopoly of offices by the followers of Wade Hampton; they demanded new blood. One of the most contentious issues was the disproportionate representation of the lowcountry in the lower house of the legislature. Francis W. Dawson, in defending the Hampton hegemony, challenged the attackers to be specific in their charges of a dominating ring.[93] The most important attack on the regime came from Ben Tillman, who addressed the state Grange and State Agricultural Society, demanding in his own fiery style that measures be undertaken to give relief to the farmers, who became poorer each year. Specifically Tillman demanded the establishment of an agricultural farm, reorganization of South Carolina College as an agricultural college, and the addition of farmers to the board of trustees of the college and to the state Board of Agriculture.[94] This was Tillman's opening barrage. While the details changed and developed through the years, his demagogic style proved to be effective in South Carolina.

The general assembly in 1886 gave the dissidents ammunition by enacting a lien law giving the first preference to landowners, the next preference to laborers, and final preference to merchant suppliers.[95] The populists argued that first preference should go to the laborers. Ben Tillman, in addressing the Farmers' Convention in Columbia in April 1886, attacked the lien law as another evidence of the political "leprosy" of the state leadership.[96]

The attacks continued. The Farmers' Convention adopted a platform advocating an agricultural college, an experimental farm, abolition of the Citadel, the establishment of a school for girls, a general primary to replace nominations by conventions, and a constitutional convention.[97] The *News and Courier* served as the main line of defense for the leadership under attack. Editor Dawson replied to Tillman, who was posing as the representative for the underdog farmers, by pointing out that the majority of members of the legislature were farmers; that over half of the students in South Carolina College were sons of farmers; that the same was true at the Citadel; that farmers received four-fifths of the benefit of the school tax; that farmers do not return for taxation more than 40 percent of the property taxed in the state; and that most states had adopted plans to combine their agricultural colleges with their universities.[98] Senator Hampton was not at this time in the direct line of fire, but he symbolized the "ring" under attack.

R. Means Davis, journalist and later college professor, invited Senator Hampton to address the Free Trade Association. Hampton declined the invitation, but sent a letter instead. The senator indicated to the association that he did not think it practicable to seek free trade at that time. Rather, the senator pledged that he would work within the Democratic Party to achieve a downward adjustment, especially since the current tariffs were fundamentally unfair to those dependent on agriculture.[99]

Grover Cleveland, the first Democrat in the White House since James Buchanan, sought to appease the South by appointing a number of Southerners to offices, the most prominent appointment being L. Q. C. Lamar as secretary of the interior. In the summer of 1886 the president appointed Governor Hugh Thompson assistant secretary of the treasury. Both Senators Hampton and Butler supported the confirmation of Thompson, which was achieved July 6, 1886.[100]

In May 1886 Hampton gave his support to a "back to Africa" interest, which attracted attention in the last years of the nineteenth century. He presented a petition from a number of black citizens of South Carolina seeking financial assistance in immigrating to Africa.[101] Since this initiative came from black citizens, it was probably an indication of the level of frustration among the black community. The interest of whites in colonization of blacks was an attempt to settle the race problem by removing one race from the scene or by reducing the numbers of one race. This interest was of course closely related to the colonization movement of earlier times. Recall that both Thomas Jefferson and Abraham Lincoln had been interested in removing blacks from this country.

The Democratic Party in their convention of 1886 nominated John Peter Richardson of an aristocratic family of Clarendon County for the office of governor. J. C. Sheppard had served as governor since the resignation of Thompson. It is likely that the convention turned away from Sheppard because he was associated with the emerging and controversial Farmers' Movement.

In August 1886 a group of thirty-nine U.S. senators gave a portrait of Hampton to the state of South Carolina. Among the donors were Joseph E. Brown of Georgia, Henry W. Blair of New Hampshire, Leland Stanford of

California, William E. Everest of New York, and M. C. Butler of South Carolina.[102] The donors were an interesting lot: Brown was the controversial governor of Georgia during the Civil War, Blair was a scion of a famous family and author of the controversial education bill that would have distributed federal aid to states in proportion to their illiterate population, Stanford was the railroad baron who served as governor and then senator of California, Everest had become famous in aiding in the acquittal of Andrew Johnson, and Butler was of course the other senator from South Carolina.

In late October, Senator Hampton campaigned for the Democratic ticket, appearing on platforms in Chester, Summerville, and Charleston. He campaigned vigorously for Richardson and for William Elliott, who was trying to unseat black congressman Robert Smalls. Hampton spoke to his Charleston audience movingly of their recent earthquake disaster.[103] The election was a victory for the Democrats: both Richardson and Elliot won.[104]

On November 15 the senator suffered another hunting accident, this time on family lands in Mississippi. He had become separated from the rest of the hunting party. Becoming entangled in brush and vines, jerking his gun to free it, he accidentally discharged it into his horse. The horse then fell on Hampton, who freed himself only after a painful struggle. He had to walk about five miles to find help. The senator was confined to bed for several days.[105] Hampton was either accident-prone, or he simply took chances unwise for someone of his age and condition. In April 1888 the senator, while riding a lively horse in Washington, was bruised when the horse stumbled and fell.[106]

Albeit a paternalist, the senator from time to time demonstrated genuine concern for black citizens. In February 1887 he supported the bill to reimburse freed slaves for funds lost in the failed Freedmen's Bank.[107]

On October 27, 1887, Hampton served as the chief marshal in ceremonies attending the unveiling of the Lee equestrian statue in Richmond. The Marine Band led an extensive parade, with Hampton riding side-by-side with his old rival Fitzhugh Lee. The Marine Band played "Dixie," "Yankee Doodle," and "The Star-Spangled Banner."[108]

The senator continued his independent ways. The Blair Education Bill passed the Senate on February 16, 1888, Hampton voting aye and Butler nay.[109] The Blair bill never passed the House. This same senator from New Hampshire introduced a bill to give a measure of preference for civil service jobs to Confederate veterans. Senator Hampton spoke to thank Senator Blair for the gesture but to say that he would vote against the bill because he opposed all arbitrary discrimination in selecting people for public service.[110] There was in this decade considerable interest in reform of the civil service.

Hampton was not a delegate to the state Democratic convention, which met in May 1888. The South Carolina Democrats unanimously supported the nomination of Grover Cleveland for a second term as president. The convention backed the Cleveland move to lower tariff rates.[111] The national convention nominated Cleveland and Allen Thurman of Ohio.

Hampton often participated in events intended to conciliate the North and South. In May 1888 the senator voted for the bill to restore the rank of full general and to bestow that rank on his old adversary Phil Sheridan.[112] In the following August the president of the Senate appointed Hampton to represent the Senate at the funeral of General Sheridan.[113]

Ben Tillman honed his style of demagoguery by participating in the South Carolina campaign of 1888. He spoke on the platform with gubernatorial candidate Richardson at a rally in Hodges. The Edgefield demagogue told his audience that since the blacks had been "pitched overboard" he was free to question which Democrat ruled. He went on to charge that an aristocracy ruled the state. The editor of the *News and Courier* commented that Tillman went out of his way to attack "some of the best elements of this state."[114] One of Tillman's targets was the Columbia Club of which Hampton was an honorary member. He accused the Columbia Club of seducing new legislators by giving them new suits.[115] In a speech in Charleston, Tillman accused Charlestonians of being an "arrant set of cowards" when they did not kill "even one nigger" in revenge for the Cainhoy massacre. Tillman bragged about his role in the Hamburg riot, where he "dared even the devil to save the state." Senator Hampton commented on Tillman in an interview with a reporter from the *News and Courier*, stating that he was surprised that the city of Charleston "permitted such blackguardism without resenting it more emphatically than they did." The senator predicted that Tillman was aiming to be governor and that if the Edgefield demagogue gained control of the legislature, then he would replace M. C. Butler in the U.S. Senate with George Tillman, Ben's brother.[116] The irony is in the near accuracy of Hampton's predictions.

Hampton spoke at a number of Democratic rallies, urging all to vote Democratic, specifically praising Richardson and Cleveland. He declared Cleveland to be "as brave, as honest, and conscientious and as true a man . . . as ever sat in the presidential chair." In an attack on Tillman the senator praised the city of Charleston for its courage and self-restraint in avoiding violence after the Cainhoy affair, and thereby avoiding the possibility of martial law.[117] Hampton told his black listeners that Cleveland in his first term had appointed more black people to office than all the Republican presidents. The results of the 1888 election were mixed for Hampton.[118] Cleveland lost; Richardson won; and the state legislature reelected M. C. Butler to the U.S. Senate.

The *New York Times* reflected the changing national opinion of the black race when it described the ignorant black vote as hanging like a pall over South Carolina. The writer approvingly quoted the *News and Courier* in supporting an educational qualification for voting. The Charleston paper admitted that the eight box law served as a check on illiterate voting, but such a law, being a "subterfuge," was "beneath the dignity of the state." The *News and Courier* noted that the state was reluctant to enact an educational qualification for fear of losing a seat in Congress.[119] On the next day the *New York Times* described the newly elected Governor Richardson as placing a high priority on white supremacy and being determined that the state never again be subject to a black majority.[120] Several days later a *New York Times* editorial sympathized with the South's fear of black dominance, a condition the South had suffered years ago.[121]

In February 1889, Senator Hampton supported the Mills bill to reduce tariff rates. His goal was to reduce rates but retain modest rates for revenue and protection.[122] The South was not solid on the issue of tariffs; several states actually favored tariff protection. Hampton's position was moderate, between the free traders and the protectionists.

It is interesting to consider Hampton's actions on one of the emotional issues of the times. In June 1887 President Grover Cleveland approved an order to return to the Southern states the battle flags captured in the recent war. The Grand Army of the Republic (GAR) led in a highly publicized and emotional attack on the president's patriotism. So effective was the GAR's effort that Cleveland ultimately revoked the order. This event became one of the factors in the Democratic defeat in 1888.[123] In March 1889, Senator Hampton wrote to Sen. S. Quay of Pennsylvania to indicate that he had been given two flags captured from Pennsylvania regiments, and he wished to have them returned to the original owners. The Pennsylvania colleague replied to express his gratitude and to say that Hampton's action was "one of the multiplying evidences that the issues and animosities of the Civil War are fading."[124]

Hampton joined in the efforts to get his fellow South Carolinian Hugh Thompson, assistant secretary of the treasury in the first Cleveland administration, another federal appointment. He went with Thompson to call on the Republican president, Benjamin Harrison. Within a short time the president appointed Thompson to the Civil Service Commission.[125]

In May 1889 the senator participated in the dedication of a monument to German Confederates erected in the Bethany Cemetery. His speech, especially when one recalls the occasion, was remarkable in urging an attitude of reconciliation. "We must remember that now all, North, South, East, and West, have but one country and one constitution, to both of which our allegiance is due." Perhaps most remarkable in a time when Southern leaders were actively redefining the causes of the war, Hampton told his audience, "The war, which was a misfortune, may have been likewise a grave mistake."[126]

Despite progressive statements on some issues, the senator also represented the conservative South, and much of the North, on issues of race. Senator Butler was advocating that the federal government give financial aid to assist blacks in "returning" to Africa. Butler introduced a bill to appropriate

$5 million to facilitate this exodus.[127] Hampton told a reporter from the *New York Times* that he was willing to see blacks leave the South, even if it resulted in a loss of seats in Congress. "I would gladly vote to appropriate $50,000,000 for the purchase of Cuba or some other place for them to settle in."[128] Apparently, Hampton later felt some discomfort on this issue. He told a correspondent from the *News and Courier* that he meant the blacks no harm. He did not favor compulsion. He remembered that President Grant had a similar exodus in mind when he advocated acquiring Santo Domingo.[129] In January 1890 Hampton addressed the Senate on this issue, telling his colleagues, "I do not wish any harm to the Negroes but I would sacrifice their votes if they would settle in New England. . . . It would be of best interest for the races to be separated, leaving each to work out his own destiny." Hampton saw the presence of blacks as "The sole disturbing cause, preventing the realization of the labors and hopes of our fathers, when they sought to establish a more perfect union between the states." He still advocated equal suffrage for the two races.[130]

It was stated earlier that Hampton retained ownership of some land in Mississippi. In November 1889 Hampton wrote to Senator Butler that he was trying to sell his land in Glen Allen, where he and his son McDuffie had been deer hunting. "There is much more fun in doing that than listening to long speeches."[131] Apparently, Hampton passed the land on to McDuffie.

Senator Hampton joined with Sen. John T. Morgan of Alabama in publishing an article titled "What Negro Supremacy Means" in the March 1890 issue of the *Forum,* in which the Southern senators argued that dominance by black voters led inevitably to absolute ruin. The article retold the story of radical Reconstruction in its most negative interpretation, often using Pike's *The Prostrate State* as a source. The article closed with an 1858 quotation of Lincoln, opposing social and political equality for blacks and whites.[132]

Lest there be any doubt about Hampton's racism, albeit moderate and generally in accord with the national mood of the time, he wrote another article published in the July 1890 issue of the *Arena* titled "The Race Problem." He argued that miscegenation always led to the degradation of both races and that blacks had progressed only because of contact with the white race. While he admitted many individual blacks had proved themselves to be exceptional, still, he stated that the black race was not fitted to rule whites. The crux of his article was that the South could not again undergo the experience of Reconstruction. He hoped that the black race would be dispersed thereafter, either by some going to Africa or by some moving to other parts of the United States.[133] In supporting Butler's bill to encourage black emigration, Hampton reminded the Senate that both Thomas Jefferson and Abraham Lincoln had supported the concept of colonization of blacks.[134] These two articles probably reflected the senator's aging and the mood of the nation at that time.

In Hampton's remaining months as a senator, he continued his stance as a sound money man, and he became involved in opposing an effort to involve the federal government in supervising elections, presumably to protect black suffrage. In July 1890 Senator Hampton voted against a bill to require the Treasury Department to issue currency notes for the silver bullion in the federal possession.[135] The last important issue for Hampton was the so-called Force Bill, introduced by Henry Cabot Lodge of Massachusetts, to have the federal government supervise elections. The Lodge bill never came to a vote in the Senate, in part because the national mood had changed. The former Reconstruction governor of South Carolina probably best expressed the new attitude. D. H. Chamberlain in an address to the Massachusetts Reform Club, in a note of bitterness and prophetic accuracy, advised his listeners to leave the blacks alone. "The party which left him [the Negro] to his fate in 1876 in order to save the presidency for the Republican Party is not the party he can trust now or ever in the future."[136]

The Blair bill to provide federal aid for education came up again for a vote in March 1890. Hampton voted aye, but the bill failed. By this time the editor of the *News and Courier*—no longer Francis Dawson, who had died—was labeling the Blair bill as the "bill to promote mendicancy,"[137] in keeping with the increasingly dominant Southern attitude toward any federal intervention that might disturb their racial relations.

Meanwhile in South Carolina events were moving to a crisis dooming the reign of the Hampton bourbons and setting the state on a course of immoderate racism, a course the state held for the next seventy years. In January 1890 Capt. G. W. Shell, representing the executive committee of the state Farmers' Association, issued a call for a convention to meet on March 27 to select a slate of nominees committed to the farmers' causes to be supported in the forthcoming Democratic conventions. The "Shell Manifesto," generally believed to be the product of Ben Tillman, accused the current state government of corruption and demanded drastic reform. The farmers of Edgefield County met early and decided to promote their neighbor Ben Tillman as the farmers' champion for governor.[138] In compliance with the Shell Manifesto thirty-four counties held conventions to select delegates for the Farmers' Convention.[139]

The Shell-Tillman Farmers' Convention met in March and chose Tillman as their nominee for the Democratic nomination and adopted a platform to be pushed at the Democratic convention. The platform

1. appealed for Anglo-Saxon unity;
2. advocated reapportionment of representation to strengthen the upcountry counties;
3. urged the state to abolish the state Board of Agriculture, its tax support, and its agricultural experiment farm and shift all to the emerging Clemson College;

4. recommended support for South Carolina College as a classical and literary institution;
5. recommended a rigid economy;
6. recommended strengthening the Rail Road Commission;
7. urged greater state control over the phosphate mines;
8. recommended a new constitutional convention; and
9. recommended requiring statewide candidates to canvass the entire state and to speak in every county.[140]

The regular Democrats—those of the Hampton legacy—were startled by the threat from the Tillman-led Farmers' Association. They had good reason to be concerned, because Tillman led a remarkably effective campaign of demagoguery; he attacked those in power with accusations of corruption and extravagance, of being an outdated aristocracy with contempt for the fate of the poor masses, almost never offering any proof to support his charges.[141] The farmers of the state, like most farmers of the nation, were indeed in tough financial straits, and ready to listen to the emotional appeals of one who promised cures for their troubles. Indeed, Tillman's appeals were not unlike those of Hitler to the troubled Germany of the 1930s, and no less effective. Conservative leaders met and issued a statement appealing to the state's Democrats "to support its own protest against the aggrandizement of one man at such a cost to the state."[142]

In the midst of the turmoil caused by the Tillman campaign, the *Washington Post* reported the rumor that Wade Hampton would attempt to staunch the Tillman movement by offering himself as a candidate for governor. The *News and Courier* reported that it was authorized to deny this rumor, and then added, "It must not be understood from this statement, however, that Senator Hampton sympathizes in any way with the candidacy of Captain Tillman or that he will fail to respond to whatever calls may be made upon him by the Democratic Party in South Carolina." The editor concluded by assuring his readers that the senator opposed Tillman and that he would do what he could to defeat the radical candidate from Edgefield.[143]

The executive committee of the South Carolina Democratic Party issued a call for the convention to meet in Columbia on August 5, 1890. The committee asked each county committee to arrange a meeting for all candidates to speak in a preliminary canvass of the state. After the preliminary campaign each county was to elect delegates to the state convention.[144] This series of county hustings gave Tillman his opportunity to appeal to the masses. The anti-Tillman Democrats sought to gather their forces to meet the radical onslaught. They convened in Columbia on May 20 and selected Gen. John Bratton of Fairfield County as their choice for governor. Bratton accepted their pleas and announced his candidacy.[145]

There was speculation early in the campaign that Tillman's long-range plan was to unseat and replace Hampton in the Senate. The *News and Courier* stated, "We have reason to believe that he [Tillman] has a grudge against Senator Hampton and that he will use his influence to defeat Hampton's re-election to the Senate." The editor then rather ruefully added, "It will be too late to save Hampton after Tillman has captured the legislature."[146] There was no doubt about the stance of the state's most influential newspaper. The editor of the *News and Courier* accurately characterized the Tillman campaign as one of slander.[147]

It is not surprising that the senator was now dividing his time between Washington and his embattled home state. He came from Canada to participate in a public meeting at the state fairgrounds on June 24. A. C. Haskell, the most prominent opponent of Tillman, presided. Hampton addressed the audience and expressed his regret that some of the pro-Tillman crowds had insulted General Bratton. The senator tried to appeal to Confederate nostalgia. He reminded the listeners that Bratton had fought bravely for the South. "Good God! Have the memories of '61 and '65, have they been obliterated and all that has been done by the men who have tried to save South Carolina? Has it been forgotten?" Hampton recognized that there was an agricultural depression, but he asked what a legislature could do about that. He denied that there was any ruling aristocracy.[148] Haskell spoke and taunted Tillman for not having served in the Southern army. Tillman scored a success by telling the crowd that he was an invalid and calling on the much-respected Bishop Ellison Capers to describe the role of the Tillman family in the war. The bishop replied that James Tillman was the "oriflamme of my regiment." Tillman then dared to turn on Hampton himself: "The grand mogul here, who ruled supremely and grandly, cannot think to come here and intimidate me." This was just the right show of daring to excite the Tillman mob.[149]

Two days later Tillman again confronted the senator before an excited audience in Aiken. This time the farmers' candidate actually rode to the platform on the shoulders of his followers. When Hampton attempted to speak he was faced with a tactic developed in the campaign of 1876; he was "howled down" to the point that he gave up and took his seat. Tillman urged Hampton to stay out of this "family quarrel," which was not relevant to the senator. In other words Hampton was irrelevant.[150]

The anti-Tillman Democrats met again, now under the leadership of A. C. Haskell. They decided to try to get the party to require primary elections to choose nominees to be ratified at a second convention to meet in September. With apparently unconscious irony these regulars called themselves "straight-out Democrats."[151]

Tillman had conducted his campaign too well to be frustrated by the last-ditch efforts of the old regulars. The party executive committee directed that the sole purpose of the August convention was to decide whether the delegates to the state convention scheduled for September should be chosen by primary elections. When the convention met on August 15 it was under the domination of Ben Tillman. The delegates ignored the executive committee and adopted a new party constitution, which required primaries beginning with the elections of 1892. The convention also elected a new executive committee. The delegates for the September convention were to be chosen by county conventions, by then well under control of the Tillmanites. A number of outraged straight-outs, led by A. C. Haskell, walked out of the convention.[152]

The Democrats convened in the House chamber in September for the business of choosing their nominees for state offices. Tillman's dominance was complete. The convention nominated Tillman for governor and Eugene B. Gary for lieutenant governor. This Gary was a relative of the late Martin Gary, under whom the nominee had read law. The party platform condemned the McKinley Tariff and the Lodge Force Bill and advocated relief for farmers in the throes of the agricultural depression, abolition of national banks, inflation of the nation's currency, adoption of an income tax, the strengthening of the state railroad commission, and a new constitutional convention.[153] It is worth noting that Senator Hampton was in agreement with much of the platform. He had opposed the McKinley Tariff, which raised rates; he opposed the Lodge bill; he was not active in relief of farmers because he saw no role for the government in such matters; and he had not opposed the income tax. The differences were in that the senator was a sound money man, opposed to attempts to cure the economic troubles by inflating the currency, and he saw no need for a new constitution.

The anti-Tillman Democrats conducted a number of county conventions and then convened in a statewide convention on October 9. The delegates represented twenty counties; fifteen were not represented. They nominated A. C. Haskell for governor and W. D. Johnson of Marion County for lieutenant governor.[154] Hampton was initially inclined to stay out of the state campaign, obviously not liking Tillman but not wanting to contribute to splitting the party. Senator Butler announced that he would support the party's nominees, that is, the Tillman ticket.[155] The editor of the *News and Courier* urged Senator Hampton to speak out, reminding him that A. C. Haskell believed that Tillman intended to abrogate the 1876 Democratic promises to the black population.[156]

Tillman played the "race card" by accusing Haskell of seeking the black vote. Haskell replied that he indeed sought the support of all legal voters, reminding the people of the pledges of 1876: that the rights of the black population were fixed by the Thirteenth, Fourteenth and Fifteenth Amendments, and the Democrats had promised to respect those rights. Tillman told his followers, "White supremacy is what we are fighting for now and white supremacy we must and will have at all hazards." Haskell said that he wanted to win by force of mind and morals, not by violence.[157] Hampton finally stated his position in a letter to the new chairman of the State Democratic Executive Committee, Col. J. L. M. Irby, who ironically was destined to supplant Hampton in the Senate. The senator informed Irby that he intended to support the party's nominees, but he added, "In doing this I by no means endorse the grave charges which have been made against the Democratic Party of the state. Honesty and integrity have marked every administration which has governed the state since 1876." Hampton said that he could not support the rump slate, "Though I have the greatest respect for the gentlemen composing it."[158] This made the reluctance of his support of Tillman quite clear.

The Republican State Executive Committee announced that there would be no Republican ticket, and the committee suggested that black citizens vote for Haskell. A conference of black leaders also endorsed the candidacy of Haskell.[159] While such a gathering of support was encouraging in one sense, the support of Republicans and blacks also enhanced Tillman's appeals to bigotry. The Haskell effort failed partly because the leaders of the state had for too long preached that the unity of the Democratic Party was essential for the welfare of the state. Many considered the Haskell campaign unpatriotic. There is evidence that Hampton could not bring himself to vote for Tillman; he left his registration in Washington.[160] The Tillman ticket won overwhelmingly, setting the political tone of the state for the next several generations.

There were many indications of the new mood of the state, but none was more telling than the fact that the number of lynchings increased dramatically in the 1890s. Although Tillman condemned lynchings in his inaugural address, he also bragged about his role in the Hamburg and Ellenton riots.[161] His followers understood his real message. Black activist Kelly Miller thought that Tillman had unleashed the violent passions of lower-class whites, passions the conservatives of the old regime had held in check.[162] John Andrew Rice, in his remarkable commentary on the state, called the reign begun by Tillman and carried on by such as Cole Blease and Cotton Ed Smith the reign of "white trash supremacy."[163]

Soon after the Tillman victory, rumors abounded that the newly elected governor would be gunning for Wade Hampton next. One unnamed Tillmanite told a reporter that Hampton's letter to Irby and his obvious reluctance to support the Democratic ticket angered Tillman. Some even thought that Tillman himself would replace Hampton in the Senate, which he could indeed have done with his control of the general assembly. These rumors evoked support for the reelection of the senator. Johnson Hagood reminded the people of Hampton's service to the state. The editor of the *News and Courier* pleaded for "this grand old man." Senator Butler spoke to a number of legislators to encourage the reelection of Hampton.[164] Not all of the state's newspapers supported Hampton so completely. The editor of the *Columbia Daily Register* commented, "We believe there are men in the state gifted with far greater talent than Hampton."[165]

The accident-prone Hampton suffered another hunting accident while hunting with his son in Mississippi. He took a bird shot in the corner of his eye, which fortunately resulted in no permanent damage.[166] Hampton was in Mississippi when his friends were urging him to be active in lobbying on his own behalf. He refused to seek the office for himself. The general assembly voted on December 7 and elected J. L. M. Irby to replace Hampton. Walter Edgar described Irby as "an habitual drunk and accused murderer."[167] Senator Hampton actually came in third place. The *News and Courier* opined: "When he shall retire from the Senate, Wade Hampton will carry with him the affection of the people of South Carolina. . . . His place in the American pantheon is safe."[168] The *New York Times* noted, "This is a result over which there will be no rejoicing outside of South Carolina, for General Hampton has shown himself an able, dignified, and high-minded senator."[169] The Tillmanites called this a revolution, but the change in leadership brought little or no improvement in the lives of poor people to whom Tillman had effectively appealed. The most obvious change was a greater intensity in racism.

While Hampton appeared stoic to the public, he revealed his disappointment to some associates. In December he wrote to M. C. Butler that he intended to resume his life as a planter, presumably in Mississippi. "I have been trying to get matters in such condition that the next crop may make something, the Alliance friends having 'shelved' me." He confided to Butler his belief that Tillman had resorted to "misrepresentation, detraction, and lying." There was even a note of bitterness: "I am hurt that the old soldiers turned against me, for I did not expect that at their hand."[170] Hampton and Butler obviously drew closer together in their last years, in part because they faced a common enemy.

The senator was active in his lame-duck period. In January he voted for a measure to require the government to purchase silver for currency,[171] despite the fact that Hampton was for the most part a sound money man. The Senate was considering a bill to involve the federal government in the supervision of elections, often called the "Force Bill." Hampton argued against the bill in a speech to the Senate on January 16, 1891. He stated his belief that the Force Bill would lead to violence, and that while some blacks had achieved remarkable progress, "a vast majority are still in dense ignorance, an ignorance so profound as to render them not only unfit to govern great and free states, but unfit to meet the responsibilities to discharge the duties of citizenship." He reminded the Senate that he had for years stood for justice for the black race. He asked his colleagues to consider what the reaction of the Anglo-Saxons of Massachusetts would be to possible domination by a large Chinese population.

He reminded the Senate that the people of the West Coast wanted to exclude the Chinese.[172] While his claim to have been a champion of blacks has some truth, it is also apparent that his attitudes toward the black race were hardening, as were those of the general population.

On March 4, 1891, the *News and Courier* reported that Senator Hampton's second term had expired. "No other son has done so much for South Carolina. No interest has been neglected, no cause of complaint has been alleged against him."[173] Hampton returned to South Carolina, leaving elected office for good, but not public life. On March 11 he gave the commencement address at South Carolina Medical College. When Hampton was introduced, the audience applauded for nearly five minutes. The speaker told the graduates, "Believe me as one who has learned to estimate at their true value popular applause and popular fame and to know what reward often follows for duties faithfully discharged, that there is but one thing in life that gives ample compensation, whether fortune smiles or frowns, and that is the consciousness of having performed honestly all the duties committed to your charge." At the conclusion of his speech the orchestra played "Dixie."[174] On March 27 Hampton was the primary orator for the celebration of the Columbia centennial.[175] He told his Columbia audience, "My political career is ended, my public work finished. Other hands, perhaps abler, will take up that work, but not within the borders of our state will one son of hers ever be found who will serve her with a more loyal devotion, a more willing hand or a more loving heart than I have done."[176]

The paucity of family records forces us to speculate that Hampton out of office divided his time between the family farms in Mississippi and Columbia, South Carolina, but he remained interested in politics. In March 1892 he met with other conservatives to consider offering opposition to the reelection of Tillman. They decided on John C. Sheppard for governor and James L. Orr for lieutenant governor.[177] Tillman and his ticket were reelected.

Hampton had never managed his finances well. He apparently saved nothing from his years in the Senate, and it was obviously difficult to earn a living from the family lands in the 1890s, years of a prolonged agricultural depression. The price of cotton actually fell as low as six cents a pound. Hampton's friends therefore sought a political sinecure for the elder statesman. Hampton was in Washington in the early days of the new Democratic administration. Only a few days into his second administration, Cleveland told a delegation of congressmen from Nebraska and Iowa, who were recommending F. H. Morrison for the office of commissioner of the Pacific Railroads, that he intended to appoint "an old and distinguished Democrat, Wade Hampton," to that office. This was a position created to represent the federal government's interests in those railroads that had been the recipients of much governmental largesse.[178] On March 21,1892, the Charleston newspaper reported that the president had indeed appointed Hampton as commissioner of the Pacific Railroads. The editor commented, "The President could not have made a better appointment and the country, rather than General Hampton, is to be congratulated that he has been appointed."[179] The *New York Times* also applauded the appointment, noting that this was appropriate as "recognition of patriotic service, for, as no one was more zealous on the Confederate side during the Civil War, none has labored more faithfully and with less desire for reward, or less actual reward, for that matter, toward the re-establishment of good feelings between the North and the South."[180]

Both Democratic and Republican administrations treated the position of railroad commissioner as a special sinecure for former Confederate generals. President Cleveland appointed Joseph E. Johnston railroad commissioner in 1885, and the general served until 1888, when the Republican Benjamin Harrison won the presidency.[181] In 1897 Hampton was succeeded by then-Republican James Longstreet, who received his appointment from William McKinley.[182]

Hampton's favor with President Cleveland undoubtedly rankled Governor Tillman. The South Carolina governor was learning that the reform elements could expect little from the conservative Cleveland. Senator Irby, surely at the urging of his mentor Tillman, went to the White House to try to contradict some of the things that the president would have heard from Hampton and his friends.[183]

It soon became apparent that Tillman, who had earlier assured South Carolinians that he had no interest in seeking office, intended to replace M. C. Butler in the U.S. Senate. In June 1893 Senator Butler wrote to Wade Hampton to enlist his help in raising funds for the forthcoming political fight. Butler and Hampton agreed that Tillman represented a threat from the common mob. Butler told Hampton that Tillman's election to the Senate would represent "a great deal of encouragement to the same class in other states."[184]

Hampton sought to do what he could for his South Carolina supporters. He went to see Cleveland's secretary of state, Walter Gresham, to seek an appointment for N. G. Gonzales, the founder of the *State* newspaper and an ardent antagonist of the Tillman regime. Hampton urged Gonzales to organize Democratic clubs in South Carolina to assist in defeating "the present disgraceful regime" in the next election. Hampton hoped that the clubs would lead to a statewide convention that would nominate a full slate to oppose the Tillmanites.[185] In a later letter to Gonzales, Hampton described the organization of the National League, which would oppose the radicalism of the Tillmanites and their allies across the country. The clubs Hampton hoped Gonzales would help organize could be associated with the National League. Hampton also passed on to his journalist friend some gossip about the Tillmanites. John Gary Evans, nephew of Martin Gary and a Tillman ally, came to Washington on a railroad pass, and he arrived intoxicated. Hampton suggested that Gonzales find whether Tillman himself took advantage of his position by using rail passes, accepting favors from the hated rail corporations.[186]

The office of commissioner of Pacific railroads was a result of the Pacific Railroad Act of 1862, which led to a large investment of federal funds in the construction of the railroads west of the Missouri River. The commissioner was to check on those railroads and their financial responsibilities to the federal government. Hampton went to work, traveling to the Pacific Coast as required. Not at all incidentally, he enjoyed fishing off the West Coast.[187] In October of his first year in office he submitted a report indicating that some of the Pacific railroads were delinquent in submitting their required reports.[188] Hampton recommended the establishment of a commission to determine the companies' indebtedness to the government, noting that those companies were not at that time in condition to make the required payments.[189] The report of 1894 noted the effects of an economic depression and the Pullman strike. Both the Union Pacific and the Kansas Pacific were in the hands of receivers. Hampton recommended the establishment of a national board of railway arbitration, to prevent the recurrence of loss of life and destruction of property in strikes such as occurred in the Pullman strike.[190] The reports of 1895 and 1896 noted improved economic conditions and increased freight rates.[191] The commissioner managed to maintain his own sense of priorities; he delayed a business trip to the West Coast so he could attend a Confederate reunion in Richmond, and he decided to return from California by way of Texas so he could engage in tarpon fishing in the Gulf. He also varied a trip to Oregon according to whether the salmon were running.[192]

In 1894 Ben Tillman opposed M. C. Butler for the U.S. Senate. Hampton might have hoped that Butler would seek and gain the support of black voters, but the senator was afraid of the possible damage to his white support.[193] Although the decision was to be made by the general assembly, the two opponents faced each other in a series of debates across the state. They vied with each other to claim the most credit for having participated in the violence of the Hamburg riot of 1876.[194] Tillman won handily, and John Gary Evans succeeded Tillman as governor; the Tillmanites were much in control.

Hampton continued to play a leading role in celebrations of the Confederacy. In May 1895 he spoke to an audience in Oakwood Cemetery in Chicago at the dedication of a monument in honor of the several thousands of Confederates who died in a nearby prison. Hampton noted that the monument had been financed in part by Union veterans and that this was another indication of increasing friendship between the North and the South. M. C. Butler, James Longstreet, and Fitzhugh Lee were also there.[195] The old general was the main feature in a number of Confederate reunions. He was introduced to a reunion in 1895 as "the stone which the builders in 1890 refused." The *News and Courier* described Hampton's entry to the Charleston reunion of 1898: "As the old hero entered the hall every man and woman got on a chair, sent up a cheer that might have been heard on Fort Sumter on a still night."[196]

Republican William McKinley defeated Democrat William Jennings Bryan in 1896. Hampton continued in his office for almost a year in the McKinley administration. There was a concerted effort to have the old man continued in office for the simple reason that he had no other means of livelihood. The *New York Times* published a letter from a Hampton supporter from Greenville, South Carolina, pleading for the general's reappointment to office. The writer described Hampton as "too generous to be thrifty, too proud to use the generosity of his friends, and too scrupulous to make profit from his place."[197] These efforts notwithstanding, another former Confederate, James Longstreet, who had become a Republican, replaced Hampton. The South Carolinian was not gracious in yielding to his former Confederate colleague. Reportedly, he refused to speak to Longstreet and did not cooperate in the transition.[198] The general was again in financial straits.

The general was residing in Southern Cross, built after the war on the Hampton property, when tragedy struck again. On May 2, 1899, the house burned, possibly the work of incendiaries, destroying everything. The eighty-two-year-old veteran went almost immediately to a Confederate reunion in Charleston, presenting himself as undaunted by cruel fates. Much to the distress of historians, Hampton reported, "All my papers and books are gone; nothing of value was saved."[199] When he returned to Columbia he found that a group of friends were busy raising funds to build a house for the destitute hero. Hampton promptly released a letter to the state's newspapers thanking the friends for their kind intentions but asking them to abandon their efforts. He assured all that their intentions would be "prized by me more than any gift from them could ever be." His protests notwithstanding, the funds came in, and the general acquired a house on Senate Street in Columbia.[200]

On February 15, 1898, the USS *Maine* sank after an explosion in Havana Harbor. The sinking of the *Maine* was the final of a series of incidents leading to a declaration of war against Spain on April 25, 1898. Hampton opposed the war as an unjustified aggression, but, the war having been declared, he urged South Carolina to fulfill its troop quota.[201] Hampton's son Alfred was considering enlisting to serve under the command of his father's old comrade and antagonist Fitzhugh Lee. The father wrote to his son, then in Nogales, Arizona, urging him not to serve under Lee. Hampton opined, "I regard the war as an unjust one, but of course every state was bound . . . to give the quota called for."[202] Despite the negative memory of Fitz Lee, there is no doubt that in these last years of Hampton's life the memories he most cherished were those of his military experiences. One admirer asked Hampton, "How shall I call you, General, Governor, or Senator?" He replied, "Call me General; I like that title best."[203]

The gift of a home was not the only generosity the general tried to decline. In 1901 President Theodore Roosevelt, attempting to build the Republican Party in the South, sought to enlist respectable whites into his camp. Sen. John L. McLauren, who—unlike Senator Tillman—admired President Roosevelt, came to see Hampton and informed him that the president would appoint him general postmaster of Columbia in return for his political support. Hampton declined, saying that he could not be bought.[204]

In December 1901 the general attended a reunion of South Carolina College alumni in Charleston, where he contracted a cold. On returning to his home the cold persisted. In early April he became gravely ill, finally losing consciousness. It was an age when people placed great emphasis on the last words of the dying. When his mind wandered, he thought of his two wounded sons at the Battle of Burgess Mill. He muttered, "My children are on the field—heroes forever—forever." And lastly, "God bless all my people, black and white." He died on April 11, 1902, exactly twenty-five years since he assumed control of the state house.[205]

The governor declared April 13 a day of mourning. The railroads operated special trains to bring mourners from all over the state. Newspapers estimated that about twenty thousand participated in the funeral. The general's body was borne on a horse-drawn hearse, driven by a white-haired former Hampton slave. All others walked from the Hampton house to Trinity Church. Hampton had asked that there be no military funeral, but many veterans were among the mourners. About 1,200 crowded into Trinity; the others waited outside. Bishop Ellison Capers presided. The pallbearers included N. G. Gonzales, who in less than a year would be murdered by Lt. Gov. Jim Tillman, nephew of Hampton's chief antagonist, Ben Tillman, who also attended the funeral.

The funeral itself represented the end of an era. Hampton became a permanent fixture in the South Carolina pantheon, but his legacy has often been distorted. Many of the state's political leaders who preached brash racism considered themselves to be heirs of Hampton. Actually, the racially moderate governors who held office from the late 1950s were more in the Hampton tradition. In a sense it took South Carolina about seventy years to come back to the policies of Wade Hampton.

In looking back over the eventful life of Wade Hampton III, his biographer is moved by the might-have-beens. What if the life of slave-worked plantations had endured? What if the dream of the Confederacy had become a permanent reality? What if the power of the newly freed blacks had lasted? And, of course, what if the paternalistic moderation of Hampton had overcome the darker side of prejudice? Could it have matured into genuine justice? Hampton's life was one of repeated loss and tragedy, yet some grasp of those losses yields a measure of understanding of what became. In the words of T. S. Eliot,

> Time past and time future
> What might have been and what has been
> Point to one end, which is always present.[206]

Preface

    1. J. H. Easterby, "The Three Wade Hamptons: The Saga of a Family of the Old South," *State* (Columbia, S.C.), February 25, 1934, A2.

Chapter 1: From Frontiersman to Aristocracy

    1. Ronald Edward Bridwell, "The South's Wealthiest Planter: Wade Hampton I of South Carolina, 1754–1835," (Ph.D. diss., University of South Carolina, 1980), 2.

    2. Ibid.

    3. Virginia G. Meynard, *The Venturers: The Hampton, Harrison, and Earle Families of Virginia, South Carolina, and Texas* (Greenville, S.C.: Southern Historical Press, 1981), 76.

    4. Ibid., 13–41.

    5. Walter Edgar, *South Carolina: A History* (Columbia: University of South Carolina Press, 1998), 205–6.

    6. Robert M. Weir, *Colonial South Carolina* (Millwood, N.Y.: KTO Press, 1983), 330; also Bridwell, 42.

    7. Bridwell, 82.

    8. Ibid., 96.

    9. Ibid., 107.

    10. Ibid., 109–12.

    11. Ibid., 116–19.

    12. Ibid., 122.

    13. Ibid., 123–92.

    14. Ibid., 209.

    15. J. H. Easterby, "The Three Wade Hamptons: The Saga of a Family of the Old South," *State* (Columbia, S.C.), February 25, 1934, A2..

    16. Meynard, *The Venturers*, 480.

    17. Bridwell, "The South's Wealthiest Planter," 228–29.

    18. J. H Easterby, "The Three Wade Hamptons," February 25, 1934, A2.

    19. Bridwell, "The South's Wealthiest Planter," 230–35.

    20. Maximilian Laborde, *History of the South Carolina College* (Charleston: Walker, Evans, and Cogswell, 1874), 16.

    21. Daniel Walker Hollis, "South Carolina College," in *University of South Carolina*, vol. 1 (Columbia: University of South Carolina Press, 1951), 24, and Bridwell, "The South's Wealthiest Planter," 248–69.

    22. Bridwell, "The South's Wealthiest Planter," 248–70.

23. Meynard, *The Venturers*, 480–82.

24. Bridwell, "The South's Wealthiest Planter," 363–78.

25. Meynard, *The Venturers*, 133.

26. Bridwell, "The South's Wealthiest Planter," 393.

27. Easterby, "The Three Wade Hamptons," February 25, 1934, A2.

28. Bridwell, "The South's Wealthiest Planter," 394.

29. Alfred Glaze Smith, *Economic Readjustment of an Old Cotton State: South Carolina, 1829–1860* (Columbia: University of South Carolina Press, 1958), 1–18.

30. Bridwell, "The South's Wealthiest Planter," 405–16.

31. John Hammond Moore, *Columbia and Richland County: A South Carolina Community, 1740–1990* (Columbia: University of South Carolina Press, 1967), 84.

32. Bridwell, "The South's Wealthiest Planter," 498.

33. Ibid., 509–26.

34. Ibid., 558.

35. Ibid., 632.

36. Ibid., 694–747.

37. Ibid., 747–48.

38. Easterby, "The Three Wade Hamptons," February 25, 1934, A2.

39. Ibid.

40. Easterby, "The Three Wade Hamptons," March 4, 1934, A2.

41. Bridwell, "The South's Wealthiest Planter," 762–63.

42. Ibid.

43. Ibid., 770–82.

44. Ibid.

45. Wade Hampton Papers, Report from Strong at Houmas, December 27, 1834 (South Caroliniana Library, University of South Carolina—hereafter cited as SCL, USC).

46. Bridwell, "The South's Wealthiest Planter," 782; Meynard, *The Venturers*, 480–526.

47. Meynard, *The Venturers*, 480–526.

48. Hampton Papers, Wade Hampton II at Walnut Ridge to Mary Fisher Hampton (daughter) in South Carolina, December 26, 1850 (SCL, USC).

49. William Kauffman Scarborough, *Masters of the Big House, Elite Slaveholders of the Mid-Nineteenth Century South* (Baton Rouge: Louisiana State University Press, 2003), 181–82.

50. Slave Schedule 1850, Issaquena County, Mississippi. Mississippi Department of Archives and History, Jackson, Mississippi.

51. *Biographical Directory of the Senate of South Carolina, 1776–1964* (Columbia: South Carolina Archives Department, 1964), 231.

52. Lacy K. Ford, *Origins of Southern Radicalism: The South Carolina Upcountry, 1800–1860* (New York: Oxford University Press, 1988), 267.

53. Charles M. Wiltse, *John C. Calhoun, Nullifier, 1829–1834* (New York: Russell and Russell, 1949), 334.

54. Smith, *Economic Readjustment*, 161–66.

55. Ibid., 168–69.

56. Benjamin F. Perry, *The Writings of Benjamin F. Perry*, vol. 2: *Reminiscences of Public Men* (Spartanburg, S.C.: Reprint Company, 1980), 933.

57. Helen Kohn Hennig, *Columbia, Capital City of South Carolina, 1786–1936* (Columbia: The Columbia Sesqui-Centennial Commission, 1936), 330.

58. Meynard, *The Venturers*, 527.

59. Easterby, "The Three Wade Hamptons," March 4, 1934.

60. William T. Porter, sr. ed., *Porter's Spirit of the Times*, vol. 4 (New York, 1858).

61. Perry, *The Writings of Benjamin F. Perry*, vol. 2, 933.

62. Hennig, *Columbia, Capital City*, 183–84.

63. Ibid.

64. Drew Gilpin Faust, *James Henry Hammond and the Old South* (Baton Rouge: Louisiana State University Press, 1982), 241–90.

65. Perry, *The Writings of Benjamin F. Perry*, vol. 2: *Reminiscences of Public Men*, 104–11.

66. Ford, *Origins of Southern Radicalism*, 200–202.

67. Philip M. Hamer, *The Secessionist Movement in South Carolina, 1847–1852* (Allentown, Pa.: H. Ray Hass and Co., 1918), 33–35.

68. Hampton Papers, Letter from Wade Hampton II to James Chesnut, June 5, 1853 (SCL, USC).

69. Easterby, "The Three Wade Hamptons," March 4, 1934.

70. Wade Hampton Papers, Letter from Wade Hampton II at Wild Woods to Mary Fisher Hampton in Columbia, March 8, 1858 (SCL, USC).

71. Indenture between Wade Hampton II and Wade Hampton III and Christopher Hampton, dated August 27, 1855; promissory notes to the Bank of Louisiana, and protests indicating failure to make payments, beginning January 1, 1861; and Chancery Court order transferring Wild Woods and Bayou Place in bankruptcy to Stephen Duncan, who had acquired the notes, signed by Wade III. Center for American History, University of Texas, Austin, Texas; and Will Book, Estate of Wade Hampton, Petition and Final Settlement, Christopher Hampton, June 28, 1861, Issaquena County Court House, Mississippi.

72. Meynard, *The Venturers*, 192.

Chapter 2: The Mantle Passes to the Third Wade Hampton

1. Horace, "It is sweet and proper to die for one's country," from Laurence Perrine, *Sound and Sense* (New York: Harcourt, Brace, and World, 1969), 8–9.

2. Wade Hampton Papers, Photostat copy from *Scientific American*, February 1860 (Southern Historical Collection, University of North Carolina, Chapel Hill).

3. Maximilian LaBorde, *History of the South Carolina College* (Charleston: Walker, Evans, and Cogswell, 1874), 206.

4. Frank Freidel, *Francis Lieber: Nineteenth Century Liberal* (Baton Rouge: Louisiana State University Press, 1947), 136.

5. Thomas Sergeant Perry, *The Life and Letters of Francis Lieber* (Boston: James R. Osgood and Company, 1882), 300–304.

6. Ibid., 306.

7. LaBorde, *History of the South Carolina College*, 538.

8. Virginia G. Meynard, *The Venturers: The Hampton, Harrison, and Earle Families of Virginia, South Carolina, and Texas* (Greenville: Southern Historical Press, 1981), 138, 197.

9. Richard Aubrey McLemore, *A History of Mississippi* (Hattiesburg: University and College Press of Mississippi, 1973), 1:343–50; and Meynard, *The Venturers*, 92.

10. McLemore, *A History of Mississippi*, 342–50.

11. D. Clayton James, *Antebellum Natchez* (Baton Rouge: Louisiana State University Press, 1968), 150.

12. Wade Hampton Papers, Letter from Wade Hampton III to Stephen Duncan, May 19, 1874 (Center for American History, University of Texas, Austin).

13. Meynard, *The Venturers*, 198–200.

14. "Bears and Bear-Hunting," *Harper's New Monthly Magazine* 65 (October 1855), 599.

15. Paul Schullery, *The Bear Hunter's Century* (New York: Dodd, Mead, and Company, 1988), 63–87.

16. Hampton Papers, Letter from Wade Hampton III at Wild Woods to Mary Fisher Hampton in Columbia, February 27, 1859 (SCL, USC).

17. Hampton Papers, Wade Hampton III in Columbia to Alexander Wilson at Cashiers Valley, October 28, 1860 (SCL, USC).

18. Harry Hampton, *Woods and Waters and Some Asides* (Columbia, S.C.: State Printing Company, 1975), 380.

19. Meynard, *The Venturers*, 977.

20. Wade Hampton Papers, Letter from Hampton in England to his wife Margaret Hampton, July 27, 1846 (Southern Historical Collection, University of North Carolina).

21. Hampton Papers, Wade Hampton III in England to his wife Mary in Columbia, July 27, 1846 (SCL, USC); and Meynard, *The Venturers*, 199.

22. Meynard, *The Venturers*, 200.

23. *Daily South Carolinian*, November 5, 1852.

24. *Journal of the House of Representatives of the State of South Carolina, Annual Session, 1852* (Columbia: R. W. Gibbs, State Printer, 1852).

25. Walter Edgar, *South Carolina: A History* (Columbia: University of South Carolina Press, 1998), 331. This is the statement made by Thomas Cooper in considering the effects of tariffs on South Carolina.

26. Lillian Adele Kibler, *Benjamin F. Perry: South Carolina Unionist* (Durham: Duke University Press, 1946), 265–66.

27. *Journal of the House of Representatives of the State of South Carolina, Session of 1852* (Columbia: R. W. Gibbes, State Printer, 1852).

28. Hampton Papers, Letter from Wade Hampton III, Columbia, to James H. Thornwell, South Carolina College, May 4, 1853 (SCL, USC).

29. *Journal of the House of Representatives of the State of South Carolina, Annual Session of 1853* (Columbia: R. W. Gibbes, State Printer, 1853).

30. *Journal of the House of Representatives of the State of South Carolina, Session of 1854* (Columbia: R. W. Gibbes, State Printer, 1854).

31. *Journal of the House of Representatives of the State of South Carolina, Session of 1856* (Columbia: E. H. Bratton, State Printer, 1856).

32. *Biographical Directory of the South Carolina Senate, 1776–1985*, vol. 1 (Columbia: University of South Carolina Press, 1986), 656–59.

33. Laura A. White, *Robert Barnwell Rhett: Father of Secession* (New York: American Historical Association, 1931), 139.

34. *Journal of the House of Representatives of the State of South Carolina, Session of 1856.*

35. John Hammond Moore, *Columbia and Richland County: A South Carolina Community, 1790–1990* (Columbia: University of South Carolina Press, 1993), 30–31.

36. B. M. Palmer, *The Life and Letters of James Henley Thornwell* (Richmond, Va.: Whitlet and Shepperson, 1875), 422–23.

37. Letter from Lieber to Hampton, September 5, 1858. Perry, *The Life and Letters of Francis Lieber*, 300–301.

38. Hampton Papers, Copy from the *New Orleans Bulletin* 1854, printed in the *Mercury*, December 7, 1854 (SCL, USC).

39. Hampton Papers, Speech of Sen. Wade Hampton, delivered in the Senate, December 10, 1859 (SCL, USC).

40. Hampton Papers, copy from *DeBow's Review* 26 (1859), 52 (SCL, USC).

41. *Journal of the Senate of the State of South Carolina, 1858* (Columbia: R. W. Gibbes, State Printer, 1858).

42. Hampton Papers, Letter from Wade Hampton III written from Wild Woods in Mississippi to Miss Mary McDuffie, March 11, 1856 (Perkins Library, Duke University).

43. Hampton Papers, Manuscript poem titled "To Miss Mary McDuffie," dated February 14, 1857 (SCL, USC).

44. Benjamin F. Perry, *Biographical Sketches of Prominent American Statesmen with Speeches, Addresses, and Letters* (Philadelphia: Free Press, 1887), 564.

45. Hampton Papers, "Note to Endorsers," Bank of the State of South Carolina, April, 1855 (SCL, USC).

46. James M. McPherson, *Battle Cry of Freedom, the Civil War Era* (New York and Oxford: Oxford University Press, 1988), 318.

47. Slave Schedules, 1850 and 1860, U.S. Census for Richland County, South Carolina, South Carolina Archives, Columbia; Slave Schedule, 1860,U.S. Census for Issaquena County, Mississippi, Mississippi Archives, Jackson; William Kauffman Scarborough, *Masters of the Big House, the Elite Slaveholders of the Mid–Nineteenth Century South* (Baton Rouge: Louisiana State University Press, 2003), 390; Hampton Papers, Letter from Hampton to F. Ham, Esq., January 1, 1877 (SCL, USC).

48. Letter of T. W. Probyn in Nice, France, to Hampton, January 4, 1860, Hampton Papers (SCL, USC).

49. T. Harry Williams, *Romance and Realism in Southern Politics*, 11.

50. Henry Adams, *The Education of Henry Adams, An Autobiography*, 131.

51. Ann Fripp Hampton, ed., *A Divided Heart, Letters of Sally Baxter Hampton, 1853–1862* (Columbia: Phantom Press, 1994), 76.

52. Ibid, letter from Sally Baxter Hampton to George Baxter, December 29, 1855, 29–30, 40.

53. Hampton Papers, Sally in Columbia to her father in New York, April 15, 1855 (Southern Historical Collection, University of North Carolina).

54. Hampton, *Divided Heart*, 53; and Julia Ward Howe, *Reminiscences*, 234–35.

55. Hampton, *Divided Heart*, 75–78.

56. Ibid., 74–75.

57. Ibid., 67–72.

58. *Daily South Carolinian*, September 30, 1855 (SCL, USC).

59. Lacey K. Ford, *Origins of Southern Radicalism: The South Carolina Upcountry, 1800–1860* (New York: Oxford University Press, 1988), 300–301.

Chapter 3: Of Arms and the Man

1. The title of this chapter is taken from Virgil's *Aeneid* ("I sing of arms and of the man.").

2. Walter Edgar, *South Carolina* (Columbia: University of South Carolina Press, 1998), 342–46.

3. Lacey K. Ford, *Origins of Southern Radicalism: The South Carolina Upcountry, 1800–1860* (New York: Oxford University Press, 1988), 200–202.

4. Lillian Adele Kibler, *Benjamin F. Perry: South Carolina Unionist* (Durham: Duke University Press, 1946), 327.

5. Benjamin F. Perry, *Biographical Sketches of Prominent American Statesmen with Speeches, Addresses, and Letters* (Philadelphia: Free Press, 1887), 564.

6. Douglas Southall Freeman, *Lee's Lieutenants: A Study in Command* (New York: Charles Scribner's Sons, 1942-1944), 1:91–95; J. H. Easterby, "The Three Wade Hamptons: A Saga of a Family of the Old South," *State* (Columbia, S.C.), March 4, 1934.

7. Ann Fripp Hampton, ed., *A Divided Heart, Letters of Sally Baxter Hampton, 1853–1862* (Columbia, S.C.: Phantom Press, 1994), 97.

8. Edward L. Wells, *Hampton and Reconstruction* (Columbia: State Company, 1907), 40. Wells had access to some Hampton papers that were destroyed in the burning of his home in 1899.

9. Richard Aubrey McLemore, *A History of Mississippi* (Hattiesburg: University and College Press of Mississippi, 1973), 1:343–50.

10. Wade Hampton Papers, Letter from Hampton in Montgomery to Mary Fisher Hampton in Columbia, April 24, 1861 (SCL, USC).

11. Manly Wade Wellman, *Giant in Gray: A Biography of Wade Hampton of South Carolina* (Dayton, Ohio: Morningside Book Shop, 1988), 50–51; Edward L. Wells, *Hampton and His Cavalry in 1864* (Richmond, Va.: B. F. Johnson Publishing Company, 1899), 71.

12. *Journal of the Congress of the Confederate States of America, 1861–1865*, vol. 1, 434, 437, 839.

13. Kibler, *Benjamin F. Perry*, 348–49.

14. Freeman, *Lee's Lieutenants*, 1:91–95.

15. Francis Butler Simkins and James Welch Patton, *The Women of the Confederacy* (Richmond and New York: Garrett and Massie, 1936), 26.

16. *South Carolina Women in the Confederacy*, Records Collected by Mrs. A. T. Smythe, Miss M. B. Poppenheim, and Mrs. Thomas Taylor (Columbia: State Company, 1903), 18–19.

17. Ibid., 56.

18. Ibid., 71.

19. Richard N. Current, editor in chief, *Encyclopedia of the Confederacy* (New York: Simon Schuster, 1993), 733–34.

20. Edward L. Wells, *Hampton and Reconstruction* (Columbia: State Company, 1907), 51.

21. *Journal of the Senate of the State of South Carolina, 1861* (Charles P. Pelham, State Printer, 1861), 8.

22. Wade Hampton Papers, Letter from Hampton to General Beauregard, Columbia, June 10, 1861 (Perkins Library, Duke University).

23. James M. McPherson, *Battle Cry of Freedom: The Civil War Era* (New York and Oxford: Oxford University Press, 1988), 337–44.

24. *Official Records of the War of the Rebellion* (hereafter referred to as ORs), vol. 2: Report of Col. Wade Hampton, July 29, 1861 (Washington, D.C.: Government Printing Office, 1880–1901), 2:566–67; Freeman, *Lee's Lieutenants*, 1:91–95.

25. Freeman, *Lee's Lieutenants*, 1:91–95.

26. Joseph E. Johnston, *Narrative of Military Operations Directed during the Late War Between the States* (New York: D. Appleton and Company, 1874), 46.

27. Wellman, *Giant in Gray*, 65.

28. Hampton Papers, Letter from Mary Fisher Hampton at Camp Johnson, Manassas, Va., to Mrs. William Martin, August 12, 1861 (SCL, USC).

29. Wells, *Hampton and Reconstruction*, 39.

30. Speech of Gen. M. C. Butler in *Final Report of the Commission to Provide for a Monument to the Memory of Wade Hampton* (Columbia: Gonzales and Bryan, 1906–1907), 10.

31. Johnston, *Narratives*, 77.

32. W. P. Miles Papers, Letter from Colonel Hampton to Rep. W. P. Miles, August 19, 1861 (Southern Historical Collection, University of North Carolina).

33. *ORs*, 1, vol. 5, Report of Adjutant General S. Cooper, October 22, 1861, 913–14; Report of Adjutant General S. Cooper, November 16, 1861, 960.

34. *ORs*, 1, vol. 5, Report of Colonel Hampton to General Johnston, December 8, 1861, 986–87.

35. Miles Papers, Letter from Colonel Hampton to Congressman Miles, December 10, 1861 (Southern Historical Collection, University of North Carolina).

36. *ORs*, 1, vol. 5, Report of Hampton to General Whiting, December 20, 1861, 1002.

37. Hampton Papers, Hampton III to Mary Fisher Hampton, from Camp Wigfall in January (n.d.), 1862 (SCL, USC).

38. *ORs*, 1, vol. 5, Report of J. E. Johnston to J. P. Benjamin, secretary of war, January 14, 1862, 1028–1030; Letter from J. E. Johnston to General S. Cooper, adjutant and inspector general, February 2, 1862, 1058.

39. Hampton Papers, Hampton III to Mary Fisher Hampton, from Camp Wigfall, March 2, 1862 (SCL, USC).

40. *ORs*, 1, vol. 5, Letter from Wade Hampton at Camp Bartow to General Whiting, March 21, 1862, 533–34.

41. *ORs*, 1, vol. 5, Order from General Whiting to Hampton, March 7, 1862, 1093–94; Letter from General Whiting to Major General Holmes, Commanding the Aquia District, March 21, 1862, 528–31.

42. *ORs*, 1, vol. 11, Report of Maj. Gen. D. H. Hill, January 1863, 601–6.

43. *ORs*, 1, vol. 11, pt. 3, 479.

44. D. S. Freeman, *Lee's Lieutenants*, 1:195.

45. *ORs*, 1, vol. 11, pt. 1, Report of Gen. W. H. C. Whiting, May 8, 1862, 169.

46. *ORs*, 1, vol. 11, pt. 1, Report of Col. Wade Hampton, no date, 632–33.

47. *ORs*, 1, vol. 2, pt. 3, Report of Gen. J. E. Johnston to Gen. R. E. Lee, May 28, 1862, 499–500.

48. *Journal of the Congress of the Confederate States of America*, 2:299, 343, 392.

49. Hampton Papers, Hampton III to Mary Fisher Hampton, May 21, 1862 (SCL, USC).

50. Hampton Papers, Hampton III to Mary Fisher Hampton, May 26, 1862 (SCL, USC).

51. *ORs*, 1, vol. 11, pt. 2, Tables of Casualties, 506.

52. Clyde N. Wilson, *Carolina Cavalier, the Life and Mind of James Johnston Pettigrew* (Athens and London: University of Georgia Press, 1990), 162–69.

53. *ORs*, 1, vol. 11, Report of Gen. Gustavus W. Smith, June 23, 1862, 989–94.

54. Ibid.

55. Hampton Papers, Wade III to Mary Fisher Hampton, from Richmond, June 3, 1862 (SCL, USC); *ORs*, 1, vol. 11, Report of Gen. Gustavus W. Smith, June 23, 1862, 993.

56. Mary Boykin Chesnut, *A Diary from Dixie*, edited by Isabel D. Martin and Myrta Lockett (Gloucester: Peter Smith, 1961), 190–93.

57. Freeman, *Lee's Lieutenants*, 1:571–79.

58. Byron Farwell, *Stonewall: A Biography of General Thomas J. Jackson* (New York and London: W. W. Norton and Company, 1992), 356–63.

59. *ORs*, 1, vol. 11, pt. 3, Special Order #173, Assist. Adj. Gen. Jno. Withers, July 26, 1862, 625.

60. *ORs*, 1, vol. 11, pt. 3, Letter from Johnston to R. E. Lee, May 25, 1862, 543.

61. *ORs*, 1, vol. 11, pt. 3, R. E. Lee to Gen. A. P. Hill, June 11, 1862, 589.

62. *ORs*, 1, vol. 11, pt. 3, Special Order #165, R. H. Chilton, assistant adjutant general, July 28, 1862, 657.

63. *ORs*, 1, vol.11, pt. 3, Letter from R. E. Lee to Gustavus W. Smith, August 14, 1862, 677.

64. *ORs*, 1, vol. 12, pt. 2, Report of General Lee to General S. Cooper, adjutant and inspector general, April 18, 1862, 177.

65. *ORs*, 1, vol. 12, pt. 3, Letter from R. E. Lee to President Jefferson Davis, August 14, 1862, 942.

66. *ORs*, 1, vol. 12, pt. 3, R. E. Lee to George W. Randolph, secretary of war, August 25, 1862, 944.

67. Edward G. Longacre, *The Cavalry at Gettysburg: A Tactical Study of Mounted Operations during the Civil War's Pivotal Campaign* (Lincoln and London: University of Nebraska Press, 1986), 23.

68. Grady McWhiney and Perry D. Jamieson, *Attack and Die: Civil War Tactics and the Southern Heritage* (University, Alabama: University of Alabama Press, 1982), 130–39.

69. U. R. Brooks, *Stories of the Confederacy* (Camden, S.C.: J. J. Fox, 1991), 67; *ORs*, 1, vol. 12, pt. 11, Report of Maj. Gen. J. E. B. Stuart to Col. R. H. Chilton, chief of staff, Army of Northern Virginia, February 13, 1863, 743–45.

70. Emory M. Thomas, *Bold Dragoon: The Life of J. E. B. Stuart* (Norman and London: University of Oklahoma Press, 1999), 140–41.

71. Brooks, *Stories of the Confederacy*, 78–84.

72. Freeman, *Lee's Lieutenants*, 2:167.

73. *ORs*, 1, vol. 12, pt. 2, Report of J. E. B. Stuart to R. H. Chilton, December 20, 1862, 119.

74. U. R. Brooks, *Butler and His Cavalry in the War of Secession, 1861–1865* (Columbia: State Company, 1909), 80–84.

75. Freeman, *Lee's Lieutenants*, 2:281; and *ORs*, 1, vol. 19, pt. 2, Letter from Wade Hampton to General Stuart, October 21, 1862, 12–14.

76. Hampton Papers, Letter from Wade Hampton to Mary Fisher Hampton, January 2, 1863 (SCL, USC).

77. Thomas, *Bold Dragoon*, 190–91.

78. Freeman, *Lee's Lieutenants*, 2:385–90.

79. Ibid., 399.

80. Brooks, *Butler and His Cavalry*, 85–86.

81. Wade Hampton to Mary Fisher Hampton, December 25, 1862, in *Family Letters of the Three Wade Hamptons, 1782–1901*, ed. Charles E. Cauthen (Columbia: University of South Carolina Press, 1953), 89–90.

82. Freeman, *Lee's Lieutenants*, 2:399–407.

83. *ORs*, 1, vol. 21, letter from R. E. Lee to J. E. B. Stuart, December 20, 1862, 671.

84. *ORs*, 1, vol. 21, J. A. Seddon to R. E. Lee, December 6, 1862, 1051.

85. *ORs*, 1, vol. 21, General Orders #29, February 28, 1863, 1114–15.

86. Freeman, *Lee's Lieutenants*, 2:694.

87. Hampton Papers, Letter from Hampton to Mary Fisher Hampton, January 27, 1863 (SCL, USC).

88. Thomas, *Bold Dragoon*, 140–41.

89. Hampton Papers, Letter from Hampton to Mary Fisher Hampton, January 2, 1863 (SCL, USC).

90. *ORs*, 1, vol. 25, pt. 1, Report of General Lee, September 21, 1863, 795.

91. *ORs*, 1, vol. 25, pt. 1, Report of Brigadier General Hampton to Major General Stuart, February 7, 1863, 9.

92. Brooks, *Stories of the Confederacy*, 143–44.

93. *ORs*, 1, vol. 25, pt. 2, Report of Brig. Gen. George M. Stoneman to General Pleasonton, February 25, 1863, 104.

94. *ORs*, 1, vol. 25, pt. 2, Report of Maj. Gen. Daniel Butterfield, April 28, 1863, 273.

95. Brooks, *Stories of the Confederacy*, 127–43.

96. Longacre, *The Cavalry at Gettysburg*, 46.

97. *ORs*, 1, vol. 25, pt. 2, Letter from General Lee to General Stuart, June 2, 1863, 449–50.

98. Edwin B. Coddington, *The Gettysburg Campaign: A Study in Command* (New York: Charles Scribner's, 1968), 44; and Thomas, *Bold Dragoon*, 217–26.

99. *ORs*, 1, vol. 27, pt. 2, Report of Hampton to Major H. B. McClellan, assistant adjutant general, June 12, 1863, 721–24; and Coddington, *The Gettysburg Campaign*, 54–60.

100. Longacre, *The Cavalry at Gettysburg*, 149.

101. Coddington, *The Gettysburg Campaign*, 107–14; and Thomas, *Bold Dragoon*, 232–46.

102. Thomas, *Bold Dragoon*, 232–46.

103. Ibid., 180–98.

104. Longacre, *The Cavalry at Gettysburg*, 154–78.

105. Ibid., 199–202.

106. *ORs*, 1, vol. 27, pt. 1, Report of Brig. Gen. J. Kilpatrick to Capt. A. J. Coheen, assistant adjutant general, Cavalry, August 10, 1863, 992.

107. Longacre, *The Cavalry at Gettysburg*, 198–99.

108. Coddington, *The Gettysburg Campaign*, 520.

109. Thomas, *Bold Dragoon*, 246–253.

110. *ORs*, 1, vol. 27, pt. 2, Report of Hampton to Maj. H. B. McClellan, assistant adjutant general, August 13, 1863, written from Columbia, S.C., 724–25; Brooks, *Stories of the Confederacy*, 152–77; and Longacre, *The Cavalry at Gettysburg*, 237–39.

111. Freeman, *Lee's Lieutenants*, 3:211.

112. *ORs*, 1, vol. 27, pt. 2, Report of General Lee on the Gettysburg Campaign, January 20, 1864, 312–25.

113. Brooks, *Stories of the Confederacy*, 174–88.

114. Longacre, *The Cavalry at Gettysburg*, 246.

115. Coddington, *The Gettysburg Campaign*, 535–74.

116. *ORs*, 1, vol. 27, Report of Casualties: The Army of Northern Virginia, 334.

Chapter 4: The Abyss of Horror

1. The title of this chapter is a description of the war to come from Sally Baxter Hampton, in *A Divided Heart, Letters of Sally Baxter Hampton, 1853–1862*, ed. Ann Fripp Hampton (Columbia, S.C.: Phantom Press, 1994), 75–78.

2. Doug Southall Freeman, *Lee's Lieutenants: A Study in Command* (New York: Charles Scribner's Sons, 1942–1944), 3:195; and Mrs. D. Giraud Wright, *A Southern Girl in '61: The War Times Memories of a Confederate Senator's Daughter* (New York: Doubleday, Page and Company, 1905), 31–32.

3. *OR*, 1, vol. 27, pt. 2, Report of Brig. Gen. Wade Hampton to Maj. H. B. McClellan, assistant adjutant general, August 13, 1863, 724–25.

4. Gary W. Gallagher, *The Peninsula Campaign* (Baton Rouge: Louisiana State University Press, 1998), 49.

5. Francis Butler Simkins and James Welch Patton, *The Women of the Confederacy* (Richmond and New York: Garrett and Massie, 1936), 84–85.

6. Lillian Adele Kibler, *Benjamin F. Perry: South Carolina Unionist* (Durham: Duke University Press, 1946), 363.

7. Freeman, *Lee's Lieutenants*, 3:209.

8. *Journal of the Congress of the Confederate States* (Washington, D.C.: Government Printing Office, 1904), 1:530, 618.

9. Emory Thomas, *Bold Dragoon: The Life of J. E. B. Stuart* (Norman and London: University of Oklahoma Press, 1999), 260–61.

10. U. R. Brooks, *Stories of the Confederacy* (Camden, S.C.: J. J. Fox, 1991), 189–90; and *ORs*, 1, vol. 27, pt. 2, Report of Gen. R. E. Lee to Gen. S. Cooper, adjutant and inspector general, August 2, 1863, 317.

11. U. R. Brooks, *Butler and His Cavalry in the War of Secession, 1861–1865* (Columbia: State Company, 1909), 192–95.

12. *ORs* 1, vol. 29, pt. 2, Field Returns of October 31, 1863, Army of Northern Virginia, 817.

13. *ORs*, 1, vol. 29, pt. 2, Special Orders No. 261, November 3, 1863, Jonathan Withers, assistant adjutant general, 817.

14. Wade Hampton Papers, Letter from Hampton to Mary Fisher Hampton December 3, 1863, written from Guiney's Station, Va. (SCL, USC).

15. Brooks, *Stories of the Confederacy*, 213-14.

16. *ORs*, 1, vol. 29, pt. 2, Report of Gen. Robert E. Lee, December 2, 1863, 825-26.

17. Freeman, *Lee's Lieutenants*, 3:278-79.

18. Thomas, *Bold Dragoon*, 275.

19. Ibid., 280-81.

20. *ORs*, 1, vol. 33, Field Returns of the Army of Northern Virginia, January 10, 1864, 1075.

21. Thomas, *Bold Dragoon*, 270-71.

22. *ORs*, 1, vol. 29, pt. 2, Letter from Hampton to Gen. R. E. Lee, December 7, 1863, 862-63.

23. Hampton Papers, Letter from Hampton to Mary Fisher Hampton, January 14, 1864 (SCL, USC).

24. *ORs*, 1, vol. 31, pt. 1, Letter from Gen. J. E. Johnston to President Jefferson Davis, November 26, 1863, 588-89.

25. *ORs*, 1, vol. 32, pt. 2, General Orders No. 2, Headquarters, Department of Tennessee, January 15, 1864, 560.

26. *ORs*, 1, vol. 31, pt. 3, President Jefferson Davis to Gen. J. E. Johnston, December 13, 1863, 816-17.

27. *ORs*, 1, vol. 32, pt. 3, Letter from Gen. James Longstreet to Gen. S. Cooper, adjutant and inspector general, January 29, 1864, letter written from Russellville, Tennessee, 632.

28. Richard M. McMurry, *Two Great Rebel Armies: An Essay in Confederate Military History* (Chapel Hill and London: University of North Carolina Press, 1989), 56-73.

29. *ORs*, 1, vol. 33, Hampton to General Lee, February 12, 1864, 1162-63.

30. *ORs*, 1, vol. 33, Letter from General Lee to General Hampton, January 23, 1864, 1117-18.

31. *ORs*, 1, vol. 33, Letter from Hampton to Major McClellan, General Stuart's adjutant, February 1, 1864, 1140.

32. *ORs*, 1, vol. 33, General Hampton to Secretary of War James A. Seddon, February 13, 1864, 1163-64.

33. C. Vann Woodward, ed., *Mary Chesnut's Civil War* (New York: Book-of-the-Month Club, 1981), 588.

34. Hampton Papers, Letter from Hampton to Mary Fisher Hampton, February 28, 1864 (SCL, USC).

35. Thomas, *Bold Dragoon*, 283.

36. *ORs*, 1, vol. 33, Hampton's Report to Major McClellan, March 8, 1864, 201-2; and *ORs*, 1, vol. 33, Report of Brig. Gen. Judson Kilpatrick, March 16, 1864, 183-87.

37. *ORs*, 1, vol. 33, Report of Gen. George G. Meade, April 8, 1864, 170-71.

38. *ORs*, 1, vol. 33, Gen. R. E. Lee to Maj. Gen. George G. Meade, April 1, 1864, 178-80.

39. Freeman, *Lee's Lieutenants*, 3:334.

40. *ORs*, 1, vol. 33, Hampton to Gen. J. E. B. Stuart, March 6, 1864, 199–200.

41. *ORs*, 1, vol. 33, Special Orders No. 65, Adjutant and Inspector General's Office, March 18, 1864, 1231–32.

42. *ORs*, 1, vol. 33, Hampton to Brigadier General Jordan, assistant adjutant general, April 1, 1864, 1260.

43. *ORs*, 1, vol. 33, Hampton to Gen. S. Cooper, adjutant and inspector general, March 29, 1864, 1243–44.

44. John Hammond Moore, *Southern Homefront, 1861–1865*, 644.

45. C. Vann Woodward, *Mary Chesnut's Civil War* (New York: Book-of-the-Month Club, 1981), 678.

46. John Hammond Moore, *Southern Homefront* (Columbia, S.C.: Sumner House Press, 1998), 34–36.

47. *ORs*, 1, vol. 33, Hampton to General Cooper, April 4, 1864, 1258–60.

48. *ORs*, 1, vol. 36, pt. 1, Field Returns, May 1864, 1027.

49. E. P. Alexander, *Military Memoirs of a Confederate*, ed. T. Harry Williams (Bloomington: Indiana University Press, 1962), 325.

50. James M. McPherson, *Battle Cry of Freedom the Civil War Era* (New York and Oxford: Oxford University Press, 1988), 724–33.

51. McPherson, *Battle Cry of Freedom*, 728; and Thomas, *Bold Dragoon*, 283.

52. Edward L. Wells, *Hampton and His Cavalry in '64* (Richmond, Va.: B. F. Johnson Publishing Company, 1899), 126–55.

53. Thomas, *Bold Dragoon*, 297; and Jeffrey D. Wirt, "Wade Hampton," in *The Confederate General*, ed. William C. Davis (Harrisburg, Pa.: National Historical Society, 1991), 3:52–53.

54. Freeman, *Lee's Lieutenants*, 3:436.

55. Ibid., 3:499–500.

56. Ibid., 3:499–500; and Wells, *Hampton and His Cavalry in 1864*, 164–70.

57. McPherson, *Battle Cry of Freedom*, 735; and Robert Wood Underwood and Clarence Clough Buel, eds., *Battles and Leaders of the Civil War* (New York: Thomas Yoseloff, 1956), 4:137–38.

58. Wells, *Hampton and His Cavalry in 1864*, 93–94, 155.

59. McPherson, *Battle Cry of Freedom*, 737–39.

60. Freeman, *Lee's Lieutenants*, 3:522–23; Wells, *Hampton and His Cavalry in 1864*, 187–210; and *ORs* 1, vol. 36, pt. 1, Report of Major General Hampton, July 9, 1864, 1095–98.

61. Wade Hampton Papers, Dispatch from Hampton near Tunstall's, June 20, 1864, to Gen. Braxton Bragg (Perkins Library, Duke University).

62. Noah Andre Trudeau, *The Last Citadel: Petersburg, Virginia, June 1864–April 1865* (Toronto and London: Little, Brown, 1991), 29–55.

63. *ORs*, 1, vol. 36, pt. 3, Gen. R. E. Lee to Wade Hampton, June 16, 1864, Lee to Hampton, June 17, 1864, Lee to Hampton, June 18, 1864, 901.

64. *ORs*, 1, vol. 40, pt. 1, Gen. R. E. Lee to the Secretary of War, June 25, 1864, 750–51.

65. Trudeau, *The Last Citadel*, 87–90.

66. *ORs*, 1, vol. 40, pt. 2, Maj. Gen. George G. Meade to Lt. Gen. U. S. Grant, June 21, 1864, 267.

67. *ORs*, 1, vol. 40, pt. 2, Brigadier General Wilson to Maj. Gen. A. A. Humphreys, chief of staff, Army of the Potomac, June 21, 1864, 286.

68. Wells, *Hampton and His Cavalry in 1864*, 229-49; *ORs*, 1, vol. 40, pt. 1, Report of C. A. Dana from City Point, Virginia, July 1, 1864, 29-30; and *ORs*, 1, vol. 40, pt. 1, Report of Major General Hampton to Lieutenant Colonel Taylor, assistant adjutant general, July 10, 1864, 807-10.

69. Hampton Papers, Letter from Wade Hampton to Mary Fisher Hampton, written from Stony Creek, Virginia, July 4, 1864 (SCL, USC).

70. *ORs*, 1, vol. 40, pt. 3, Hampton to Lieutenant Colonel Taylor, assistant adjutant general, July 13, 1864, and Lieutenant Colonel Taylor to Hampton, July 16, 1864, with endorsement by Gen. R. E. Lee, July 20, 1864, 772-73.

71. *ORs*, 1, vol. 38, pt. 5, Gen. J. B. Hood to James A. Seddon, secretary of war, July 19, 1864, 892.

72. Wells, *Hampton and His Cavalry in 1864*, 249.

73. U. R. Brooks, *Butler and His Cavalry*, 223.

74. *ORs*, 1, vol. 42, pt. 2, Special Orders No. 189, Gen. W. H. Taylor, assistant adjutant general, August 11, 1864, 1171.

75. Douglas Southall Freeman, ed., *Lee's Dispatches: Unpublished Letters of General Robert E. Lee* (New York: G. P. Putnam and Sons, 1957), 268-69, letter from General Lee to President Davis, July 2, 1864.

76. Richard Duer, "Generals in the Saddle," in *Southern Historical Society Papers*, vol. 19, edited by Richard Duer (Richmond: Southern Historical Society, 1891), 170-71.

77. McPherson, *Battle Cry of Freedom*, 756-57.

78. *ORs*, 1, vol. 42, pt. 2, General Lee to Wade Hampton, August 11, 1864, 1171-72; and Trudeau, *The Last Citadel*, 149-52.

79. *ORs*, 1, vol. 42, pt. 2, General Lee to General Hampton, August 14, 1864, 1177.

80. *ORs*, 1, vol. 42, pt. 1, Report of General Lee to James A. Seddon, secretary of war, August 26, 1864, 851.

81. Wells, *Hampton and His Cavalry in 1864*, 270-86.

82. Freeman, *Lee's Lieutenants*, 3:549.

83. *ORs*, 1, vol. 42, pt. 1, Itinerary of the Army of the Potomac, August–December 1864, 82.

84. Hampton Papers, Letter from Hampton in Richmond to Mary Fisher Hampton, August 20, 1864 (SCL, USC).

85. Edward Boykin, *Beefsteak Raid* (New York: Funk and Wagnalls, 1960), 156-68, 183-86.

86. *ORs*, 1, vol. 42, pt. 1, Report of Maj. Gen. Wade Hampton, September 27, 1864, 944-47; Wells, *Hampton and His Cavalry in 1864*, 267-87; Boykin, *The Great Beefsteak Raid*, 191-210; and Trudeau, *The Last Citadel*, 195-201.

87. Boykin, *The Great Beefsteak Raid*, 280.

88. *ORs*, 1, vol. 42, pt. 3, Lt. Col. G. M. Sorrell, assistant adjutant general, to division commanders, October 20, 1864, 1155. The meaning of "mistreat Federal deserters" is not clear.

89. *ORs*, 1, vol. 42, pt. 1, Report of Maj. Gen. Wade Hampton, November 21, 1864, 947-48.

90. Hampton Papers, Letter from Hampton to Mary Fisher Hampton, written from his headquarters near Petersburg, October 11, 1864 (SCL, USC).

91. *ORs*, 1, vol. 42, pt. 1, Report of Maj. Gen. Wade Hampton, November 21, 1864, 949–50.

92. Ibid.

93. 2 Sam. 19:33; Wells, *Hampton and His Cavalry in 1864*, 344–50; Mary Boykin Chesnut, *A Diary from Dixie*, eds., Isabel D. Martin and Myrta Lockett (Gloucester: Peter Smith, 1961), 332–33.

94. Vann Woodward, *Mary Chesnut's Civil War*, 497; Brooks, *Butler and His Cavalry*, 359.

95. Brooks, *Butler and His Cavalry*, 351; and Wells, *Hampton and His Cavalry in 1864*, 323–44.

96. Hampton Papers, Campaign narrative written by Hampton for General Lee in 1867, presumably for a book Lee intended to write (SCL, USC).

97. Hampton Papers, Letter from Hampton to Mary Fisher Hampton, written from near Petersburg, November 14, 1864 (SCL, USC).

98. Freeman, *Lee's Dispatches*, 305.

99. Wells, *Hampton and Reconstruction* (Columbia: State Company, 1907), 60.

100. Wells, *Hampton and His Cavalry in 1864*, 352.

101. Hampton Papers, letter from Hampton to Mary Fisher Hampton, December 14, 1864, written from Stony Creek (SCL, USC).

102. *ORs*, 1, vol. 42, pt. 1, Report of Maj. Gen. Wade Hampton, January 21, 1865, 950–52; and Freeman, *Lee's Lieutenants*, 3:616; and Trudeau, *The Last Citadel*, 270–84.

103. Hampton Papers, Letter from Hampton to Mary Fisher Hampton, written from Petersburg, January 10, 1865 (SCL, USC).

104. *ORs*, 1, vol. 42, pt. 2, Josiah Gorgas, chief of ordnance to Gen. Wade Hampton, November 28, 1864, 1231.

105. *ORs*, 1, vol. 43, pt. 3, H. B. McClellan, assistant adjutant general to Lt. Col. John S. Mosby, Virginia Partisan Rangers, battalion commander, November 24, 1864, 926.

106. Hampton Papers, Hampton to Mary Fisher Hampton, January 10, 1865 (SCL, USC).

107. Hampton Papers, Hampton to Gov. Milledge L. Bonham, written from cavalry headquarters near Petersburg, December 4, 1864 (SCL, USC).

108. Freeman, *Lee's Lieutenants*, 3:622.

109. *ORs*, 1, vol. 42, pt. 3, General Grant to General Meade, November 30, 1864, 749.

110. *ORs*, 1, vol. 44, Maj. Gen. Wade Hampton to the commanding officer at Augusta, Georgia, November 24, 1864, 589 (instructing that officer to insert a dispatch in all *newspaper*s in Augusta, ordering that "All men of my command in Georgia will rendezvous forthwith at Augusta and then in South Carolina at Columbia and await orders.").

111. *ORs*, 1, vol. 42, pt. 3, General Lee to President Jefferson Davis, December 5, 1864, 1254–55.

112. *ORs*, 1, vol. 46, pt. 1, Field Returns of the Army of Northern Virginia, January 19, 1865, 1273.

113. *ORs*, 1, vol. 46, pt. 2, Gen. M. C. Butler to Lt. Col. W. H. Taylor, assistant adjutant general, Army of Northern Virginia, January 2, 1865, 1003–1004 (endorsement by Gen. R. E. Lee).

114. Hampton Papers, Report of General Hampton written in 1867 and submitted to General Lee for his use in a projected book about the war (SCL, USC).

115. *ORs*, 1, vol. 46, pt. 3, Special Orders No. 8, Headquarters of the Cavalry Corps, Army of Northern Virginia, H. B. McClellan, assistant adjutant general, January, 19, 1865, 1101; and *ORs*, 1, vol. 46, pt. 3, Gen. R. E. Lee to Gen. S. Cooper, adjutant and inspector general, Richmond, January 19, 1865, 1100–1101.

116. *ORs*, 1, vol. 46, pt. 3, Field Returns of the Army of Northern Virginia, February 28, 1865, 1273.

117. Hampton Papers, Wade Hampton III to Mary Fisher Hampton, written from cavalry headquarters near Petersburg, January 18, 1865 (SCL, USC).

118. Mrs. D. Giraud Wright, *A Southern Girl in '61: The War Times Memories of a Confederate Senator's Daughter* (New York: Doubleday, Page and Company, 1905), 222–24.

119. McPherson, *Battle Cry of Freedom*, 825–26.

120. Marion B. Lucas, *Sherman and the Burning of Columbia* (Columbia: University of South Carolina Press, 2000), 36.

121. Ibid., 26–29.

122. Ibid., 41–43.

123. Ibid., 45.

124. *ORs*, 1, vol. 47, pt. 2, Special Orders No. 32, Headquarters, Department of South Carolina, Georgia, and Florida, H. W. Fielden, assistant adjutant general, February 7, 1865, 1112.

125. *ORs*, 1, vol. 47, pt. 2, General Beauregard to General Hardee, February 11, 1865, 1157.

126. *ORs*, 1, vol. 47, pt. 2, Beauregard to Gen. R. E. Lee, February 12, 1865, 1165.

127. Hampton Papers, Letter from Hampton in Columbia to "Dear Johnson," November 9, 1899 (Perkins Library, Duke University).

128. *ORs*, 1, vol. 47, pt. 2, letter from Garnett McMillen, captain in charge of sub terra defenses, to Brig. Gen. G. T. Rains, chief of torpedo bureau, March 1, 1865, endorsed by General Hampton, 1299–1300.

129. *ORs*, 1, vol. 47, pt. 2, General Hampton to General Beauregard, February 14, 1865, 1185.

130. *ORs*, 1, vol. 47, pt. 2, Beauregard to Hampton, February 14, 1865, 1186.

131. *ORs*, 1, vol. 47, pt. 2, Maj. Theodore G. Barker, assistant adjutant general, to Colonel Grigsby of General Wheeler's staff, February 15, 1865, 1199.

132. *Journal of the Congress of the Confederate States* (Washington, D.C.: Government Printing Office, 1904), 4:563–64.

133. *ORs*, 1, vol. 47, pt. 2, President Davis to Wade Hampton, February 16, 1865, 1207.

134. Lucas, *Sherman and the Burning of Columbia*, 46–49.

135. Ibid., 1–80.

136. *ORs*, 1, vol. 47, pt. 2, General Hampton to General Wheeler, February 17, 1865, 1212; and Lucas, *Sherman and the Burning of Columbia*, 51–71.

137. Earl Schenck Miers, ed., *When the World Ended: The Diary of Emma LeConte* (New York and Oxford: Oxford University Press, 1957), 29.

138. *ORs*, 1, vol. 47, pt. 2, General Hampton to General Beauregard, February 18, 1865, 1218–19.

139. *ORs*, 1, vol. 47, pt. 2, General Beauregard to General Hampton, February 21, 1865, 1245.

140. *ORs*, 1, vol. 47, pt. 1, Maj. Gen. W. T. Sherman to Maj. Gen. H. W. Halleck, chief of staff, April 4, 1865, 17–29.

141. *ORs*, 1, vol. 47, pt. 1, Report of Brig. Gen. E. W. Rice to Capt. L. H. Evarts, assistant adjutant general, Fourth Division, 15th Corps, March 31, 1865, 342–43.

142. *ORs*, 1, vol. 47, pt. 2, General Beauregard at Chester, South Carolina, to President Jefferson Davis, February 21, 1865, 1238.

143. *ORs*, 1, vol. 47, pt. 1, Report of Maj. Gen. John W. Geary to Col. H. W. Perkins, assistant adjutant general, 20th Corps, March 26, 1865, 680–99.

144. *ORs*, 1, vol. 47, pt. 2, General Lee to Gen. J. E. Johnston, February 22, 1865, 1248.

145. Ibid.

146. Lucas, *Sherman and the Burning of Columbia*, 163–67.

147. *ORs*, 1, vol. 47, pt. 1, Maj. Gen. W. T. Sherman to Maj. Gen. H. W. Halleck, chief of staff, April 9, 1865, 17–29.

148. *Memoirs of General William T. Sherman* (New York and London: D. Appleton and Company, 1875), 2:287.

149. *ORs*, 1, vol. 47, pt. 1, Maj. Gen. W. T. Sherman to Maj. Gen. H.W. Halleck, chief of staff, April 4, 1865, 17–29.

150. *ORs*, 1, vol. 47, pt. 3, General Hampton to General Beauregard, February 25, 1865, 1277–78.

151. *ORs*, 1, vol. 47, pt. 2, Maj. Gen. W. T. Sherman to Lt. Gen. Wade Hampton, February 24, 1865, 546.

152. *ORs*, 1, vol. 47, pt. 2, General Hampton to General Sherman, February 27, 1865, 596–97.

153. *ORs*, 1, vol. 47, pt. 1, Gen. J. E. Johnston to Gen. R. E. Lee, February 23, 1865, 1050.

154. *ORs*, 1, vol. 47, pt. 1, Return of April 9, 1865, 1065.

155. Chesnut, *Diary from Dixie*, 343.

156. *ORs*, 1, vol. 47, pt. 2, Wade Hampton, Jr., to Gen. J. E. Johnston, March 18, 1865, 1429.

157. Russell F. Weigley, *A Great Civil War* (Bloomington: Indiana University Press, 2000), 418.

158. *ORs*, 1, vol. 47, pt. 2, General Lee to Gen. J. E. Johnston, February 22, 1865, 1247.

159. *ORs*, 1, vol. 47, pt. 2, Johnston to Lee, February 22, 1865, 1247.

160. *ORs*, 1, vol. 47, pt. 2, General Beauregard to General Hampton at Chester, South Carolina, February 23, 1865, 1262.

161. *ORs*, 1, vol. 47, pt. 2, Hampton to Beauregard, February 25, 1865, 1277.

162. *ORs*, 1, vol. 47, pt. 2, General Kilpatrick to Maj. L. M. Dayton, March 4, 1865, 682.

163. *ORs*, 1, vol. 47, pt. 2, H. B. McClellan to Major General Wheeler, March 5, 1865, 1326–27.

164. *ORs*, 1, vol. 47, pt. 2, J. E. Johnston to R. E. Lee, March 10, 1865, 1361.

165. *ORs*, 1, vol. 47, pt. 2, Judson Kilpatrick to Maj. L. M. Dayton, assistant adjutant general, Military District of Mississippi, March 11, 1865, 786–87.

166. Wells, *Hampton and Reconstruction*, 62–65.

167. *Memoirs of General William T. Sherman*, 2:294.

168. *ORs*, 1, vol. 47, pt. 1, Report of Gen. O. O. Howard to Maj. L. M. Dayton, assistant adjutant general, April 1, 1865, 191–209.

169. *ORs*, 1, vol. 47, pt. 2, W. J. Hardee to J. E. Johnston, March 15, 1865, 1392–97.

170. *Memoirs of General William T. Sherman*, 2:302.

171. Ibid., 204.

172. *ORs*, 1, vol. 47, pt. 1, J. E. Johnston to R. E. Lee, March 27, 1865, 1054–57; and an article by Wade Hampton in "The Battle of Bentonsville," *Battles and Leaders of the Civil War*, 4:700–705.

173. *Memoirs of General William T. Sherman*, 2:306.

174. Ibid., 324–27.

175. *ORs*, 1, vol. 47, pt. 3, Hampton to General Johnston, March 24, 1865, 684.

176. *ORs*, 1, vol. 47, pt. 3, Hampton to J. E. Johnston, March 27, 1865, 704.

177. Hampton Papers, Telegram from Hampton to all commissioned officers, April 5, 1865 (Perkins Library, Duke University).

178. *ORs*, 1, vol. 47, pt. 3, Field Returns, 707.

179. *ORs*, 1, vol. 47, pt. 3, Hampton to J. E. Johnston, March 27, 1865, 705.

180. Hampton Papers, Letter from Wade Hampton to Mary Fisher Hampton, March 30, 1865 (SCL, USC).

181. *Journal of the Congress of the Confederate States of America*, 4: 676, 721, 737.

182. *ORs*, 1, vol. 47, pt. 3, Wade Hampton to Judson Kilpatrick, April 16, 1865, 334.

183. *ORs*, 1, vol. 47, pt. 3, Kilpatrick to Maj. L. M. Dayton, April 16, 1865, 233–34.

184. Hampton Papers, Message from Hampton from cavalry headquarters to General Kilpatrick, April 20, 1865 (Perkins Library, Duke University).

185. *ORs*, 1, vol. 47, pt. 3, Kilpatrick to Maj. L. M. Dayton, April 29, 1865, and Dayton to Kilpatrick, April 29, 1865, 261.

186. *ORs*, 1, vol. 47, pt. 3, Gov. Z. B. Vance to Gen. J. E. Johnston, April 19, 1865, 810–11.

187. *ORs*, 1, vol. 47, pt. 3, Gov. Z. B. Vance to Gen. J. E. Johnston, April 20, 1865, 815.

188. *ORs*, 1, vol. 47, pt. 3, Gen. U. S. Grant to Gen. W. T. Sherman, April 21, 1865, 263–64.

189. *ORs*, 1, vol. 47, pt. 3, Hampton to Jefferson Davis, April 22, 1865, 829–30.

190. *ORs*, 1, vol. 47, pt. 3, Davis to Hampton, April 22, 1865, 830.

191. *ORs*, 1, vol. 47, pt. 3, John C. Breckinridge to J. E. Johnston, April 24, 1865, 835.

192. *ORs*, 1, vol. 47, pt. 3, Mallory to Davis, April 24, 1865, 832–34.

193. *ORs*, 1, vol. 47, pt. 3, Jefferson Davis to J. E. Johnston, April 24, 1865, 834–35.

194. *ORs*, 1, vol. 47, pt. 3, J. E. Johnston to John C. Breckinridge, April 25, 1865, 836–37.

195. *ORs*, 1, vol. 47, pt. 3, Breckinridge to Johnston, April 25, 1865, 837.

196. *ORs*, 1, vol. 47, pt. 3, Johnston to Breckinridge, April 25, 1865, 837.

197. *ORs*, 1, vol. 47, pt. 3, Davis to Hampton, April 26, 1865, 841.

198. *ORs*, 1, vol. 47, pt. 3, General Orders Number 18, Army of Tennessee, April 27, 1865, 837.

199. *ORs*, 1, vol. 47, pt. 3, Hampton to Johnston, April 26, 1865, 841.

200. *ORs*, 1, vol. 47, pt. 3, Hampton to Breckinridge, April 27, 1865, 845.

201. *ORs*, 1, vol. 47, pt. 3, Breckinridge to Hampton, April 28, 1865, sent from the Broad River in South Carolina, 851.

202. *ORs*, 1, vol. 47, pt. 3, Archer Anderson, assistant adjutant general, to Lieutenant General Hunter, April 27, 1865, 847.

203. *ORs*, 1, vol. 47, pt. 3, Hampton to Gen. J. E. Johnston, April 27, 1865, 46.

204. *ORs*, 1, vol. 47, pt. 3, Archer Anderson, assistant adjutant general, to General York at the Catawba River Bridge in South Carolina, no date, 854.

205. *ORs*, 1, vol. 47, pt. 3, General Sherman to General Rawlins, April 29, 1865, 345–46; and *Memoirs of General William T. Sherman*, 2:365–67.

206. *Columbia Phoenix*, May 5, 1865 (SCL, USC).

207. "Address of Governor Wade Hampton, February 22, 1878," *Southern Historical Papers*, vol. 6, September 1878, 130–32.

208. Joseph Wheeler, "An Effort to Rescue Jefferson Davis," *Century Magazine*, vol. 56 (May 1898): 85–91; and letter published in *The Southern Historical Society Papers*, 27:132.

209. Freeman, *Lee's Lieutenants*, 3:638–39.

210. Hampton Papers, Letter from Hampton to "Dear Captain," May 10, 1865 (SCL, USC).

211. Wells, *Hampton and Reconstruction*, 67.

Chapter 5: The Prostrate State

1. Stephen V. Ash, *When the Yankees Came, Conflict and Chaos in the Occupied South, 1861–1865* (Chapel Hill: University of North Carolina Press, 1995), 565.

2. Sidney Andrews, *The South since the War, as Shown By Fourteen Weeks of Travel and Observation in Georgia and the Carolinas* (Boston: Ticknor and Fields, 1866), 33.

3. Ibid., 36–37.

4. Marion Lucas, *Sherman and the Burning of Columbia* (Columbia: University of South Carolina Press, 2000), 128

5. Francis Butler Simkins and Robert Willard Woody, *South Carolina during Reconstruction* (Chapel Hill: University of North Carolina Press, 1932), 4–5.

6. *Columbia Phoenix*, May 12, 1865.

7. Mary Boykin Chesnut, *A Diary from Dixie*, eds. Isabel D. Martin and Myrta Lockett (Gloucester: Peter Smith, 1961), 404.

8. *Columbia Phoenix*, May 9, 1865.

9. John S. Reynolds, *Reconstruction in South Carolina* (Columbia: State Publishing Company, 1905), 1–27.

10. Chesnut, *Diary From Dixie*, 399.

11. *Columbia Phoenix*, May 12, 1865.

12. Ibid., May 26, 1865.

13. Ibid.

14. Ibid., July 3, 1865.

15. *Columbia Daily Phoenix*, June 15, 1865 (SCL, USC).

16. Lillian Adele Kibler, *Benjamin F. Perry, South Carolina Unionist* (Durham: Duke University Press, 1946), 390.

17. John Hope Franklin, *Reconstruction after the Civil War* (Chicago and London: University of Chicago Press, 1961), 23.

18. Reynolds, *Reconstruction in South Carolina*, 1–27.

19. Simkins and Woody, *South Carolina during Reconstruction*, 4–5; *Columbia Daily Phoenix*, June 6, 1865 (SCL, USC); and Willie Lee Rose, *Rehearsal for Reconstruction: The Port Royal Experiment* (Indianapolis, New York, Kansas City: Bobs-Merrill Company, 1964), 200–216.

20. Reynolds, *Reconstruction in South Carolina*, 1–27.

21. *Daily Phoenix*, October 17, 1865.

22. *Daily Phoenix*, September 27, 1865.

23. Wade Hampton Papers, Letter from an unnamed authority in New York to Gen. Wade Hampton, July 25,1865 (SCL, USC).

24. Hampton Papers, Hampton to the editor of *Columbia Phoenix*, July 27, 1865 (SCL, USC).

25. *Nation*, August 17, 1865, 195.

26. Eric Foner, *Reconstruction, America's Unfinished Revolution, 1863–1877* (New York: Harper and Row, 1988), 192.

27. Hampton Papers, Wade Hampton to Mayor James G. Gibbes, August 20, 1865 (SCL, USC).

28. Eric L. McKitrick, *Andrew Johnson and Reconstruction* (Chicago and London: University of Chicago Press, 1960), 91.

29. *Columbia Daily Phoenix*, May 24, 1865.

30. Ibid., June 26, 1865.

31. *Daily Phoenix*, November 30, 1865.

32. Andrews, *The South since the War*, 391.

33. Hampton Papers, Hampton to the editors of *Day Book* of New York, July 15, 1865 (SCL, USC).

34. Henry T. Thompson, *Ousting the Carpetbagger from South Carolina* (Columbia: R. L. Bryan Company, 1926), 44–45.

35. *Columbia Daily Phoenix*, July 10, 1865.

36. Foner, *Reconstruction*, 55.

37. Ibid., 65.

38. *Columbia Daily Phoenix*, September 5, 1865.

39. Simkins and Woody, *Reconstruction in South Carolina*, 37–55.

40. Quoted in Foner, *Reconstruction*, 192.

41. *Daily Phoenix*, September 7, 1865.

42. *Nation*, October 4, 1865, 524.

43. *Daily Phoenix*, September 5, 1865.

44. Ibid.

45. Ibid.

46. Ibid., September 23, 1865.

47. Ibid., September 28, 1865.

48. Simkins and Woody, *South Carolina during Reconstruction*, 37–55.

49. *Daily Phoenix*, November 8, 1865.

50. Ibid., September 16, 1865.

51. Ibid., September 26, 1865.

52. Ibid., October 11, 1865.

53. Ibid., November 26, 1865.

54. Reynolds, *Reconstruction in South Carolina*, 1–27.

55. Simkins and Woody, *South Carolina during Reconstruction*, 37–55; and Thomas Holt, *Black over White: Negro Political Leadership in South Carolina during Reconstruction* (Urbana, Chicago, and London: University of Illinois Press, 1977), 10.

56. Walter Edgar, *South Carolina: A History* (Columbia: University of South Carolina Press, 1998), 348.

57. *Daily Phoenix*, November 15, 1865.

58. Wade Hampton Papers, Protest of No Payment on Debts to the Bank of Louisiana, January 4, 1862 (Center for American History, University of Texas, Austin, Texas).

59. Hampton Papers, Letter from Jno. F. Irvine, cashier, to Hampton, February 24, 1865 (Center for American History, University of Texas, Austin).

60. *Daily Phoenix*, October 10, 1865.

61. Foner, *Reconstruction*, 124–75.

62. *Daily Phoenix*, January 21, 1866.

63. Hampton Papers, Letter from Hampton to Mary Fisher Hampton, December 18, 1865 (SCL, USC).

64. Hampton Papers, Letter from Hampton to Mary Fisher Hampton, January 1, 1866 (SCL, USC).

65. Foner, *Reconstruction*, 162.

66. Hampton Papers, Letter from Hampton to Mary Fisher Hampton, January 31, 1866 (SCL, USC).

67. Hampton Papers, Letter from Hampton while in New Orleans to Mary Fisher Hampton, March 19, 1866 (SCL, USC).

68. Hampton Papers, Hampton at Wild Woods to Mary Fisher Hampton, March 28, 1866 (SCL, USC).

69. Hampton Papers, Hampton from cavalry headquarters in Virginia, January 14, 1864 (SCL, USC). The Duncans had been indemnified by the Union government for damage done to their property by guerrillas.

70. *Daily Phoenix*, June 27, 1866.

71. Ibid., March 22, 1866.

72. Hampton Papers, Hampton to General Beauregard, April 22, 1866 (SCL, USC); and *Daily Phoenix*, May 6, 1866.

73. *Daily Phoenix*, May 13, 1866.

74. *Daily Phoenix*, May 29, 1866.

75. Hampton Papers, Hampton at Wild Woods to Chancellor Carroll, May 25, 1866 (SCL, USC).

76. Hampton Papers, Hampton at Wild Woods to Mary Fisher Hampton, June 3, 1866 (SCL, USC).

77. Virginia G. Meynard, *The Venturers: The Hampton, Harrison, and Earle Families of Virginia, South Carolina, and Texas* (Greenville, S.C.: Southern Historical Press, 1981), 983.

78. Hampton Papers, Hampton in Columbia to Gen. R. E. Lee, July 21, 1866 (SCL, USC).

79. *Daily Phoenix*, July 24, 1866.

80. Ibid., August 2, 1866.

81. Ibid., August 15, 1866.

82. Hampton to President Andrew Johnson, August 25, 1866, quoted in *Family Letters of the Three Wade Hamptons, 1782-1901*, ed. Charles E. Cauthen (Columbia: University of South Carolina Press, 1953), 124-41.

83. *Daily Phoenix*, November 14, 1866.

84. Ibid., October 17, 1866.

85. Ibid., October 25, 1866.

86. Ibid., December 9, 1866.

87. Ibid., August 16, 1866.

88. Foner, *Reconstruction*, 243-51.

89. Alfred H. Kelly and Winfred A. Harbison, *The American Constitution, Its Origins and Development* (New York: W. W. Norton and Company, 1963), 466-68.

90. Simkins and Woody, *South Carolina during Reconstruction*, 63.

91. Quoted in *Daily Phoenix*, March 23, 1867.

92. Quoted in *Daily Phoenix*, March 26, 1867.

93. Julie Saville, *The Work of Reconstruction, from Slave to Wage Laborer in South Carolina, 1860-1870* (Cambridge: Cambridge University Press, 1994), 152.

94. *Hampton Family Letters*, Letter from Hampton to John Mullaly, March 31, 1867, 141-42.

95. Russell Kirk, *The Conservative Mind* (South Bend, Ind.: Gateway Editions, 1953), 52.

96. *Daily Phoenix*, March 28, 1867.

97. Hampton Papers, Hampton to James Conner (Charleston), March 24, 1867 (SCL, USC).

98. Quoted in the *Daily Phoenix*, May 16, 1867.

99. Simkins and Woody, *South Carolina during Reconstruction*, 74-77.

100. Hampton Papers, Hampton to John Mullaly, April 11, 1867 (SCL, USC).

101. Hampton Papers, Wade Hampton to Mrs. Edward Carrington, March 28, 1867 (SCL, USC).

102. Meynard, *The Venturers*, 192, 284.

103. *Daily Phoenix*, April 2, 1867.

104. Ibid., April 25, 1867.

105. Ibid., July 16, 1867.

106. Hampton Papers, Hampton to Thomas S. Gains, office of Conner and Sexias, New Orleans, April 17, 1867 (SCL, USC).

107. Hampton Papers, Ledger Book of Bond I'on, 1782-1859, including a letter from Hampton to Charles J. Lowndes, executor of the estate of Bond I'on, June 8, 1867 (SCL, USC).

108. Hampton Papers, Mortgage to Henry W. Conner, April 18, 1868 (SCL, USC).

109. *Daily Phoenix*, August 28, 1867.

110. Quoted in *Daily Phoenix*, September 6, 1867.

111. Quoted in *Daily Phoenix*, October 22, 1867.

112. Ibid., September 1, 1867.

113. Sir Llewellyn Woodward, *The Age of Reform, 1815-1870* (Oxford: Clarendon Press, 1938), 141.

114. *Daily Phoenix*, September 1, 1867.

115. Reynolds, *Reconstruction in South Carolina*, 60–62.

116. Simkins and Woody, *South Carolina during Reconstruction*, 74–77; and W. Lewis Burke, Jr., "The Radical Law School," in *At Freedom's Door: African American Founding Fathers and Lawyers in Reconstruction South Carolina*, eds. James Lowell Underwood and W. Lewis Burke, Jr. (Columbia: University of South Carolina Press, 2000), 100. Cardozo became a graduate of the University of South Carolina Law School.

117. *Daily Phoenix*, October 18, 1867.

118. Ibid., November 8, 1867.

119. Simkins and Woody, *South Carolina during Reconstruction*, 90–111; Reynolds, *Reconstruction in South Carolina*, 76–84; and Eric Foner, "South Carolina's Black Elected Officials during Reconstruction," in *At Freedom's Door*, eds. Underwood and Burke, 172.

120. Reynolds, *Reconstruction in South Carolina*, 86–88; and *Daily Phoenix*, March 13, 1868.

121. Reynolds, *Reconstruction in South Carolina*, 88–96; and Simkins and Woody, *South Carolina during Reconstruction*, 90–111.

122. Reynolds, *Reconstruction in South Carolina*, 996–98.

123. *Daily Phoenix*, April 16, 1868.

124. Ibid., May 14, 1868.

125. Ibid., June 6, 1868.

126. Ibid., June 10 and June 12, 1868.

127. Hampton Papers, Published in Columbia by Phoenix Book and Job Power Press, 1868 (SCL, USC).

128. *Daily Phoenix*, June 18, 24, and 26, 1868.

129. Ibid., July 8, 1868.

130. Ibid., July 12, 1868.

131. Ibid., July 14, 1868.

132. Ibid.

133. Ibid., July 26, 1868.

134. James G. Blaine, *Twenty Years in Congress, from Lincoln to Garfield* (Norwich: Henry Bill Publishing Company, 1886), 400–401.

135. *Daily Phoenix*, July 30, 1868.

136. Ibid., August 7, 1868.

137. Ibid., August 15, 1868.

138. Ibid., July 23, 1868.

139. Ibid., September 4, 1868.

140. Ibid., October 4, 1868.

141. Ibid., October 11, 1868.

142. Hampton Papers, Manuscript notes in Hampton Family Papers (SCL, USC); and *Daily Phoenix*, October 13, 1868.

143. Hampton Papers, Copy of Hampton Address, dated October 12, 1868 (SCL, USC).

144. *Daily Phoenix*, October 23, 1868.

145. *Daily Phoenix*, October 23, 1868; Reynolds, *Reconstruction in South Carolina*, 102–5; Robert Zuczek, *State of Rebellion; Reconstruction in South Carolina* (Columbia:

University of South Carolina Press, 1996), 51–52; and Foner, "South Carolina's Black Elected Officials," 175.

146. Zuczek, *State of Rebellion*, 60.

147. *Daily Phoenix*, November 13, 1868.

148. Ibid., November 14, 1868.

149. Ibid., November 15, 1868; the *New York Times* is quoted in the *Phoenix*.

150. The Central Committee published a letter in the *Daily Phoenix*, December 5, 1868, in answer to a question about its stance on labor problems, and Hampton's name was absent from the list of members.

151. Wade Hampton Papers, Letter from Hampton at Wild Woods in Mississippi to A. Burt, March 13, 1868 (Perkins Library, Duke University).

152. Hampton Papers, Digest Bankruptcy, No. 1103, Done by B. L. Todd, clerk of court, Southern District of Mississippi, awarded March 22, 1870 (SCL, USC); Meynard, *The Venturers*, 255–56; and Wade Hampton Papers, abstract of land transactions in Mississippi, dating from 1855 to 1888 (Library of Congress).

153. Hampton Papers, Letter from Hampton to Col. L. D. Childs, February 22, 1869 (SCL, USC).

154. Hampton Papers, Letter from Hampton at Wild Woods to A. Burt, January 2, 1871 (Perkins Library, Duke University).

155. William Kauffman Scarborough, *Masters of the Big House, The Elite Slaveholders of the Mid-Nineteenth Century South* (Baton Rouge: Louisiana State University Press, 2003), 385.

156. Ibid., 391–92.

157. Records of the Chancery Court, Greenville County, Mississippi.

158. Copy from Records of the Chancery Court, Greenville County, Mississippi, (Center for American History, University of Texas, Austin).

159. Letter from Hampton to Stephen Duncan, May 10, 1874 (Center for American History, University of Texas, Austin).

160. Ibid.

161. Deed Records, Book N, Issaquena County Court House, Mississippi, 478–79.

162. Will dated December 22, 1879, Record of Wills, Will Book 1, Washington County Court House, Mississippi.

163. Deed Book P, 329–220 and Deed book Q, 454, Issaquena County Court House, Mississippi. In 1888 Kate Hampton was borrowing money to harvest cotton on the Walnut Ridge Plantation. Deed Book Q, 454, Issaquena County, Mississippi.

164. Deed Book X, 1899, 395, 586–87, Issaquena County Court House, Mississippi.

165. Hampton Papers, Letter from Hampton to James Conner, April 1, 1869 (SCL, USC).

166. Hampton Papers, Printed Brochure, Bureau of Records, Survivors Association of the State of South Carolina, July 1, 1870 (SCL, USC).

167. Ralph Lowell Eckert, *John Brown Gordon: Soldier, Southerner, American* (Baton Rouge: Louisiana State University Press, 1989), 135.

168. M. C. Butler Papers, Letter from M. C. Butler to Col. E. G. W. Butler, July 14, 1871 (on stationery of Carolina Life Insurance Co.) (SCL, USC).

169. Hampton Papers, Letter from Hampton to Mrs. Parker, March 1, 1872 (SCL, USC).

170. Hampton Papers, Letter from Wade Hampton to Dr. D. H. Trezevant, October 2, 1872 (SCL, USC).

171. Meynard, *The Venturers*, 256–57, 563–64.

172. Lt. Gen. Wade Hampton, *Address on the Life and Character of General Robert E. Lee, Delivered on 21st October, 1871, before the Society of Confederate Soldiers and Sailors in Maryland* (Baltimore: John Murphy and Company, 1871). The Virgil quotation is translated: "Dreadful Queen the woe thou bidst me to recall, I myself saw in all its horror."

173. James M. McPherson, *Battle Cry of Freedom, the Civil War Era* (New York and Oxford: Oxford University Press, 1988), 244.

174. *Southern Historical Society Papers*, vol. 11, 390.

175. Hampton Papers, Article written for *Greenville (Miss.) Times*, August 2, 1872 (SCL, USC).

176. Craig L. Symonds, *Joseph E. Johnston: A Civil War Biography* (New York and London: W. W. Norton and Company, 1992), 361.

177. Hampton Papers, Letter from Hampton to Dr. D. H. Trezevant, written in Baltimore, December 27, 1872 (SCL, USC).

178. Wade Hampton, "Memorial Address," *Southern Magazine*, August 1873, 225–32.

179. "Speech of Wade Hampton to the Southern Historical Society," Richmond, October 29, 1873, *Southern Magazine*, January 1874, 11–18.

180. Eckert, *John Brown Gordon*, 135; and Hudson Strode, *Jefferson Davis, Tragic Hero: The Last Twenty-five Years, 1864–1889* (New York: Harcourt, Brace, and World, 1964), 357.

181. Hampton Papers, Letter from Hampton in Baltimore to A. Burt, December 28, 1872 (Perkins Library, Duke University).

182. Hampton Papers, Hampton to Anna Preston, April 7, 1873 (SCL, USC).

183. Hampton Papers, Letter from Wade Hampton to Thomas Preston, March 29, 1873 (SCL, USC).

184. Hampton Papers, Hampton to John Mullally, February 18, 1874 (SCL, USC).

185. Meynard, *The Venturers*, 258.

186. Hampton Papers, Letter from Hampton in Columbia to A. Burt, April 12, 1874 (Perkins Library, Duke University).

187. Simkins and Woody, *South Carolina during Reconstruction*, 112–20.

188. Thomas Holt, *Black over White: Negro Political Leadership in South Carolina during Reconstruction* (Urbana, Chicago, and London: University of Illinois Press, 1977), 10.

189. Simkins and Woody, *South Carolina during Reconstruction*, 112–20.

190. Reynolds, *Reconstruction in South Carolina*, 118.

191. Edgar, *South Carolina*, 396; and Carol K. Rothrock Bleser, *The Promised Land: The History of the South Carolina Land Commission, 1869–1890* (Columbia: University of South Carolina Press, 1969), 27–29, 157.

192. Steven Hahn, *A Nation under Our Feet: Black Political Struggles in the Rural South from Slavery to the Great Migration* (Cambridge, Mass., and London: Belknap Press of Harvard University Press, 2003), 303–4.

193. Zuczek, *State of Rebellion*, 72–76.

194. Walter Allen, *Chamberlain's Administration in South Carolina* (New York: G. P. Putnam's Sons, 1888), vii.

195. Simkins and Woody, *South Carolina during Reconstruction*, 112-20.

196. George C. Rogers, *Generation of Lawyers: A History of the South Carolina Bar* (Columbia: South Carolina Bar Foundation, 1992), 59-60.

197. Zuczek, *State of Rebellion*, 135-36.

198. Reynolds, *Reconstruction of South Carolina*, 121.

199. Allen, *Chamberlain's Administration*, 5-6.

200. Simkins and Woody, *South Carolina during Reconstruction*, 148-63.

201. Zuczek, *State of Rebellion*, 81.

202. Ibid., 93-96.

203. Hampton Papers, Letter from Hampton to A. Burt, October 22, 1871 (Perkins Library, Duke University).

204. Zuczek, *State of Rebellion*, 98.

205. *Testimony Taken by the Joint Committee to Inquire into the Condition of Affairs in the Late Insurrectionary State, South Carolina*, vol. 2 (Washington, D.C.: Government Printing Office, 1872), 1218-34.

206. Zuczek, *State of Rebellion*, 120-24.

207. Joel Williamson, *After Slavery: The Negro in South Carolina during Reconstruction, 1861-1877* (New York: W. W. Norton Company, 1965), 148-49.

208. Edgar, *South Carolina*, 394.

209. Williamson, *After Slavery*, 151-54.

210. Foner, *Reconstruction*, 374-77.

211. Ibid., 236; and Stanley P. Hirshon, *Farewell to the Bloody Shirt: Northern Republicans and the Southern Negro, 1877-1893* (Chicago: Quadrangle Books, 1968), 10 and passim.

212. Hugh Seton-Watson, *The Russian Empire, 1801-1917* (Oxford: Clarendon Press, 1967), 347-48.

213. *News and Courier*, July 7, 1876.

214. Reynolds, *Reconstruction in South Carolina*, 162-71.

215. Zuczek, *State of Rebellion*, 120-27.

216. Hampton Papers, Letter from Hampton to John Mullaly, May 19, 1872 (SCL, USC).

217. Reynolds, *Reconstruction in South Carolina*, 468-70.

218. Martin Gary Papers, Speech of Gen. M. U. Gary before the Taxpayers' Convention, Columbia, February 19, 1874 (SCL, USC).

219. Peggy Lamson, *The Glorious Failure, Black Congressman Robert Brown Elliott and the Reconstruction in South Carolina* (New York: W. W. Norton and Company, 1973), 174-85.

220. Zuczek, *State of Rebellion*, 137.

221. *News and Courier*, December 10, 1874.

222. James S. Pike, *The Prostrate State, South Carolina under Negro Rule*, ed. Robert F. Durden (1874; repr., New York: D. Appleton and Company, 1960), 12-15, 61.

223. Robert F. Durden, *James S. Pike, Republicanism and the American Negro, 1850-1882* (Durham: Duke University Press, 1957), 188.

224. Simkins and Woody, *South Carolina during Reconstruction*, 470-73

225. E. Culpepper Clark, *Francis Warrington Dawson: South Carolina, 1874-1889* (University: University of Alabama Press, 1980), 38-39.

226. Zuczek, *State of Rebellion*, 143.

227. *News and Courier*, December 12, 1874.

228. *News and Courier*, December 18, 1874.

229. Lamson, *The Glorious Failure*, 205-207.

230. James Lowell Underwood, "African American Founding Fathers: The Making of the South Carolina Constitution of 1868," in *At Freedom's Door*, eds. Underwood and Burke, 10-12.

231. Lamson, *The Glorious Failure*, 211-12.

232. Simkins and Woody, *South Carolina during Reconstruction*, 474-83.

233. Allen, *Governor Chamberlain's Administration*, 8-14.

234. Ibid., 21-22.

235. Ibid., 55-56.

236. Ibid., 68-70; and *News and Courier*, January 6, 1875.

237. *News and Courier*, January 21, 1875.

238. Allen, *Chamberlain's Administration*, 80-87.

239. *News and Courier*, March 3, 1875.

240. Ibid., March 11, 1875.

241. Ibid., May 27, 1875.

242. Allen, *Chamberlain's Administration*, 96-103.

243. Quoted in *News and Courier*, July 2, 1875.

244. Allen, *Chamberlain's Administration*, 108-13.

245. *News and Courier*, September 3, 1875.

246. *News and Courier*, July 21, August 5, and August 18, 1875; and Allen, *Chamberlain's Administration*, 145.

247. *News and Courier*, September 9, 1875.

248. *News and Courier*, September 21, 1875.

249. *Columbia Register*, October 20, 1875.

250. *Union Herald*, July 5, 1876.

251. *Columbia Register*, September 13, 1875.

252. John A. Leland, *A Voice from South Carolina: Twelve Chapters before Hampton and Two Chapters after Hampton* (Charleston: Walker, Evans, and Cogswell, 1879), 51-74.

253. *News and Courier*, September 20, 1875.

254. Allen, *Chamberlain's Administration*, 163-66.

255. *News and Courier*, September 4 and 22, 1875.

256. Ibid., October 16, 1875.

257. Quoted in *News and Courier*, November 12, 1875.

258. Ibid., November 24, 1875.

259. Ibid., December 1, 1875.

260. Ibid., September 23, 1875.

261. Allen, *Chamberlain's Administration*, 253-56.

262. *News and Courier*, December 24, 1875.

263. Allen, *Chamberlain's Administration*, 192-201; and *News and Courier*, December 17, 20, 22, and 24, 1875.

264. Simkins and Woody, *South Carolina during Reconstruction*, 474-83, and Edward A. Miller, Jr., *Gullah Statesman, Robert Smalls from Slavery to Congress, 1839-1915* (Columbia: University of South Carolina Press, 1995), 113.

265. *News and Courier*, December 27, 1875.

266. Allen, *Chamberlain's Administration*, 202-3.

267. Ibid., 220–21.

268. *Columbia Register*, January 12, 1876.

269. Allen, *Chamberlain's Administration,* 220–21.

270. *Family Letters of the Three Wade Hamptons,* Letter from Hampton to John Mullaly, February 18, 1874.

271. *News and Courier,* November 24, 1874.

272. Hampton Papers, Hampton to Mrs. Thomas L. Preston, April 27, 1875 (SCL, USC).

273. *News and Courier,* July 8, 1875.

274. Hampton Papers, Letter from Hampton to Mrs. Thomas L. Preston, undated (SCL, USC).

275. *News and Courier,* February 17, 1875.

276. Ibid., July 22, 1875.

277. Ibid., July 29, 1875.

Chapter 6: The Election of 1876

1. John S. Reynolds, *Reconstruction in South Carolina* (Columbia: State Publishing Company, 1905), 337–39; *News and Courier,* January 8, 1876; *Columbia Register,* January 6 and 8, 1876.

2. *Columbia Register*, February 13, 1876.

3. Ibid., February 26, 1876.

4. Ibid., March 3, 1876.

5. E. Culpepper Clark, *Francis Warrington Dawson: South Carolina, 1874–1889* (University of Alabama: University of Alabama Press, 1980), 57–60.

6. Ibid.

7. *News and Courier,* January 6, 1876.

8. Ibid., January 10, 1876.

9. Ibid., January 10 and 15, 1876.

10. William J. Cooper, *The Conservative Regime, South Carolina, 1877–1890* (Baltimore: Johns Hopkins Press, 1968), 17.

11. *Columbia Register*, November 2, 1875.

12. Ibid., November 16, 1875.

13. Martin Gary Papers, Letter from S. M. Ferguson of Mississippi to T. G. Parker of Charleston, January 7, 1876 (South Caroliniana Library, University of South Carolina—hereafter cited as SCL, USC).

14. *Columbia Register*, December 30, 1875.

15. *Union Herald,* July 5, 1876.

16. Eric Foner, *Reconstruction, America's Unfinished Revolution, 1863–1877* (New York: Harper and Row, 1988), 559.

17. Gary Papers, Petition to R. F. W. Allston, 1857 (SCL, USC).

18. Gary Papers, MS document, dated August 5, 1871, signed by Gary and Patterson (SCL, USC).

19. Gary Papers, Editorial from the *(New York) Sun,* February 1, 1878 (Perkins Library, Duke University).

20. Gary Papers, Undated letter from Gary to the *(Abbeville, S.C.) Medium* (Perkins Library, Duke University).

21. *Columbia Register*, January 16, 1876.

22. Ibid., January 30, 1876.

23. *News and Courier*, January 19, 1876.

24. Walter Allen, *Chamberlain's Administration in South Carolina* (New York: G. P. Putnam's Sons, 1888), 259–71.

25. *News and Courier*, April 12, 1876.

26. Ibid., February 7, 1876.

27. Ibid., February 18, 1876.

28. Wade Hampton Papers, Manuscript resolution, undated (SCL, USC).

29. Mary Conner Moffett, ed., *Letters of General James Conner* (Columbia, S.C.: R. L. Bryan Company, 1950), 210–14.

30. Ibid., 198–99, Letter from Conner to Wade Hampton, April 9, 1876.

31. Ibid., 198–99, Letter from Wade Hampton to James Conner, April 9, 1867.

32. *News and Courier*, February 21, 1874.

33. Gary Papers, (Augusta, Georgia) *Constitutionalist*, April 7, 1874 (SCL, USC).

34. *News and Courier*, February 24, 1876.

35. Alfred B. Williams, *Hampton and His Red Shirts, South Carolina's Deliverance in 1876* (Charleston: Walker, Evans, and Cogswell, 1933), 261.

36. *News and Courier*, July 4, 1876.

37. *Columbia Register*, March 25, 1876.

38. Ibid.

39. Andrew Slap, "The Spirit of '76: The Reconstruction of History in the Redemption of South Carolina," *The Historian* 63 (Summer 2001): 769–76.

40. *News and Courier*, March 13, 1876.

41. Alfred H. Kelly and Winfred A. Harbison, *The American Constitution, Its Origins and Development* (New York: W. W. Norton and Company, 1963), 483.

42. *News and Courier*, April 1, 1876.

43. Ibid., April 8, 1876.

44. *Columbia Register*, April 11, 1876.

45. Ibid., April 13, 1876.

46. *Documents of the House of Representatives*, 44th Cong., 2nd session, 1876–1877 (Washington, D.C., 1877), 28–29.

47. *News and Courier*, May 4, 1876.

48. *Columbia Register*, May 5, 1876.

49. Ibid., May 6, 1876.

50. *News and Courier*, May 6, 1876.

51. Ibid., May 9, 1876.

52. DeWitt Grant Jones, "Wade Hampton and the Rhetoric of Race: A Study of the Speaking of Wade Hampton on the Race Issue, 1865–1878" (Ph.D. diss., Louisiana State University and Agricultural and Mechanical College, 1988), 112.

53. *Columbia Register*, May 14, 1876.

54. Ibid., May 21, 1876.

55. *News and Courier*, May 23, 1876.

56. Ibid., May 24, 1876; and *Columbia Register*, May 24, 1876.

57. *Columbia Register*, May 25, 1876.

58. *News and Courier*, May 29, 1876.

59. Thomas Holt, *Black over White: Political Leadership in South Carolina during Reconstruction* (Urbana, Chicago, and London: University of Illinois Press, 1977), 168–69; *News and Courier*, August 24, 1876; and Steven Hahn, *Gullah Statesman: A Nation under Our Feet: Black Political Struggles in the Rural South from Slavery to the Great Migration* (Cambridge, Mass., and London: Belknap Press of Harvard University Press, 2003), 348–49.

60. *News and Courier*, May 26, 1876.

61. *Columbia Register*, May 28, 1876.

62. Edgefield advertiser, quoted in *Columbia Register*, June 2, 1876.

63. Ibid., June 7, 1876.

64. Ibid., May 30, 1876.

65. Ibid.

66. Ibid., June 28, 1876.

67. Ibid., June 3, 1876.

68. Quoted in *News and Courier*, June 24, 1876.

69. *Columbia Register*, July 4, 1876.

70. Ibid., June 24, 1876.

71. *News and Courier*, July 8, 1876.

72. *Columbia Register*, July 11, 1876; and *News and Courier*, July 10, 1876.

73. Francis Butler Simkins, *Pitchfork Ben Tillman, South Carolinian* (Baton Rouge: Louisiana State University Press, 1944), 62–63.

74. Quoted in the *Columbia Register*, July 12, 1876.

75. *Union Herald*, July 14, 1876; and Peggy Lamsen, *The Glorious Failure Black Congressman Robert Brown Elliott and the Reconstruction in South Carolina* (New York: W. W. Norton and Company, 1873), 216.

76. *News and Courier*, July 10, 1876.

77. Ibid., July 12, 1876.

78. Ibid., July 14, 1876; and Samuel J. Martin, *Southern Hero: Matthew Calbraith Butler, Confederate General, Hampton Red Shirt, and U.S. Senator* (Mechanicsburg, Pa.: Stackpole Books, 2001), 207–11.

79. *Union Herald*, July 12, 1876.

80. Ibid.; and *Columbia Register*, July 14, 1876.

81. *News and Courier*, July 13, 1876.

82. Jones, "Wade Hampton and the Rhetoric of Race," 128.

83. *News and Courier*, July 20, 1876.

84. *Columbia Register*, July 18, 1876.

85. Allen, *Chamberlain's Administration*, 322–24.

86. Ibid., 325.

87. Kenneth Stampp, "Triumph of the Conservatives," in *Reconstruction*, ed. Staughton Lynd (Evanston and London: Harper and Row, 1967), 159.

88. Allen, *Chamberlain's Administration*, 328–29.

89. *News and Courier*, August 2, 1876.

90. *Columbia Register*, July 13, 1876.

91. *News and Courier*, July 15 and July 21, 1876.

92. Ibid.

93. *Columbia Register*, July 15, 1876.

94. *News and Courier*, July 27, 1876; and *Union Herald*, July 19, 1876.

95. *Union Herald*, July 29, 1876.

96. *Columbia Register*, July 20, 1876.

97. *Union Herald*, July 20, 1876.

98. *Columbia Register*, July 21, 1876.

99. Gary Papers, Letter from Hampton in Cashiers Valley, North Carolina, July 25, 1876, to Martin Gary (SCL, USC).

100. *News and Courier*, August 5, 1876.

101. *Columbia Register*, July 18, 1876.

102. Clark, *Francis Warrington Dawson*, 6.

103. *News and Courier*, August 7, 1876.

104. *Columbia Register*, August 9, 1876.

105. Ibid.

106. Ibid., July 30, 1876.

107. Simkins, *Pitchfork Ben Tillman*, 270.

108. *Columbia Register*, August 15, 1876.

109. Williams, *Hampton and His Red Shirts*, 167.

110. *Union Herald*, August 5, 1876.

111. Simkins, *Pitchfork Ben Tillman*, 262–72.

112. Gary Papers, Unsigned and undated paper in the collection (SCL, USC).

113. Gary Papers, Undated paper written by William M. Barnwell (SCL, USC).

114. Slap, "The Spirit of '76," 769–76.

115. *News and Courier*, August 8, 1876.

116. *Union Herald*, August 9, 1876.

117. Allen, *Chamberlain's Administration*, 325–26.

118. *News and Courier*, August 21 and 22, 1876.

119. *Columbia Register*, August 4, 1876.

120. Martin, *Southern Hero*, 211–12.

121. *Columbia Register*, August 9, 1876.

122. *News and Courier*, August 10, 1876.

123. *Columbia Register*, August 15, 1876.

124. *News and Courier*, August 17, 1876.

125. Ibid., August 18, 1876.

126. Ibid., August 19, 1876; and Reynolds, *Reconstruction in South Carolina*, 347–55.

127. *Columbia Register*, August 15, 1876.

128. *Union Herald*, August 16, 1876.

129. *Columbia Register*, August 16, 1876.

130. Reynolds, *Reconstruction in South Carolina*, 354–55.

131. *Columbia Register*, August 16 and 17, 1876.

132. Edwards L. Wells, *Hampton and Reconstruction* (Columbia: State Company, 1907), 115–16.

133. *Columbia Register*, August 17, 1876.

134. Keith Ian Polakoff, *The Politics of Inertia: The Election of 1876 and the End of Reconstruction* (Baton Rouge: Louisiana State University Press, 1973), 192–93.

135. *News and Courier*, August 26, 1876.

136. Slap, "The Spirit of '76," 769–76.

137. *Union Herald*, August 18, 1876.

138. Martin, *Southern Hero, Matthew Calbraith Butler*, 212–18.

139. Hampton Papers, Pamphlet, "Free Men! Free Ballots!! Free Schools!!!, The Pledge of General Wade Hampton, Democratic Candidate for Governor to the Colored People of South Carolina," undated (SCL, USC).

140. T. Harry Williams, *Romance and Realism in Southern Politics* (Athens: University of Georgia Press, 1961), 40.

141. W. W. Ball, *The State That Forgot: South Carolina's Surrender to Democracy* (Indianapolis: Bobbs-Merrill, 1932), 157.

142. *Columbia Register*, August 18, 1876.

143. *Union Herald*, August 19, 1876.

144. Ibid., August 30, 1876.

145. *Columbia Register*, August 23, 1876.

146. *News and Courier*, August 29, 1876.

147. Edmund L. Drago, *Hurrah for Hampton! Black Red Shirts in South Carolina during Reconstruction* (Fayetteville: University of Arkansas Press, 1998), 1–16.

148. Ibid., 43.

149. Ball, *The State That Forgot*, 163–64.

150. Drago, *Hurrah for Hampton*, 38–43.

151. *Columbia Register*, August 25, 1876.

152. *Union Herald*, August 10, 1876.

153. *News and Courier*, October 2, 1876.

154. *Report on the Denial of the Elective Franchise in South Carolina at the State and National Election of 1876, the United States Senate Subcommittee of the Committee of Privileges and Election* (Washington, D.C.: Government Printing Office, 1877), 138.

155. Drago, *Hurrah for Hampton*, 32; and *Columbia Register*, September 19, 1876.

156. *News and Courier*, August 28, 1876.

157. *Columbia Register*, August 20, 1876.

158. *News and Courier*, September 7, 1876; and Reynolds, *Reconstruction in South Carolina*, 374–81.

159. *Union Herald*, September 9, 1876.

160. Ibid., September 12, 1876.

161. *News and Courier*, July 13, 1876.

162. Ibid., July 20, 1876.

163. Clark, *Francis Warrington Dawson*, 67.

164. *Columbia Register*, September 1, 1876.

165. Ibid., September 2, 1876.

166. Ibid., September 5, 1876.

167. Ibid., September 8, 1876.

168. Ibid., September 9, 1876.

169. Ibid., September 13, 1876.

170. Jones, "Wade Hampton and the Rhetoric of Race," 151.

171. *Columbia Register*, September 10, 1876.

172. *News and Courier*, September 15 and 16, 1876.

173. Allen, *Chamberlain's Administration*, 504–5; and *News and Courier*, September 16, 1876.

174. Eric Foner, "South Carolina's Black Elected Officials during Reconstruction," in *At Freedom's Door*, eds. James Lowell Underwood and W. Lewis Burke, 171.

175. D. H. Chamberlain, "Reconstruction in South Carolina," *Atlantic Monthly* (April 1901): 473–84.

176. Allen, *Chamberlain's Administration*, 346.

177. Ibid., 352–53.

178. Hampton Papers, *Chronicle and Sentinel*, Augusta, Georgia, January 11, 1878, photostatic copy (SCL, USC).

179. William Gillette, *Retreat from Reconstruction, 1867–1879* (Baton Rouge: Louisiana State University Press, 1979), 314.

180. Polakoff, *The Politics of Inertia*, 197.

181. Gary Papers, A letter to an unnamed editor, never published, undated, and letter from Gary to Hugh of Cokesbury, March 10, 1878 (SCL, USC).

182. Jones, "Wade Hampton and the Rhetoric of Race," 156.

183. *Columbia Register*, September 17, 1876.

184. Robert Zuczek, *State of Rebellion: Reconstruction in South Carolina* (Columbia: University of South Carolina Press, 1996), 174–75; *Columbia Register*, September 21, 1876; and *Union Herald*, September 28, 1876.

185. *News and Courier*, October 4, 1876.

186. Zuczek, *State of Rebellion*, 176.

187. *News and Courier*, October 6, 1876.

188. Ibid., October 9, 1876.

189. Simkins and Woody, *South Carolina during Reconstruction*, 492.

190. *Report on the Denial of the Elective Franchise in South Carolina*, 157–58.

191. Allen, *Chamberlain's Administration*, 367.

192. *Union Herald*, October 6, 1876.

193. *News and Courier*, October 16, 1876.

194. Ibid., October 18, 1876.

195. Ibid., October 20, 1876.

196. Manly Wade Wellman, *Giant in Gray: A Biography of Wade Hampton of South Carolina* (Dayton, Ohio: Morningside Book Shop, 1988), 265.

197. *News and Courier*, October 20, 1876.

198. Allen, *Chamberlain's Administration*, 467.

199. Ibid., 418–19.

200. *Union Herald*, October 12, 1876.

201. Jones, "Wade Hampton and the Rhetoric of Race," 142.

202. Drago, *Hurrah for Hampton*, 1.

203. *News and Courier*, October 26, 1876.

204. Ibid., October 26 and 30, 1876.

205. Reynolds, *Reconstruction in South Carolina*, 387.

206. *Union Herald*, October 19, 1876.

207. Ibid., October 20, 1876.

208. Moffitt, *Letters of General James Conner*, 229–31, letter from Conner to Mrs. Conner, October 24, 1876; and Jones, "Wade Hampton and the Rhetoric of Race," 123.

209. Jones, "Wade Hampton and the Rhetoric of Race," 142.

210. *Columbia Register,* October 8, 1876.

211. Ibid., October 19, 1876.

212. *Union Herald,* November 22, 1876.

213. Ibid., October 18, 1876.

214. Ibid., October 27, 1876.

215. *News and Courier,* November 6, 1876; and *Columbia Register,* October 31, 1876.

216. Jones, "Wade Hampton and the Rhetoric of Race," 125.

217. *Documents of the House of Representatives,* 44th Cong., 2nd session, 1876–1877 (Washington, D.C., 1877), 181–82.

218. Ibid., 422–23.

219. Ibid., 266–67.

220. Gary Papers, Affidavits submitted by Wiley J. Williams and Abraham Lauhan, managers of Box #1 of Edgefield, November 9, 1876 (Perkins Library, Duke University).

221. Williams, *Hampton and His Red Shirts,* 379.

222. Reynolds, *Reconstruction in South Carolina,* 397; and *News and Courier,* November 14, 1876.

223. Allen, *Chamberlain's Administration,* 428.

224. *News and Courier,* November 11 and 15, 1876.

225. Ibid., November 14, 1876.

226. *Columbia Register,* November 9, 1876.

227. Ibid., November 11, 1876.

228. *News and Courier,* November 18, 1876.

229. *Columbia Register,* November 23, 1876.

230. *News and Courier,* November 28, 1876.

231. Reynolds, *Reconstruction in South Carolina,* 408–42; Hampton M. Jarrell, *Wade Hampton and the Negro: The Road Not Taken* (Columbia: University of South Carolina Press, 1950), 109; and Governor Hampton Papers, Letter from G. A. Neuffer to Governor Hampton, December 15, 1876 (South Carolina Department of Archives and History—hereafter cited as South Carolina Archives).

232. Zuczek, *State of Rebellion,* 195.

233. Hampton Papers, Telegram from Hampton to President Grant, dated November 30, 1876 (South Carolina Archives).

234. Hampton Papers, Telegram from Hampton to Hamilton Fish, December 3, 1876 (South Carolina Archives).

235. Jarrell, *Wade Hampton and the Negro,* 109–10; and *News and Courier,* November 29, 1876.

236. *Union Herald,* December 6, 1876.

237. Allen, *Chamberlain's Administration,* 445–47.

238. *Columbia Register,* December 7, 1876; and *News and Courier,* December 7, 1876.

239. *News and Courier,* December 9, 1876.

240. Hampton Papers, The executive Messages of Governor Hampton, December 14, 1876, 1–5 (South Carolina Archives); and *Columbia Daily Register Extra,* December 14, 1876.

241. *Columbia Register,* December 15, 1876.

242. *News and Courier,* December 16, 1876.

243. Ibid., December 28, 1876.

244. *Columbia Register,* December 20, 1876.

245. *News and Courier,* December 19, 1876.

246. Ibid., December 20, 1876.

247. Hampton Papers, Letter from ——, December 16, 1876 (South Carolina Archives).

248. Hampton Papers, Letter from Thompson Earle to Governor Hampton, December 28, 1876 (South Carolina Archives).

249. Hampton Papers, Letters Received, Box 2 (South Carolina Archives).

250. Hampton Papers, Letter from J. Robert Boyles of Fairfield County, March 8, 1877 (South Carolina Archives).

251. *News and Courier,* December 20, 1876.

252. Ibid.

253. *Columbia Register,* December 21, 1876.

254. *News and Courier,* December 22, 1876.

255. *Union Herald,* January 4, 1877.

256. Jarrell, *Wade Hampton and the Negro,* 112.

257. Hampton Papers, Letter from Wade Hampton to R. B. Hayes and to S. J. Tilden, December 23, 1876 (South Carolina Archives).

258. *Columbia Register,* January 7, 1877.

259. *Union Herald,* January 5, 1877.

260. *News and Courier,* December 29, 1876.

261. Ibid., January 3, 1877; and *Columbia Register,* January 2, 1877.

262. Hampton Papers, *(Augusta, Georgia) Chronicle and Sentinel,* January 10, 1877, photostatic copy (SCL, USC).

263. *Columbia Register,* January 6, 1877.

264. Hampton Papers, Petition from Savannah River Rice Planters, January 12, 1877, Box 2 (South Carolina Archives).

265. *News and Courier,* January 6, 8, and 9, 1877.

266. Ibid., January 10, 1877.

267. *Columbia Register,* January 9, 10, 11, and 12, 1877.

268. *News and Courier,* January 16, 1877.

269. Hampton Papers, Letter from Jno. Scoggins, private secretary, to G. W. Offley, January 9, 1877, Miscellaneous Papers (South Carolina Archives).

270. Hampton Papers, Letter from Hampton to Larrick Cossell, January 11, 1877, Miscellaneous Papers (South Carolina Archives).

271. Hampton Papers, Letter from John A. Hamilton to Governor Hampton, January 2, 1877 (South Carolina Archives).

272. Hampton Papers, Undated Petition from Sumter County (South Carolina Archives).

273. Hampton Papers, Letter from James H. Rion to Governor Hampton, January 11, 1877 (South Carolina Archives).

274. *Union Herald,* January 15, 1877.

275. Hampton Papers, Letter from Mrs. D. E. Conner of Reevesville to Governor Hampton, January 10, 1877 (South Carolina Archives).

276. *News and Courier,* January 12, 1877.

277. *Union Herald,* January 17, 1877.

278. Ibid., January 18, 1877.

279. *Columbia Register*, January 18, 1877.

280. *Union Herald*, February 17, 1877.

281. *Columbia Register*, February 1, 1877.

282. Ibid., February 15, 1877.

283. *Columbia Daily Register*, February 28, 1877.

284. Quoted in *News and Courier*, February 20, 1877.

285. *Daily Register*, March 20, 1877.

286. Ibid., February 21, 1877, and Hampton Papers, "Proclamation of Governor Hampton, February 20, 1877," Miscellaneous Letters, Letter Book 83–84 (South Carolina Archives).

287. *News and Courier*, February 27, 1877.

288. C. Vann Woodward, *Reunion and Reaction, the Compromise of 1877 and the End of Reconstruction* (New York: Little, Brown, and Company, 1951), 235–67.

289. Ibid., 138–42.

290. Allen, *Chamberlain's Administration*, 469–70.

291. *Daily Register*, March 31, 1877.

292. *News and Courier*, March 7, 1877.

293. Ibid.

294. Hampton Papers, Telegram from Mackey in Washington to Governor Hampton, March 10, 1877 (South Carolina Archives).

295. Hampton Papers, Telegram from Hampton in Columbia to Butler in Washington, March 7, 1877 (South Carolina Archives).

296. Woodward, *Reunion and Reaction*, 238–39.

297. Hampton Papers, Telegram from Mackey in Washington to Hampton, March 26, 1877 (South Carolina Archives).

298. Hampton Papers, Telegram from Hampton to President Hayes, March 26, 1877 (South Carolina Archives).

299. *Union Herald*, March 7, 1877.

300. Hampton Papers, Letter from Hampton to Moses, January 15, 1877, Miscellaneous Papers (South Carolina Archives).

301. *News and Courier*, March 26, 28, 29, and 30, 1877.

302. Hampton Papers, Letter from Wade Hampton at Willard's Hotel to President R. B. Hayes, March 29, 1877 (South Carolina Archives).

303. *News and Courier*, March 30, 1877.

304. Reported in *News and Courier*, March 31, 1877.

305. Hampton Papers, *New York Tribune*, March 30, 1877, photostatic copy (SCL, USC).

306. Hampton Papers, Letter from Wade Hampton at Willard's Hotel to President Hayes, March 31, 1877 (South Carolina Archives).

307. Vincent P. DeSantis, *Republicans Face the Southern Question—The New Departure Years, 1877–1897* (Baltimore: Johns Hopkins Press, 1959), 7.

308. *Daily Register*, April 4, 1877.

309. *News and Courier*, April 3 and 4, 1877.

310. Ibid., April 6 and 7, 1877.

311. Hampton Papers, *New York Tribune*, April 3, 1877, photostatic copy (SCL, USC).

312. Allen, *Chamberlain's Administration*, 472–73.

313. *News and Courier*, April 9 and 11, 1877.

314. Ibid., April 12, 1877.

315. *Columbia Register*, April 12, 1877.

316. D. H. Chamberlain, "Reconstruction in South Carolina," 473–84; and Jarrell, *Wade Hampton and the Negro*, 103.

Chapter 7: *In Office*

1. Thomas Holt, *Black over White: Negro Political Leadership in South Carolina during Reconstruction* (Urbana, Chicago, and London: University of Illinois Press, 1977), 208–10.

2. Governor Hampton Papers, Letter from W. H. Manning to T. C. Dunn et al, April 14, 1877, Miscellaneous Papers (South Carolina Department of Archives and History, hereafter cited as South Carolina Archives); and *News and Courier*, April 16 and 17, 1877.

3. Hampton Papers, Letter from Atty. Gen. R. B. Elliott to Wade Hampton Manning, private secretary to Governor Hampton, April 16, 1877, also signed by J. R. Tolbert and James Kennedy (South Carolina Archives); and *Columbia Register*, April 17, 1877.

4. *News and Courier*, April 19 and 20, 1877.

5. George Brown Tindall, *South Carolina Negroes, 1877–1906* (Columbia: University of South Carolina Press, 1952), 22–23; and *Daily Register*, August 23, 1877.

6. Hampton Papers, Manuscript compilation, Letters of Appointment (South Carolina Archives).

7. *News and Courier*, April 14, 1877.

8. *Columbia Register*, April 12, 1877.

9. Martin Gary Papers, Letter from Martin Gary to Hugh ——, March 10, 1878, and letter from Gary to Hugh ——, May 3, 1878 (South Caroliniana Library, University of South Carolina—hereafter cited as SCL, USC).

10. Belton O'Neal Townsend, "The Political Condition of South Carolina," *Atlantic Monthly* 29 (February 1877): 177–94.

11. *News and Courier*, April 23 and 24, 1877.

12. Ibid., April 27, 1877.

13. Hampton Papers, Letter from Governor Hampton to A. W. Cummings, chairman of the University of South Carolina, August 7, 1877, Letterbook, Miscellaneous Letters, vol. 1, 85 (South Carolina Archives); and Daniel Walker Hollis, "South Carolina College," in *University of South Carolina*, vol. 1 (Columbia: University of South Carolina Press, 1951), 78–79.

14. Hampton Papers, Executive Message, #1, April 26, 1877 (South Carolina Archives); and Holt, *Black over White*, 69.

15. *Journal of the House of Representatives of the State of South Carolina, Special Session, Commencing April 24, 1877* (Columbia: Presbyterian Publishing House, 1877), 3.

16. *News and Courier*, April 27, 1877.

17. Ibid., May 3, 1877.

18. Tindall, *South Carolina Negroes*, 23.

19. Hampton Papers, Letter from James F. Izlar to Governor Hampton, April 21, 1877 (South Carolina Archives).

20. William J. Cooper, Jr., *The Conservative Regime, South Carolina, 1877–1890* (Baltimore: Johns Hopkins Press, 1968), 24–25.

21. *News and Courier*, April 28, 1877.

22. Ibid., May 6, 1877.

23. Ibid., May 10, 1877.

24. Ibid., May 16, 1877.

25. *Columbia Register*, May 5, 1877.

26. *News and Courier*, May 22, 1877.

27. Hampton Papers, Letter from Hampton to Secretary of State Evarts, May 13, 1877 (South Carolina Archives).

28. Hampton Papers, Letter from Hampton to Secretary of State Evarts, May 15, 1877 (South Carolina Archives).

29. DeWitt Grant Jones, "Wade Hampton and the Rhetoric of Race," (Ph.D. diss., Louisiana State University and Agricultural and Mechanical College, 1988), 97; and *Columbia Daily Phoenix*, April 3, 1876.

30. Hampton Papers, Letter from Governor Hampton to President Hayes, April 22, 1877 (South Carolina Archives).

31. Clarence C. Clendenin, "President Hayes' 'Withdrawal of Troops'—An Enduring Myth," *South Carolina Historical Magazine* 70 (1969): 240-43.

32. *Journal of the House of Representatives of the State of South Carolina, Special Session Commencing April 24, 1877*, 354; and *News and Courier*, May 15, 1877.

33. Hampton Papers, Letter from President Hayes to Governor Hampton, May 12, 1877 (South Carolina Archives).

34. Holt, *Black over White*, 210-11.

35. Hampton Papers, Letter from Hampton to President Hayes, June 24, 1877 (South Carolina Archives).

36. Hampton Papers, Letter from Hampton to President Hayes, September 25, 1877 (South Carolina Archives).

37. Hampton M. Jarrell, *Wade Hampton and the Negro: The Road Not Taken* (Columbia: University of South Carolina Press, 1950), 137-38.

38. *Columbia Register*, May 26 and 27, 1877.

39. *News and Courier*, June 4, 1877.

40. *Columbia Register*, June 3, 1877.

41. *News and Courier*, June 5, 1877.

42. Ibid., June 11, 1877.

43. *Columbia Register*, June 7, 1877.

44. *News and Courier*, June 8, 1877.

45. George C. Rogers, *Generations of Lawyers: A History of the South Carolina Bar* (Columbia: South Carolina Bar Foundation, 1992), 69.

46. Richard Gergel and Belinda Gergel, "To Vindicate the Cause of the Downtrodden," in *At Freedom's Door: African American Founding Fathers and Lawyers in Reconstruction South Carolina*, eds. James Lowell Underwood and W. Lewis Burke (Columbia: University of South Carolina Press, 2000), 64.

47. *News and Courier*, June 11, 1877.

48. Hampton Papers, Letter from George W. Yuck to Governor Hampton, April 28, 1877 (South Carolina Archives).

49. Hampton Papers, Letter from Governor Hampton to Speaker W. A. Wallace, June 8, 1877, Letterbook (South Carolina Archives).

50. *Daily Register*, June 12, 1877.

51. *News and Courier*, June 11, 1877.

52. *Journal of the House of Representatives of State of South Carolina for the Regular Session of 1877–1878*, 333.

53. *News and Courier*, June 13, 1877.

54. Ibid., June 20 and 23, 1877; and James B. Murphy, *L. Q. C. Lamar, Pragmatic Patriot* (Baton Rouge: Louisiana State University Press, 1973), passim. Lamar seized the opportunity of delivering a eulogy for the late Sen. Charles Sumner and thereby achieved recognition as a leading spokesman for the reconciled South.

55. *Daily Register*, June 22, 1877.

56. Ibid., June 30, 1877.

57. *News and Courier*, June 26, 1877.

58. Ibid., July 9, 1877.

59. Ibid., June 20, 1877.

60. Hampton Papers, Letter from M. A. Warren to Governor Hampton, June 5, 1877 (South Carolina Archives).

61. Joel Williamson, *After Slavery: The Negro in South Carolina during Reconstruction, 1861–1877* (New York: W. W. Norton Company, 1965), 224–29; Francis Butler Simkins and Robert H. Woody, *South Carolina during Reconstruction* (Chapel Hill: University of North Carolina Press, 1932), 443; and Cooper, *The Conservative Regime*, 112.

62. *Acts and Joint Resolutions of the General Assembly of South Carolina, Passed at the Special Session of 1877* (Columbia: Calvo and Patton, State Printers, 1877), 315.

63. Jarrell, *Wade Hampton and the Negro*, 126–27.

64. Hampton Papers, Resolutions from the Central Democratic Club of Abbeville, May 7, 1877 (South Carolina Archives).

65. Hampton Papers, Letter from J. N. Garner, Intendant of Timmonsville, to Governor Hampton, June 15, 1877 (South Carolina Archives).

66. Hampton Papers, Letter from Rev. H. H. Hunter to Governor Hampton, June 16, 1877 (South Carolina Archives).

67. Hampton Papers, Letter from Carlos Tracy to Governor Hampton, May 27, 1877 (South Carolina Archives).

68. Hampton Papers, Letter from M. M. Thompson to Governor Hampton, June 25, 1877 (South Carolina Archives).

69. Hampton Papers, Letter from Alfred Williams to Governor Hampton, June 18, 1877 (South Carolina Archives).

70. *News and Courier*, June 23, 1877; and Jones, "Wade Hampton and the Rhetoric of Race," 224.

71. *News and Courier*, July 16, 1878.

72. *Daily Register*, August 22, 1877.

73. Kenneth Stampp, "Triumph of the Conservatives," in *Reconstruction*, ed. Staughton Lynd (Evanston and London: Harper and Row, 1967), 157.

74. *Daily Register*, August 23, 1877.

75. Hampton Papers, Letter from Mayor Charles D. Jacob to Governor Hampton, August 21, 1877 (South Carolina Archives).

76. Hampton Papers, Telegrams from L. C. Northrop to Governor Hampton, October 3, 1877, and November 19, 1877 (South Carolina Archives).

77. Rogers, *Generations of Lawyers*, 63; *Daily Register*, October 17, 1877; and Hampton Papers, Letters from Northrop to Governor Hampton, October 3, 1877 and November 8, 1877 (South Carolina Archives).

78. Cooper, *The Conservative Regime*, 28.

79. Vincent P. DeSantis, *Republicans Face the Southern Question—The New Departure Years, 1877-1897* (Baltimore: Johns Hopkins Press, 1959), 86-87.

80. *News and Courier*, September 17, 19, 20, 24, and 28, 1877.

81. Ibid., September 7 and October 6, 1877.

82. Hampton Papers, Extradition request from Governor Hampton to the chief justice of the District of Columbia, October 10, 1877 (South Carolina Archives); and *Daily Register*, November 1, 1877.

83. *News and Courier*, August 30, 1877.

84. Ibid., September 17, 1877.

85. Ibid., September 8, 1877.

86. Hampton Papers, Letter from William E. James to Governor Hampton, September 24, 1877, and letter from Tillman Watson to Governor Hampton, October 21, 1877 (South Carolina Archives).

87. Hampton Papers, Letter from J. N. Ballard to Governor Hampton, October 24, 1877 (South Carolina Archives); and *News and Courier*, February 2, 1878.

88. *News and Courier*, October 22, 1877.

89. Ibid., November 5, 1877.

90. Ibid., November 29, 1877.

91. *Daily Register*, December 9, 1877.

92. *News and Courier*, December 20, 1877.

93. Ibid., December 1, 1877.

94. Ibid., December 6 and 7, 1877, and February 5, 1878.

95. Hampton Papers, Hathaway and Pond of Boston to Governor Hampton, December 6, 1877 (South Carolina Archives).

96. Hampton Papers, Letter from James B. Brickell to Governor Hampton, December 8, 1877 (South Carolina Archives).

97. Hampton Papers, Letter from Benjamin Moorhouse to Governor Hampton, December 13, 1877 (South Carolina Archives).

98. Hampton Papers, Governor's Message #36 to the Senate, December 15, 1877, Miscellaneous Letters (South Carolina Archives).

99. Hampton Papers, Petition from citizens of Newberry County to Governor Hampton, undated (South Carolina Archives).

100. Hampton Papers, Petition of sundry citizens of Lancaster County, May 27, 1878 (South Carolina Archives).

101. Hampton Papers, Letter from Robert Aldrich to Governor Hampton, March 23, 1878 (South Carolina Archives).

102. Hampton Papers, Petition from citizens of Georgetown County, August 9, 1878 (South Carolina Archives).

103. *Daily Register*, December 29 and December 13, 1877.

104. *News and Courier*, January 22, 1878.

105. Cooper, *The Conservative Regime*, 26; and *News and Courier*, January 23, 1878.

106. Ibid., February 14, 1878.

107. *Acts and Joint Resolutions of the General Assembly of the State of South Carolina, Passed at the Extra Session of 1877*, 314–15; and *News and Courier*, January 30, 1878.

108. Hampton Papers, Letter from Governor Hampton to the House of Representatives, February 14, 1878, Miscellaneous Letters (South Carolina Archives); and *News and Courier*, February 15 and 16, 1878.

109. *News and Courier*, February 8, 1878.

110. Ibid., February 11, 1878.

111. Cooper, *The Conservative Regime*, 45–46.

112. *News and Courier*, February 23 and 25, 1878.

113. Ibid., March 2, 1878.

114. Martin Gary Papers, Letter from Martin Gary to Hugh Farley, March 10, 1878 (SCL, USC).

115. Gary Papers, Letter from Senator Butler to Martin Gary, April 3, 1878 (SCL, USC).

116. Gary Papers, Letters from Martin Gary to Hugh Farley, April 8 and 20, and May 3, 1878 (SCL, USC).

117. Hampton Papers, Letter from J. D. Allen of Barnwell to Governor Hampton, March 11, 1878 (South Carolina Archives). Allen warned Hampton that Gary would try to unseat him.

118. *News and Courier*, February 8, 1878.

119. Hampton Papers, Letter from W. W. Humphreys of Anderson to Governor Hampton, March 7, 1878 (South Carolina Archives).

120. Cooper, *The Conservative Regime*, 45–47; and *News and Courier*, March 11 and April 2, 1878.

121. *Daily Register*, March 15, 1878.

122. *News and Courier*, June 4, 1878.

123. *Acts and Joint Resolutions of the General Assembly of the State of South Carolina, Passed at the Regular Session of 1877–78*, 405–6; and *News and Courier*, March 14, 1878.

124. *Acts and Joint Resolutions of the General Assembly of the State of South Carolina, Passed at the Special Session of 1877*, 251–54, and *Acts and Joint Resolutions, 1877–1878*, 342.

125. *Acts and Joint Resolutions, 1877–1878*, 792.

126. Hampton Papers, Letter from Governor Hampton to W. J. Magrath, president of the South Carolina Railroad, June 20, 1878, Miscellaneous Papers (South Carolina Archives).

127. *Acts and Joint Resolutions, Special Session of 1877*, 266 and 375–76. The legislature created Berkeley County in 1882 and Florence County in 1888.

128. *Daily Register*, March 21, 1878.

129. Ibid., March 22, 1878.

130. Hampton Papers, Letter from Jacob Mauldin, sheriff of Pickens County, to Governor Hampton, March 11, 1878 (South Carolina Archives).

131. Hampton Papers, Letter from Judge T. J. Mackey to Governor Hampton, March 14, 1878 (South Carolina Archives).

132. Hampton Papers, Sheriff Mauldin to Governor Hampton, March 17, 1878 (South Carolina Archives).

133. *News and Courier*, March 25, 1878.

134. Hampton Papers, Affidavit of J. J. Lewis, clerk of court of Common Pleas for Pickens County, and Jacob Mauldin, sheriff of Pickens County, July 17, 1878 (South Carolina Archives).

135. *News and Courier*, July 18, 1878.

136. Hampton Papers, Letter from E. M. Brayton to Governor Hampton, May 8, 1878 (South Carolina Archives).

137. Hampton Papers, Letter from G. B. Raum, commissioner of Internal Revenue, to Governor Hampton, March 18, 1878 (South Carolina Archives).

138. *News and Courier*, September 2, 1878; and Hampton Papers, Letter from George J. Southern to Governor Hampton, September 12, 1878 (South Carolina Archives).

139. Hampton Papers, Letter from R. V. Gist to Governor Hampton, March 19, 1878 (South Carolina Archives).

140. *News and Courier*, March 27, 1878.

141. Ibid., April 1, 1878.

142. Ibid., April 3, 1878.

143. *Daily Register*, April 6, 1878.

144. *News and Courier*, April 10 and 11, 1878.

145. Ibid., April 12, 1878.

146. Ibid., April 18, 1878.

147. Miller, *Gullah Statesman, Robert Smalls from Slavery to Congress, 1839-1915* (Columbia: University of South Carolina Press, 1995), 112, 121.

148. Ibid., May 21, 1878.

149. Cooper, *The Conservative Regime*, 231; and E. Culpepper Clark, *Francis Warrington Dawson: South Carolina, 1874-1889* (University of Alabama: University of Alabama Press, 1980), 81.

150. Hampton Papers, Letter from John S. Bratton to Governor Hampton, June 4, 1878 (South Carolina Archives); and Allen W. Trelease, *White Terror: The Ku Klux Klan Conspiracy and Southern Reconstruction* (Baton Rouge: Louisiana State University Press, 1999), 418.

151. Hampton Papers, Letter from Governor Hampton to Colonel Bratton, June 14, 1878 (South Carolina Archives); and Jarrell, *Wade Hampton and the Negro*, 181.

152. *Daily Register*, May 19, 1878.

153. Ibid., June 7, 1878; and *News and Courier*, March 17, 1879.

154. *News and Courier*, June 4, 1878.

155. Ibid., June 10, 1878.

156. Ibid., June 17, 1878.

157. *Daily Register*, June 17, 1878.

158. *News and Courier*, July 5 and 6, 1878; and *Daily Register*, July 7, 1878.

159. *Daily Register*, July 11, 1878.

160. Gary Papers, Letter from Gary to Hugh ____, July 17, 1878 (SCL, USC).

161. Gary Papers, Letter from George Johnstone to Martin Gary, July 27, 1878 (SCL, USC). Johnstone had learned that Hampton had assured Lieutenant Governor Simpson that circumstances would have to change drastically for him to be interested in the Senate. Simpson wanted to be elected to the Supreme Court and did not want to be sidetracked by succeeding Hampton as governor, should the latter be elected to the Senate.

162. *Daily Register,* July 21, 1878.

163. *News and Courier,* July 20, 1878.

164. Ibid., July 19, 1878.

165. *Daily Register,* July 25, 1878.

166. Ibid., August 2, 1878; and *News and Courier,* July 29, 1878.

167. *News and Courier,* August 2, 1878.

168. *Daily Register,* August 8, 1878.

169. *News and Courier,* August 12, 1878.

170. Ibid., August 14, 1878.

171. W. A. Sheppard, *Red Shirts Remembered, Southern Brigadiers of the Reconstruction Period* (Atlanta: Ruralist Press, 1940), 261.

172. *News and Courier,* August 19, 1878.

173. Hampton Papers, Letter from Superintendent Parmele to Governor Hampton, August 9, 1878 (South Carolina Archives); and *News and Courier,* August 14, 1878.

174. Hampton Papers, Letter from C. Thomas to Governor Hampton, August 10, 1878 (South Carolina Archives).

175. Sheppard, *Red Shirts Remembered,* 263–64.

176. *News and Courier,* August 31, 1878.

177. *Daily Register,* August 24, 1878.

178. Sheppard, *Red Shirts Remembered,* 263–64; and *News and Courier,* August 29, 1878.

179. Gary Papers, Letter from Ellis G. Graydon to Martin Gary, August 9, 1878 (SCL, USC).

180. Jones, "Wade Hampton and the Rhetoric of Race," 200; and *Daily Register,* September 20, 1878.

181. *News and Courier,* September 20, 1878.

182. Gary Papers, Letter from Martin Gary to Hugh ——, October 4, 1878 (SCL, USC).

183. Hampton Papers, Letter from Hampton at Cashiers, North Carolina (the Valley) to James Conner, September 5, 1878 (SCL, USC).

184. Gary Papers, Letter from C. Baring Farmer to Martin Gary, October 4, 1878 (SCL, USC).

185. Gary Papers, Letter from T. G.Clemson of Fort Hill to Martin Gary, October 8, 1878 (SCL, USC).

186. Clark, *Francis Warrington Dawson,* 83–85.

187. *News and Courier,* September 23, 1878.

188. Ibid., October 3, 1878.

189. *Daily Register,* October 22, 1878.

190. *News and Courier,* October 29, 1878.

191. *New York Times,* October 31, 1878.

192. Hampton Papers, Letter from William S. Drayton to Governor Hampton, September 28, 1878 (South Carolina Archives).

193. *Columbia Register,* November 7, 1878.

194. *News and Courier,* November 15, 1878.

195. Ibid., November 28, 1878.

196. *New York Times,* April 23, 1881.

197. *News and Courier,* November 9, 1878; and *New York Times,* November 18, 1878.

198. *News and Courier*, November 27, 1878.

199. *Daily Register*, November 30, 1878.

200. Gary Papers, Letter from Henry Farley to Mart Gary, October 11, 1878 (SCL, USC).

201. *News and Courier*, November 18, 1878.

202. Ibid., December 2, 1878.

203. Ibid., December 5, 1878; and *New York Times*, December 8, 1878.

204. *News and Courier*, December 6, 1878.

205. Ibid., December 11, 1878; and *New York Times*, December 10, 1878.

206. Ibid., December 11, 1878; *News and Courier*, December 11, 1878; and *Daily Register*, December 11, 1878.

207. *New York Times*, March 3, 1879.

208. *News and Courier*, February 8, 1879.

209. Ibid., February 12 and 24, and March 10, 1879.

210. Ibid., March 26, 1879.

211. Gary Papers, Letter from E. B. Cash to Martin Gary, October 27, 1878 (SCL, USC).

212. Gary Papers, undated manuscript in Martin Gary's handwriting (SCL, USC).

213. *News and Courier*, February 20, 1879.

214. Clark, *Francis Warrington Dawson*, 85–86.

215. *News and Courier*, January 9, 1879.

216. Ibid., January 10, 1879.

217. Ibid., January 20, 1879.

218. Ibid., January 20 and 31, 1879.

219. Ibid., March 1, 1879.

220. James G. Blaine, "Forum on Race," *North American Review*, 268 (1879), 231–44.

221. *News and Courier*, April 16, 1879.

Chapter 8: The Senate and Beyond

1. *News and Courier*, April 19, 1879.

2. *Congressional Record*, 46th Cong., 1st sess. (1879), 48.

3. Ibid., 7337.

4. *News and Courier*, June 5 and 6, 1879.

5. *New York Times*, June 6, 1879.

6. *Congressional Record*, 46th Cong., vol. 9 (1879), 1358.

7. *News and Courier*, June 12, 1879; and *Congressional Record*, 46th Cong., vol. 9 (1879), 1779–1781.

8. Ibid.

9. *News and Courier*, November 4, 1879.

10. Ibid., November 14, 1879.

11. Ibid., December 12, 1879.

12. *New York Times*, November 21, 1879.

13. Wade Hampton Papers, Letter from Hampton to Mrs. Thomas L. Preston, March 20, 1880 (SCL, USC).

14. Hampton Papers, Letter from Hampton to his sister Anne, March 20, 1880 (SCL, USC).

15. *New York Times*, December 26, 1879.

16. Martin Gary Papers, Letter from T. R. Gaines to Gary, March 27, 1880 (SCL, USC).

17. *News and Courier*, December 15, 1879.

18. D. D. Wallace, "The Question of the Withdrawal of the Democratic Presidential Electors in South Carolina in 1876," *Journal of Southern History* 8 (August 1942): 374–85.

19. *News and Courier*, December 20, 1879.

20. Ibid., December 22, 1879.

21. Manly Wade Wellman, *Giant in Gray: A Biography of Wade Hampton of South Carolina* (Dayton, Ohio: Morningside Book Shop, 1988), 289.

22. *News and Courier*, December 29, 1879.

23. Ibid., January 28 and February 2, 1880.

24. The *News and Courier* reprinted an article from the *(Sumter, S.C.) Watchman* to this effect, March 4, 1880; and George Brown Tindall, *South Carolina Negroes, 1877–1900* (Columbia: University of South Carolina Press, 1952), 222–23.

25. *Congressional Record*, 46th Cong., 2nd sess., vol. 10 (1880), 1618.

26. Ibid., March 25, 1880, 1868.

27. Ibid., May 18, 1880, 3452–53.

28. Ibid., May 13, 1880, 3313–16.

29. Ibid., May 25 and 26, 1879, 3755 and 3811.

30. *New York Times*, January 2, 1880.

31. Ibid., February 7, 1880.

32. Gary Papers, Letter from Gary to Hugh Thompson, from Hot Springs, August 8, 1879 (SCL, USC).

33. Gary Papers, Gary's Speech to the 1880 Democratic Convention (SCL, USC).

34. *News and Courier*, May 5, 1880.

35. Gary Papers, Undated letter written by Gary and apparently never mailed (SCL, USC).

36. Gary Papers, Letter from "Douglas" to the editor of the *Medium*, December 4, 1879 (SCL, USC).

37. *News and Courier*, June 2 and 3, 1880.

38. Ibid., June 4, 1880.

39. *New York Times*, February 10, 1880.

40. Ibid., June 12, 1880

41. *Congressional Record*, 47th Cong., 1st sess., vol. 13 (1882), pt. 1:146 and pt. 7:6876.

42. Ibid., pt. 1:937.

43. *News and Courier*, June 23 and 25, 1880.

44. *New York Times*, July 31 and September 14, 1880.

45. *News and Courier*, August 2 and 3, 1880.

46. Ibid., September 27, 1880.

47. Ibid., October 5, 1880.

48. *New York Times*, October 19, 1880.

49. *News and Courier*, October 13, 20, and 28, 1880.

50. Charles J. Holden, "'The Public Business is Ours': Edward McCrady, Jr. and Conservative Thought in Post–Civil War South Carolina, 1865–1900," *South Carolina*

Historical Magazine, 100 (April 1999): 124-42. McCrady saw the imposition of a literacy qualification as means of pre*serving* civilization. Short of such a restriction whites would have to resort to either fraud or violence, and McCrady preferred violence to fraud. Use of fraud would, he believed, reduce South Carolina to a less-than-civilized people. Violence was less degrading than fraud. *News and Courier*, May 5, 1881.

51. Quoted in Heather Cox Richardson, *The Death of Reconstruction, Race, Labor, and Politics in the Post-Civil War North, 1865-1901* (Cambridge: Harvard University Press, 2001), 209.

52. *News and Courier*, November 13, 1880.

53. Ibid., April 11, 1881.

54. Ibid., December 1, 1880.

55. Ibid., November 30, 1880.

56. Joel Williamson, *The Negro in South Carolina during Reconstruction, 1861-1877* (New York: W. W. Norton Company, 1965), 224-29; and William J. Cooper, *The Conservative Regime, South Carolina, 1877-1890* (Baltimore: Johns Hopkins Press, 1968), 112.

57. Ibid., 236.

58. Tindall, *South Carolina Negroes*, 291-92.

59. John Hammond Moore, ed., *Before and After, or the Relations of the Races at the South*, by Isaac DuBose Seabrook (Baton Rouge: Louisiana State University Press, 1967), 10-11.

60. *Congressional Record*, 47th Cong., 1st sess., vol. 13, pt. 4 (May 3, 1882), 3538.

61. *News and Courier*, April 26, 1881.

62. Ibid., September 13, 1881.

63. Ibid., January 13, 1882.

64. Stephen Kantrowitz, *Ben Tillman and the Reconstruction of White Supremacy* (Chapel Hill: University of North Carolina Press, 2000), 84.

65. *New York Times*, August 6, 1883.

66. Ibid., January 22, 1882.

67. *News and Courier*, May 8, 1882.

68. *New York Times*, August 5, 1883; and *News and Courier*, February 25, 1882.

69. *News and Courier*, January 27, 1882.

70. *New York Times*, June 22, 1882.

71. *News and Courier*, July 14, 1882.

72. William J. Cooper, *The Conservative Regime*, 65-71; and *New York Times*, August 11, 1882.

73. *News and Courier*, October 21, 1882.

74. Ibid., November 11, 1882.

75. Ibid., February 17 and March 3, 1883.

76. *New York Times*, June 21, 1883; and *News and Courier*, June 21, 1883.

77. *News and Courier*, June 29, 1883.

78. *Congressional Record*, 47th Cong., 2nd sess., vol. 14, pt. 2 (June 23, 1883), 1472.

79. *News and Courier*, October 16 and 24, 1883.

80. Ibid., November 5, 1883.

81. Ibid., March 22 and 29, April 21, and May 9, 1884; and *Congressional Record*, 48th Cong., 1st sess., vol. 15, pt. 3 (March 27, 1884), 2329-31.

82. *News and Courier*, June 23, 1884.

83. *Congressional Record*, 48th Cong., 2nd sess., vol. 16 (February 4, 1885), 1254.

84. *News and Courier*, June 30, 1884.

85. William J. Cooper, *The Conservative Regime*, 62.

86. *News and Courier*, September 27, 1884.

87. Ibid., October 3, 1884.

88. Ibid., October 14, 16, 17, and 27, 1884.

89. Ibid., November 15, 1884.

90. Ibid., December 1 and 10, 1884.

91. Ibid., March 28, 1885.

92. Ibid., June 2, 1885.

93. William J. Cooper, *The Conservative Regime*, 73–78.

94. *News and Courier*, April 6 and 7, 1885.

95. Ibid., February 25, 1886.

96. Ibid., April 29, 1886.

97. Ibid., May 1, 1886.

98. Ibid., April 29, 1886.

99. Ibid., June 1, 1886.

100. Ibid., June 30 and July 7, 1886.

101. *Congressional Record*, 49th Cong., 1st sess., vol. 17, pt 5 (May 17, 1886), 4568.

102. *News and Courier*, August 17, 1886.

103. Ibid., October 14, 17, and 18, 1886.

104. Ibid., November 15, 1886.

105. Ibid., November 24, 1886, and *New York Times*, November 25, 1886.

106. *News and Courier*, April 29, 1888.

107. *Congressional Record*, 49th Congress, 2nd Session, vol. 18, pt. 3 (February 26, 1887), 2326.

108. *News and Courier*, October 25 and 28, 1887.

109. Ibid., February 16, 1888.

110. *Congressional Record*, 50th Cong., 1st sess., vol. 19, pt. 3 (March 20, 1888), 2947.

111. *New York Times*, May 18, 1888; and *News and Courier*, May 17 and 18, 1888.

112. Ibid., June 1, 1888.

113. *Congressional Record*, 50th Cong., 1st sess., vol. 19, pt. 8 (August 6, 1888), 7270.

114. *News and Courier*, July 21 and 22, 1888.

115. Ibid., August 8, 1888.

116. Ibid., August 29 and 30 and September 29, 1888.

117. Ibid., October 17, 24, 25, 27 and November 1, 1888.

118. Ibid., December 13, 1888.

119. *New York Times*, December 6, 1888.

120. Ibid., December 7, 1888.

121. Ibid., December 10, 1888.

122. *News and Courier*, February 1, 1889.

123. Allan Nevins, *Grover Cleveland: A Study in Courage* (New York: Dodd, Mead, 1932), 332–36.

124. *News and Courier*, March 23, 1889.

125. Ibid., March 10 and May 9, 1889.

126. Ibid., May 16, 1889.

127. M. C. Butler Papers, Butler's Address to the U.S. Senate, April 10, 1890 (SCL, USC).

128. *New York Times*, August 22, 1889.

129. *News and Courier*, October 3, 1889.

130. Hampton Papers, Copy of Speech to the Senate, January 30, 1890 (SCL, USC).

131. Hampton Papers, Letter from Wade Hampton to M. C. Butler, from Glen Allan, November 16, 1889 (SCL, USC).

132. Wade Hampton and John T. Morgan, "The Race Problem in the South," *Forum Extra*, March 1890, 2–14.

133. Wade Hampton, "The Race Problem," *Arena* (July 1890): 132–38.

134. *News and Courier*, January 31, 1890.

135. *Congressional Record*, 51st Cong., 1st sess., vol. 21, pt. 8 (July 10, 1890).

136. *News and Courier*, February 11, 1890.

137. Ibid., March 21, 1890.

138. Ibid., February 25 and March 4, 1890.

139. Ibid., March 5, 1890.

140. Ibid., March 28, April 3, 1890; and Kantrowitz, *Ben Tillman*, 128–29.

141. *News and Courier*, 132–39.

142. *New York Times*, April 26, 1890.

143. *News and Courier*, May 15, 1890.

144. Ibid., May 17, 1890.

145. Ibid., May 22 and 29, 1890.

146. Ibid., June 9, 1890.

147. Ibid., June 12, 1890.

148. Ibid., June 25, 1890.

149. Ibid., June 26, 1890.

150. Ibid., June 28, 1890.

151. Ibid., July 11, 1890.

152. Ibid., August 11 and 16, 1890, and Kantrowitz, *Ben Tillman*, 132–39.

153. *News and Courier*, September 11 and 12, 1890.

154. Ibid., October 6, 9, and 10, 1890.

155. *New York Times*, August 27, 1890.

156. *News and Courier*, October 18, 1890.

157. Ibid., October 24, 1890.

158. Ibid., October 25, 1890.

159. Ibid., October 26, 1890.

160. Letter from Lizzie Perry to "Dearest Friend," November 6, 1890 (SCL, USC).

161. Kantrowitz, *Ben Tillman*, 165–70.

162. Ibid., 277–78.

163. John Andrew Rice, *I Came Out of the Eighteenth Century* (New York: Hillery House, 1951), 16–17.

164. *News and Courier*, November 17, 27, and 28, 1890.

165. *Columbia Daily Register*, December 9, 1890.

166. *New York Times*, November 27, 1890.

167. Walter Edgar, *South Carolina* (Columbia: University of South Carolina Press, 1998), 439.

168. *News and Courier*, December 12, 1890.

169. *New York Times*, December 12, 1890.

170. Hampton Papers, Letter from Hampton to Sen. M. C. Butler, December 13, 1890 (SCL, USC).

171. *News and Courier*, January 9 and 25, 1891.

172. Hampton Papers, Speech of Wade Hampton in the Senate, January 16, 1891, the Force Bill, HR 11045 (SCL, USC).

173. *News and Courier*, March 4 and 5, 1891.

174. Ibid., March 11, 1891.

175. Ibid., March 27, 1891.

176. *Columbia Daily Register*, May 14, 1891.

177. George C. Rogers, *Generations of Lawyers: A History of the South Carolina Bar* (Columbia: South Carolina Bar Foundation, 1992), 105-6.

178. *News and Courier*, March 11, 1893.

179. Ibid., March 21, 1893.

180. *New York Times*, March 21, 1893.

181. Craig L. Symonds, *Joseph E. Johnston: A Civil War Biography* (New York and London: W. W. Norton and Company, 1992), 378-79.

182. William Garrett Piston, "Lee's Tarnished Lieutenant: James Longstreet and His Image in American Society" (Ph.D.diss., University of South Carolina, 1982), 598.

183. *News and Courier*, March 11, 1893.

184. Butler Papers, Letter from M. C. Butler to Wade Hampton, June 19, 1893 (SCL, USC).

185. Hampton Papers, Letter from Wade Hampton in Washington to N. G. Gonzales, August 30, 1893 (SCL, USC).

186. Hampton Papers, Letter from Hampton in Washington to N. G. Gonzales in Columbia, February 9, 1894 (SCL, USC).

187. Edwards L. Wells, *Hampton and Reconstruction* (Columbia: State Company, 1907), 210-11. Wells knew Hampton well; he had served with the general in the Civil War, and he had access to many papers that were destroyed in the fire of 1899.

188. *New York Times*, October 13, 1893.

189. *Report of the Commissioner of Railroads to the Secretary of the Interior, 1893*, 3-13.

190. *Report of the Commissioner of Railroads to the Secretary of the Interior, 1894*, 3-12.

191. *Report of the Commissioner of Railroads to the Secretary of the Interior, 1895*, 3; *Report of the Commissioner of Railroads to the Secretary of the Interior, 1896*, 10-11.

192. Hampton Papers, Letter from Hampton to W. G. Curtis, assistant to the general manager of the Southern Pacific Railroad, June 12, 1896 (SCL, USC).

193. Samuel J. Martin, *Southern Hero: Matthew Calbraith Butler, Confederate General, Hampton Red Shirt, and U.S. Senator* (Mechanicsburg, Pa.: Stackpole Books, 2001), 271.

194. Ibid., 280.

195. *New York Times*, May 31, 1895.

196. Charles J. Holden, *In the Great Maelstrom* (Columbia: University of South Carolina Press, 2002), 68-69.

197. *New York Times*, May 13, 1897.

198. Piston, "Lee's Tarnished Lieutenant," 598.

199. Hampton Papers, Letter from Hampton to General Munford, May 22, 1899 (SCL, USC); and *New York Times*, May 3, 1899.

200. Wells, *Hampton and Reconstruction*, 216–17.

201. Ibid., 217.

202. Hampton Papers, Letter from Wade Hampton to Alfred Hampton, May 7, 1898 (SCL, USC).

203. Hampton Papers, Paper read by Margaret Crawford Adams at Hampton's eighty-first birthday party, March 25, 1899 (SCL, USC).

204. *New York Times*, May 10, 1901.

205. Wells, *Hampton and Reconstruction*, 224–25; and *New York Times*, April 14, 1902.

206. T. S. Eliot, "Burnt Norton," *The Complete Poems and Plays, 1909–1950* (New York: Harcourt, Brace, 1952), 117–22.

A Note on Sources

The most valuable of Hampton's papers are in the South Caroliniana Library of the University of South Carolina. Others are scattered from the Library of Congress to the Center for American History at the University of Texas. The *Official Records of the War of the Rebellion* is of course essential for the Civil War era. The South Carolina Department of Archives and History has a well ordered and apparently complete collection of records of Hampton's *service* as governor. I of course made significant use of the *Congressional Record* for the senatorial years. The land records in Mississippi depositories are useful, but do not answer all questions pertaining to the fate of the Hampton holdings.

Virginia Meynard's genealogical study was essential in considering details of the Hampton family. Ronald Bridwell's dissertation on Wade Hampton I was of fundamental importance in understanding Wade III's antecedents. I found useful a number of works contemporaneous to Hampton's life, such as Edward Wells' treatment of Hampton in the war and Reconstruction, Sidney Andrews on postwar South Carolina, and Walter Allen on the Chamberlain administration. Francis Butler Simkins and Robert Hilliard Woody's book continues to be essential in studying South Carolina in Reconstruction. William Cooper's study of the era of Bourbon dominance gives an essential understanding of the influence of Hampton and his followers. I found Eric Foner's treatment of Reconstruction the best of recent general studies of Reconstruction. The best work on Sherman's conquest of Columbia is by Marion Lucas.

In considering the problems of race I relied heavily on the works of George Brown Tindall, Joel Williamson, Thomas Holt, Allen Trelease, and Robert Zuczek. I used these studies in conjunction with the *newspaper*s to gain some grasp of the complexities of race relations.

Biographies of Hampton's contemporaries helped fill the gaps left by the absence of those papers destroyed in the several Hampton fires. I made special use of Culpepper Clark's biography of Francis W. Dawson, Stephen Kantrowitz on Ben Tillman, Emory Thomas on J. E. B. Stuart, and Lilian Kibler's biography of Benjamin F. Perry.

There are two recent biographical studies of Hampton III. Edward G. Longacre's book is especially strong on Hampton's military experience, but he gave slight treatment to the postwar years. Walter Brian Cisco's study is quite good in details and color; he does not give much attention to Hampton's weaknesses.

Manuscript Collections

Butler, M. C. Papers. South Caroliniana Library, University of South Carolina.
Deed Books and Wills Books. Chancery Court Records. Washington County Court House, Mississippi.

Gary, Martin. Papers. Perkins Library, Duke University.

———. Papers. South Caroliniana Library, University of South Carolina.

Hampton, Governor Wade. Papers. South Carolina Department of Archives and History.

Hampton, Wade. Papers. Center for American History. University of Texas, Austin.

———. Papers. Library of Congress.

———. Papers. Perkins Library, Duke University.

———. Papers. South Caroliniana Library, University of South Carolina.

———. Papers. Southern Historical Collection, University of North Carolina.

Miles, W. P. Papers. Southern Historical Collection, University of North Carolina.

Slave Schedules, Census of 1850 and 1860. Will Books and Deed Books, Issaquena County Court House, Mississippi. Mississippi Department of Archives and History (the Slave Schedule for Washington County, 1860, is not extant).

Books

Acts and Joint Resolutions of the General Assembly of South Carolina, Passed at the Extra Session of 1877. Columbia: Calvo and Patton, State Printers, 1877.

Acts and Joint Resolutions of the General Assembly of the State of South Carolina, Passed at the Regular Session of 1877–1878. Columbia: Calvo and Patton, State Printers, 1878.

Adams, Henry. *The Education of Henry Adams*. Boston: The Riverside Press for the Massachusetts Historical Society, 1918.

Alexander, E. P. *Memoirs of a Confederate*, Edited by T. Harry Williams. Bloomington: Indiana University Press, 1962.

Allen, Walter. *Chamberlain's Administration in South Carolina*. New York: G. P. Putnam's Sons, 1888.

Andrews, Sydney. *The South since the War, as Shown By Fourteen Weeks of Travel and Observation in Georgia and the Carolinas*. Boston: Ticknor and Fields, 1866.

Ash, Stephen V. *When the Yankees Came: Conflict and Chaos in the Occupied South, 1861–1865*. Chapel Hill: University of North Carolina Press, 1995.

Baily, N. Louise, Mary L. Morgan, and Carolyn R. Taylor. *Biographical Directory of the South Carolina Senate, 1776–1985*. Columbia: University of South Carolina Press, 1986.

Ball, W. W. *The State That Forgot: South Carolina's Surrender to Democracy*. Indianapolis: Bobbs-Merrill, 1932.

Biographical Directory of the Senate of the State of South Carolina, 1776–1964. Columbia: South Carolina Archives Department, 1964.

Blaine, James G. *Twenty Years in Congress, from Lincoln to Garfield*. Norwich: Henry Bill Publishing Company, 1886.

Bleser, Carol K. Rothrock. *The Promised Land: The History of the South Carolina Land Commission, 1869–1890*. Columbia: University of South Carolina Press, 1969.

Boykin, Edward. *Beefsteak Raid*. New York: Funk and Wagnalls, 1960.

Brock, R. A., ed. *The Southern Historical Society Papers*. Vol. 27. Richmond: Southern Historical Society, 1899.

Brooks, U. R. *Butler and His Cavalry in the War of Secession, 1861–1865*. Columbia: The State Company, 1909.

———. *Stories of the Confederacy*. Camden, S.C.: J. J. Fox, 1991.

Butler, M. C. Speech in *Final Report of the Commission to Provide for a Monument to the Memory of Wade Hampton*. Columbia: Gonzales and Bryan, 1906–7.

Cauthen, Charles E., ed. *Family Letters of the Three Wade Hamptons, 1782-1901*. Columbia: University of South Carolina Press, 1953.

Chesnut, Mary Boykin. *A Diary from Dixie*. Edited by Isabel D. Martin and Myrta Lockett. Gloucester: Peter Smith, 1961.

Clark, E. Culpepper. *Francis Warrington Dawson: South Carolina, 1874-1889*. University: University of Alabama Press, 1980.

Coddington, Edwin B. *The Gettysburg Campaign: A Study in Command*. New York: Charles Scribner's, 1968.

Congressional Record. 46th Cong., 1st sess. Washington, D.C., 1879.

Congressional Record. 46th Cong., 2nd sess. Vol. 10. Washington, D.C., 1880.

Congressional Record. 47th Cong., 1st sess. Vol. 13, pt. 1. Washington, D.C., 1882.

Congressional Record. 47th Cong., 1st sess. Vol. 13, pt. 4. Washington, D.C., 1882.

Congressional Record. 47th Cong., 1st sess. Vol. 13, pt. 7. Washington, D.C., 1882.

Congressional Record. 47th Cong., 2nd sess. Vol. 14, pt. 2. Washington, D.C., 1882.

Congressional Record. 48th Cong., 1st sess. Vol. 15, pt. 3. Washington, D.C., 1884.

Congressional Record. 48th Cong., 2nd sess. Vol. 16. Washington, D.C., 1885.

Congressional Record. 49th Cong., 1st sess. Vol. 17, pt. 5. Washington, D.C., 1886.

Congressional Record. 49th Cong., 2nd sess. Vol. 18, pt. 3. Washington, D.C., 1887.

Congressional Record. 50th Cong., 1st sess. Vol. 19, pt. 3. Washington, D.C. 1888.

Congressional Record. 50th Cong., 1st sess. Vol. 19, pt. 8. Washington, D.C., 1888.

Congressional Record. 51st Cong., 1st sess. Vol. 21, pt. 3. Washington, D.C., 1889.

Congressional Record. 51st Cong., 1st sess. Vol. 21, pt. 8. Washington, D.C., 1890.

Cooper, William J. *The Conservative Regime, South Carolina, 1877-1890*. Baltimore: Johns Hopkins Press, 1968.

Current, Richard N, editor in chief. *Encyclopedia of the Confederacy*. New York: Simon Schuster, 1993.

DeSantis, Vincent P. *Republicans Face the Southern Question—The New Departure Years, 1877-1897*. Baltimore: Johns Hopkins University Press, 1959.

Documents of the House of Representatives. 44th Cong., 2nd session, 1876-1877. Washington, D.C., 1877.

Drago, Edmund L. *Hurrah for Hampton! Black Red Shirts in South Carolina during Reconstruction*. Fayetteville: University of Arkansas Press, 1998.

Duer, Richard. "Generals in The Saddle." *Southern Historical Society Papers*, vol. 19. Edited by R. A. Brack. Richmond: Southern Historical Society, 1891.

Durden, Robert F. *James S. Pike, Republicanism and the American Negro*. Durham: Duke University Press, 1957.

Eckert, Ralph Lowell. *John Brown Gordon: Soldier, Southerner, American*. Baton Rouge: Louisiana State University Press, 1989.

Edgar, Walter. *South Carolina: A History*. Columbia: University of South Carolina Press, 1998.

Eliot, T. S. "Burnt Norton." *The Complete Poems and Plays, 1909-1950*. New York: Harcourt, Brace, 1952.

Farwell, Byron. *Stonewall: A Biography of General Thomas J. Jackson*. New York and London: W. W. Norton and Company, 1992.

Faust, Drew Gilpin. *James Henry Hammond and the Old South*. Baton Rouge: Louisiana State University Press, 1982.

Foner, Eric. *Reconstruction, America's Unfinished Revolution, 1865-1877*. New York: Harper and Row, 1988.

Ford, Lacy K. *Origins of Southern Radicalism: The South Carolina Upcountry, 1800-1860*. New York: Oxford University Press, 1988.

Franklin, John Hope. *Reconstruction after the Civil War*. Chicago and London: University of Chicago Press, 1961.

Freeman, Douglas Southall. *Lee's Lieutenants: A Study in Command*, vols. 1-3. New York: Charles Scribner's Sons, 1942-1944.

———. *Lee's Dispatches: Unpublished Letters of General Robert E. Lee*. New York: G. P. Putnam and Sons, 1957.

Friedel, Frank. *Francis Lieber: Nineteenth Century Liberal*. Baton Rouge: Louisiana State University Press, 1947.

Gallagher, Gary W. *The Peninsula Campaign*. Baton Rouge: Louisiana State University Press, 1998.

Gillette, William. *Retreat from Reconstruction, 1867-1879*. Baton Rouge: Louisiana State University Press, 1979.

Hahn, Steven. *A Nation under Our Feet: Black Political Struggles in the Rural South from Slavery to the Great Migration*. Cambridge, Mass., and London: Belknap Press of Harvard University Press, 2003.

Hamer, Philip M. *The Secessionist Movement in South Carolina, 1847-1852*. Allentown, Pa.: H. Ray Hass and Co., 1918.

Hampton, Ann Fripp, ed. *A Divided Heart, Letters of Sally Baxter Hampton, 1853-1862*. Columbia, S.C.: Phantom Press, 1994.

Hampton, Harry. *Woods and Waters and Some Asides*. Columbia, S.C.: State Printing Company, 1975.

Hampton, Lt. Gen. Wade. *Address on the Life and Character of General Robert E. Lee, Delivered on 21st October, 1871, before the Society of Confederate Soldiers and Sailors in Maryland*. Baltimore: John Murphy and Company, 1871.

Hennig, Helen Kohn. *Columbia, Capital City of South Carolina, 1786-1936*. Columbia: The Columbia Sesqui-Centennial Commission, 1936.

Hirshon, Stanley P. *Farewell to the Bloody Shirt: Northern Republicans and the Southern Negro, 1877-1893*. Chicago: Quadrangle Books, 1968.

Holden, Charles J. *In the Great Maelstrom: Conservatism in Post–Civil War South Carolina*. Columbia: University of South Carolina Press, 2002.

Hollis, Daniel Walker. "South Carolina College." In *University of South Carolina*, vol. 1. Columbia: University of South Carolina Press, 1951.

———. "University of South Carolina, College to University. In *University of South Carolina*, vol. 2. Columbia: University of South Carolina Press, 1956.

Holt, Thomas. *Black over White: Negro Political Leadership in South Carolina during Reconstruction*. Urbana, Chicago, and London: University of Illinois Press, 1977.

Howe, Julia Ward. *Reminiscences, 1819-1899*. New York: Negro Universities Press, 1899.

James, D. Clayton. *Antebellum Natchez*. Baton Rouge: Louisiana State University Press, 1968.

Jarrell, Hampton M. *Wade Hampton and the Negro: The Road Not Taken*. Columbia: University of South Carolina Press, 1950.

Johnston, Joseph E. *Narratives of Military Operations Directed during the Late War Between the States*. New York: D. Appleton and Company, 1874.

Journal of the Congress of the Confederate States of America, 1861–1865. Vol. 1. Washington, D.C.: Government Printing Office, 1904.

Journal of the House of Representatives of the State of South Carolina, Annual Session of 1852. Columbia: R. W. Gibbes, State Printer, 1852.

Journal of the House of Representatives of the State of South Carolina, Annual Session of 1853. Columbia: R. W. Gibbes, State Printer, 1853.

Journal of the House of Representatives of the State of South Carolina, Annual Session of 1854. Columbia: R. W. Gibbes, State Printer, 1854.

Journal of the House of Representatives of the State of South Carolina, Annual Session of 1855. Columbia: E. H. Bratton, State Printer, 1855.

Journal of the House of Representatives of the State of South Carolina, Annual Session of 1856. Columbia: E. H. Bratton, State Printer, 1856.

Journal of the House of Representatives of the State of South Carolina, Annual Session of 1857. Columbia: E. H. Bratton, State Printer, 1857.

Journal of the House of Representatives of the State of South Carolina, Annual Session of 1858. Columbia: R. W. Gibbes, State Printer, 1858.

Journal of the House of Representatives of the State of South Carolina, Annual Session of 1860. Columbia: R. W. Gibbes, State Printer, 1860.

Journal of the House of Representatives of the State of South Carolina, Regular Session Beginning November 28, 1876. Columbia: Presbyterian Publishing House, 1877.

Journal of the House of Representatives of the State of South Carolina, Commencing April 24, 1877. Columbia: Presbyterian Publishing House, 1877.

Journal of the House of Representatives of the State of South Carolina, Special Session, 1877–78. Columbia: Calco and Patton, State Printer, 1878.

Journal of the House of Representatives of the State of South Carolina for the Regular Session of 1877–78. Columbia: Calco and Patton, State Printers, 1878.

Journal of the Senate of the State of South Carolina, 1858. Columbia: R. W. Gibbes, State Printer, 1858.

Journal of the Senate of the State of South Carolina, 1859. Columbia: R. W. Gibbes, State Printer, 1859.

Journal of the Senate of the State of South Carolina, 1860. Columbia: R. W. Gibbes, State Printer, 1860.

Journal of the Senate of the State of South Carolina, 1861. Charles P. Pelham, State Printer, 1861.

Kantrowitz, Stephen. *Ben Tillman and the Reconstruction of White Supremacy.* Chapel Hill: University of North Carolina Press, 2000.

Kelly, Alfred H., and Winfred A. Harbison. *The American Constitution, Its Origins and Development.* New York: W. W. Norton and Company, 1963.

Kibler, Lillian Adele. *Benjamin F. Perry: South Carolina Unionist.* Durham: Duke University Press, 1946.

Kirk, Russell. *The Conservative Mind.* South Bend, Ind.: Gateway Editions, 1953.

LaBorde, Maximilian. *History of the South Carolina College.* Charleston: Walker, Evans, and Cogswell, 1874.

Lamson, Peggy. *The Glorious Failure, Black Congressman Robert Brown Elliott and the Reconstruction in South Carolina.* New York: W. W. Norton and Company, 1973.

Leland, John A. *A Voice from South Carolina: Twelve Chapters before Hampton and Two Chapters after Hampton.* Charleston: Walker, Evans, and Cogswell, 1879.

Longacre, Edward G. *The Cavalry at Gettysburg, A Tactical Study of Mounted Operations during the Civil War's Pivotal Campaign.* Lincoln and London: University of Nebraska Press, 1986.

Lucas, Marion. *Sherman and the Burning of Columbia.* Columbia: University of South Carolina Press, 2000.

Lynd, Staughton. *Reconstruction.* New York: Harper and Row, 1967.

Martin, Samuel J. *Southern Hero: Matthew Calbraith Butler, Confederate General, Hampton Red Shirt, and U.S. Senator.* Mechanicsburg, Pa.: Stackpole Books, 2001.

McKitrick, Eric. *Andrew Johnson and Reconstruction.* Chicago and London: University of Chicago Press, 1960.

McLemore, Richard Aubrey. *A History of Mississippi*, vol. 1. Hattiesburg: University and College Press of Mississippi, 1973.

McMurry, Richard M. *Two Great Rebel Armies: An Essay in Confederate Military History.* Chapel Hill and London: University of North Carolina Press, 1989.

McPherson, James M. *Battle Cry of Freedom, the Civil War Era.* New York and Oxford: Oxford University Press, 1988.

McWhinney, Grady, and Perry D. Jamieson. *Attack and Die: Civil War Tactics and the Southern Heritage.* University, Alabama: University of Alabama Press, 1982.

Meynard, Virginia G. *The Venturers: The Hampton, Harrison, and Earle Families of Virginia, South Carolina, and Texas.* Greenville, S.C.: Southern Historical Press, 1981.

Miers, Earl Schenck, ed. *When the World Ended: The Diary of Emma LaConte.* New York and Oxford: Oxford University Press, 1957.

Miller, Jr., Edward A. *Gullah Statesman: Robert Smalls from Slavery to Congress, 1839–1915.* Columbia: University of South Carolina Press, 1995.

Moffett, Mary Conner, ed. *Letters of General James Conner.* Columbia, S.C.: R. L. Bryan Company, 1950.

Moore, John Hammond. *Columbia and Richland County: A South Carolina Community, 1740–1990.* Columbia: University of South Carolina Press, 1993.

———. *Southern Homefront, 1861–1865.* Columbia, S.C.: Sumner House Press, 1998.

Murphy, James B. *L. Q. C. Lamar, Pragmatic Patriot.* Baton Rouge: Louisiana State University Press, 1973.

Nevins, Allan. *Grover Cleveland, A Study in Courage.* New York: Dodd, Mead, 1932.

Official Records of the War of the Rebellion, 128 volumes. Washington, D.C.: Government Printing Office, 1880–1901.

Palmer, B. M. *The Life and Letters of James Henley Thornwell.* Richmond, Va.: Whitlet and Shepperson, 1875.

Perrine, Laurence. *Sound and Sense: An Introduction to Poetry.* New York: Harcourt, Brace, and World, 1969.

Perry, Benjamin F. *Biographical Sketches of Prominent American Statesmen with Speeches, Addresses, and Letters.* Philadelphia: Free Press, 1887.

———. *Reminiscences of Public Men.* Philadelphia: John D. Avil and Company, 1883.

———. *The Writings of Benjamin F. Perry.* Vol. 2, *Reminiscences of Public Men.* Spartanburg, S.C.: Reprint Company, 1980.

Perry, Thomas Sergeant. *The Life and Letters of Francis Lieber.* Boston: James R. Osgood and Company, 1882.

Pike, James S. *The Prostrate State: South Carolina under Negro Rule.* Edited by Robert F. Durden. 1874; New York: D. Appleton and Company, 1960.

Polakoff, Keith Ian. *The Politics of Inertia: The Election of 1876 and the End of Reconstruction.* Baton Rouge: Louisiana State University Press, 1973.

Porter, William T., sr. ed. *Porter's Spirit of the Times,* vol. 4. New York, 1858.

Report of the Commissioner of Railroads to the Secretary of the Interior, 1893. Washington, D.C.: Government Printing Office, 1893.

Report of the Commissioner of Railroads to the Secretary of the Interior, 1894. Washington, D.C.: Government Printing Office, 1894.

Report of the Commissioner of Railroads to the Secretary of the Interior, 1895. Washington, D.C.: Government Printing Office, 1895.

Report of the Commissioner of Railroads to the Secretary of the Interior, 1896. Washington, D.C.: Government Printing Office, 1896.

Report on the Denial of the Elective Franchise in South Carolina at the State and National Election of 1876, the United States Senate Subcommittee of the Committee of Privileges and Election. Washington, D.C.: Government Printing Office, 1877.

Reynolds, Emily Bellinger and Joan Reynolds Faunt, eds. *Biographical Directory of the Senate of South Carolina.* Columbia: South Carolina Archives Department, 1964.

Reynolds, John S. *Reconstruction in South Carolina.* Columbia: The State Publishing Company, 1905.

Rice, John Andrew. *I Came Out of the Eighteenth Century.* New York: Hillery House, 1951.

Richardson, Heather Cox. *The Death of Reconstruction: Race, Labor, and Politics in the Post-Civil War North, 1865-1901.* Cambridge: Harvard University Press, 2001.

Rogers, George C. *Generations of Lawyers: A History of the South Carolina Bar.* Columbia: South Carolina Bar Foundation, 1992.

Rose, Willie Lee. *Rehearsal For Reconstruction, the Port Royal Experiment.* Indianapolis, New York, Kansas City: Bobbs-Merrill Company, 1964.

Saville, Julie. *The Work of Reconstruction, from Slave to Wage Labor in South Carolina, 1860-1870.* Cambridge: Cambridge University Press, 1994.

Scarborough, William Kauffman. *Masters of the Big House: The Elite Slaveholders of the Mid-Nineteenth Century South.* Baton Rouge: Louisiana State University Press, 2003.

Schullery, Paul. *The Bear Hunter's Century.* New York: Dodd, Mead, 1988.

Seabrook, Isaac Dubose. *Before and After, or the Relations of the Races at the South,* ed. John Hammond Moore. Baton Rouge: Louisiana State University Press, 1967.

Seton-Watson, Hugh. *The Russian Empire, 1801-1917.* Oxford: Clarendon Press, 1967.

Sheppard, W. K. *Red Shirts Remembered: Southern Brigadiers of the Reconstruction Period.* Atlanta: Ruralist Press, 1940.

Sherman, William T. *Memoirs of General William T. Sherman.* New York and London: D. Appleton and Company, 1875.

Simkins, Francis Butler. *Pitchfork Ben Tillman, South Carolinian.* Baton Rouge: Louisiana State University Press, 1944.

Simkins, Francis Butler, and Robert H. Woody. *South Carolina during Reconstruction.* Chapel Hill: University of North Carolina Press, 1932.

Simkins, Francis Butler, and James Welch Patton. *The Women of the Confederacy.* Richmond and New York: Garrett and Massie, 1936.

Smith, Alfred Glaze. *Economic Readjustment of an Old Cotton State: South Carolina, 1829–1860.* Columbia: University of South Carolina Press, 1958.

South Carolina in 1876, Report on the Denial of the Elective Franchise in South Carolina at the State and National Election of 1876 by the U. S. Senate Subcommittee of the Committee on Privileges and Elections. Washington, D.C.: Government Printing Office, 1877.

South Carolina Women in the Confederacy. Records collected by Mrs. A. T. Smythe, Miss M. B. Poppenheim, and Mrs. Thomas Taylor. Columbia: State Company, 1903.

Southern Historical Society Papers, vol. 11. Richmond, Va.: Southern Historical Society, 1883.

Stampp, Kenneth. "Triumph of the Conservatives." In *Reconstruction.* Edited by Staughton Lynd. Evanston and London: Harper and Row, 1967.

Strode, Hudson. *Jefferson Davis, Tragic Hero, 1864–1889.* New York: Harcourt, Brace, and World, 1964.

Symonds, Craig L. *Joseph E. Johnston: A Civil War Biography.* New York and London: W. W. Norton and Company, 1992.

Testimony Taken by the Select Committee to Inquire into the Condition of Affairs in the Late Insurrectionary State, South Carolina, vol. 2. Washington, D.C.: Government Printing Office, 1872.

Thomas, Emory M. *Bold Dragoon: The Life of J. E. B. Stuart.* Norman and London: University of Oklahoma Press, 1999.

Thompson, Henry T. *Ousting the Carpetbagger from South Carolina.* Columbia: R. L. Bryan Company, 1926.

Tindall, George Brown. *South Carolina Negroes, 1877–1906.* Columbia: University of South Carolina Press, 1952.

Trelease, Allen W. *White Terror: The Ku Klux Klan Conspiracy and Southern Reconstruction.* Baton Rouge: Louisiana State University Press, 1999.

Trudeau, Noah Andre. *The Last Citadel: Petersburg, Virginia, June 1864–April 1865.* Toronto and London: Little, Brown, 1991.

Underwood, James Lowell, and W. Lewis Burke, eds. *At Freedom's Door: African American Founding Fathers and Lawyers in Reconstruction South Carolina.* Columbia: University of South Carolina Press, 2000.

Underwood, Robert Wood, and Clarence Clough Buel, eds. *Battles and Leaders of the Civil War,* vol. 4. New York: Thomas Yoseloff, 1956.

Weigley, Russell F. *A Great Civil War.* Bloomington: Indiana University Press, 2000.

Weir, Robert M. *Colonial South Carolina.* Millwood, N.Y.: KTO Press, 1983.

Wellman, Manly Wade. *Giant in Gray: A Biography of Wade Hampton of South Carolina.* Dayton, Ohio: Morningside Book Shop, 1988.

Wells, Edward L. *Hampton and His Cavalry in '64.* Richmond, Va.: B. F. Johnson Publishing Company, 1899.

———. *Hampton and Reconstruction.* Columbia: The State Company, 1907.

Wheeler, Joseph. Letter published in *The Southern Historical Society Papers,* edited by R. A. Brock, vol. 27. Richmond: Southern Historical Society, 1899, 132.

White, Laura A. *Robert Barnwell Rhett: Father of Secession.* New York: The American Historical Association, 1931.

Williams, Alfred. B. *Hampton and His Red Shirts, South Carolina's Deliverance, 1876.* Charleston: Walker, Evans, and Cogswell, 1933.

Williams, T. Harry. *Romance and Realism in Southern Politics.* Athens: University of Georgia Press, 1961.

Willaimson, Joel. *After Slavery: The Negro in South Carolina During Reconstruction, 1861-1877.* New York: W. W. Norton Company, 1965.

Wilson, Clyde N. *Carolina Cavalier, the Life and Mind of James Johnston Pettigrew.* Athens and London: University of Georgia Press, 1990.

Wiltse, Charles M. *John C. Calhoun, Nullifier, 1829-1834.* New York: Russell and Russell, 1949.

Wirt, Jeffrey D. "Wade Hampton." In *The Confederate General,* vol. 3, edited by William C. Davis. Harrisburg, Pa.: National Historical Society, 1991.

Woodward, C. Vann. *Mary Chesnut's Civil War.* New York: Book-of-The-Month Club, 1981.

———. *Reunion and Reaction: The Compromise of 1877 and the End of Reconstruction.* New York: Little, Brown, and Company, 1951.

Woodward, Sir Llewellyn. *The Age of Reform, 1815-1870.* Oxford: The Clarendon Press, 1938.

Wright, D. Giraud. *A Southern Girl in '61: The War Times Memories of a Confederate Senator's Daughter.* New York: Doubleday, Page, and Company, 1905.

Zuczek, Robert. *State of Rebellion: Reconstruction in South Carolina, 1996.* Columbia: University of South Carolina Press, 1996.

Articles

"Bears and Bear-Hunting." *Harpers New Monthly Magazine* 65 (October 1855): 599.

Blaine, James, G. "Forum on Race." *North American Review* 268 (1879): 231-44.

Chamberlain, D. H. "Reconstruction in South Carolina." *Atlantic Monthly* (April 1901): 473-84.

Clendenin, Clarence C. "President Hayes' 'Withdrawal of Troops'—An Enduring Myth." *South Carolina Historical Magazine* 70 (1969): 240-43.

Easterby, J. H. "The Three Wade Hamptons: A Saga of a Family of the Old South." *State* (Columbia, S.C.), February 3 and 25, March 4, 1934.

Hampton, Wade. "Address of General Wade Hampton," February 22, 1878. *Southern Historical Papers,* vol. 6, 130-32.

———. "The Battle of Bentonville." *Battles and Leaders of the Civil War.* New York: Thomas Yoreloff, 1956, vol. 4, 700-703.

———. "Memorial Address." *Southern Magazine* (August 1873): 225-49.

———. "The Race Problem." *Arena* (July 1890): 132-38.

———. "Speech to the Southern Historical Society." *Southern Magazine* (January 1874): 11-18.

Hampton, Wade, and John T. Morgan. "The Race Problem in the South." *Forum Extra* (March 1890): 2-14.

Holden, Charles J. "'The Public Business Is Ours': Edward McCrady, Jr. and Conservative Thought in Post-Civil War South Carolina, 1865-1900." *South Carolina Historical Magazine* 100 (April 1999): 124-42.

Nation 1 (August 17, 1865): 95; (October 4, 1865): 524.

Slap, Andrew. "The Spirit of '76: The Reconstruction of History in the Redemption of South Carolina." *Historian* 63 (Summer 2001): 769-76.

Townsend, Belton O'Neal. "The Political Condition of South Carolina." *Atlantic Monthly* 29 (February 1877): 177-94.

Wallace, D. D. "The Question of the Withdrawal of the Democratic Presidential Electors in South Carolina in 1876." *Journal of Southern History* 8 (August 1942): 374-85.

Wheeler, Joseph. "An Effort to Rescue Jefferson Davis." *Century Magazine* 56 (May 1898): 85-91.

Dissertations

Bridwell, Ronald Edward. "The South's Wealthiest Planter: Wade Hampton I of South Carolina, 1754-1835." Ph.D. diss., University of South Carolina, 1980.

Jones, DeWitt Grant. "Wade Hampton and The Rhetoric of Race: A Study of The Speaking of Wade Hampton on The Race Issue, 1865-1878." Ph.D., diss., Louisiana State University and Agricultural and Mechanical College, 1988.

Piston, William Garrett. "Lee's Tarnished Lieutenant: James Longstreet and His Image in American Society." Ph.D.diss., University of South Carolina, 1982.

Newspapers

All newspapers listed here are South Carolina publications unless otherwise noted.
Columbia Register, 1875-77.
Columbia Daily Phoenix, 1865.
Columbia Daily Register, 1877-91.
Columbia Phoenix, 1865.
Constitutionalist, 1874 (Augusta, Georgia).
Daily Phoenix, 1865-77.
Daily Register, 1877-78.
Daily South Carolinian, 1855.
New York Times, 1878-1901.
News and Courier, 1874-1893.
State, 1934- .
Union Herald, 1876-77.

DeVeaux, James, 9
Diamond Hill, 22, 125
Dill, Solomon Washington, 124
Donovant, John, 58
Drago, Edmund L., 176–77
Drayton, William S., 234
Duncan, Dr. Stephen, 15, 56
Duncan, Stephen, Jr., 27, 104, 125–26
Dunn, T. C., 179–80, 188, 202

Earle, Thompson, 193
Early, Jubal, 49, 62, 65, 72
Easterby, James H., 6
Edgefield plan, 168–69
Edgefield rally, of 1876, 167
Edmunds, George Franklin, 241–42
Edward McCrady, Jr., 158
eight box law, 249
election of 1868, 118
election of 1876, 156, 187–89
election of 1878, 233–34, 246
Eliot, T. S., 272
Ellenton riot, 182–83, 186, 227
Elliot, R. B., 137, 140–41, 146, 155, 165,
    179–80, 182, 184, 188, 201, 203
Elliott, William, 257
Enforcement Acts of 1870 and 1871,
    133, 157
Ensor, J. F., 193
Erskine College, 143
Eutaw Springs, Battle of, 3
Evans, John Gary, 250, 268–69
Evans, Shanks, 30–31
Evarts, W. M., 199, 209
Everst, William E., 257
Ewell, Richard S., 48, 61

Falling Waters, 51
Farley, Henry, 235
Farmer, C. Baring, 233
Farmers' Association, 262
Farmers' Convention, 261–62
fence laws, 223–24, 235, 251
Ferguson, Samuel, 153, 172–73
Festerville incident, 79–80
fire eaters, 26
First Foreign Battalion, 59
Fish, Hamilton, 191

Five Forks, Battle of, 69, 71
Foner, Eric, 153
Force Bill, 261, 266
Forrest, Nathan Bedford, 30, 76
Fort Granby, 3
Fredericksburg, Battle of, 43
Free Trade Association, 256
freedmen, attitude towards field labor,
    103
Freedmen's Bank, 257
Freedmen's Bureau, 90, 107, 109
Freeman, Douglas Southall, 31, 61, 89
fusion politics, 151, 154, 158–59, 162,
    169–70, 215

Gaillard, P. B., 196
Gaines, T. R., 243
Garfield, James A., 201, 248–49, 251
Garrison, William Lloyd, 180
Gary, Eugene B., 264
Gary, Martin, 30, 181, 198, 206, 209,
    211, 215, 217, 219–24, 226, 228–32,
    235–37, 243–44, 246, 249–50, 264;
    charges that Hampton ditched Tilden
    campaign, 244–45; general charges
    against Hampton, 246–47
Gettysburg, Battle of, 48–51
Getzen, Henry, 162
Gibbes, James, 95, 113
Gibbes, Robert W., 7, 105
Gilmore, Quincy, 99
Gleaves, R. H., 116, 137, 139–40, 180,
    205, 215
Globe Tavern, 66
Gonzales, N. G., 268–69, 271
Goodwyn, Kit, 29
Goodwyn, Thomas Jefferson, 77
Gordon, John B., 101, 110, 127, 144,
    170, 179, 199–200, 217, 228
Gorgas, Josiah, 71
Gowen, Samuel, 243–44
Grand Army of the Republic (GAR), 259
Grant, U. S., 60, 72, 81, 120, 133, 140,
    158, 164–65, 170, 180, 184, 191, 194
Gray, J. W., 232
Graydon, Ellis G., 232
Greeley, Horace, 137
Green, John T., 139–40

Greenback Party, 252
Gregg, David M., 46, 66, 69
Gregg, Maxcy, 44
Guiteau, Charles J., 251

Hagood, Johnson, 136, 150, 168, 171,
    182, 186, 219, 222, 229, 243, 245, 247,
    250–51, 265
Halleck, Henry, 133
Hamburg riot, 162–78, 269
Hamfield, 1
Hammond, Catherine Fitzsimons, 6, 10
Hammond, James H., 6, 10
Hampton, Alfred (son of Wade I), 4
Hampton, Alfred (son of Wade III), 127,
    270
Hampton, Anthony, 1
Hampton, Anne Fitzsimons, 6, 8
Hampton, Caroline, 9
Hampton, Catherine, 8
Hampton, Catherine Fisher, 111, 127
Hampton, Christopher (Kit), 8, 11, 14,
    216
Hampton, Elizabeth Preston, 1
Hampton, Frank (son of Wade I), 4, 5
Hampton, Frank (son of Wade II), 9, 24,
    29, 41, 47
Hampton, George McDuffie, 22
Hampton, Harriet (daughter of Marga-
    ret Preston Hampton), 17
Hampton, Harriet (daughter of Mary
    Cantey Hampton), 4
Hampton, Harriet Flud, 3, 4
Hampton, Kate, 127
Hampton, Louisa Wade, 4
Hampton, Mary McDuffie, 70–71, 104,
    127; death of, 130; marriage of, 21–22
Hampton, Margaret Preston: marriage
    of, 14; death of, 17
Hampton, Martha Goodwin Howell, 3
Hampton, Mary Cantey, 4, 6–7, 16, 52
Hampton, Mary Fisher, 8–9, 44, 111
Hampton, Mary Singleton (Daisy), 127
Hampton, Mary Sumter, 4
Hampton, McDuffie, 104, 127
Hampton, Preston, 17, 29, 41, 69–70,
    248
Hampton, Sally, 17

Hampton, Sally Baxter, 24–25, 27
Hampton, Susan Frances, 4
Hampton, Wade, I, 1–6; death of, 14
Hampton, Wade, II, 4–9, 10–11, 26;
    death of, 22
Hampton, Wade, III, 92–95, 99, 118,
    149–50, 153, 156, 161, 187, 190, 197–
    99, 241–42, 262–69; accident of
    November 1878, 233–36; address at
    Richland Fork, 103; appointment of
    blacks to office, 205; appointment of
    chief justice, 206, 208–9, 213; assumes
    command in Columbia, 75; assumes
    power as governor, 201–2; attitude
    toward early Reconstruction, 95–96;
    attitude toward race, 175–78, 250, 260,
    237–38; bankruptcy, 125–26; Beef-
    steak Raid, 67–68; Bentonville, Battle
    of, 82–83; birth of, 8,13; black suf-
    frage, 110–11, 114; Blackville rally,
    1878, 229; Blair Bill, 253; Brandy Sta-
    tion, Battle of, 46–47; brigadier gen-
    eral, promotion to, 35–39; burning of
    Columbia, controversy concerning,
    96–97; Butler, M. C., rift with, 220;
    campaign of 1876, 174–75, 179; cam-
    paign of 1878, 225–26, 232–33; cav-
    alry, joins, 38; cavalry mounts, concern
    for welfare of, 45, 55–57; cavalry,
    named commander of, 65; Chambers-
    burg raid, 42; charges of ditching Til-
    den ticket, 197; Charlottesville,
    residing in, 130; Columbia, fall of, 76–
    77; as commisioner of Pacific Rail-
    roads, 240, 267–69; Confederate Con-
    gress' resolution, 84; Conservative
    Convention of 1867, 115–16; consoli-
    dates power of office of governor, 204;
    convention of 1865, 93; death, 271;
    declared elected governor, 192;
    declines to run for governor, 102;
    Democratic Convention of 1876, 171;
    dinner at Claflin, 228–29, 232, 237;
    education, 14; elected governor, 189;
    expatriation, possibilities of, 94; expira-
    tion of senatorial term, 267; first mar-
    riage, 14; Gettysburg, Battle of, 47–51;
    Hawes Shop, 62; hunting accident of

1886, 257; inauguration to second term as governor, 235–36; indebtedness of, 102, 112–13; KKK defendants, defense of, 133–34; letter from Democratic Executive committee to public, 1868, 124; letter to Pres. Johnson, 107–8; letter to public in August of 1867, 113–14; letters to Tilden and Hayes, 194; lieutenant general, promotion to, 75 ; major general, promotion to, 53; Manassas, Battle of, 30–32; Mine Run, Battle of, 54; Mississippi lands, 260; National Democratic Convention of 1868, 119–20; nomination for governor, 168; North Carolina campaign, 81–88; outdoorsman, 13, 15–16; pardons, policy of, 231–32, 219–20; patronage as governor, 205; Petersburg, siege of, 63; Pickens bootleggers, 225; political leader, emergence as, 91; portrait of, 256–57; Pres. Hayes, friendship with, 209–10, 217; Pres. Hayes, negotiations with, 195, 199–201; public education, 213–15, 218–19, 227, 250; raid near Fayetteville, 81–82; raids above Fredericksburg, 42–44; ranking cavalry officer, 61; reply to John Quincy Adams's address, 123; return to S.C., in 1864, 58–59; return to S.C. in 1865, 72–73, 90; second marriage, 22; solid South, 95; sound money policies, 261; S.C. House and Senate, 17–18; speaking engagements, 219; speech in memory of Gen. Lee, 127–28; speech at Walhalla, 108; speech at Washington College, 119; surrender of the Army of Tennessee, 85–89; state executive committee, chairman of, 117–18, 121; tariffs, 252, 259; tax strategy against Chamberlain, 194–96; Tilden campaign, 181; time in the wilderness, 148; tour with Pres, Hayes, 217; travel abroad, 16; travels beyond S.C., 213; Trevilion Station, 62–63; U.S. Senate, election to, 235–36; U.S. Senate, reelected to, 254–55; violence in campaign, 183–84; wounded at Gettysburg, 50–51; wounded at Seven Pines, 35

Hampton, Wade, IV, 17, 24, 29, 38, 56, 70, 80, 126–27, 130, 240
Hampton administration, inefficiency of, 218
Hampton and Tilden Musical Club, 184
Hampton County, 224
Hampton Legion, 28–29, 31
Hampton massacre, 2
Hampton-Preston, House, 6, 7
Hancock, Winfield Scott, 69, 120, 248
Hardee, William J., 73–75, 80, 82
Harlee, Mrs. Alonzo, 182
Harmon, Mr. and Mrs., 160
Harrison, Benjamin, 259, 268
Hart, J. F., 29, 39, 46, 70
Hart's Battery (Washington Artillery), 29, 72, 88
Haskell, A. C., 158, 182–84, 190, 197, 200, 219, 244–45, 247, 262, 264–65
Haskell, John C., 91, 130, 247
Haskell, Sally Hampton, 91
Haskell, Sophia Lovell Cheves, 59
Hayes, Rutherford B., 160, 180–82, 198–201, 209, 216, 226–27, 231, 237, 241, 247
Hayne, H. E., 188, 202–3
Hemphill, Robert H., 158
Hendricks, T. A., 161
Hendricks, Thomas J., 172
Hill, A. P., 47–48, 66, 69, 71
Hoar, George F., 246
Hood, John B., 34, 52, 65, 72, 78, 81
Hooker, Joe, 48
Houghton, N., 92
Houmas, 4, 16
Howard, O. O., 74, 76
Howe, Samuel Gridley (and Julia), 24
Howe, W. B. W., 185
Hunkadory Club, 178, 191
Hunter, David, 62
Hunter, H. H., 215

Imboden, John D., 51
incendiary cases, 156–57, 193–94
Independent Republicans, 139
Ingalls, John J., 251

Redpath, James, 144, 153
Reed, J. P., 141
Respectful Remonstrance on Behalf of the White People of South Carolina, 1868 (Democratic State Executive Committee), 118–19
Republican Convention of 1876, 179–80
Republican Convention of 1878, 230–31
Republican Printing Company, 132
Rice, John Andrew, 265
Richardson, John S., 150
Richardson, J. P., 218, 247, 256–59
Richardson, Willard, 196
rifle clubs, 133, 157–58, 183; disbandment of, 184; estimated strength of, 184–85
Riley, Stephen, 185
Rivers, Prince, 162
Robertson, Beverly, 47–48
Robertson, Thomas J., 116, 132, 165, 193, 195, 198, 219
Roosevelt, Theodore, 16, 271
Rose, Billy, 217
Rosser, Thomas Lafayette, 67–68
Ruger, Thomas H., 182, 185–86, 190–91
Rutledge, B. H., 58

Sanders, Sandy, 176
Sawyer, Frederick A., 132
scalawags, 117
Scarborough, William Kauffman, 7
Schofield, John M., 81
Scott, Robert K., 116, 121, 124, 130–33, 137, 186, 200, 204, 216–17
scouts, 59–60, 68
secession convention, 27
Seddon, J. A., 57
Seton-Watson, Hugh, 135
Seven Pines, Battle of, 35–37
Seymour, Horatio, 120
Shadburne, George B., 66–67
Shannon, William, 176
sharecropping, 126
Sharpsburg (Antietam), Battle of, 41–42
Shaw, A. J., 220–21
Shell, G. W., 261
Shell Manifesto, 261–62
Sheppard, J. C., 161, 219, 252, 256, 267

Sheridan, Philip, 57, 60–63, 67, 72, 258
Sherman, John, 248
Sherman, W. T., 60, 71–73, 76–79, 81, 84–86, 88, 90, 96–97, 108, 133, 184
Sickles, Daniel, 102, 108–10, 112, 115
Simkins, Francis Butler, 116
Simmons, Thomas Y., 150
Simpson, William D., 150, 171, 179, 201, 208, 222, 235–36
Sims, R. M., 171, 218, 247
Sims, W. Gilmore, 174
Sinking Fund Commission, 144
slave trade, 19–21
Slocum, Henry, 79
Smalls, Robert, 116, 147, 160, 174, 193, 211, 217, 227, 257
Smith, Cotton Ed, 265
Smith, Gustavus W., 39
South Carolina College, 4, 6, 14, 18, 25, 255–56
Southern Cross, 106, 126, 270
Southern Historical Society, 129
Southern Life Insurance Company, 130
Spotsylvania, Battle of, 60–61
Stanberry, Henry, 134
Stanford, Leland, 256–57
Stanton, Edwin, 85, 88
Starke, William Pinkney, 161
State Board of Canvassers, 204–5
state indebtedness, 132–33, 140, 206–7, 211–13, 218, 221, 223
Stephens, Alexander, 128
Stevenson, Carter, 75, 77
Stewart, B. F., 80
Stone, William, 188
Stoneman, George M., 45–46
straight-out policy, 145–47, 151–52, 155–56, 166, 169–71
strike, of rice field workers, 160
Stuart, J. E. B., 32, 38, 41, 44, 46, 50, 54, 60; and the Gettysburg campaign, 47–51
Sumner, Charles, 27, 123, 137
Sumter, Thomas, 2
Supreme Court, state, 192
Survivors Association, 127
Swails, S. A., 155, 190, 234
Sweetwater Sabre Club, 163